Educational Communications and Technology: Issues and Innovations

Series Editors
Michael Spector
M.J. Bishop
Dirk Ifenthaler

More information about this series at http://www.springer.com/series/11824

Anthony A. Piña • Victoria L. Lowell
Bruce R. Harris

Editors

Leading and Managing e-Learning

What the e-Learning Leader Needs to Know

 Springer

Editors
Anthony A. Piña
Sullivan University
Louisville, KY, USA

Victoria L. Lowell
Purdue University
West Lafayette, IN, USA

Bruce R. Harris
Dixie State University
Saint George, UT, USA

Educational Communications and Technology: Issues and Innovations
ISBN 978-3-319-61779-4   ISBN 978-3-319-61780-0   (eBook)
https://doi.org/10.1007/978-3-319-61780-0

Library of Congress Control Number: 2017950875

Printed on acid-free paper

This Springer imprint is published by Springer Nature
The registered company is Springer International Publishing AG
The registered company address is: Gewerbestrasse 11, 6330 Cham, Switzerland

Preface

There is an abundance of literature for those who wish to teach, take, or develop online courses. There are far fewer resources for those who have been called to lead and manage online/distance education programs within their organizations and for those who oversee e-learning that is blurring the distinction between online and on-ground learning.

Leading and Managing e-Learning: What the e-Learning Leader Needs to Know provides insights and expertise from more than 50 instructional technology leaders and professionals from over 30 different institutions across the country. While faculty, instructional designers, and others can benefit from the information in this work, it has been designed primarily to assist the educational leader or manager who does not come from a background of formal training in educational technology, instructional design, or distance education.

Written for the practitioner—rather than the scholar—this book provides information on the most salient topics of online/distance education and e-learning and provides guidance for making decisions that will result in successful e-learning implementation. It is the most comprehensive guide for practice currently available for e-learning leaders and managers.

Louisville, KY, USA   Anthony A. Piña
West Lafayette, IN, USA   Victoria L. Lowell
Saint George, UT, USA   Bruce R. Harris

Acknowledgements

Tony Piña: I wish to express my gratitude to my supervisors who, over the years, have led by example, while giving me the space to grow, progress, and achieve: Dr. Edward Morante, Ms. Kennedy Rocker, Dr. Edmund Hansen, and leaders at Sullivan University, including Dr. A. R. Sullivan, Dr. Glenn Sullivan, Mr. Thomas Davisson, Dr. Jay Marr, Dr. Kenneth Miller, Dr. Diana Lawrence, and Mr. Michael Johnson.

Victoria Lowell: I would like to thank Tony Piña for his mentoring and support in the development of this book. I am appreciative of Jim Lehman, who provided advice and support. She wishes to give sincere gratitude to the authors who contributed their time and their expertise to this book so that others can learn from each one.

Bruce Harris: To Laurie.

Contents

Contributors

Meg Van Baalen-Wood University of Wyoming, Laramie, WY, USA

Olga Belikov Brigham Young University, Provo, UT, USA

Meridith Z. Bergeron Franciscan Missionaries of Our Lady University, Formerly Our Lady of the Lake College, Baton Rouge, LA, USA

Christi Boggs University of Wyoming, Laramie, WY, USA

Alfonso Bradoch Oregon State University, Corvallis, OR, USA

Tara Bunag University of the Pacific, Stockton, CA, USA

Alison Carr-Chellman University of Idaho, Moscow, ID, USA

Thomas B. Cavanagh University of Central Florida, Orlando, FL, USA

Lauren Cifuentes Texas A&M University–Corpus Christi, Corpus Christi, TX, USA

Marie A. Cini University of Maryland University College, Upper Marlboro, MD, USA

Camille Dickson-Deane University of Melbourne, Melbourne, VIC, Australia

Jessica DuPont Oregon State University, Corvallis, OR, USA

Brian P. Fodrey University of North Carolina at Chapel Hill, Chapel Hill, NC, USA

Sarah C. Fornero Adler University, Chicago, IL, USA

Camille Funk University of Southern California (USC), Los Angeles, CA, USA

Andrea Gregg The Pennsylvania State University, State College, PA, USA

Stephanie Harff University of South Florida, Tampa, FL, USA

Cathy Holsing The Pennsylvania State University, State College, PA, USA

Alexandra Janney Texas A&M University–Corpus Christi, Corpus Christi, TX, USA

Mary Kickham-Samy McDonough Geschke Library, Marygrove College, Detroit, MI, USA

Royce Kimmons Brigham Young University, Provo, UT, USA

Japheth Koech Columbus State University, Columbus, GA, USA

Swapna Kumar University of Florida, Gainesville, FL, USA

Kathryn E. Linder Oregon State University, Corvallis, OR, USA

Olysha Magruder Johns Hopkins University, Gainesville, FL, USA

Florence Martin University of North Carolina Charlotte, Charlotte, NC, USA

Sandra C. McCarthy Washtenaw Community College, Ann Arbor, MI, USA

Tracy McMahon Loyola University, Parkville, MD, USA

Robert L. Moore University of North Carolina at Chapel Hill, Chapel Hill, NC, USA

Cheryl A. Murphy University of Arkansas, Fayetteville, AR, USA

Megan C. Murtaugh Dara-Oak Academic Community, Alva, FL, USA

Sanghoon Park University of South Florida, Tampa, FL, USA

Anthony A. Piña Sullivan University, Louisville, KY, USA

Matthew Prineas Athabasca University, Athabasca, Canada

Victoria Raish Penn State University, University Park, PA, USA

Stevie Rocco The Pennsylvania State University, PA Furnace, PA, USA

Stephenie Schroth Penn State University, University Park, PA, USA

Jacqueline H. Singh Qualitative Advantage, LLC, Fishers, IN, USA

Deborah S. Slaughter Dara-Oak Academic Community, Sherwood, MI, USA

Michael G. Strawser Bellarmine University, Louisville, KY, USA

Rinki Suryavanshi Texas A&M University–Corpus Christi, Corpus Christi, TX, USA

Lisa L. Templeton Oregon State University, Corvallis, OR, USA

Kelvin Thompson University of Central Florida, Orlando, FL, USA

Amy Thornton Columbus State University, Columbus, GA, USA

Thomas J. Tobin Tobin Consulting, State College, PA, USA

Denise Tolbert National University, Costa Mesa, CA, USA

Amy Valente Cayuga Community College, Auburn, NY, USA

Dian Walster Wayne State University, Detroit, MI, USA

Kyle Whitehouse Oregon State University, Corvallis, OR, USA

About the Editors

Anthony A. Piña is Associate Provost at Sullivan University, Louisville, Kentucky, where he oversees academics and development for 30 fully online degree programs (including a Ph.D.) and over 600 online and hybrid courses taught by more than 150 faculty. He is Past-President of the Division of Distance Learning of the Association for Educational Communications and Technology (AECT) and has served on the AECT Board of Directors. Tony has been a consultant to Fortune 500 corporations, small businesses, local government agencies, educational institutions, and the US Military. He is author or editor of four books and has over 50 academic publications. He serves on the editorial boards of three scholarly journals and has been a guest editor of *Tech Trends* and of the *Quarterly Review of Distance Education.* Tony received his undergraduate and master's degrees from Brigham Young University, did postgraduate work at Arizona State University, completed his doctorate at La Sierra University, and earned a postdoctoral master's degree from Sullivan University. He is married and the father of six children—four biological and two adopted.

Victoria L. Lowell is Program Convener of the Online Master of Science in Education (M.S.Ed.), in Learning Design and Technology program at Purdue University, Indiana's second largest university, where she oversees 45+ professors and 230+ students. She holds a Ph.D. in Education, with a dual concentration in Distance Education and Higher Education Institutional Policy Planning and a M.Ed. in Educational Technology. At Purdue she conducts research on issues pertaining to online learning and teaching, instructional strategies, and leading online programs. She has authored and edited numerous articles and presented over 50 presentations related to online learning and educational technology. She has worked in the field of education for 20 years teaching, researching, advising students, and serving in various higher education administration roles, including Director of Professional Licensure Programs and Director of Instructional and Web Technologies at Regent University. For Regent University, she led the development of the university's online continuing education programs. She has served as a consultant for higher education institutions, developed and evaluated online programs, and has taught at K-12 and university levels, face-to-face, blended/hybrid and online. She has served on the Board of Directors for the Division of Distance Learning (DDL) of the Association for Educational Communications & Technology (AECT).

Bruce R. Harris has worked as an instructional designer for several companies and organizations and has consulted with many clients such as Motorola, Sullivan University, Illinois State Museum, and K-12 school districts. He completed his doctorate in Instructional Science at Brigham Young University. For 24 years he was a professor of Instructional Design and Technology and served in several leadership roles at Western Illinois University. He has published over 20 academic publications and has presented over 130 papers at professional conferences on such topics as self-regulated learning, effective online learning programs and strategies, and evaluating quality online teaching. He developed and taught his first online course in 1994 and has been teaching online courses every semester since that first course. He is currently the Executive Director of Academic Innovation and Leadership in which he oversees the Department of Distance & Digital Learning and is also the Director of the Center for Teaching & Learning at Dixie State University.

Introduction: What the e-Learning Leader Needs to Know

Abstract During the past two decades, we have witnessed the rise of online education as it has overtaken all other forms of distance education and has moved from the outer reaches of continuing education departments to the mainstream of higher education. Despite recent downturns in overall college and university enrollments, online enrollments have continued to increase and online learning is still the fastest growing sector in US higher education (Allen, Seaman, Poulin, & Straut, 2016). As e-learning permeates all aspects of college and university campus (and, increasingly, K-12) through blended/hybrid, web-enhanced, and flipped courses, the boundaries between "online" and "on-campus" courses are becoming ever more blurred (Glance, 2014). We consider "e-learning" as broadly defined to encompass online/distance education and, increasingly, the use of digital learning, regardless of whether students are local or remote.

Keywords e-Learning • Distance Education • Educational Administration • Administration • Educational Leadership

The Need for This Book

Market researchers have noted the rapid rise of new online degree and certificate programs at US colleges and universities (e.g., Clinefelter & Aslanian, 2015). With many new online degree programs, there will be a need for a prominent leader within the school's ranks. However, while some e-learning leaders come with some background or training in the field of instructional design and technology, most are taken from the ranks of faculty or administration with little orientation into online distance education. Some of these new leaders may not be prepared for the dynamic nature of online distance education and its differences from traditional methods of teaching, course development, student services, infrastructure, and support.

The lack of experience or knowledge can affect the success of e-learning programs under their leadership. Therefore, leaders taking the helm need to recognize that schools "are and exist within a complex socio-technological ecology" requiring an understanding of the "diverse set of interests of the various stakeholders in the process" (Misha, Henriksen, Boltz, & Richardson, 2016, p. 254).

The vast majority of books currently available on online/distance education are written for students or faculty and deal primarily with designing and developing online courses, teaching online, or promoting online student success. This emphasis is understandable, since the majority of the authors of these books are college and university faculty, who tend to research and write on the topics closer to where they "live" (Huett & Piña, 2016). Administrators, for their part, tend to have little time to write and often do not have institutional incentive to do so.

The available literature has not kept up with the need to prepare those called to lead and manage e-learning at an institution or organizational level. A book that we have found most helpful is *An Administrator's Guide to Online Education* (Shelton & Saltsman, 2005); however, it is now over a decade old. *Leading the e-Learning Transformation of Higher Education* (Miller et al., 2014) is a useful volume that provides sage advice on managing organizational change, but does not deal with a number of the "nuts and bolts" issues that drive administrative decisions. Other related works are very specialized and consider a single aspect of e-learning. These include *Managing Online Instructor Workload* (Conceição & Lehman, 2011), *Assuring Quality in Online Education* (Shattuck, 2014), and *Quality Assurance and Accreditation in Distance Education and e-Learning* (Jung & Latchem, 2012). Finally, there is *Beyond the Online Course: Leadership Perspectives on e-Learning* (Piña & Huett, 2016), which is a collection of scholarly articles on leading various aspects of e-learning, including innovation and change, course and program design, development and support of online students, development and support of online faculty and staff, and legal and accreditation issues.

At the present time, there is no single comprehensive "ready reference" that provides top-level academic leaders/administrators/managers with a way to get up-to-speed on the various topics surrounding e-learning. We envisioned *Leading and Managing e-Learning: What the e-Learning Leader Needs to Know* to be that ready reference, not to be a scholarly treatise or a handbook of research, but a practical way to get the information leaders and managers need to make sound decisions. To maximize the book's usefulness, we asked our authors to compose their chapters in the following format:

- Abstract
- Decision-making guidance
- What you need to know
- What you can do
- Further information
- References

Who Should Read This Book

This book is written for those who have been promoted or hired to serve in prominent high-level administration roles that include leading and managing online learning across their institutions (or who are interested in serving in this capacity). Faculty and others interested in a comprehensive treatment of e-learning from an administrative point of view will also benefit. It includes a representative set of e-learning topics that leaders will likely encounter at their institutions. It is filled with advice for those who need to know the best practices for building and overseeing online education. The next 25 chapters in this book present a diverse set of opinions and ideas. By reading this book, leaders will have knowledge of what is needed to develop and manage online learning at their institutions. Leaders will find the advice in this book to be both practical and timely, as they work through the various challenges and successes of developing and running online learning programs. As Confucius said, "Education without understanding is a futile exercise."

What You Will Find

We are so fortunate to have had so much enthusiasm about this project from our colleagues within the Association for Educational Communications and Technology (AECT) and from others across the country. The AECT Division of Distance Learning endorsed this book as the Division's contribution to the Springer Books and Briefs initiative for AECT. The number of high-quality submissions in response to our call for chapters could have easily filled three books, so the process of determining what should and should not be included in the book was a taxing one for the three of us. We are blessed to be able to include the wisdom and advice from dozens of our colleagues from institutions around the country. These are scholars and practitioners who "walk the walk" of e-learning in their daily lives.

Thomas B. Cavanagh and Kelvin Thompson open the discussion by differentiating short-range and long-range vision and the nature of innovation. The authors introduce and explain the FIRRST framework—a set of principles for assisting e-learning leaders to make strategic decisions.

Next, Andrea Gregg, Cathy Holsing, and Stevie Rocco present a series of five guidelines that leaders should consider when planning, developing, and maintaining institutional online learning. The authors illustrate these principles using many examples from their own institution.

Meridith Z. Bergeron and Sarah C. Fornero explore the topic of centralized and decentralized approaches to managing online programs. For e-learning leaders these two different approaches are discussed in detail, with examples of each method to assist in selecting an approach that will meet the culture and needs of their institution, as well setting up standards and policies for managing e-learning programs. The authors also discuss conducting a needs assessment to determine the feasibility of a formal centralized and decentralized approach and the best practices for addressing the needs of technology, faculty, administration, curriculum, and support services when leading and managing e-learning at an institution.

Lisa L. Templeton and Kathryn E. Linder discuss the important considerations and various issues that can be a part of the development of an e-learning division. This chapter will assist e-learning leaders in addressing the various considerations for developing and structuring an e-learning division and collaborating across an institution to ensure the success of an e-learning division. Topics including budget models, incentives, models for course and program design, considerations regarding promotion and marketing, and structuring student services are presented.

Camille Dickson-Deane, Denise Tolbert, Tracy McMahon, and Camille Funk provide an alternative view for the implementation of an e-learning unit, including different strategies for establishing the unit, maintaining expertise, developing personnel and course design.

Amy Thornton and Japheth Koech explore the design and development of an e-learning center to support the instructional and learning needs of faculty and students. This chapter provides leaders with relevant advice from other leaders who have been through this process.

Robert L. Moore and Brian P. Fodrey look at the design of a distance education technology infrastructure. The authors discuss important topics such as the hardware and software used in e-learning, the relationship between the software tools and systems for online distance education delivery, the personnel that will work within this infrastructure, the objectives of the infrastructure, and the evaluation of distance education delivery.

Co-editor Anthony A. Piña begins the discussion on e-learning technologies with a primer for leaders on learning management systems (LMS). He walks readers through the characteristics of the systems, considerations for selecting and adopting a new LMS, and guidelines for maximizing the effectiveness of an LMS.

Christi Boggs and Meg Van Baalen-Wood continue the technology discussion with guidelines for implementing a university-wide LMS. In this chapter, they discuss both the benefits and considerations for implementing an LMS, as well as the major consideration of changing the way instructors and programs may have previously delivered their instruction either in an online or traditional format.

Mary A. Kickham-Samy and Sandra C. McCarthy engage in a discussion on information literacy within an e-learning program. For e-learning leaders, developing a strong library presence within e-learner's programs can provide an enriching experience. This chapter addresses the need for including librarians as stakeholders in this process and the development of resources to meet the needs of online learners and instructors.

Dian Walster delves into information policy, an important topic for e-leaders who will be working with and supporting e-learning programs with large amounts of information that is presented online and collected about students, instructors, and programs. Important topics that are included in this chapter include policies regarding intellectual property, the collection or dissemination of personal and public information, and the storage of information.

Olga Belikov and Royce Kimmons discuss the topics of copyright laws, public domain, fair use, open licensing for education, and developing open literacies. Without proper understanding materials may be underutilized or improperly used without regard to copyright laws. This chapter will assist e-learning leaders by providing a basic review of the laws regulating the use of educational materials including copyright, public domain, fair use, and open licensing for teaching and course development.

Cheryl A. Murphy discusses the process and structure needed to prepare for accreditation. This chapter provides a framework for data collection and analysis and details the types of data an e-learning leader will need to be collecting and methods to organize and systematically collect the data that will address key concerns of accreditors.

Lauren Cifuentes, Rinki Suryavanshi, and Alexandra Janney present e-learning leaders with methods to motivate administrators and instructors to adopt e-learning. Through identifying what motivates instructors and administrators to either avoid or adopt e-learning, e-learning leaders are provided with information to assist them in encouraging campus-adoption of e-learning.

Michael G. Strawser and Tara Bunag start the discussion of faculty development. This chapter provides e-learning leaders with advice on hiring e-learning instructors, addressing common barriers and challenges with converting traditional courses to e-learning courses, and developing a faculty training plan.

Olysha Magruder McRae and Swapna Kumar continue the discussion on faculty training and professional development, through providing e-learning leaders with a strong understanding of the major roles and competencies faculty will need to teach online. They also discuss the benefits and drawbacks of providing faculty training with a focus on technology or pedagogy.

Thomas J. Tobin moves the faculty agenda to evaluating online teaching. This important topic for e-learning leaders presents leaders with three sets of tools for creating, implementing, and operating an evaluation program for online teaching at your campus. E-learning leaders will better understand criteria that should be considered when evaluating online learning, who should be involved in the evaluation process of online teaching, bias that need to be removed from the evaluation process, and the evaluation measures that should be used to promote and re-hire the best online faculty members.

Deborah S. Slaughter and Megan C. Murtaugh discuss the design and development of e-learning with collaboration among all stakeholders. E-learning leaders are presented with advice on creating and managing a streamlined, effective, and collaborative design process for working with subject matter experts.

Florence Martin and Swapna Kumar present e-learning leaders with an overview of frameworks, benchmarks, guidelines, and instruments to assess e-learning courses and programs. E-learning leaders are provided with seven quality indicators such as institutional support, technology infrastructure, course design, learner and instructor support, learning effectiveness, faculty and student satisfaction, and course assessment and evaluation, so they can make key decisions and implement those decisions.

Jacqueline H. Singh provides a comprehensive look at strategic front-end evaluation planning and shows how formative evaluation can ultimately save time and money and assist in policy development and program implementation. This chapter differentiates program evaluation from other types of inquiry and provides guidance on the selection of an evaluation design.

Marie A. Cini and Matthew Prineas highlight the issue of scaling when developing and running online programs. This chapter focuses on how to organize and build an institutional infrastructure that will facilitate scale, including faculty training and development, student services, managing the process of change, and balancing quality and cost, to prevent the potential for ballooning expenses.

Jessica DuPont, Stephanie Harff, Sanghoon Park, and Kathryn E. Linder discuss university services needed for a successful e-learning strategy at a university. This chapter delves into the key strategies when marketing online degrees to adult learners. Many universities have centralized marketing strategies that are focused on marketing traditional on-campus programs. Developing a marketing strategy for e-learners will be key to your e-learning programs success. Other topics include the staff and resources necessary for marketing.

Alfonso Bradoch, Kyle Whitehouse, and Kathryn E. Linder discuss the important topic of student support and retention services for e-learners. This chapter includes a discussion of accreditation and policy guidelines at universities that have led to e-learning student success and a review of recommendations from accrediting bodies for services and systems. Collaboration between university departments and institutional partners to provide these services and systems is central to this process.

Amy Valente provides a look at how to successfully lead e-learning within the unique environment of the community college. She presents a case study of a community college to investigate and analyze organizational culture, leadership, planning, and management and identify critical success factors.

Finally, Victoria Raish, Stephenie Schroth, and Alison Carr-Chellman present important factors for those leading an online K-12 program or school. Leaders are presented with a systematic approach to e-learning leadership in a K-12 setting, including addressing various needs such as supporting students attending the e-learning program, setting clear expectations for parents or guardians, addressing curriculum development and delivery from orientation to assessment, being innovative and responsive to needs of transparency for all stakeholders, and providing equitable access.

Conclusion

Together, the chapters in this book provide a wealth of information and tools that can be customized and implemented to meet the needs of a developing or established online learning plan at an organization. It is our hope that *What the e-Learning Leader Needs to Know: Leading and Managing e-Learning* will provide leaders with the knowledge and tools they need to know to successfully lead e-learning at their schools.

Louisville, KY, USA   Anthony A. Piña
West Lafayette, IN, USA   Victoria L. Lowell
Saint George, UT, USA   Bruce R. Harris

References

Allen, I. E., Seaman, J., Poulin, R., & Straut, T. T. (2016). *Online report card: Tracking online education in the United States*. Babson Park, MA: Babson Survey Research Group and Quahog Research Group.

Clinefelter, D. L., & Aslanian, C. B. (2015). *Online college students 2015: Comprehensive data on demands and preferences*. Louisville, KY: The Learning House.

Conceição, S. C. O., & Lehman, R. M. (2011). *Managing online instructor workload: Strategies for finding balance and success*. San Francisco, CA: Jossey-Bass.

Glance, D. (2014). *Online vs. online on campus: What's the difference?* Retrieved from http://www.socialsciencespace.com/2014/04/online-vs-online-on-campus-whats-the-difference/.

Huett, J. B., & Piña, A. A. (2016). Beyond the online course. In A. A. Piña, & J. B. Huett (Eds.) *Beyond the online course: Leadership perspectives on e-Learning*. Charlotte, NC: Information Age Publishing.

Jung, I., & Latchem, C. (2012). *Quality assurance and accreditation in distance education: Models, policies and research*. New York, NY: Routledge.

Miller, G., Benke, M., Chaloux, B., Ragan, L. C., Schroeder, R., Smutz, W., & Swan K. (2014). *Leading the e-learning transformation of higher education*. Sterling, VA: Stylus.

Mishra, P., Boltz, L., Henriksen, D., & Richardson, C. (2016). E-Leadership and teacher development using ICT. In R. Huang, Kinshuk, & J. K. Price (Eds.), *ICT in education in global context: Comparative reports of innovations in K-12 education*. Berlin: Springer.

Piña, A. A., & Huett, J. B. (2016). *Beyond the online course: Leadership perspectives on e-Learning*. Charlotte, NC: Information Age Publishing.

Shattuck, K. (2014). *Assuring quality in online education: Practices and processes at the teaching, resource, and program levels*. Sterling, VA: Stylus.

Shelton, K., & Saltsman, G. (2005). *An administrator's guide to online education*. Greenwich, CT: Information Age Publishing.

Keeping FIRRST Things First: The Delicate Dance of Leading Online Innovation at Your Institution

Thomas B. Cavanagh and Kelvin Thompson

Abstract Perhaps one difference between managers and leaders is that the former play the hands they are dealt while the latter exert their influence to make changes for the better (i.e., innovate). In this chapter we address the need for online education leaders to keep their organizations nimble to respond to changing institutional realities as they choose when to adopt a new technology/resource called for by others and when to initiate change themselves. This involves understanding the status quo at one's own institution while also staying current on developments in the broader online education community. Leaders must read the signs of the times and position themselves accordingly to exert positive influence on their institutions through their organizations. We ground our discussion within a framework called FIRRST, which is an acronym describing a set of principles that have proven to be effective in helping online higher education leaders make strategic decisions. FIRRST can serve as a useful heuristic for all those who must cultivate innovation in their eLearning contexts.

Keywords Online learning • Leadership • FIRRST • eLearning • Innovation

Decision-Making Guidance

This chapter will help you make decisions in accomplishing the following tasks.

- Establishing long-range vs. short-range technology innovation strategies.
- Prioritizing competing options about technology-based innovation.
- Determining effective investments of time and resources in technology and innovation on your campus.

T.B. Cavanagh (✉) • K. Thompson
University of Central Florida, 3100 Technology Pkwy, Ste 234, Orlando, FL 32826, USA
e-mail: cavanagh@ucf.edu; kelvin@ucf.edu

© Association for Educational Communications and Technology 2018
A.A. Piña et al. (eds.), *Leading and Managing e-Learning*, Educational
Communications and Technology: Issues and Innovations,
https://doi.org/10.1007/978-3-319-61780-0_1

1

What You Need to Know

A key difference between a manager and a leader is that the former only reacts to events and direction from others while the latter exerts his/her influence to proactively make changes for the better (i.e., innovate). Online education leaders must keep their organizations nimble to respond to changing institutional realities as they choose when to adopt a new technology/resource called for by others and when to initiate change themselves. This involves understanding the status quo at one's own institution while also staying current on developments in the broader online education community. Leaders must read the signs of the times and position themselves accordingly to exert positive influence on their institutions through their organizations.

Short- and Long-Range Vision

Leaders must accomplish the difficult task of maintaining simultaneous oversight of short-range opportunities while also being aware of emerging long-range trends. It is understandable for online learning leaders to be concerned with the success of their operations in the here and now. It is also defensible to set performance targets and stretch goals based on a here and now snapshot. However, if one's vision for the future is constrained by how things are only in the here and now, that is a problem. It can lead one to envision continuing on as is with nothing but (hopefully) steady improvements in performance metrics and the occasional requisite system upgrade to interrupt the status quo. However, like Johnson's (1998) Littlepeople in the Maze, sooner or later one's cheese will be moved.

To avoid this unsettling prospect and, indeed, to prepare for a more strategic and rewarding visioning of the future, online learning leaders should cultivate a perspective that is not limited to the here and now but that is, instead, informed by "there and then." That is, much like Covey, Merrill, and Merrill's (1994) admonition of using a 2 × 2 matrix (urgent/important; not urgent/important; urgent/not important; not urgent/not important) for appropriate time management to avoid the "tyranny of the urgent" (Hummel, 1967, cited in Covey et al., 1994), we might suggest imagining a similar matrix to avoid what we might call the Tyranny of the Here and Now (see Fig. 1). It is important to give sufficient attention to the there and then (i.e., global context and trend forecasting) to avoid an overly provincial perspective. Each quadrant in this matrix (here/now; there/now; here/then; there/then) has some value in helping the online learning leader be effective in leading innovation. Having already commented briefly on the value of the Here/Now quadrant, we'll note opportunities for gaining perspective from the other quadrants and the value of doing so.

There/Now. There is obvious value in consulting with our colleagues at other institutions, whether those schools are aspirational peers or whether they are very similar demographically but just doing things differently. Teleconferences or site visits allow the online learning leader to build upon the brief coffee break

Fig. 1 Contextual
visioning quadrants

	Here	There
Now	Operations	Collegial Consultation
Then	Strategic Planning	Distant Vision

conversations at conferences to get a better understanding of innovations that are working somewhere else right now.

There/Then. The antithesis of the Here/Now and perhaps most associated with "vision," the global, long-term perspective of There/Then allows one to get needed distance from one's immediate context and brings depth to one's vision. Perhaps one of the best-known resources for cultivating this global, long view is the annual New Media Consortium's (NMC) Horizon Report distributed freely online (see http://www.nmc.org/nmc-horizon). Based upon an extensive compilation of primary and secondary sources filtered by an expert panel, each year's Higher Education Edition of the NMC's Horizon Report (Johnson et al., 2016) identifies "six key trends, six significant challenges, and six important developments in educational technology" with "likely impact on the core missions of universities and colleges" across a 5-year time frame that are then "detailed in succinct, non-technical, and unbiased presentations" (p. 3).

Here/Then. Ultimately, one must be able to envision how things will or, perhaps, how things *should* play out over time in one's local context. Again, without being informed by the There/Now and There/Then quadrants, it is easy to assume that events will unfold incrementally in the Here/Then. One of the most obvious examples of cultivating Here/Then is in the strategic planning process. Ideally, the online learning leader is a part of the institutional strategic planning process during which a broader institutional perspective is maintained but online education can most assuredly be instrumental. If not directly a part of strategic planning for the institution, the online learning leader can still carry out strategic planning for his/her own area *in alignment* with the institutional strategic plan. (This alignment might be facilitated by consultation with one or more individuals involved in the institutional planning.) Innovation should be factored into the strategic planning for online education at the institution.

Nature of Innovation

For the purposes of this chapter, we'll consider innovation as the implementation of new ideas in online education in order to bring about better outcomes. As we've discussed above, this involves a vision of the future that is informed by what's working where we are, what is working elsewhere, what trends and technologies are rippling through higher education in coming years, and what senior leaders envision for the local institution in the future. We might synthesize the overarching process as one of monitoring trends, noting applicability (for a valued outcome) in the local context, and then gauging the probability of successful implementation locally. This process underlies all that follows in this chapter. Cavanagh and Thompson (2015, November 2) note that there is a "delicate dance" (14:22) between countervailing forces such as here/there and now/then. "Leaders… read the signs of the times and then position themselves accordingly in order to exert positive influence" (20:45) in their settings. In the remainder of this chapter we focus on the steps involved in this delicate dance of leading online innovation.

What You Can Do

To lead or follow is a key decision for any educational technology leader, and online learning leaders are no different. While there are advantages to being on the cutting edge (or even the bleeding edge) of a technology adoption, there are also advantages to waiting for others to leap first and work out the inevitable problems (and costs) that may arise. Likewise, the decision to build vs. buy can be a "make or break" scenario for an institution that is striving to succeed in an increasingly competitive higher education landscape.

However, no two situations are identical, as are no two institutional contexts. How is an online learning leader to navigate the complex sets of variables associated with a high-stakes decision? The following methodology, known by the acronym FIRRST, can serve as a useful heuristic for both short- and long-term decision-making.

- Follow the Energy.
- Invent the Future.
- Research and Make a Decision.
- Recognize Resource Limitations.
- Solve the Big Problems.
- Take Action.

The FIRRST methodology can be applied by both online learning leaders and those aspiring to leadership positions to make decisions about technology on campus. While leadership decisions are certainly more art than science, having a heuristic can help to mitigate risk and improve the chance of a successful outcome. The FIRRST methodology is described below.

Follow the Energy

Inspired by Peter Senge's advice to "follow the energy," (Senge, Hamilton, & Kania, 2015, "Guides for Moving Along the Path," para. 4) it's important for leaders of technology innovation in higher education to identify pockets of opportunity where critical mass is forming and capitalize on those "rising tides" of institutional energy. The key and the challenge is to influence the nascent energy and direct it at institutional goals.

If, for example, an online learning leader learns of various individual faculty members across her institution implementing adaptive learning courseware into their online courses, that may be an opportunity to organize a disconnected set of lone actors into a much more impactful enterprise initiative. Scale can be a powerful component of a narrative when requesting resources and trying to positively impact student success and institutional efficiency. Another example might be an online learning leader volunteering for a cross-institutional task force on data analytics and ensuring that learning management system (LMS) data are a central component of an emerging analytics strategy. In this example, the leader sees the growing energy on campus surrounding data analytics and capitalizes on that to ensure that online learning is not only a beneficiary of the resource investment but also a contributor to the effort's success.

Yet, determining a legitimate coalescence of opportunities from a temporary fad can be a challenge. A key question for a leader to ask himself/herself is: will pursuing this opportunity potentially result in tangible benefits for my organization? Even if those benefits are not yet quantifiable or completely defined yet, there must be a clear goal in mind that could benefit the leader's institution. If an opportunity has no obvious benefits, yet there seems to be a lot of media or other attention concerning it, the leader should seriously question its pursuit—especially if significant resources must be expended. If the energy surrounding an opportunity is simply a case of "keeping up with the Joneses," then it may not be prudent to pursue it. Very few institutions have resources to spare on purely experimental endeavors not related to its core mission. In most cases, the resources that would have been spent could be better applied elsewhere.

Invent the Future

An important aspect of leadership is to also recognize potential opportunities and have the courage and fortitude to envision a future state that does not yet exist and keep an organization moving toward that vision even amid inevitable setbacks. As Kay (n.d.) has said, sometimes the best way to predict the future is to invent it. Blazing a trail can include inherent risk but it can also lead to considerable rewards.

Consider this context: the EDUCAUSE Learning Initiative (ELI) has been facilitating the articulation of aspirational goals related to a "next generation digital learning environment" (NGDLE) for several years now (EDUCAUSE Learning Initiative, 2014, September 17). The core idea is the establishment of a standards-based ecosystem affording greater flexibility and personalization for learners than current learning management systems (LMSs) offer (EDUCAUSE Learning Initiative, 2015, December 9). While the NGDLE construct was identified by a survey of over 900 educational technology leaders in higher education as a "key issue" for higher education in 2016 (EDUCAUSE Learning Initiative, 2016), themes emerging from an interactive online symposium of nearly 150 higher education faculty, designers, and administrators indicated that there was lack of agreement on what an NGDLE is, how an NGDLE should be created, and how an institution might position itself to move toward the vision of an NGDLE (Alexander, Cooper, & Thompson, 2016, April 28).

Against this backdrop, it is easy to imagine an online learning leader refusing to commit institutional personnel and other resources toward the development of such an ill-defined construct. Perhaps it would be much more sound to wait until products enter the market and a legitimate build-versus-buy decision can be framed. However, if instead a leader focuses on the institutional payoff of achieving the end-goals of a more sustainable, more extensible learning environment that better meets the needs of learners and faculty, he might decide to begin marshalling his forces now toward this eventual end-state. For instance, perhaps he encourages developers to embrace standards such as learning tools interoperability (LTI) and challenges LMS administrators to ensure that integrations between LTIs and the LMS work seamlessly. Maybe he goes even further to establish a multi-tiered governance structure through which third-party LTIs and homegrown tools are vetted and tested through agile processes without the bottlenecks common to traditional IT projects.

While inventing the future starts with the online learning leader having a vision, it is carried out by inspiring others to see this vision and prompting myriad action steps in pursuit of it. Indeed, Certo and Chesney (2016, March 2) and Certo and Harrington (2016, March 7) have identified *inspiration* as a hallmark of effective senior leaders. "[P]eople need to believe there is a better place, believe there is a better way" (Certo & Chesney, 2016, March 2, 15:19). When is such inspiration more important than when asking a team to join you in inventing the future?

Research and Make a Decision

The risk associated with inventing the future can be mitigated to some degree by gathering as much data as possible. Unfortunately, leaders are often faced with situations in which there are insufficient data to know precisely what to do. It has been said that a decision is what a leader makes when the data don't present themselves. After all, if the data were so clear as to tell you exactly what to do, then anyone could be a leader. Gather as much information as you can and then don't be afraid to make a decision.

Of course, there is a certain amount of data awareness involved in the leader's general, ongoing background processes of monitoring trends, listening for applicability to his/her local context, and gauging the probability of success. However, once relevance for institutional needs is recognized, it is important to establish a local line of inquiry. At the very least this will involve one or more pilots, but it might also involve formal research studies. In either event, the goal should be "to obtain different but complementary data on the same topic" (Morse, 1991, p. 122), most likely through collecting a combination of quantitative and qualitative data. This is in the service of the fundamental purpose of building a case that convinces oneself and other stakeholders that there is a preponderance of evidence pointing to the probability of success.

For instance, in the case of piloting an adaptive learning platform, one might invite a small number of faculty from different disciplines to work with designers to redesign existing online courses for this new modality. Data sources during the development phase might include time logs of designers and data from the system on the number and type of lesson nodes created. Once a course is ready the adaptive learning system can be leveraged for various kinds of user performance data (e.g., interactions and outcomes), but these data can be complemented with surveys of students and instructors. If particular issues warrant further investigation, individual interviews or focus groups can be carried out (depending upon the design of the questionnaires). If the online learning leader continues to insist on data collection and analysis, eventually he/she will have "enough" data to convince herself (and others) that the pilot is worth expanding to a few more cases, transitioning to a full scale institutional rollout, or abandoning. That being said, leaders must remind themselves that a perfect data set is never coming. We are dealing in probabilities, not absolutes. The leader must convince himself/herself that a project is likely to succeed or likely to fail. The leader must not be duped into spending costly personnel hours in pursuit of a sure thing. Leaders take educated risks and are prepared to accept the consequences.

Recognize Resource Limitations

No organization has unlimited resources. The key to effective leadership is deciding where to apply the resources you have. As Arthur Kirk, former president of Saint Leo University, has said: "It's not about resources… it's about how resourceful you are" (Kirk, 2013, 46:57). Of course, deciding to apply resources in one area also implies that you won't have resources available in another. That's why vision and strategy are so important. Make an informed decision about a future direction and then do all you can to adequately resource that venture for success.

Beyond the important step of trimming any fat and the simple-but-cold calculus of letting one initiative go hungry in order to feed a start-up, other alternatives might involve partnering with another institutional unit to co-fund a project or to devise a financial model that is self-sustaining. For instance, in an effort to better serve students and grow online-exclusive enrollments, an online learning leader might propose a revised fee schedule for such students in which they do not pay for campus-based services they do not receive. If the financial model is sound and demonstrates that this initiative can pay for itself within an acceptable time frame, it has a greater likelihood of seeing the light of day. Extending this scenario a bit, perhaps the financial model is still not workable if it depends solely upon the fiscal resources of the online learning unit. However, a persevering online learning leader might partner with another unit if mutual benefit can be established. As an example, perhaps student support services are needed for exclusively online students and a regional campus office has excess capacity and knowledgeable personnel who can serve these students. Such a partnership can mutually benefit both departments, help accomplish the broader institutional mission, and ultimately (and most-importantly) better serve students.

The phrase "resource limitations" undoubtedly triggers visions of budget spreadsheets, personnel rosters, and inventory lists. However, especially in relation to innovation, the creative potential and passion of team members are often overlooked resources that might be sitting untapped within each and every employee.

Turgeon (2016, January 26) offers the example of technology companies that set aside time for their employees to pursue creative problem solving (e.g., hack days, hackathons, or 20% time) and tells the story of overcoming resistance to such a concept in a university setting thanks to an online learning leader with vision. "We just couldn't convince anyone to dedicate a week of our department's time to the idea. Honestly, that is a hard sell, especially if you're in an 'enterprisey' environment. We just didn't have the persuasion skills to convince our managers to sign off on that many hours of unknowns. Fortunately that all changed [due to the intervention of the online learning leader], and we got started something that's become a fruitful tradition" (para. 3).

While some might scoff at such a concept, Turgeon (2016, January 26) paints a picture of highly engaged employees who carry out "really useful ideas" (para. 5) that had been abandoned previously. A look at the growing online gallery of hack day projects shared by Turgeon (see https://trello.com/b/fboKZjst/cdl-hack-day-history) reveals that many of these individual and small group projects are rapid prototypes associated with leading educational technology trends. While some emerge from part-time student felt needs, a number of these are related to broader institutional challenges. Imagine being the leader that sparks such passion in pursuit of institutional needs!

Solve the Big Problems

While it's important to continually assess performance against internal measures such as adoption, educational technology leaders in general and online learning leaders specifically won't truly be able to claim significant impact unless they are aligning digital innovation efforts with the larger institutional goals and challenges. Using online learning and other digital innovations to solve global issues such as retention, access, and cost will place online learning leaders at the table with other key institutional decision-makers and ensure that their work is focused on maximum impact.

Leaders will never achieve institutional impact by only measuring against internal goals. While, for example, the number of online sections offered may be important and should certainly be tracked, it is only meaningful as a measure in the service of larger institutional objectives. How does the number of sections impact institutional access, revenue, retention, student debt, and student success? Senior leaders will only invest in technology initiatives if they see them as solutions for their own, larger challenges. The key word in the preceding sentence is "invest." Initiatives must be positioned as investments with a valued return rather than as mere expenses. If online leaders cannot link their initiatives to the primary challenges facing the broader institution, then they will not see the level of resource investment they want. Nor should they receive significant investment when other strategies may be more compelling solutions to institutional challenges. However, if online learning leaders succeed in tying their initiatives to broader institutional goals, effective senior leadership will welcome their suggestions and contributions.

Take Action

Recall that a key difference between a manager and a leader is the decision-making process. A manager is more often called upon to implement a decision on a primarily tactical basis. A leader, however, must be comfortable enough with risk to make strategic decisions that others will implement. These leadership decisions rarely offer a clearly defined pathway to success.

Yet, leaders must act and move forward. As educational technology and pedagogical practice continue to advance, being satisfied with the status quo risks the potential of being left behind. The challenge facing an online learning leader is recognizing both that an opportunity is one worth pursuing and knowing the timing of making such a decision to act. Further, once a leader has decided that the time is right for a particular decision, he/she must ensure that the financial, infrastructure, and human resources are aligned to make it successful. This can be no small task.

Because the stakes can be so high, a potential risk is for a leader to become frozen in an attempt to gather all the data possible—what is colloquially known as "analysis paralysis." She may convince herself that an additional survey, one more focus group, a committee, a task force, will provide the necessary information to eliminate all risk and reveal the proper course of action. However, the proper course of action will never be 100% clear. An online learning leader must make friends with the concept of acceptable risk and not let fear prevent her from acting.

While it is especially important in a higher education context to gather data and build consensus before embarking upon a digital innovation project, leaders also need to recognize that there are sometimes limited windows of opportunity. Please allow us as authors to address you personally for a moment. As a leader you will never have all the data you need, and you will rarely ever have unanimous consensus. However, at a certain point, as a leader, you must decide to act with the data you have available and with the team you have built. Eschew the paralysis of analysis and remember that doing nothing is itself a decision.

Conclusion

There are numerous leadership training programs available for professional development, many of which are specifically focused on the higher education sector generally or even the higher education technology sector specifically. However, no matter how much training a leader receives, leadership can only be accomplished in practice. To be a leader one must actually lead, with all the concomitant messiness associated with difficult decisions. This is especially true for online learning leaders, where the pace of change in technology, pedagogy, and practice seems to accelerate on a daily basis.

Organizations want to achieve impactful results and it's a leader's job to recognize opportunities, marshal resources, know when to act, and accept risk. This can be difficult in highly-complex, often political environments. Yet, it is often in the crucible of especially-charged contexts that the most effective work can be done. A leader must understand his/her context, including his/her allies, obstacles, and stakeholders.

This context includes both short- and long-range considerations. Keeping up with rapidly-emerging trends while simultaneously attending to the responsibilities of daily operations requires a particular set of leadership skills. The concepts and FIRRST heuristic offered in this chapter are intended to serve as a potential structure for online learning leaders as they navigate the steps of the "delicate dance" of strategic decision-making.

For More Information

Technology Trend Briefs

Horizon Report (Higher Education Edition) http://www.nmc.org/publication-type/horizon-report
Issued annually as a collaboration between the New Media Consortium (NMC) and the EDUCAUSE Learning Initiative (ELI), this is a go-to resource for gauging technologies with the potential to have a meaningful impact on higher education within a 5-year time frame.

7 Things You Should Know About Series http://www.educause.edu/research-and-publications/7-things-you-should-know-about Each two-page primer within this ongoing series produced by the EDUCAUSE Learning Initiative (ELI) offers a brief-but-substantive look at technologies becoming impactful within higher education.

Leadership Podcasts

TOPcast: The Teaching Online Podcast http://topcast.online.ucf.edu

A monthly podcast for online and blended learning leaders hosted by Thomas Cavanagh and Kelvin Thompson over a shared cup of coffee. Each 30 min episode takes a fun and informative look at the various trends, best practices and technologies affecting online education.

Chasing Wisdom Podcast

https://www.chasewisdom.com/podcast

This weekly 20 min podcast hosted by Rollins College business professor Sam Certo offers practical wisdom for real world business challenges through interviews with CEOs and other leaders from various fields.

References

Alexander, B., Cooper, A., & Thompson, K. (2016, April 28). *Community observations on the next-generation digital learning environment.* Invited session within the EDUCAUSE Learning Initiative Online Focus Session: Exploring the Next-Generation Learning Environment. Retrieved from https://events.educause.edu/eli/focus-sessions/2016/eli-online-focus-session-exploring-the-next-generation-digital-learning-environment/proceedings/discussion-community-observations-on-the-next-generation-digital-learning-environment.

Cavanagh, T. & Thompson, K. (Hosts). (2015, November 2). The "delicate dance" of leaders: Shaping the future of online learning [Episode 7]. *Topcast: The teaching online podcast* [Audio podcast]. Retrieved from http://cdl.ucf.edu/topcast-s01e07.

Certo, S. (Host) & Chesney, L. (Guest). (2016, March 2). The difference between manager and leader [Episode 21]. *Chasing wisdom podcast* [Audio podcast]. Retrieved from http://www.chasewisdom.com/podcast.

Certo, S. (Host) & Harrington, R. (Guest). (2016, March 7). Managers do things right, leaders do the right thing [Episode 22]. *Chasing wisdom podcast* [Audio podcast]. Retrieved from http://www.chasewisdom.com/podcast.

Covey, S. R., Merrill, A. R., & Merrill, R. R. (1994). *First things first: To live, to love, to learn, to leave a legacy.* New York: Simon & Schuster.

EDUCAUSE Learning Initiative. (2014, September 17). Next generation digital learning environment. Retrieved from https://library.educause.edu/resources/2014/9/next-generation-digital-learning-environment-initiative.

EDUCAUSE Learning Initiative. (2015, December 9). *7 things you should know about ngdle.* Retrieved from https://library.educause.edu/resources/2015/12/7-things-you-should-know-about-ngdle.

EDUCAUSE Learning Initiative. (2016). *Key issues in teaching and learning 2016.* Retrieved from https://www.educause.edu/eli/initiatives/key-issues-in-teaching-and-learning-2016.

Johnson, L., Adams Becker, S., Cummins, M., Estrada, V., Freeman, A., & Hall, C. (2016). *NMC Horizon Report: 2016 Higher Education Edition*. Austin, Texas: The New Media Consortium. Retrieved from http://www.nmc.org/publication/nmc-horizon-report-2016-higher-education-edition.

Johnson, S. (1998). *Who moved my cheese?: An amazing way to deal with change in your work and in your life*. New York: Putnam.

Kay, A. (n.d.). Retrieved from https://web.archive.org/web/19991008040012/http://www.small-talk.org/alankay.html.

Kirk, A. (2013) The online tsunami: go big, go home, or go away. *Connect 2013 Keynote*. Retrieved via video from https://www.youtube.com/watch?v=mnAnr_1FwAg.

Morse, J. M. (1991). Approaches to qualitative-quantitative methodological triangulation. *Nursing Research, 40*, 120–123.

Senge, P., Hamilton, H., & Kania, J. (2015). The dawn of system leadership. *Stanford Social Innovation Review, 13*(1). Retrieved from http://ssir.org/articles/entry/the_dawn_of_system_leadership.

Turgeon, I. (2016, January 26). *Inviting innovation. Running hack days at UCF's center for distributed learning* [Web log post]. Retrieved from https://medium.com/@iturgeon/inviting-innovation-500d8efa4342.

Quality Online Learning: e-Learning Strategies for Higher Education

Andrea Gregg, Cathy Holsing, and Stevie Rocco

Abstract This chapter is structured to target what we have identified as five key dimensions of planning, developing, and maintaining successful online learning specific to your educational institution. This chapter is written to be helpful to you whether you are just getting started with online learning or already have a strategy in place that you want to refine or further develop. In order to best maximize your efforts, we recommend that you (1) establish quality as a top priority; (2) customize your e-Learning approach for your institution; (3) invest in learning design and faculty development; (4) work strategically with educational technology and its vendors; and (5) leverage the e-Learning community. Each of the sections includes a brief overview of the essential information you need to know about the topic and then provides concrete suggestions for what you can do at your institution in order to make progress in that area. The authors of this chapter have over 40 years of combined experience in online education, starting as learning designers and moving into leadership roles. We have structured this chapter based on our professional experiences and our personal commitment to and passion for quality in e-Learning.

Keywords Quality • Online learning • Higher education • Learning design • Faculty development • Customized strategies • Financial models • Educational technology • e-Learning community

A. Gregg (✉)
The Pennsylvania State University, 840 Galen Dr., State College, PA 16803, USA
e-mail: axg251@psu.edu

C. Holsing
The Pennsylvania State University, 365 High Point Cove., State College, PA 16801, USA
e-mail: cjh145@psu.edu

S. Rocco
The Pennsylvania State University, 134 W. Blade Drive, PA Furnace, PA 16865, USA
e-mail: sxr133@psu.edu

© Association for Educational Communications and Technology 2018   13
A.A. Piña et al. (eds.), *Leading and Managing e-Learning*, Educational Communications and Technology: Issues and Innovations,
https://doi.org/10.1007/978-3-319-61780-0_2

Decision-Making Guidance

This chapter will help you make decisions about how to:

1. Establish quality as a top priority.
2. Customize your e-Learning approach for your institution.
3. Invest in learning design and faculty development.
4. Work strategically with educational technology and its vendors.
5. Leverage the e-Learning community.

What You Need to Know

In this first major section, What You Need to Know, we provide a brief overview for each of our five suggested strategies for quality e-Learning. Then, in the next major section, What You Can Do, we offer concrete steps to enact those suggested strategies.

Establish Quality as a Top Priority

Establishing quality as a top priority for online learning at your institution can be both a differentiator and a useful focal point for your overall e-Learning strategy. In the many e-Learning conversations pertaining to technology, infrastructure, and scaling innovation, an explicit focus on quality in teaching and learning sometimes gets overlooked. We believe, however, that quality should be a top priority and not an afterthought. While many of the specifics regarding how to do online learning will vary based on unique factors at your institution, a commitment to quality transcends institution type.

We also start here in large part pragmatically because it continues to be the most challenged domain of online learning. Many still have questions and doubts about online learning such as "Can students *really* learn online?" or "Isn't it the case that online courses are easier?" And, to be sure, there are some examples of low quality online courses or online instructors who were derelict in their teaching duties. That said, examples of poor quality can be found in residential education as well. Therefore, rather than discount online learning based on selected poor examples, we suggest committing to quality at your institution for your online offerings and then working to make it true in practice. In the What You Can Do section, we offer specific suggestions for how to establish quality as a top priority.

Customize your e-Learning Approach for Your Institution

In order to enable quality online teaching and learning to take place, there is much that needs to be in place at your institution in terms of infrastructure, administration, and corresponding policies and procedures. This is especially true if you are planning to offer these courses at a distance. To do this well requires adopting a systems approach that includes finances, marketing, IT, learning design, faculty development, and academic and student support services like enrollment management and academic advising (Moore & Kearsley, 2012). The infrastructure you develop, or extend, will be dependent on whether you are focusing primarily on residential online courses or extending to a new distance audience. In the What You Can Do section, we offer specific suggestions for what you can do to evaluate the infrastructure needed at your institution.

Invest in Learning Design and Faculty Development

Offering quality learning experiences online requires both well-designed online courses and qualified, confident instructors to teach those courses. Within the larger system of online education, there are two concrete ways you can work toward those ends. These include developing a strong, skilled learning design staff and implementing effective online faculty development programs. An easy way to understand the distinction between learning design and faculty development is that learning design typically takes place *before the course is offered* and faculty development takes place in order to empower individuals to teach *as the course is running*. While learning design and faculty development are sometimes carried about by the same set of individuals, we discuss them separately for clarification purposes. Learning designers (also called instructional designers) collaborate with faculty members in order to design and develop online courses. Many institutions rely on what is described as a master course model, which is one of the predominant models throughout the field of online education (Magda, Poulin, & Clinefelter, 2015). In this model, a master course is developed in collaboration between a learning designer and a faculty member and then multiple sections of that master course are taught, often over multiple semesters, by individual instructors *who were often not the initial course authors*.

Learning designers and faculty development experts are essential to the success of this model. A core competency of learning designers is the ability to design effective learning experiences *whatever the delivery modality*. While an increasing number of students are taking courses online, there are still a significant number of faculty members who have no online teaching experience. Consider that "[r]esearch shows most teachers teach as they were taught. However, distance educators lack a model or benchmark for online teaching because many of them have not taken online courses as students" (Schmidt, Tschida, & Hodge, 2016). Faculty development is especially important, therefore, in order to empower faculty members to be competent, qualified online instructors as the course is running.

Work Strategically with Educational Technology and Its Vendors

While we have taken care throughout this chapter to emphasize that online learning should ultimately be concerned with quality education, it is also the case that working in the online learning realm will likely involve various educational technologies and vendor relationships. In fact, some universities have taken advantage of the move to e-Learning to create greater efficiencies regarding technology throughout their institutions (Davidson, 2014). While you might decide to develop some of your technology solutions in-house, it is nearly inevitable when working in the world of online learning that you will end up working with some educational technology vendors. Accordingly, melding the fast-paced, sales cycle-driven world of educational technology entrepreneurs with the decision-by-committee, highly regulated world of higher education can be challenging. In the What You Can Do section, we offer specific suggestions to help you successfully navigate this complex terrain.

Leverage the e-Learning Community

The larger e-Learning professional community abounds with resources. You can reach out to this community with regard to institutional leadership, technology, learning design strategies, teaching online, policies impacting online higher education, and much more. While there will certainly be exceptions to this general trend, we have found that rather than being competitive and holding information "close to the vest" the e-Learning community is remarkably open, helpful, and interested in sharing best practices. Perhaps it is the shared commitment to wanting to do online learning right that makes this such a productive professional community of which to be a part. Some concrete suggestions for leveraging this community follow in the What You Can Do section.

What You Can Do

The previous section, What You Need to Know, provided a brief overview of each of the five suggested strategies. Here we offer specific action steps for each of those strategies.

Table 1 Pursuing online learning—Penn State example

Pursuing Online Learning
Penn State Example
For Penn State, the decision to pursue online learning evolved in large part from within a long-standing distance education infrastructure. Penn State's distance education began in 1892 with the advent of one of the first correspondence courses through rural free delivery. Moving into online learning in 1997 was a natural next step given Penn State's commitment to meeting the needs of learners, wherever their location. Currently, Penn State World Campus is the fully online, distance education campus of the distributed campus system at Penn State

Establish Quality as a Top Priority

Clarify why you are pursuing online learning. We believe in starting here because if you have a good sense of why you are pursuing online learning, it will be easier for you to define and operationalize quality. There are many valid reasons to get into online learning and it is likely that your motivation is some combination of the following. Using online offerings to:

- Extend the capacity of your curriculum offerings beyond the constraints of your physical campus.
- Respond to your students' requests for online experiences before they graduate.
- Build on an already established infrastructure of distance and continuing education.
- Generate new revenue for your institution.

For an example of Penn State's reasons to pursue online learning, see Table 1. Whatever your specific reason(s), it is ultimately the educational experience that should warrant your attention.

Commit to standards of quality for online learning. We cannot tell you how to specifically operationalize quality at your institution given that this will likely vary based on your institutional mission, structure, and culture. Areas in which standards for quality commonly exist pertain to the achievement of learning outcomes, depth or level of thinking expected within various course levels, achievement of applicable skills, job acquisition upon graduation, and exposure to cocurricular experiences. We suggest that you should have the *same standards and expectations for online learning* as you do for your residential courses. This includes viewing and treating your online students as *real,* rather than *virtual*, students. While *virtual* can suggest a disconnect from the humanness of your distance learners, thinking of them as *real* emphasizes that while they may participate in your University differently than your residential students, they are equally deserving of high quality education and the relevant corresponding student support services. Two useful frameworks to help guide your thinking about online quality are:

- *OLC Quality Framework:* A holistic, systems-based framework for evaluating quality in online learning that considers learning effectiveness, scale, access,

Table 2 Academic quality in online learning—Penn State example

Academic Quality in Online Learning
Penn State Example
When the World Campus was initially formed in 1997, it was the vision of the senior administrators that World Campus courses have the same academic rigor in terms of teaching and learning as residential courses. This commitment means that there is no distinction between the courses offered residentially and those offered online. They are designed and taught by Penn State faculty and instructors, and curriculum and academic hiring decisions remain in the domain of the academic departments and colleges
Penn State also views online learners as *real* students. While the needs of adult distance learners are not identical to those of their traditional-aged residential counterparts, they still warrant advising, student affairs, career counseling, tutoring services, financial aid assistance, and many of the other services that are commonplace for residence education

student satisfaction, and faculty satisfaction. (More information can be found at http://onlinelearningconsortium.org/about/quality-framework-five-pillars/)

- *Quality Matters:* A research-based rubric for specifically evaluating online course design that emphasizes eight general areas including the course overview, learning objectives, assessment, materials, course activities, technology, support, and accessibility and usability. (More information can be found at https://www.qualitymatters.org/)

In order to establish quality in your online offerings it is essential that you make a commitment that is sincere and consistent with your practices. This quality commitment can be included in your strategic plan for online offerings, in how you talk about online learning throughout your institution, and in how you support the online infrastructure through staffing, professional development, and technology investments (Table 2).

Plan to invest in online learning. Because online learning is likely different than what is currently taking place at your institution, in order to do this *right*, you are going to need to invest in new types of positions, new technologies, and new forms of professional development. As an example, this is not something you can accomplish by simply asking faculty members to convert their courses to an online format "over the summer." Achieving quality online learning requires time, resources, and specialized expertise that will be discussed throughout this chapter.

Customize Your e-Learning Approach for Your Institution

Evaluate your structure and mission. Every higher education institution has unique characteristics that will shape its e-Learning efforts. These include, but are not limited to, your institutional funding model; public or private status; STEM, liberal arts, or other specialized curriculum emphases; research emphasis (e.g., R1, R2, R3); 2-year or 4-year status; target demographics (e.g., HBCU, military, gender specific, adult learner focus); multi- or single-campus; residential or commuter; and centralized or decentralized administration. For instance, at an institution where there is a board of regents and campuses are more independent, structures may be in place that create difficulties for individuals to cooperate across locations to offer online programs. Likewise, if your mission is to serve the individuals of a particular region, you will need to consider whether and how to undertake marketing efforts outside that region. An institution whose mission is to serve the people in a particular city, for example, will likely not want to begin online recruiting efforts outside that city. In the end, the e-Learning strategy you adopt will depend on your mission and the way your institution is organized.

Consider your culture. A related issue, but also distinct because it is often less formalized, is a consideration of the culture of your institution. Does your institution value risk and innovation, or does a commitment to tradition hold greater import? Is faculty buy-in required to make changes, as it may be for systems with shared governance? Does your institution have top-down governance? Who are your stakeholders? Will faculty members' work in delivering online courses be valued in the promotion and tenure process? Understanding this culture helps to identify realistic opportunities and constraints as you create and/or assess your e-Learning efforts. For example, if online course authoring and teaching will not "count" in the promotion and tenure process, then you may need to forgo the use of tenure-line faculty until they have achieved tenure or until online learning is central enough to the institutional mission to be counted. Intellectual property is another area of important consideration. If your institution does not have a policy regarding intellectual property of courseware, you should consider developing one that incentivizes both the institution and the faculty member to participate in online learning. It is also important that you work closely with your legal team. Ultimately your institution's implicit culture can be just as impactful in shaping your e-Learning efforts as its explicit structure and mission. For a brief overview of structure, mission, and culture at Penn State, see Table 3.

Table 3 Structure, mission, and culture—Penn State example

Structure, mission, and culture
Penn State Example
Penn State is a large, geographically distributed organization comprising multiple campuses throughout the state. Therefore the idea of having another campus focusing solely on online, distance learning, made sense within the existing structure of Penn State. When the World Campus was founded in 1997 it became like another campus but only in some respects. A key difference between the World Campus and other Penn State campuses is that the academic authority for the courses offered through the World Campus still reside within the academic units offering the courses. If a college or department wants to offer online courses at a distance, however, they must be delivered through the World Campus. This is both to maintain decentralized academic authority and a centralized system of distance course delivery

Develop appropriate financial models. You cannot assume that you will necessarily make money from undertaking e-Learning at your institution. Even if you plan to extend your offerings to attract new learners or to generate revenue from online residential courses, it can take years to recoup the costs of launching a new online program. This is especially true if you have invested in the necessary faculty time, learning design, faculty development, and other support staff. In some cases, costs can be recovered and revenue generated once initial costs for online program launch are paid. For example, you may choose to have all tuition revenue gathered centrally and distributed. If buy-in is an issue, though, it might be better to allow participating academic units to benefit from their efforts. For example, if tuition for online learning, or some percentage of that tuition, goes to the academic unit to be used to fund graduate students, special projects, or even other faculty members, those units may be more willing to participate. Regardless of the specifics, the financial models you adopt for e-Learning are important.

Be flexible and adapt to change. Whether because of the impact of technology and/or the increasingly dynamic nature of higher education, you will need to adapt your e-Learning approach to meet the needs of your institution, students, and faculty. Over time, the types of courses and programs you offer, faculty willingness to participate, your ability to invest, and regulatory policies will shift, causing you to revisit your e-Learning strategy. Be willing and open to look for any "pain points" that signal a need to revisit what you've been doing. For example, if faculty willingness to participate is lower because of your intellectual property policy, be willing to look at that policy. If your financial models are making it too difficult for particular units to participate, then be willing to look at that as well. Flexibility over time will be key to your success. For examples of changes within online learning at Penn State over the years, see Table 4.

Table 4 Adapting to change—Penn State Example

Adapting to change
Penn State Example
Penn State's initial model for online learning was largely centralized in the administrative delivery unit of the World Campus, which included a single learning design shop. Over the years, learning design became more diffused throughout the university and individual colleges and departments established embedded design units
Online learning at Penn State has also grown to encompass much more than just online distance education. As of today, there are fully online, distance courses and programs taken by students distributed all over the world; blended courses that include a balance of online and residential components; and fully online courses offered residentially. Penn State has continued to evolve its e-Learning administrative policies and structures in order to allow for a balance of growth, innovation, and college independence as well as consistency and collaboration among such a large distributed community

Invest in Learning Design and Faculty Development

Hire and support qualified learning design and faculty development staff. For both faculty development and learning design positions, we recommend hiring people who are educators first, technologists second. This is because, from our perspective, technology is the means to the educational end. Therefore it is essential that people working in the areas of learning design and faculty development understand the fundamentals of teaching and learning. Learning designers and faculty development staff might possess a master's degree in fields like instructional design, educational technology, adult education, curriculum and instruction, and/or be qualified for these positions through other skills and experiences. Learning designers and faculty development staff should be able to design for and support instruction in multiple modalities, including fully online courses, hybrid experiences, and technology-enhanced residential courses. It is, important that you hire qualified staff with the requisite degree(s) and/or experience and support their professional development. See the last section of this chapter for details on how you can leverage the e-Learning community to advertise for jobs, consult on job descriptions, and identify appropriate professional development opportunities for your learning design and faculty development staff.

Avoid bloating the positions. For many institutions, these are new roles within an existing university structure, and as such, can naturally be conflated or confused with other positions that are more familiar. For instance, it is not uncommon for learning designers to be confused with web designers. We recommend you take care not to bloat the learning design and faculty development positions and try not to require them to also be multimedia specialists, programming experts, or teaching assistants.

Encourage meaningful collaboration. Both faculty development and learning design work best when it is truly a collaborative endeavor with faculty members (Aleckson & Ralston-Berg, 2011). Your faculty members are experts in their subject matter, know their discipline, are aware of what needs to be taught, and where students typically encounter challenges. Your learning designers should partner with those faculty members, as they know how to align learning objectives, content design, assessments, activities, and other supporting materials in order to create the most effective and engaging teaching and learning experiences. Additionally, your faculty development experts can help faculty members effectively teach their subject matter in an online context. It helps to establish that learning designers, faculty development staff, and faculty members are all professionals in their own right, having corresponding educational degrees, skillsets, and well-established professional network. For an overview of learning design and faculty development at Penn State, see Table 5.

Table 5 Learning design and faculty development—Penn State example

Learning Design and Faculty Development
Penn State Example
Learning Design and Faculty Development at Penn State reflects the structure and culture of the University in that there are both centralized and decentralized elements
With Learning Design, while there is a centralized learning design shop housed within the World Campus, there are also many individual learning design shops within campuses, colleges, and departments. Similarly, there is a centralized faculty development unit within the World Campus that works closely with faculty development units and personnel throughout the University
There is a large, active Learning Design community across Penn State and some general consistency of requirements for hiring instructional design staff. For example, the instructional designers are typically required to have a master's degree in an educational discipline and previous teaching or training experiences are highly desired

Work Strategically with Educational Technology and Its Vendors

Evaluate when to develop in-house and when to use vendor solutions. In moving forward with your online learning endeavors, you will be faced with multiple decision points concerning whether to work with outside vendors or develop technology solutions internally. The decision to "build" or "buy" can be a challenging one with a variety of factors to consider. When incorporating a new technology, there may be situations in which building an entirely in-house solution is the best pathway. At other times, working with open source software that is not "owned" by any one entity can enable talented programmers within your organization to create software solutions to exactly fit your organization's needs. There will also be cases where purchasing a technology solution, "out of the box," directly from a vendor has clear advantages, including cost, functionality, maintenance, reliability, and regular upgrades. The education technology advisory company Eduventures has a list of recommendations to help inform your decision-making in this area (Davidson, 2014). (More information can be found at http://www.eduventures.com/2014/09/higher-education-landscape/).

Include faculty members as key stakeholders. This may seem obvious, but it is easy to make decisions based on the best ideas of your technology professionals or learning designers without involving faculty members in the process. As your goal is quality online education, you will need to work successfully with technology solutions to provide the best experience for your faculty and students. Educational technology leader Michael Feldstein explains that,

> Higher education needs to get better at academic needs assessment. That requires an entirely different and deeper set of questions than which features are important to put on a checklist. It requires an in-depth exploration of how teaching and learning happens in various corners of the campus community and what capabilities would be most helpful to support those efforts. (Feldstein, 2016)

Know that a one-size-fits-all solution may not work for both engineering and the humanities. Faculty members also may not realize that there is a solution that would meet their needs already available at your university. Finding ways to accurately assess faculty requirements and keep them updated and invested in decision-making can help to both increase adoption of a technology once it is implemented and familiarize the faculty with the intricacies of the required procurement process. A novel approach for needs assessment and production evaluation is the Learning Technology Commons recently built by the University of North Carolina. Using this open rating system, vendors who agree to the university's terms and conditions can upload information about their products to the Commons site while faculty members can use the site to provide feedback regarding which technologies improve student learning across diverse disciplines. (More information can be found at http://unc.learntrials.com).

Streamline (or at least clearly document) your procurement process. Depending on the size and centralization of your institution, this step may be more or less necessary. In many large institutions or systems, the process to buy an educational technology software solution can be difficult to navigate, with few having a good understanding of all of the steps involved. Risk Management, Purchasing, and IT all play crucial roles and may not always work together seamlessly. Risk Management will be tasked with assessing how well a vendor meets a long list of legal requirements, while Purchasing will have a standard Request for Information (RFI) and Request for Proposals (RFP) process requiring varying levels of pilots and review before a vendor can be selected. IT will need to make sure the new solution integrates with existing systems and understand the user support that will be needed. Making these processes as transparent as possible will help to prevent false starts. That way, time is not spent by Risk Management to vet a system only to find it will not work with existing technologies, and IT will be careful not to find a perfect software solution that fails to abide by necessary legal requirements such as FERPA or the need for the solution to be accessible. Once you have the process documented, gather the stakeholders together to see where efficiencies can be found or communication improved.

Collect information regarding which technologies are already adopted independently. You may be surprised to find out the number of technologies that are currently being used across your institution through separate licenses with individual faculty members or departments. In some cases, these may be unique use cases that only apply within a specific discipline, so a license for an individual or just a few users may be appropriate. However, you may also discover that a large number of separate entities within the University have contracted with the same vendor for the same product and that by negotiating a campus-wide license you can get a less expensive per-user rate and may actually save money overall. Ultimately, be sure you take the time to step back and evaluate how well the technology you have adopted contributes to the fundamental goal of high quality teaching and learning.

Leverage the e-Learning Community

Become familiar with the history of online education. In addition to being a more informed leader in this domain, acclimating yourself with some of the history of online education can also help you identify which professional networks make the most sense for your needs. It also gives you a shared language and understanding of which questions have already been widely addressed and largely settled (e.g., "Can students *really* learn online?") and those that are still being actively tackled (e.g., "How do we best do hands-on science labs with distributed, asynchronous learners?"). Since 2003, an annual study has been conducted identifying demographics, enrollment trends, and other key issues of concern to online higher education. Reviewing these and noting the changes over time is an important starting point. (These reports can be found at http://www.onlinelearningsurvey.com/highered.html). Additionally, while this chapter is not meant to be a literature review, if you are embarking into the online learning realm and are met with skepticism about its efficacy, it can help to be familiar with some of the meta-analyses in this area (see, for example, Bernard et al., 2004; Means, Toyama, Murphy, Bakia, & Jones, 2010; Russell, 1999).

Keep up with regulations regarding online learning. Because online learning and online distance education are less understood at the governmental regulatory level, keeping up with emerging policies and their potential impact on your practice is important for someone in your leadership. Some especially powerful organizations in this regard are University Professional and Continuing Education Association (UPCEA), United States Distance Learning Association (USDLA), Online Learning Consortium (OLC), and Western Cooperative for Educational Telecommunications (WCET).

Develop informal communities within your own institution. If your institution is distributed and there are enough people to participate, you can cultivate an e-Learning community within your own organization. Often these communities are most effective when they are organized at the grassroots level and emerge out of the needs of the members (e.g., learning designers, online instructors). However, if just getting started, you may benefit from establishing a community around online learning. Much of the success of e-Learning comes through sharing best practices and overcoming silos. Yammer, Facebook, email listservs, internal meetings, and even mini-conferences can all contribute toward this as they can nurture spaces of constant informal learning. For examples of the learning design community at Penn State, see Table 6.

Benchmark with peer institutions. Invite colleagues at peer institutions to come to your institution for a day or two and meet with your key stakeholders in order to understand how they have approached their online learning—and be willing to share your own story as well.

Identify appropriate professional networks. The e-Learning community includes conferences, professional organizations, blogs, listservs, and comprises professional staff, research faculty, online instructors, and many others. While some of

Table 6 Informal learning design community—Penn State example

Informal Learning Design Community
Penn State Example
One of Penn State's strengths with Learning Design, given that learning designers are housed within different Campuses, Colleges, Departments, and the World Campus, is its large, informal, highly active distributed learning design community
Ways this community of practice has been developed and supported over the years include Yammer groups, email listservs, annual conferences like Teaching with Technology (TLT), an ID-to-ID mentoring program, and other collaborations among learning design staff across administrative reporting lines
Consistent with the centralized and decentralized structure and culture at Penn State, some of these initiatives have been developed and managed centrally, while many others are grassroots-based and grow up in individual colleges and units

these are applicable across higher education, many are specific to the online learning arena. Some of these organizations offer listservs that are often free, provide industry-targeted news stories and information, and are easy to unsubscribe from if it turns out they are not relevant to your needs. You'll want to identify conferences and professional organizations where you can participate and network. As well, it will be important to connect through different organizations based on the needs of your staff. For example, your administrative leadership will likely benefit from different professional networks than your learning designers, advisors, faculty members, or faculty development personnel. Examples of e-Learning professional networks include:

- Association of Educational Communications and Technology (AECT) Distance Learning Division
- Distance Teaching and Learning Conference in Madison, WI
- EDUCAUSE
- e-Literate blog (http://mfeldstein.com)
- EDUCAUSE Learning Initiative (ELI)
- European Distance and e-Learning Network (EDEN)
- International Council for Open and Distance Education (ICDE)
- Inside Higher Ed (http://insidehighered.com)
- Kapp Notes (http://karlkapp.com/kapp-notes)
- Online Learning Consortium (OLC, formerly Sloan-C)
- University Professional and Continuing Education Association (UPCEA)
- United States Distance Learning Association (USDLA)
- Western Cooperative for Educational Telecommunications (WCET)

Conclusion

Congratulations on being a part of the e-Learning community! This is a well-developed, knowledgeable, and helpful professional group of which to be a part. Perhaps this is because it initially evolved from a type of education that was very much on the margins and treated with great skepticism. Conversely, perhaps it just happens to be made up of smart, helpful people. Whatever the reason, one of the benefits to starting (or growing) your University's work in online learning at this point in time is that there is now a well-established online learning community and many resources on which you can rely. This book on e-Learning leadership is just one example.

In the above, we have emphasized five key areas of import in starting or growing your e-Learning strategy at your institution. In brief, we believe you should commit to high quality online learning, intentionally develop a strategy that fits your unique institution, invest in both learning design and faculty development, work strategically with educational technology and its vendors, and leverage the vast and powerful e-Learning professional network. Whether you are just starting out or well into your implementation of e-Learning at your institution, we wish you the best of luck in your endeavor!

For More Information

Larreamendy-Joerns, J., & Leinhardt, G. (2006). Going the distance with online education. *Review of Educational Research, 76*(4), 567–605.

Miller, G., Benke, M., Chaloux, B., Ragan, L. C., Schroeder, R., Smutz, W., & Swan, K. (2014). *Leading the e-learning transformation of Higher Education: Meeting the challenges of technology and distance education.* Steerling, VA: Stylus Publishing, LLC.

Willcox, K. E., Sarma, S., & Lippel, P. H. (2016). Online education: A catalyst for higher education reforms. *MIT Online Education Policy Initiative.* Retrieved from https://oepi.mit.edu/sites/default/files/MIT%20Online%20Education%20Policy%20Initiative%20April%202016_0.pdf.

References

Aleckson, J. D., & Ralston-Berg, P. (2011). *MindMeld: Micro-collaboration between e-Learning designers and instructor experts.* Madison, WI: Atwood Publishing.

Bernard, R. M., Abrami, P. C., Lou, Y., Borokhovsk, E., Wade, A., Wozney, L., … Huang, B. (2004). How does distance education compare with classroom instruction? A meta-analysis of the empirical literature. *Review of Educational Research, 74*(3), 379–439.

Davidson, S. (2014, September 16). Making sense of the higher education technology landscape. *Eduventures.* Retrieved from http://www.eduventures.com/2014/09/higher-education-landscape/.

Feldstein, M. (2016, March 8). What's really to blame for the failures of our learning-management systems. *Chronicle of Higher Education.* Retrieved from http://chronicle.com/article/What-s-Really-to-Blame-for/235620.

Magda, A. J., Poulin, R., & Clinefelter, D. L. (2015). *Recruiting, orienting, & supporting online adjunct faculty: A survey of practices.* Louisville, KY: The Learning House, Inc..

Means, B., Toyama, Y., Murphy, R., Bakia, M., & Jones, K. (2010, September). *Evaluation of evidence-based practices in online learning: A meta-analysis and review of online learning studies*. Monograph. Retrieved February 1, 2014, from http://www.ed.gov/about/offices/list/opepd/ppss/reports.html.

Moore, M. G., & Kearsley, G. (2012). *Distance education: A systems view of online learning* (3rd ed.). Belmont, CA: Cengage Learning.

Russell, T. L. (1999). *The no significant difference phenomenon*. Chapel Hill: Office of Instructional Telecommunications, University of North Carolina.

Schmidt, S. W., Tschida, C. M., & Hodge, E. M. (2016). How faculty learn to teach online: What administrators need to know. *Online Journal of Distance Learning Administration, 19*(1), n1.

Centralized and Decentralized Approaches to Managing Online Programs

Meridith Z. Bergeron and Sarah C. Fornero

Abstract It is necessary for institutions to have a formal approach to overseeing the design and delivery of online programs. The selected approach will fall on the spectrum between centralized and decentralized. This chapter will explore the differences between centralized and decentralized approaches, best practices, and necessary components that need to be considered, regardless of the method selected. Whether centralized or decentralized, all institutions offering online learning need to consider the following areas, related to best practices: technology, faculty, administration, curriculum, and support services. From there, establishing guidelines and standards are explored, and suggestions for implementation are considered.

Keywords e-Learning • Centralized • Decentralized • Standards • Design • Delivery • Online • Distance

Decision-Making Guidance

This chapter will help you make decisions about:

- Selecting a formal approach to managing online programs on the spectrum between centralized and decentralized
- Conducting a needs assessment to establish your institutional culture and status quo
- Identifying, selecting, and monitoring institutional guidelines and standards related to managing online programs

M.Z. Bergeron (✉)
Franciscan Missionaries of Our Lady University, Formerly Our Lady of the Lake College,
5414 Brittany Drive, Baton Rouge, LA 70808, USA
e-mail: Meridith.Bergeron@ololcollege.edu

S.C. Fornero
Adler University, 17 N. Dearborn Street, Chicago 60602, IL, USA
e-mail: SFornero@adler.edu

© Association for Educational Communications and Technology 2018   29
A.A. Piña et al. (eds.), *Leading and Managing e-Learning*, Educational
Communications and Technology: Issues and Innovations,
https://doi.org/10.1007/978-3-319-61780-0_3

What You Need to Know

Distance education continues to be a growing area in higher education; Allen and Seaman (2015) indicate that in 2013 there were 5,257,279 students enrolled in a distance education courses, up 3.7% from 2012. There is, however, still scrutiny regarding the quality of the design and delivery of online courses and programs. To offer sustainable online programs, in a number of states higher education institutions will likely need state authorization, which will result in the need for identifying how they plan to sustain, provide academic oversight, maintain a rigorous curriculum, evaluate effectiveness, and train and support faculty delivering online programming (NC-SARA, 2015). In addition, regional accreditation is necessary to procure Title IV funding, federal financial aid for institutions, which similarly requires institutions to identify how they are developing their curriculum and instructional design for online courses, their plans to support students and faculty, and evaluate online learning (Higher Learning Commission, 2015). Beyond the individual requirements for the National Council for State Authorization Reciprocity Agreement (NC-SARA) or the Higher Learning Commission of the North Central Association (HLC), the Council of Regional Accrediting Commissions (C-RAC) has issued a series of guidelines for the evaluation of distance education programs which include requirements for the oversight of the design and delivery of distance, or online, programs (Middle States Commission on Higher Education, 2002, 2011; New England Association of Schools and Colleges Commission on Institutions of Higher Education, 2013). Further, online learning creates a setting where there is a record of all activity that takes place in the classroom, and the e-learning leader can no longer get by hoping that no one notices when there is a poor learning experience.

For the reasons listed above, it is necessary for institutions to have a formal approach to overseeing the design and delivery of online programs. The selected approached will fall on the spectrum between centralized and decentralized.

A Centralized Approach

Definition. A fully *centralized* approach to overseeing the design and delivery of online programs utilizes a primary unit within the institution to coordinate and facilitate related processes, or a series of institution-wide departments that provide consistent services across all online offerings. All oversight and policies for the design and delivery of online programs are housed in a single office or department for all online offerings in the institution, and specialized faculty and staff focus on the various aspects of online learning.

What does a fully centralized approach look like? A fully centralized approach has one or more institutional departments charged with managing the design and delivery of online programs. The department or departments coordinate all functional aspects considered in this chapter for online learning across the entire institution, including technology, faculty, administration, curriculum, and support services. Specialized employees work with academic program leads and respective faculty to set design standards and expectations for online programs. They work with program leads to develop training materials, course content, and course and program assessment, making the online program both operational and functional. Additionally, the centralized departments assist in the development of formal faculty observations and a course evaluation process that is carried out by academic supervisors. The technology chosen for delivering online programs is standardized through a single learning management system (LMS) for the institution and all support inquiries are funneled to one place to streamline communication and feedback.

Pros and cons of a centralized approach. When considering a *centralized* approach to overseeing the design and delivery of online programs, the e-learning leader must evaluate the overall needs and expectations of the institution. Housing all functional considerations within institution-level departments allows for commonality and structure throughout the institution by providing consistency in program design and delivery. However, a centralized approach must be thoughtfully considered, as it will require buy-in from faculty, staff, and administration across the institution. The e-learning leader must recognize and implement a formal process for creating and delivering online programs. Policies must be created, following best practices, and the institution must embrace the fully centralized department across the board. From program leads, faculty, and support services, the e-learning leader must implement a centralized approach that is comparable and equivalent to that of a residential program.

A Decentralized Approach

Definition. A different approach, more *decentralized* in nature, involves each academic or program area making their own decisions as it relates to online programming. In some instances, key individuals from different departments may come together as a team to oversee the design and delivery of online programs, but may work independently from one another. The defining characteristic of a decentralized approach is present when online offerings in different program areas of an institution function differently than others. Program leads and academic deans oversee the design and delivery of online programs, including policies and procedures. These leads, in turn, work with departments across campus for support services to design and deliver online programs.

What do fully decentralized support services look like? A fully decentralized approach to managing the design and delivery of online programs falls on the opposite spectrum of full centralization. The decentralized approach places emphasis on program leads and their ability to coordinate oversight for online program design and delivery. However, it is not to say programs do this *on their own.* When implementing a decentralized approach, it is essential to work collaboratively with other departments to define, delineate, and coordinate the technology, administrative functions, faculty training and support, curriculum design, and support services needed to maintain an online program. Without this, program leads can find themselves working in a silo, unbeknownst to others who can assist with such oversight and ease the burden placed upon the e-learning leader in charge.

Pros and cons of a decentralized approach. When considering a *decentralized* approach to overseeing the design and delivery of online programs, the e-learning leader must still consider the overall needs and expectations of the institution, placing emphasis on individual online programs. Does the institution pride itself on *individuality*? Do programs want the choice of building their own *online image*? A decentralized approach affords individual programs the opportunity for uniqueness. It offers the ability to choose different types of technology, and individual control over various design and delivery aspects. When implementing a decentralized approach, the e-learning leader must proceed cautiously. Program leads must be knowledgeable in overseeing *all* aspects of designing and delivering the online program, for missing crucial elements could result in loss of accreditation and diminished reputation.

Best Practices

Whether centralized or decentralized, all institutions offering online learning need to consider the following areas, related to best practices: technology, faculty, administration, curriculum, and support services. Consideration must be given to the needs and demands of each component, how the areas differ for an online learning environment versus a residential environment, and how each area will be managed and funded. We will discuss the areas and components related to best practices, and describe how the setup may vary based on how centralized or decentralized the implementation is.

Technology. To deliver online learning, there are a variety of technical components that need to be addressed: systems and infrastructure, support, and integration. The e-learning leader will need to evaluate the existing systems and infrastructure already in place to determine the capability of expanding to an online or remote population. When it comes to technology support, it is important to ensure resources are available to assist students and faculty at times they are most likely to be working on coursework. In addition, technicians must be well versed in the situations that online students and faculty will encounter, such as uploading files or videos, or needing to have special plugins installed to access course content. A centralized technology solution will have a single technology team providing services to all online constituents, whereas a decentralized approach may have different groups providing support to the various colleges, departments, or programs that offer online learning.

Faculty. For faculty to be successful in the online learning environment, they need access to training, support, and evaluation. These components are necessary for residential learning experiences as well but have unique requirements in the online environment. Training for faculty needs to cover the technology used in teaching and learning online, and processes for communicating with various departments on a nonstandard schedule. Many institutions provide an in-house training course or courses; however, there are also some programs available for purchase such as the Certificate for Online Adjunct Teaching (Quality Matters, 2016a) from Quality Matters or the Certificate Programs (Online Learning Consortium, 2016a) through the Online Learning Consortium.

Closely related to training is support. How will faculty members get support while teaching in the online environment? Support includes technical services for them and their students, access to writing services, administrative support for dealing with student issues, and mentoring to guide faculty through the transition to teaching online.

Finally, a system needs to be developed to evaluate faculty who are teaching in the online environment. What expectations or standards are the faculty expected to meet? How will you ensure that those expectations are met? Providing faculty with specific expectations and how they'll be assessed will foster an evaluation process that is fair and transparent.

In a fully centralized solution, all online offerings will utilize the same training, support, and evaluation approaches. Decentralized solutions will have varying setups for the different units that provide online learning. A hybrid approach may share training and support services but have different evaluation methods by college or program.

Administration. Administration is, in some senses, a broad catch-all category for other things that occur in an online environment. The main components are management, support staff, and policies and procedures. Having a dedicated management and leadership team for online programs will help ensure those teaching and learning in the online environment have the resources and support necessary for success. Policy and procedure is an area often overlooked by institutions when they first start offering online learning. The use-cases, or needs and life circumstances, of the online learner, are often different from those of the residential student. Online students tend to be working adults with additional obligations such as family and career (Aversa & MacCall, 2013; Baptista, 2011; Street, 2010). Online learners are often not able to interact with institutional departments during standard business hours. Additionally, online learning sometimes shifts the timing of when courses are offered, and all policies should be reviewed to make sure they have the student's best interest in mind. Regulation of online learning, in the eyes of regulatory bodies, is often stricter as well, and the e-learning leader must review institutional policies for providing financial aid, monitoring attendance, and verifying student identity to ensure these policies are transferable to the online environment.

Centralized administration approaches have designated offices that are responsible for providing services and maintaining policies and procedures for all online students. Decentralized solutions will have more variation across departments. One challenge to a decentralized approach, as it relates to administration, is during accreditation self-studies or reviews, documentation will need to be collected from each unit providing services or maintaining policies. Institutions that will pursue State Authorization or membership in NC-SARA may want to identify a single office that will manage this process for all academic units.

Curriculum. In the most general sense, curriculum development for online and residential learning is very similar. Where online learning takes a turn is in the implementation and development of specific courses and degree requirements. In the online learning environment, there is stricter scrutiny in regard to alignment between program objectives, course objectives, activities, technology, and resources. Many institutions engage instructional designers and other support staff to develop the actual courses to a set standard, such as those outlined by Quality Matters (2016a) or the International Association for K-12 Online Learning (International Association for K-12 Online Learning, 2015). Further, it is necessary to ensure there is a procedure for program assessment, including a comprehensive review of student learning outcomes, program and course efficacy, and student feedback.

Similar to other functional areas, centralized solutions will have one team of instructional designers for the entire institution and a single curriculum review group. Approaches that are more decentralized in nature may have instructional designers that are assigned to the different academic units and report directly to the program dean or chair instead of a head of instructional design.

Support Services. Students and faculty in an online learning environment need to have the same access to support services as residential constituents. Service areas, including but not limited to writing services, library services and support, financial aid, registrar, bursar, and office hours must be thoughtfully considered. It is important for institutions to revisit support service policies and procedures to ensure services are truly available to online students when they need them most. For support services, in particular, having a centralized group that can provide services to all online students and faculty will increase the institution's ability to offer extended hours.

What You Can Do

Select an Approach

In this chapter, we outline approaches to managing online programs, specifically centralized and decentralized approaches. The e-learning leader may find themself conflicted as to what approach to take. Does one have to choose a fully centralized or decentralized approach? Can programs function successfully as a mixture of both? Professional practice literature hasn't suggested one approach greater than the other. Rather, the literature suggests the selected approach, whether centralized, decentralized, or a combination of both, is dependent upon institutional and program needs. Choosing an approach to managing online programs may seem daunting. However, if the e-learning leader takes appropriate steps to determining a centralized or decentralized approach to managing online programs, he will find himself following a similar path as the one outlined in detail below.

Conduct a Needs Assessment

To determine where the e-learning leader should start, he needs to understand the institution's current state by conducting a needs assessment and defining goals for distance education. The e-learning leader may ask themselves, "why are we venturing into the online learning arena?" Reasons for starting down the path of online learning will help determine the setup of the online program and resources needed to be successful. Questions to be considered include, "what resources are currently available?" and "what resources are still needed?" When considering the needs assessment, the e-learning leader must keep institutional needs, culture, and the population it serves in mind. Otherwise, the leader may find that they are facing adopters who are resistant to change.

Where to start. The first area the e-learning leader needs to research is the demand for the online learning in the field or area of a possible online program. Then, determine whether the institution has the faculty, staff, and technology available to create a successful online learning experience. One way to do this is with a scorecard—such as the *OLC Quality Scorecard* (Shelton & Saltsman, 2014) or the *Distance Learning Programs: Interregional Guidelines for the Evaluation of Distance Education (Online Learning)* (Middle States Commission on Higher Education, 2002, 2011) or the *Quality eToolkit* (eCampus Alberta, n.d.) to assess status quo. For funding, the e-learning leader should inquire with institutional leadership about the budget available. To evaluate actual costs e-learning leaders may want to consult with other institutions offering online programming or hire an individual who has established an online program before. Items to consider in the needs assessment include:

- Technology needs
- Support staff availability
- Faculty load and time available to dedicate to course development and teaching online
- Course and curriculum design
- Funding for course development—both the content expert (faculty member) and support staff to build and maintain the course and assist with multimedia
- Institutional & Faculty Policies, such as Intellectual Property
- Library services, consult the *Standards for Distance Learning Library Services* (Association of College & Research Libraries, 2008) for more information
- Student services—student organizations, financial aid, student accounts, registrar, advising

- State Authorization for offering online courses and programs

Based on the findings from the needs assessment, the e-learning leader will evaluate whether these areas can be fulfilled in a centralized or decentralized manner. Alternatively, the e-learning leader may choose to manage some items, such as technology and support services, with a more centralized approach, while other items are overseen in a more decentralized manner.

Select a Structure and Documentation Setup

Once the e-learning leader identifies the best approach for managing online programs, they must move on to select an online program structure and documentation setup. To support and promote the smooth functioning of an online program, it is essential that all parties involved have a clear understanding of individual roles and responsibilities (Kearsley, 2013). The e-learning leader must work with administration and program leads to develop a structure that aligns with the purpose and mission of the institution, and establish clear guidelines for reporting, documentation, institutional guidelines, and standards. In doing so, one will consider the following essential for success.

Coordinating efforts across campus. Many institutions, especially those serving a large population, often take a decentralized approach to managing online programs. Even in smaller institutions, academic departments may find themselves working with little interaction amongst one another. Therefore, it is essential to coordinate efforts across campus. Kearsley (2013) suggests establishing an institutional committee to coordinate resources and policies related to online programs. This committee should meet frequently and include online program managers, representatives from service and functional units (library services, financial aid, registrar, etc.), and faculty. The charge of the committee is to coordinate resources and policies across all programs. Kearsley (2013) also suggests this committee report to a Vice President or Provost, and not Information Technology (IT) as doing so tends to keep the focus more on technology rather than resources and policies.

Coordinating efforts via a centralized office. Institutions that prefer a centralized approach tend to have a central department or office that coordinates the management of online programs. This office liaises with faculty and operational units to ensure a cohesive delivery of online learning. There may still be differences in how each program is structured, based on the pedagogical needs and demands of the discipline, but the central department is able to establish standards and baseline expectations for all online programs. Often, for a central department or office to be successful, it will require strong institutional support from the academic and operational leadership, to ensure buy-in from the various academic units and functional groups. The central department should include academic personnel, such as instructional designers and curriculum coordinators, along with operational roles including project managers, logistical coordinators, multimedia developers, and possibly system administrators. The variety of skill sets within this department will allow them to fully understand all aspects of online programming and provide cohesiveness to the institution. Institutions which select a centralize approach often enjoy cost savings via the ability to leverage the academic and support staff across multiple units or departments without having to hire separate FTEs for each area.

Even with a central office or department coordinating efforts across the institution, the creation of an institutional committee to advise the office and help establish standards is extremely helpful to ensure there is a formal opportunity for all stakeholders to share their concerns and ideas. Having a central office for the management of online programming should not limit or minimize academic freedom or the unique needs of each discipline, but rather provide a scalable and sustainable structure for preserving the quality of the online learning experience.

Establish Institutional Guidelines/Standards

Forming a workgroup. In addition to coordinating resource and policy efforts, the e-learning leader must also consider establishing institutional guidelines and standards for supporting quality online programs. In this vein, the e-learning leaders who are using a centralized approach should consider forming a workgroup for establishing institutional guidelines and standards for the design of online programs and courses, along with the delivery of online learning. If an e-learning leader is pursuing a decentralized setup, a workgroup or institutional committee is still recommended to minimize duplication of work and to increase consistency across academic units.

When forming this workgroup, it is important to identify key decision makers and those needing to be consulted on such decisions. Depending on the chosen approach, centralized or decentralized, this may be decision makers at the institution, college, or programmatic level. Workgroup membership should be broad and include representatives from Central Administration, Learner Support Services, Information Technology, teaching faculty, student representatives, and relevant campus service organizations, such as library services (Boddy et al., 2013). Consider including the following areas as consultants to the workgroup: operational units, such as compliance, admissions, financial aid, and registrar. These individuals will likely provide guidance from an implementation and change management perspective. At many institutions, standards relating to academic content development and course delivery are owned by the teaching faculty or under the purview of a faculty council. If this is the case, the e-learning leader should assess the institutional culture and determine if he should engage all faculty or start with a key group of faculty who are interested in or have experience in teaching online.

Next, in addition to the key decision makers, the e-learning leader should seek local experts, who may or may not be faculty members within the institution, for inclusion in the workgroup. Experts may include instructional designers, a director of distance learning, LMS administrators, and faculty who have taught online at other institutions—even consider adjunct faculty who have taught online before. Including a diverse and comprehensive group in the process from the beginning will streamline the decision-making process and help ensure the end product is sustainable and scalable.

Review and establish standards. Once a workgroup has been formed, the e-learning leader should review standards that have been established by existing organizations. To start, the e-learning leader can review Table 1 within this chapter as it contains a list of organizations that have written standards for online or distance learning. This table includes the name of the standards, the focus level, the focus area, and website where the standards can be retrieved. Once the e-learning leader and workgroup have reviewed existing standards, the e-learning leader should lead the group in a reflection on the established standards and have the group compare and contrast different options available. Then, the e-learning leader should survey the workgroup to see if there are other standards they feel should be established that were not referenced in outside sources. From here, exact standards for the institution or academic units can be formulated with consideration to the mission and core values of the institution. If a decentralized approach is used, it may still be beneficial to share as many standards as possible across the academic units.

Reminding the workgroup to think outside the box is something the e-learning leader should take into consideration. Online teaching and learning are not identical to face-to-face instruction and thereby needs its own set of standards. The workgroup should be reminded look at the goal or purpose of the standards and accept that the means of achieving these goals may look different in the online environment. Finally, the e-learning leader should set a timeline for the standards to be implemented; the timeline should include adequate time to disseminate and train necessary individuals. Further, a timeline for the standards to be reviewed and updated needs to be developed. A minimum of 6 months to 1 year, before revisions, is recommended to allow individuals time to adjust and become comfortable with using the standards.

Implement standards. Once the workgroup has finalized a set of standards and institutional or appropriate level decision makers have approved the standards, they will need to be implemented. Some organizations choose to implement standards on a pilot basis to learn more and adjust standards before full implementation occurs. The decision to pilot or fully roll out standards should be identified in the decision-making process. Pilot processes are a great way to get buy-in from one group while allowing other groups to see how it works. This could be a method for starting with a decentralized approach and working toward a centralized one. Implementation will require training and a system for ensuring the standards are followed and met.

Before full implementation, the e-learning leader must ensure all affected individuals are fully trained on standards and any associated technology that accompanies them. For example, if a standard about providing feedback and grades within 48 h of the assignment due date is present, the e-learning leader should make sure faculty are fully trained on the tools available within the LMS for grading and feedback, along with best practices on how to efficiently give substantive feedback—such as using a rubric or developing macros in a word processor.

Table 1 Standards for online learning

Organization	Standards	Intended level	Focus	URL
Quality Matters (2016b)—QM	Higher Education Rubric; K-12 Rubric	Higher Education, K-12	Course Design	https://www.qualitymatters.org/
Online Learning Consortium (2016b)—OLC	OLC Quality Scorecard	Higher Education, K-12	Program Design, Delivery, and Structure	http://onlinelearningconsortium.org
International Association for K-12 Online Learning (2015)—iNACOL	iNACOL National Standards for Quality Online Courses; iNACOL National Standards for Quality Online Teaching	K-12	Course Design, Course Delivery	http://www.inacol.org/
Illinois Online Network (2015)—ION	Quality Online Course Initiative	Higher Education, K-12	Course Design	http://www.ion.uillinois.edu/
Institute for Higher Education Policy—IHEP Merisotis and Phipps (2000)	Quality On the Line: Benchmarks for Success in Internet-Based Distance Education	Higher Education	Course and Program Design and Delivery	http://www.ihep.org/research/publications/ quality-line-benchmarks-success-internet-based-distance-education
Middle States Commission on Higher Education (2011)—MSCHE	Distance Education Programs: Interregional Guidelines for the Evaluation of Distance Education (Online Learning)	Higher Education	Course and Program Design and Delivery	https://www.msche.org/publications/Guidelines-for-the-Evaluation-of-Distance-Education-Programs.pdf

The training provided should be timely before faculty start teaching, and just-in-time, sending out reminders and tips as they relate to the activities performed at certain times during the course. Ongoing training should also tie into the established guidelines and be consistent with standards provided. At one institution, faculty members teach from a pre-built course and cannot make edits to the course in real time. Therefore, the training provided does not include how to create or edit content in the LMS but instead on the features available to teach and provide feedback. For just-in-time training, the same institution circulates information on submitting final grades 1 week before the end of each term. At another institution, faculty members teach courses they design with assistance from instructional designers, and can make edits to the course in real time. Therefore training includes how to create or edit content in the LMS. For just-in-time training, this institution provides video and PDF tutorials on creating, editing, and managing content as well as providing feedback and submitting final grades.

Monitor standards. Once standards are implemented, a system will need to be established for monitoring and supervision. Depending on the types of standards, different approaches or tools can be used. Regardless of approach, the e-learning leader should be able to definitively answer the following question, "were standards for distance learning met?" For design standards, many institutions use a rubric or checklist to ensure all necessary components are included, supplemental business rules and standard operating procedures also help ensure consistency and compliance.

For delivery standards, reports based on data stored in the LMS can be very beneficial for tracking response time to student inquiries, frequency of logins, and timeliness of grading and feedback. Regardless of how many reports are developed, there is no substitution for true observations within the online course. One approach is to create an observation survey or tool that aligns with each standard, or group of standards, and then have a designated individual review the course and determine if standards were met. Some institutions have supervisors conduct the observations while other institutions enlist a mentor or peer.

Conduct observations. A substantial factor in whether to have supervisors or peers conduct observations will depend on how the results are being used. If the results are purely for mentoring and coaching, then peers or mentors may be the best choice. If the results have some impact on whether or not a faculty member is assigned an online course in the future, then a supervisor should be involved. Even if observations are an evaluation of performance, it is strongly encouraged this be done in a nurturing and developmental manner. If the goal is for all to achieve and be successful, substantive feedback should be provided to the faculty member. Again, the e-learning leader should consider the institutional culture and the type of approach taken when making these decisions.

Evaluate setup. Once a structure and standards have been implemented, the e-learning leader will need to evaluate how well they are working. When setting out the initial plan, the e-learning leader should include tentative timelines for evaluating the setup at key milestones, such as 6, 12, 24, and 48 months after implementation. As the e-learning leader gets started, he should be prepared for critical feedback and to make adjustments and modifications. Also, he will need to be aware that what works at the beginning when program offerings are small and contained, may not work well when online and distance offerings grow and expand. Each institution has its own internal culture that will play into how well the setup is adopted and how much room for modification is available. Evaluating the structure and standards at key milestones, and allowing for adjustment and modifications will assist the e-learning leader in establishing and maintaining guidelines that are adaptable and scalable to meet the changing needs of the institution.

Conclusion

Distance education is a growing area in higher education, and there is much scrutiny regarding the quality of the design and delivery of online courses and programs. This makes it necessary for institutions to have a formal approach to overseeing the design and delivery of online programs. A *centralized* approach to overseeing the design and delivery of online programs utilizes a primary unit, or units, within the institution to coordinate and facilitate related processes for all online offerings. A *decentralized* approach involves key individuals from different departments coming together as a team to oversee the design and delivery of online programs, but decision-making typically lies with the leaders of each academic unit.

Regardless of whether a centralized or decentralized approach to overseeing the design and delivery of online programs is chosen, the e-learning leader must ensure best practices that are present, accounted for, and perpetual. Best practices in critical areas include providing stable and robust technology, faculty training and support, transparency in administrative oversight, assistance with online curriculum development, and providing adequate support services for those teaching and learning at a distance. To implement best practices and standards in online programs, it is suggested that the e-learning leader coordinates efforts across campus and forms a workgroup to establish standards in overseeing the design and delivery of online programs at his institution. These standards should be reviewed, according to a set schedule, to ensure they are adaptable and scalable as online program offerings grow. Doing so will ensure longevity in overseeing the design and delivery of online programs, whether it be centralized, decentralized, or a combination of both formal approaches.

For More Information

For more information on managing the design and delivery of online programs, including information on centralized and decentralized approaches, please refer to:

- Moore, M. G. (2013). *Handbook of distance education (3rd Ed.)*. Routledge: New York, NY.
- Moore, M. G. & Kearsley, G. (2012). *Distance education: A systems view of online learning (3rd Ed.)*. Wadsworth: Belmont, CA.

References

Allen, I. E. & Seaman, J. (2015). *Grade level: Tracking online education in the United States.* Babson Survey Research Group. http://www.onlinelearningsurvey.com/reports/gradelevel.pdf.

Association of College & Research Libraries. (2008). *Standards for distance learning library services.* Retrieved from http://www.ala.org/acrl/standards/guidelinesdistancelearning.

Aversa, E. & MacCall, S. (2013). Profiles in retention part 1: Design characteristics of a graduate synchronous online program. *Journal of Education for Library & Information Science, 54*(2), 147–161.

Baptista, A. V. (2011). Non-traditional adult students: Reflecting about their characteristics and possible implications for higher education. *Procedia—Social and Behavioral Sciences, 30,* 752–756. doi:10.1016/j.sbspro.2011.10.147.

Boddy, C., Detellier, C., Duarte, S., Duplàa, E., Erdmer, A., Levasseur, D., … Ufholz, L.-A. (2013). *Report of the E-Learning working group.* University of Ottawa, https://www.uottawa. ca/vice-president-academic/sites/www.uottawa.ca.vice-president-academic/files/e-learning-working-report.pdf.

eCampus Alberta. (n.d.). *Quality eToolkit.* Retrieved from http://quality.ecampusalberta.ca/.

Higher Learning Commission. (2015). *Distance or correspondence education: Substantive change application.* Higher Learning Commission. https://downloadna11.springcm. com/content/DownloadDocuments.ashx?aid=5968&Selection=Document%2Ce356 a8b4-4e91-df11-9372-001cc448da6a%3B.

Illinois Online Network. (2015). *Illinois online network.* Retrieved from http://www.ion.uillinois. edu.

International Association for K-12 Online Learning. (2015). *iNACOL.* Retrieved from http://www. inacol.org/.

Kearsley, G. (2013). Management of online programs. In M. G. Moore (Ed.), *Handbook of distance education* (3rd ed., pp. 425–436). New York, NY: Routledge.

Merisotis, J. P. & Phipps, R. A. (2000). *Quality on the line: Benchmarks for success in internet-based distance education.* Institute for Higher Education Policy. Retrieved from http://www.ihep.org/ research/publications/quality-line-benchmarks-success-internet-based-distance-education.

Middle States Commission on Higher Education. (2002). *Distance learning programs: Interregional guidelines for electronically offered degree and certificate programs.* Philadelphia, PA. Retrieved November 23, 2015 from, http://eric.ed.gov/?id=ED468791.

Middle States Commission on Higher Education. (2011). *Distance education programs: Interregional guidelines for the evaluation of distance education (online learning).* Philadelphia, PA. Retrieved November 23, 2015 from, https://www.msche.org/publications/Guidelines-for-the-Evaluation-of-Distance-Education-Programs.pdf.

Moore, M. G. (2013). *Handbook of distance education* (3rd ed.). Routledge: New York, NY.

Moore, M. G. & Kearsley, G. (2012). *Distance education: A systems view of online learning* (3rd ed.). Wadsworth: Belmont, CA.

NC-SARA. (2015). *Application and approval form for institutional participation in SARA.* National Council for State Authorization Reciprocity Agreements. http://nc-sara.org/files/docs/ SARA-Institutional-Application.pdf.

New England Association of Schools and Colleges Commission on Institutions of Higher Education. (2013). *Guidelines for the evaluation of distance education (on-line learning).* Burlington, MA. Retrieved November 23, 2015 from https://cihe.neasc.org//sites/cihe.neasc.org/downloads/POLICIES/Pp90_Guidelines_for_the_Evaluation_of_Distance_Education__On-line_Learning_.pdf.

Online Learning Consortium. (2016a). *Certificate programs.* Retrieved from http://onlinelearningconsortium.org/learn/teaching-certificates/.

Online Learning Consortium. (2016b). *Online learning consortium.* Retrieved from http://onlinelearningconsortium.org.

Quality Matters. (2016a). *Certificate for online adjunct teaching.* Retrieved from https://www.qualitymatters.org/COAT.

Quality Matters. (2016b). Quality Matters. Retrieved from https://www.qualitymatters.org.

Shelton, K. & Saltsman, S. (Eds.) (2014). *OLC quality scorecard 2014.* Online Learning Consortium. Retrieved November 23, 2015 from http://onlinelearningconsortium.org/consult/quality-scorecard/olc-quality-scorecard-review/.

Street, H. D. (2010). Factors influencing a learner's decision to drop-out or persist in higher education distance learning. *Online Journal of Distance Learning Administration, 13*(4). Retrieved from http://www.westga.edu/~distance/ojdla/winter134/street134.html.

Establishing an e-Learning Division

Lisa L. Templeton and Kathryn E. Linder

Abstract Establishing an e-learning division can be a daunting task. In this chapter the authors offer a comprehensive overview of the steps needed to create an e-learning division that is financially viable and student-centered. Through a series of guiding questions, the authors provide information that e-learning leaders need to know about the campus culture regarding e-learning, the pros and cons of centralized versus decentralized structures, various models for connecting an e-learning division to the larger institutional structure, and e-learning policies. The authors also share information about potential budget models, incentives, models for course and program design, considerations regarding promotion and marketing, and how to structure student services. The chapter ends with some considerations for creating buy-in across stakeholder groups. Throughout this chapter, readers will be exposed to the breadth of issues that need to be considered when designing e-learning initiatives, programs, and degrees.

Keywords Strategic planning • e-Learning structures • e-Learning staffing • Start-up • e-Learning policy

Decision-Making Guidance

This chapter will help you make decisions about:

- Structuring an e-learning division
- How best to collaborate across your institution to ensure the success of your e-learning division

L.L. Templeton • K.E. Linder (✉)
Oregon State University, 4722 The Valley Library, Corvallis, OR 97331, USA
e-mail: lisa.l.templeton@oregonstate.edu; kathryn.linder@oregonstate.edu

© Association for Educational Communications and Technology 2018   45
A.A. Piña et al. (eds.), *Leading and Managing e-Learning*, Educational
Communications and Technology: Issues and Innovations,
https://doi.org/10.1007/978-3-319-61780-0_4

What You Need to Know

Establishing an e-learning division can be a daunting task. As Miller et al. (2013) note, the growth of distance education "has brought into leadership roles academics and other professionals for whom distance education is a new venture and who have little connection with the preexisting distance education community" (p. 3). Thus, the distance education administrator community is diverse, with a range of experience levels related to e-learning. As more and more institutions are creating e-learning divisions, administrators may be tasked with building such a division from the ground up. There are several questions that should be taken into account when establishing an e-learning division. The chapter will be organized around these questions. Below we elaborate on each one.

What Is the Campus Culture Regarding e-Learning?

Depending on the e-learning efforts already undertaken at an institution, as well as faculty perceptions of e-learning, there may be significant cultural supports or barriers to overcome when establishing a new e-learning division.

Having an established goal of why an e-learning division is being created is a fundamental component of helping to gain allies at the institution in order to move forward. For example, the goal for the creation of Ecampus at Oregon State University was to increase access and serve nonresidential learners. As a land-grant institution, serving adult learners who could not come to campus was an important piece of the institutional mission. The development of Ecampus as an e-learning division was founded on a mission of access and prioritizing the needs of Oregon's adult learner population. Similarly, your institution may also have mission-specific rationales for the creation of an e-learning division.

Additionally, knowing the perceptions of e-learning on your campus from various stakeholders, including administrators, faculty, and students, is critical. e-Learning divisions are successful because of the partnerships and the trust they build with a range of campus constituents. The more you can learn about the perceptions that people have at the outset, the better you can prepare yourself to strengthen relationships and create allies for your e-learning division.

An awareness of your campus culture regarding e-learning will also help you to develop an appropriate vision for your e-learning division. What are the long-term goals that you want the division to accomplish once it is established? What kind of influence will the division have on the institution as a whole? How will the division contribute to the institutional mission in the long term?

Should the Division Be Centralized or Decentralized?

There are two main models for e-learning divisions: centralized or decentralized. In a centralized model, the staffing resources, budget, and administration and policy decisions are made centrally and then distributed across the entire division. In a decentralized model, the staffing, budget, and policies may be located in colleges or departments where there is a more localized influence. There are pros and cons to both centralized and decentralized models for e-learning divisions (see Table 1).

Centralized models for e-learning divisions can be beneficial because they can offer more consistency. For example, if you have one team of instructional designers, the faculty who engage with that team can receive similar course design templates and training that will produce consistency for learners who engage with those courses. Centralized divisions can also offer one place for faculty and e-learners to go with questions or when they are in need of resources. When staffing an e-learning division, it is important to set up the structure to support project management. A centralized team can be managed to share responsibilities to meet many deadlines and shifting priorities so that responses can be agile and flexible.

Centralized models can also be more cost-effective because there is potential for less redundancy in purchasing of software and hardware, as well as in staffing models. Centralized divisions may be able to scale more rapidly and may have a broader marketing capacity due to combined resources.

Table 1 Pros and cons of centralized and decentralized divisions

	Centralized	Decentralized
Pros	Consistency of learner experiences	Can respond to discipline-specific concerns
	Consistency of faculty training	Can make college or department-specific policies
	Efficiency of resources and staffing	Can be nimbler for academic units
	Ability to scale more rapidly	Faculty may feel more ownership of courses and curriculum
	Cross-discipline engagement	
	Professionalization of subunits	
	Broader marketing capacity to bundle advertising	
	One place for learners and faculty to go to find resources	
	Appearance of e-learning coordination	
Cons	Less control at the department level	Redundancy of resources and staffing
	Guidelines and policy are broadly applied and may not include department or college nuances	Potential for unequal across departments
		Potential for lack of backup with illness or staff turnover
		Isolation from other e-learning professionals

Centralized models can also offer more cross-discipline engagement between the staff of the e-learning division and the faculty who engage in the e-learning division services. For example, faculty development programs and services may more naturally allow faculty participants to engage with colleagues from outside of their home discipline.

The challenges for centralized units may include less control at the department level in terms of decisions about course or program development. For example, a centralized division may decide not to develop a new program due to saturation in the market, whereas a decentralized division could decide to launch that program if they preferred. A second challenge is that the policy decisions of a centralized division may be too broadly applied and may not include specifics for departments or colleges that would address local concerns.

Decentralized models are perhaps most effective with responding to department or college-specific needs. In particular, decentralized models allow departments and colleges to set policies that are specific to them. Consistency can also be established in a decentralized environment, but it might take extra effort to ensure that all the decentralized division staff are trained appropriately and are communicating with one another. Monitoring for consistency must also be intentionally planned in decentralized units. Sometimes, because of local policies, decentralized models can be nimbler. Decentralized models may also have faculty who feel more ownership over their courses and curriculum.

However, depending on the resources available, a decentralized division may have a lean staffing structure that requires a wider breadth of expertise and experience. This staffing structure may result in a lack of backup with illness or if there is staff turnover. Staff may also feel isolated from other e-learning professionals if they are the only equivalent of their position within the department or college. In a decentralized model, there may also be a redundancy of resources across the departments or colleges or the potential for unequal support or resources across the decentralized units.

The model that you choose will depend on your campus culture, the resources available (including staff and budget), and your initial goals for launching the e-learning division.

Are the Courses and Programs Included in the e-Learning Division Going to Be Equivalent to the Campus-Based Courses and Programs? Will the Same Faculty Develop, Deliver, and Teach These Courses? Will the Diplomas for the e-Learning Programs Be Equivalent to the Campus-Based Programs?

There are different models for the role that e-learning will play as part of a larger institutional strategy. We explore three case studies and discuss the advantages and disadvantages to each.

Case Study 1: An Equivalent Model

In this model, the courses in the e-learning division are designed, developed, and delivered by the department and they belong to the academic units. There may or may not be collaboration with the e-learning division in the design and development of courses and programs, but all the courses and programs have identical learning outcomes across modalities. In this model, the courses and degrees are equivalent to on-campus courses and degrees, which means the diploma will be equivalent for e-learners. The benefits of this model include more faculty and department control over the courses in their programs and the decisions around the creation and dissemination of those courses. One challenge to this model is that faculty buy-in becomes a necessity to make it work. There are several examples of institutions that follow this model, including the University of Illinois Springfield, Penn State University, the University of Nebraska, and the University of Utah, among others.

Case Study 2: A Segregated Model

In this model, the e-learning division is created as a separate division and the faculty is hired by the e-learning division with or without input from the department. Degrees may not be equivalent, but will have the university name on them. The main benefit of this model is that it is incredibly nimble. The e-learning division will be able to move quickly and develop at scale. In part, this is because the division will not be dependent on faculty buy-in and timelines. The main challenge of this model is academic quality. For example, there may be challenges to achieving a quality ranking due to the institution's lack of faculty engagement. This model can also alienate faculty members. A few examples of institutions that use a version of this model are the University of Phoenix, the University of Wisconsin La Crosse, and Rio Salado College.

Case Study 3: The Outsourced Model

In this model, the creation of the e-learning division is built through outsourcing content creation and using an adjunct model to teach courses. Degrees may or may not be equivalent, but will have the university name on them. One benefit of this model is that development of the e-learning division can be fast. There is also a large choice of degrees, so the division can be quick to ramp up and scale. The challenges of this model are similar to those for the segregated model. There can be a lack of faculty buy-in and this model can alienate faculty. This model also gives academic departments a lack of control over the curriculum and can be expensive. In the long run, outsourcing can also hurt your brand due to the division's lack of control over the course and curriculum content. Some examples of institutions that seem to follow a version of this model are Notre Dame College (Ohio), Bay State College, Purdue University, and DeVry University.

What Types of Policies Regarding e-Learning Exist at Your Institution and What Will Need to Be Developed?

The question of policy can be a difficult one especially when establishing a new e-learning division because you may not know what you need. Here are some key policies to include in an e-learning division as well as some guiding questions to consider for each policy:

Admissions: Will the admissions policies be identical to on-campus admissions policies or will they be different?

Advising: Who will advise e-learners? Will this be done centrally or through a decentralized model?

Compensation: How will faculty members be compensated for the development of a course and the delivery of a course? Who will decide the compensation levels (the department or the e-learning division, or a combination of both)?

Course capacity and frequency: Who decides the course capacity and the frequency of offerings?

Course and program development: Who makes decisions about what courses and programs should be developed and when?

Equivalent student services: All e-learners will need the same services (such as advising, tutoring, and other forms of support) that on-campus students receive. Who will oversee the student services for the e-learning division to ensure they are equivalent to on-campus services?

Faculty load: Will the faculty load for designing and delivering a course for the e-learning division be equivalent to other campus models?

Finances: How will tuition be set? Will tuition be equivalent to on-campus credits and courses? What, if any, is the revenue-sharing model for the e-learning division?

Hiring: Who is responsible for hiring and firing e-learning instructors and faculty? Will you use campus faculty to teach courses or hire adjunct instructors?

Intellectual property rights: Who owns the materials created for e-learning courses?

Quality: What criteria will be used to assess the quality of the courses developed through the e-learning division?

Training: How will faculty be trained, if at all, to teach in or for the e-learning division? Will this training, if created, be mandatory?

Refresh and renew: Will courses be periodically refreshed and how often? Will this be a requirement of participating in the e-learning division? Who decides when a course will be cancelled or removed from the schedule?

Review and evaluation: How much and how frequently will reviews of teaching occur and how will the evaluation of teaching in or for the e-learning division be counted for promotion and tenure?

Keep in mind that this list of potential policies is not exhaustive and that these questions may lead to additional policies that need to be explored, discussed, or created at your institution. Moreover, existing policies will have been developed for site-based students and programs and all of these policies will need to be revisited to make sure they are inclusive of e-learners.

What Budget Is Available to Establish the e-Learning Division? What Kinds of Staffing Will Be Needed?

Historically, some e-learning divisions were launched with the assistance of grant funding (this was how Ecampus at Oregon State University was established with a FIPSE grant; other universities who received funds from divisions such as the Alfred P. Sloan Foundation include the University of Illinois, Penn State University, the University of Central Florida, and the University of Massachusetts). This kind of grant funding, however, is less available in the current climate, although some opportunities still exist (see, for example, funds available to support distance education from the National Institute of Food and Agriculture). Three other models for funding are more realistic for e-learning divisions that are just beginning (see also Boyd-Barrett, 2000).

Institutionally sponsored. In this first model, an e-learning division is tied to a strategic initiative within the university which the university funds. This is a common starting point for many e-learning divisions that are not yet generating revenue.

Combination of institutional and self-sponsorship. As e-learning divisions grow and scale, a second model might be a combination where some funding comes from the institution and is combined with funding from student tuition or fees as e-learning begins to generate revenue.

Self-supported. The third model has a budget that is self-supported from revenues generated through the e-learning division courses from sources such as student tuition or fees. Some examples of institutions that currently use this model are the University of North Texas, Eastern Kentucky University, and Purdue University's Masters of Learning Design and Technology.

The staffing of an e-learning division will also depend on the budget available. Based on the budget and the university structure, e-learning units often reside in academic affairs, outreach and engagement units, continuing education units, or are housed in a separate college or division. Across these structures, there is no typical staffing arrangement, but some key positions might include a director or dean of the division, a director or lead of instructional design, a director or lead of student services, and a director or lead of marketing and enrollment services.

What Kinds of Incentives Will Be Used to Engage Faculty and Departments to Join the e-Learning Division in Offering Courses and Programs?

Frequently, departments and faculty are already feeling over-taxed and e-learning efforts can feel like an (unwanted) obligation. Because of this attitude toward e-learning initiatives, incentives can be an important motivator for faculty and administrator involvement in the e-learning division.

One potential incentive is to adjust university policy to include e-learning course development and teaching as part of the promotion and tenure process. Although these policies are evolving, at many institutions these components of the e-learning division are separate from the typical promotion and tenure process.

A second potential incentive is replacing load for faculty engaging in teaching for the e-learning division. For example, an e-learning course developed and taught might replace a site-based course of the same credit structure. Many faculty members struggle when e-learning commitments are considered overload and this can cause a lack of faculty buy-in.

A third incentive can be financial incentives for faculty and/or departments. Faculty financial incentives might be tied to course development time as well as professional development related to teaching for the e-learning division. Some divisions pay faculty based on student credit hours or enrollment in the courses they teach. At the department level, financial incentives can include shared revenue, based on enrollments, of student tuition or fees.

A fourth incentive for departments can be overall growth in their program enrollments. For example, at Oregon State University, one academic department now has more online students than face-to-face in their overall enrollment. If there is revenue sharing in place, this additional enrollment can result in additional graduate student, faculty, or student support services being provided at the department level.

How Will Online Courses and Programs Be Designed? What Resources Does Your Institution Have (Financial and Expertise) to Develop Best Practice Online Materials?

Developing quality and engaging online education takes time and expertise. Most e-learning units have one of three models: (1) faculty-created content and course design, (2) a faculty/instructional designer collaboration, and (3) a content outsourcing model. Pros and cons for each model are included in Table 2 and described below.

Faculty-created content and course design. In this model, faculty members are primarily responsible for the design and development of e-learning courses and programs. This can result in more faculty buy-in and engagement and can also

Table 2 Pros and cons of three models for designing online courses and programs

	Faculty-created content and course design model	Faculty-instructional designer collaboration model	Content outsourcing model
Pros	Faculty engagement and buy-in	Faculty engagement and buy-in	Quick
	Faculty are content experts	Leverage the resources and expertise of the instructional designer	Nimble for adding new courses and programs
	Ensures a good fit with department curriculum	A baseline for quality assurance	Courses will have consistent look and feel
		Courses will have consistent look and feel	A baseline for quality assurance
		Better application of course design practices and policies such as best practices for engagement or accessibility	Better application of course design practices and policies such as best practices for engagement or accessibility
Cons	Quality assurance can be limited	Additional cost of employing instructional designers	Cost
	Faculty may have lack of resources or course design knowledge to create quality content using best practices for engagement or accessibility	Could take more time for course design	Lack of faculty engagement and buy-in
	Dependent on faculty to refresh the course regularly	Not all faculty want to collaborate on course design	Can alienate faculty
	All courses will look different, even within a department		Lack of department control over curriculum

ensure a good fit between the courses and the department curriculum. An additional benefit is the role of faculty as content experts in the creation of courses and programs, which can ensure academic quality.

Challenges to this model can include quality assurance, which can be limited. Faculty may lack the resources or expertise to create quality content and resources for e-learners in the online environment. This model is also dependent on the faculty designer to refresh or update the course on a regular basis. Lastly, this model can result in a lack of consistency across courses, even within departments, because of faculty using different course templates, technologies, and online tools. If there are policies for accessibility or other course design best practices, this model may not result in consistent implementation of those policies.

Faculty/instructional designer collaboration. In this model, faculty members partner with instructional designers in the design and development of courses and programs. As noted earlier in the chapter, these designers may be housed in a centralized or decentralized model depending on how the e-learning division has been structured. This model benefits from faculty engagement, buy-in, and content expertise, but also leverages the resources and expertise of the instructional designer, which can make for an efficient partnership. This model can also offer a baseline for quality assurance and can ensure that courses will have a consistent look and feel. If there are policies for accessibility or other course design best practices, this model may be an easier way to apply those policies.

Some of the challenges to this model can include the additional cost of employing instructional designers. Additionally, not all faculty want to collaborate on course design and may be resistant or reluctant to engage in this model.

Content outsourcing. In this third model, the e-learning division outsources the design and development of courses and programs to a third-party vendor. This model can ensure the speedy development of courses and programs and the ability to quickly add new courses and programs to create a nimble division. This model also allows courses and programs to have a consistent look and feel (assuming the same vendor is used to design all courses) and ensures a baseline for quality assurance. If there are policies for accessibility or other course design best practices, this model may be an easier way to apply those policies.

Challenges to this model include cost, as it can be expensive to outsource course and program design. This model may also create a lack of faculty engagement or buy-in since faculty are not involved in the creation of the courses they will be teaching. Indeed, this model can alienate faculty from the e-learning division. This model can also cause a lack of department and faculty control over the e-learning curriculum.

Your choice of course design model will depend on the budget and staffing resources available, the amount of local expertise that you can draw on, the culture of your institution, as well as past practices of faculty development. We recommend speaking with faculty and administrator stakeholders as you decide which model to choose.

How Will Your e-Learning Division Engage in Promotion and Marketing?

Some universities, particularly those with name recognition, may not feel that they need a separate marketing strategy for their online division. This should be reconsidered. The online education marketplace has become very competitive and resources are needed to stand out in this crowded space. At minimum, e-learning divisions need to develop a marketing plan for their courses and programs.

Most universities use one of four models for marketing e-learning courses and programs: (1) a central marketing division for the university manages and implements marketing strategies, (2) the e-learning division manages their own marketing planning and implementation, (3) the academic departments offering the programs manage their own marketing, or (4) the institution chooses to outsource the marketing for the e-learning division.

Which model you choose will depend on your budget, the staffing size and expertise within your e-learning division, the size and breadth of your programs and offerings, and how aggressively you want to enter the market place.

When you are just starting out, some key questions to ask regarding the marketing of your programs include:

– What are your enrollment goals?
– What expertise do existing staff have in creating marketing strategies, writing and implementing both broad and targeted marketing plans, design work, and Internet marketing (for example, search engine optimization)?
– What budget can you allocate to marketing?

What Student Support Services and Systems Are Available to Support Nonresidential e-Learners? Can Services and Systems that Already Exist Be Modified for e-Learners?

Creating a successful e-learning division means taking into account the differences between e-learners and campus-based students. You will want to provide the resources and support systems that e-learners need to be successful.

Many e-learning students are adult learners who are juggling many and varied responsibilities, and have extremely busy lives. Adult learners can be working full time and/or have a multitude of family and community commitments. These adult learners who decide to enroll in e-learning courses and programs tend to be very focused and motivated students. They expect to have the appropriate student support services at their fingertips whenever it is needed. Some of the critical services that greatly support these e-learning students include:

Advising. Students need phone/SKYPE numbers and e-mail addresses of their advisor so that they can contact them. Students may have critical questions, but a very busy schedule, so it is important that they can get a hold of an advisor when needed. We recommend having advisors that are specifically focused on e-learning students, because their needs are often different than traditional campus students. However, some e-learning units use the same advisors for both residential and nonresidential students.

Online tutoring. e-Learning students often do not have access to campus tutoring centers; so having online 24/7 tutoring services available is extremely beneficial.

Proctoring services. If a nonresidential student needs to get a test proctored, there should be someone in the e-learning division to help coordinate this. It can be at an approved testing center (community college, library, etc.) or through an outsourced online tutoring service.

Library resources/textbooks. It is critical that the needed library resources and textbooks/course materials are available to the students. Often items need to be mailed to the students, as they may not be able to go to the university library or bookstore.

Success coaching. Busy distance students often need some support along their educational journey. This can include coaching in time management, strategizing how to manage all of their many commitments, and goal setting.

Career services. Some e-learning students need career counseling. This should not happen when they are reaching the end of their degree program, but should happen before they actually select their program, and throughout their educational journey. e-Learning units sometimes hire their own career counselor(s) or use campus-based counselors. Also, some career centers and e-learning units offer virtual career fairs for their nonresidential students.

Residential students taking e-learning courses also need many of these services. You will need to decide if they will tap into the existing campus-based student services, or if your e-learning division will also provide student support services for the campus-based students who take occasional online courses.

Who Are the On-Campus Partners Who Can Help to Establish a Strong e-Learning Division?

A successful e-learning division will need outstanding partners across campus. Most universities are structured for campus-based students who can access physical departments or offices to talk with someone or fill out the right form. When creating an e-learning division you will need to make sure that the distance student can have access to everything needed in their educational journey without physically going to the campus. This takes a great deal of coordination across the institution. While there are many units across the entire campus that you will need to partner with, the e-learning division should plan to work closely with the following stakeholders:

Admissions office. You will want to make sure that you have an admissions process for your e-learning division and there may be components of this process that differ from the admissions process of your on-campus students. Talking with colleagues from admissions will help you ensure a smooth process for e-learners who apply and enroll in your courses and programs.

Financial aid office. A potential obstacle for adult learners who come back to school as e-learners are the financial resources they need for enrollment in courses and programs. You will want to talk with financial aid colleagues to decide if the processes for e-learners will be the same for on-campus students or if there are key differences that need to be taken into account.

Registrar's office. If the university wants to track e-learner enrollments and other student data, coding will need to be created to identify these students, courses, and programs affiliated with the e-learning division. Collaboration with the registrar's office can ensure that the e-learner data is compliant with already-existing structures for institutional data.

These units need to make sure all forms and materials are available online, that their websites communicate clearly to distance students, and that the support students will need can be given by phone or e-mail.

What You Can Do?

By answering each of the questions we have outlined in this chapter, you will be well prepared to begin the launch of your e-learning division. Here are some additional action items to consider as you plan your launch:

Form an advisory committee. We recommend answering the questions included in this chapter with the assistance of an inclusive advisory committee for your e-learning division. This advisory committee might include representatives from key academic disciplines, the provost's office, the university library, student affairs, enrollment services, and student representatives. By including this group of stakeholders from the beginning stages of your planning, you will gain allies and also ensure that you are not leaving important components out of the planning process.

Draft a strategic plan. Once you have explored these questions with various stakeholders including faculty, administrators, and students, you will need to draft a strategic plan for the creation of your e-learning division. This plan will need to include the goals of the division, the timeline of the launch, the staffing structure for the division, the space needs for the division, and how you will assess the effectiveness of the division.

For each goal within your strategic plan, you will want to draft accompanying strategies to achieve the goal and metrics to measure the goal's success. For example, if you have an enrollment goal of 1000 students enrolled within the first five years of the division launch, then you might develop strategies that are related to marketing, student support, and retention. Metrics to measure the success of this goal would include enrollment and retention data.

Create a communications strategy. In addition to your strategic plan, you will also need to develop an internal and external communications strategy to share information about the e-learning division with a range of stakeholders. This will ensure broad buy-in and support from diverse allies across your campus and externally. Similar to your strategic plan, your communication strategy needs to include goals, the stakeholders involved in implementing key strategies, and metrics to measure outcomes.

Conclusion

Putting in the time to plan out the various components of your e-learning division's structure, staffing, budget, resources, goals, and vision will help you to ensure that you are set up for a successful launch and that you have secured the necessary institutional support for your e-learning division. This planning can take some time and should, ideally, include a range of stakeholders from across your institution.

In this chapter, we offered questions to consider as you launch your e-learning division. These questions are meant to show you the breadth of issues that need to be considered when designing e-learning initiatives, programs, and degrees. It should be clear from this chapter that an e-learning division's success is a team effort that must be institutionally supported. Keeping student success at the center of your e-learning division's mission and goals is also paramount. No e-learning division can succeed if its students are not learning and thriving in their courses and programs.

In the following section, we offer additional resources that can help provide important information and context as you launch your e-learning division.

For More Information

Below, we offer some of the resources that have been most helpful to us when learning about the e-learning leadership and division landscape.

Leadership Opportunities for e-Learning Leaders

OLC and Penn State Institute for Emerging Leadership in Online Learning
   https://coil.psu.edu/ielol/
   UPCEA and ACE Summit for Online Leadership
   http://conferences.upcea.edu/SOL/
   UPCEA Online Leadership Roundtable
   http://conferences.upcea.edu/roundtable/
   WCET Leadership Summits
   http://wcet.wiche.edu/events/summits
   EDUCAUSE Leadership programs
   http://www.educause.edu/careers/advanced-programs1

Research and Advisory Services for e-Learning Divisions

The Education Advisory Board (EAB)
   https://www.eab.com/
   Eduventures
   http://www.eduventures.com/

References

Boyd-Barrett, O. (2000). Distance education provision by universities: How institutional contexts affect choices. *Information, Communication & Society*, *3*(4), 474–493. doi:10.1080/13691180010002332

Miller, G., Benke, M., Chaloux, B., Ragan, L.C., Schroeder, R, Smutz, W., & Swan, K. (2013). *Leading the e-Learning transformation of higher education: Meeting the challenges of technology and distance education*. Sterling, VA: Stylus Publishing.

Structuring and Resourcing Your eLearning Unit

Camille Dickson-Deane, Denise Tolbert, Tracy McMahon, and Camille Funk

Abstract This chapter will help you make decisions on the types of resources you will need and the qualifications of personnel that should be considered in order to create an eLearning Unit. These suggestions include considerations of an organization's mission and vision as it relates to course design, delivery, and implementation. Some course delivery processes require different needs based on where the development is occurring within the organization. If the course development is viewed as an academic process, then the skills and/or abilities of the resources will differ than those associated with course development occurring as part of a technology process. Deciding on which model benefits your organization is pertinent to the mission of the entire need for the eLearning Unit. The models described include considerations for responding to market needs as the new education models now include business needs as key goals. These do not exclude further considerations for the pedagogical nature of the unit but simply allow for an overall awareness of the field and its requirements.

Keywords Designing an eLearning unit • Resourcing an eLearning unit • Structure impacting outcomes • Alignment of strategic goals • Lessons learned database • Quality assurance of courses • Role of accreditation

C. Dickson-Deane (✉)
University of Melbourne, 111 Barry Street, Level 6, FBE Building,
Melbourne, VIC 3053, Australia
e-mail: c.dickson@unimelb.edu.au

D. Tolbert
National University, 3390 Harbor Blvd, Costa Mesa, CA 92626, USA
e-mail: dtolbert@nu.edu

T. McMahon
Loyola University, 31 Derwood Ct, Parkville, MD 21234, USA
e-mail: tdedwards@gmail.com

C. Funk
University of Southern California (USC), Los Angeles, CA, USA
e-mail: cfunk19@gwu.edu; cfunk@usc.edu

© Association for Educational Communications and Technology 2018
A.A. Piña et al. (eds.), *Leading and Managing e-Learning*, Educational
Communications and Technology: Issues and Innovations,
https://doi.org/10.1007/978-3-319-61780-0_5

Introduction

As eLearning professionals move from opportunity to opportunity, they do recognize that the structure of the organization tends to dictate the focus of the development (i.e., number of courses and specific fields/topics) as well as how the actual course/program is designed. To elaborate, organizations on one spectrum can treat the development of courses similar to that of a factory where X number of courses are designed for delivery by Y date—using a static template model. On the other extreme spectrum, courses can be developed with a more flexible design approach—based on the intended audience, the course design process can vary in design and delivery. This delineation can possibly be seen as the categorization of organizations with one maybe focusing on the delivery (i.e., including teaching), another on research, and maybe even another focusing on the various needs of the organization. This categorization can create a view that one method is better than the other, where in fact the organizational need actually promotes the design and delivery approach. Furthermore, stating that one design approach is being employed based on an organizational need does not prohibit the organization from reviewing the approach for delivery and implementation. Revisions to delivery and design approaches can include new objectives and/or an expaned/adapted response to market changes. The central focus of these decisions can also be dependent on the organizational learning methods employed as foundational tenets. These tenets may guide the course development process where the focal point promotes some belief system that was intended to make the organization successful. Thus, these form great discussions for eLearning professionals where solutions are essentially contextual but having some guidance can always help.

Decision-Making Guidance

This chapter will help you make decisions about:

- The foundational strategic approach to your unit—what strategic goals are going to guide your unit.

- If your unit/department is new you will have the opportunity to use the strategic goals of the organization to guide the development of the unit. This means that understanding how the strategic goals are related to the installation of a new unit/department will determine what is identified as a success or not. Deciding if your unit is responsible for the tools/technology or the online learning pedagogy and strategies attached to the pedagogy, is important going forward.
- What you can use to build the skills of those on your team:
- The hierarchical structure of your organization will be reflected in some way by your own unit and department. This in turn will guide what your team skills are, and how they are acquired. Understanding what skills and abilities you need on

your team will determine how you resource the team and also how those resources are to be maintained. The maintenance is important as it may fulfil the symbiotic relationship between resources and the structure in which the resources reside. Some places that may be considered to help sustain the team's knowledge are The International eLearning Association (IELA), Online Learning Consortium (OLC), Association for Educational Communications and Technology (AECT), the eLearning Guild, and European Distance and ELearning Network (EDEN), all of which have varying foci and thus produce different types of expertise, and hence content towards knowledge.

- Being innovative because *eLearning* evolves quickly—What you can do to keep your team's skills ahead of the curve:

- Being innovative is on the top of every organization's goals. Delivering eLearning is part of today's education model which for many organizations is slowly adapting to include business practices. This means that being aware of the key stakeholders and how these stakeholders needs should be met allows for a varied skilled approach to maintaining a quality product and/or service.

What You Need to Know

As an eLearning leader you should strive to understand the organizational structure as this is key to you receiving information which affects your decision-making processes. The structure of the organization will provide a visual for how the communication and support system for your unit will operate. Being part of and understanding the organizational structure will guide the expectations that are associated with this specific unit. Knowledge, like the mission and vision of the unit along with determining the relationship between the unit and the faculty, is pertinent to the unit's operations and continued existence. As such, the unit may experience political and strategic limitations which when translated means that the unit may not have a firm foundation for operating going forward.

Strategic Structure

There are two contexts which can guide the acquisition and maintenance of resources for an eLearning unit.

1. Creating a new unit out of a need that was presented
2. Modifying an existing unit to include the new need

Both of these situations can create different timelines and approaches to getting to the main goal of offering courses and programs online. They also can address the role and responsibilities attached to the leadership of the organization to ensure that the unit is fully supported to achieve its assigned goals. For the field of eLearning, the knowledge attached to providing the product and service is tied to basic management principles (Maslow, 1943). These principles are what can assist in the provisions as well as achieving the key goals for the unit. Following these decisions, understanding if the unit is located under the academic arm or under the administrative arm of the institution will guide your future behaviours. Each arm obviously has its pros and cons and can be managed based on the leader's ability, support, and institutional culture.

A New eLearning Unit

A new eLearning unit can be seen as having an easier time to create foundations based on a researched/perceived need. The unit's existence will be further guided by the overarching organization's culture and thus how projects are approached will be seen as part of proving the initiative. Part of this approach will be to:

1. Determine the purpose of the unit
2. Align the purpose with the core objectives
3. Identify the projected budget that was used to determine the unit as a need
4. Identify the key stakeholders (internal and external)
5. Identifying the resources

    (a) Determine what expertise would be needed to ensure that the need is achieved
    (b) What resources would be used to manage the immediate need
    (c) What resources/expertise would be needed to manage and sustain the unit

6. Review the budget with respect to the resourcing of the unit

When identifying the resources some organizations just have a course design team as the core members of the eLearning unit. This may include instructional designers, technologist, quality assurance reviewers, and copywriters. Others may be larger and thus include a media/production team. Having both is not rare and provides a great level of expertise whilst adding financial considerations that would not normally be present in just a design team (see Fig. 1). Also having team members who have additional expertise like instructional designers who do multimedia development or instructional technologists who can do animations is also common. As a leader, careful consideration of the teams' abilities will guide the management of your entire unit.

Modifying an eLearning Unit

An existing unit that is being modified to incorporate eLearning activities will have to review its existing processes and procedures and see where new ones are needed. This process can create many challenges not only with existing resources, but also

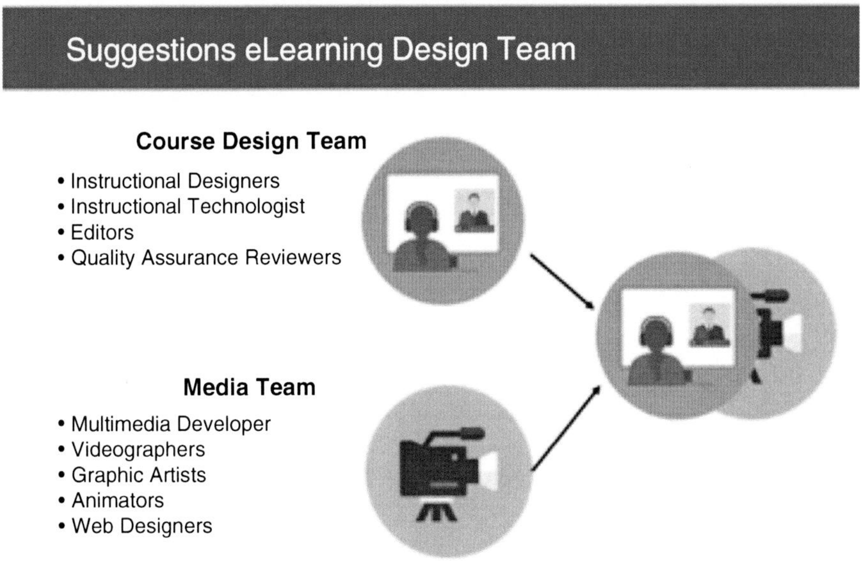

Suggestions eLearning Design Team

Course Design Team

• Instructional Designers
• Instructional Technologist
• Editors
• Quality Assurance Reviewers

Media Team

• Multimedia Developer
• Videographers
• Graphic Artists
• Animators
• Web Designers

Fig. 1 Models of eLearning design teams

with trying to adapt the new principles into the existing organizational structure. This provides additional inter- and intra-related challenges with those in the pre-existing structure. Identifying the challenges which may occur from a structure and interaction point of view will be one of the most important activities this new eLearning leader will endure. Part of this challenge is understanding the effect of modification on individual contributors, thus impacting motivation, perceptions, and the overall ability to create a new culture of operating where an old one existed (Leban & Zulauf, 2004).

Design and Delivery Perspectives

Academic Arm

eLearning units that are strategically placed under the academic arm of the organization are being guided to have direct interaction with faculty and thus pursue duties that tend to be more related to pedagogical outcomes. The academy typically focusses on achieving learning outcomes and can thus guide a unit into having the same objectives (see Fig. 2). This means that the communication between the academic area and the administrative area will focus on the implementation of the courses and programs as opposed to the design and development activities. This allows the pedagogically related activities to be within the academy and potentially can create an easier conversation between the faculty and design team. Today, some

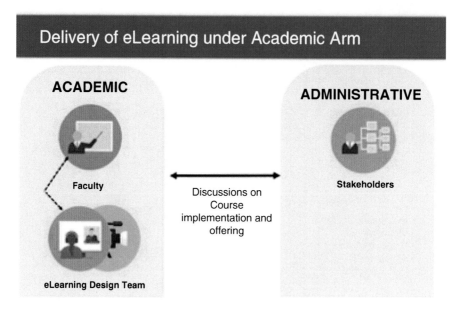

Fig. 2 Delivery of courses with eLearning under the academic arm

academies are also changing their models to accommodate more of a business model, and thus learning outcomes are now coupled with earning abilities. This adds an additional perspective to the delivery model under the academic arm where eLearning is used to attract more business and in essence seen by many as the ability for the organization to earn more. To this end, an increase in the visibility of a particular department and at most times the entire organization comes as part of the perceived reward. This can affect how the design and delivery process are enacted as there are many considerations to accommodate.

Administrative Arm

Some organizations will place their eLearning units under the administrative arm. Some branches are housed under the Information Technology Department or even under the Human Resource/Training Department. Some units are their own departments and are named for the technology used to deliver the product (i.e., Instructional technology) and then there are other [newer] management terms that are being used to position these skills—Talent Management Department. The product and service that comes out of this area may differ as the focus is now the tools that are used to deliver the service. This also means that the communication between those who deliver the content for the courses (i.e., Faculty/Subject Matter Experts) and those that design, deliver, and implement the courses and programs differs. The focus now includes discussions on the pedagogy the faculty want to employ so that everyone is

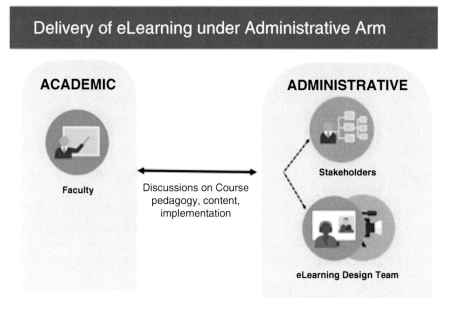

Fig. 3 Delivery of courses with eLearning under the administrative arm

on the same page and sometimes these discussions can be difficult because of the separation of the design and development process (see Fig. 3).

Mixture of Academic and Administrative

It is not without saying that some units do and can report to both arms of an organization. This can make it difficult to manage the products and services but this can also create a strength whereby all of the stakeholders are now directly incorporated into the crafting of unique products and the management of services.

When looking at where the unit is positioned in the organizational structure, a key point is knowing that most faculty (especially those outside of Colleges/Schools of Education) typically do not have a background in the design and learning theories which are specifically related to online pedagogy. The same is true of most employees who are under the technology services umbrella. When it comes to delivering courses, faculty members are very clear as to what they would like learners to know—understanding how the content should be delivered especially as it relates online can be a challenge. Being unaware of design differences between traditional (i.e., onground) and online courses can potentially create implementation problems for the institution, especially when some institutions expect their faculty to conform to the policies and procedures of the organization.

Accreditation

As the organizations plan to deliver their programs online, they now have to be careful how they proceed to offer the eLearning opportunities because defining the consumer base can be difficult. In the United States, in order to adhere to accreditation, education organizations must have agreements between the state where the organization's main business resides and the state where potential customers, in the form of learners, will originate. There are a number of organizations that provide the accreditation for provision of online courses—two of these accrediting bodies are:

1. National Council for State Authorization Reciprocity Agreements (NC-SARA)
2. Council for Higher Education Accreditation (CHEA)

The knowledge and awareness required for offering online programs do not just extend to national/international accreditation agencies, but also includes specialized organizations. Some programs are guided by certifying organizations; for example, a certification for project management may want to be aligned with the Project Management Institute's guide of knowledge (i.e., Project Management Body of Knowledge [PMBOK]). Offering such courses using the traditional methods typically do not create any challenges for accreditors but doing so online may have a different outcome.

What You Can Do

Recommendations

Organizational Structure

- Ensure that the goals of your unit are clear and that all of the stakeholders expectations on how courses will be delivered are known and understood.
- Join listservs and partner with people who have different structures so that you can compare and contrast.
- Discuss how often the eLearning unit should review their operating procedures to reflect the adjustments to market needs.
- The structure of the organization can thus determine what kind of training is required to support the faculty. Be certain that you can guide this conversation so that your unit's structure is not affected in any way.
- In some organizations the information technology department has the major voice in how courses are placed into the system and how the system is managed and functions. These differences create different views for how the online courses should be offered.

Maintaining and Managing Expertise

- Regardless of who loads courses into the LMS, training faculty and your team is important. Create a professional development plan for faculty and your team members to always be up to date with any new technology that is used to deliver courses. Plan for continuous faculty training on different features of the LMS and its updates. Training may be delivered to the group or individually.
- Create a plan and timeline for LMS updates. It is important to ensure that technology updates are not done during the semester when faculty are using the LMS to finish their courses. So timing when LMS updates occur during the academic calendar is important.
- Create a development and implementation timeline to guide the development of the courses. Ensure that the resources needed for the implementation are noted (i.e., faculty, IT staff, vendors, other administrators, and students for testing).
- Invest in training staff in the field of project management. This includes getting a tool to manage projects that will occur during your tenure in the organization.
- Through the use of project management principles you will need to assign owners and managers for each project. This means managing the risk, process and outcomes of the delivery and implementation.
- Do know that you will need other tools to help develop courses. Part of promoting what is known as active learning is to create strategies that use additional tools, and some of these tools may require additional hosting/server spaces.
- Create a budget that allows for growth especially when the unit is new.
- Provide basic instructional design training for faculty so they can more fully participate in course design.
- Create a lessons learned database so that your team can identify quick solutions even though they may be contextual. Schön (1983) discusses the reflective practitioner and a lessons learned database can help with the continued development of your team.
- Invest in your own expertise and complete not only management training but also pedagogical know-how. Understanding how faculty deliver their own courses will help you in the design and development process. Then managing a team that designs and develops also requires specific skills.

Being Innovative

- To be innovative you will have to match your area's strategic goals against many bodies, (e.g., regional, national, and international bodies). Maybe even against other topic-driven organizations.
- Acquire membership in organizations that have conferences and training sessions so that you and your team can learn as well as present/share with others.
- Being innovative does require a budget that will support risk taking (i.e., failure). If your unit is going to invest in innovation, do explain to stakeholders what being innovative truly means.

Best Practices

- Some organizations create a template for delivering the content. This allows all of the courses being delivered to follow one set navigational guide. An example of the course navigation would be
  - Syllabus
  - Schedule
  - Course Materials
  - Assignments
  - Grades
- What is the approval process before courses can be offered? (Faculty Senate, Academic Affairs Committees, Graduate or Undergraduate Councils). If there is no process one should be created and all major stakeholders submit agreements.
- Create an online orientation to train faculty and students on how to use the course delivery system.
- A course revision process needs to be created and an owner assigned. This can be linked to who is responsible for leading the course content but it can also be based on the strategic organization of the institution.
- Quality assurance is key for accreditation as well as the consistency of offerings. Decisions need to be made on what determines if a course is ready to be loaded and offered. What internal and external revision processes will be implemented.
- Consider using a rubric or other tool to plan and schedule course and program revisions.

Ideas

- How you set up your delivery unit does depend on the goals and the organizational structure and it can stem from one extreme where the eLearning unit is responsible for everything to the other extreme where the faculty are responsible for the course and the content and the eLearning unit is a service unit (see Fig. 4 below):

- Form relationships with other institutions close by and create a network to share experiences and expertise
- Create an annual workshop where you can work directly with faculty to create innovative solutions for their courses.
- Identify faculty champions who will help lead the design and delivery process—these champions are early adopters of solutions that can sell the great experiences your unit offers.

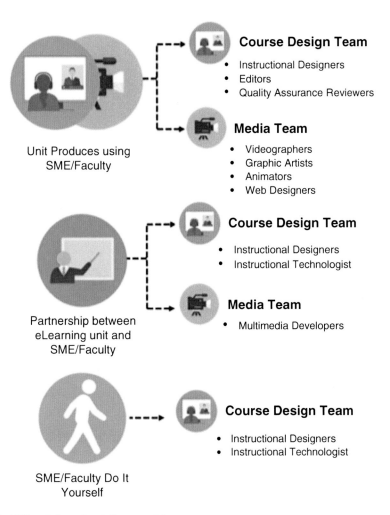

Fig. 4 Different eLearning delivery models

- Have your entire team (including yourself) teach at least one course a year and present at one conference a year. Having views from different perspectives of the design and development processes will assist you as you interact with faculty and administrators.

Conclusion

This chapter is filled with personal experiences and advice from the authors which means that it is not exhaustive. The experiences captured provide a range of suggestions from the faculty, design, and delivery perspective. Being prepared to offer eLearning can be a difficult task if the strategic goals for the unit are not clear. Understanding that the field of eLearning is dynamic and thus will require much flexibility, emotional awareness, structured determination, and perseverance. Managing a team and their abilities are the most important part of the eLearning process. Underestimating your resources' skills and abilities can be a severe hindrance to the success of such a group. Managing an entire unit will differ from organization to organization and thus will produce different successes.

For More Information

- Clark, R. C., & Mayer, R. E. (2016). *E-learning and the science of instruction: Proven guidelines for consumers and designers of multimedia learning.* John Wiley & Sons.
- eLearning Guild—Subscription.
- Khan, B. H. (2015). Introduction to e-learning. *International Handbook of E-Learning Volume 1: Theoretical Perspectives and Research, 2,* 1.
- Kulmann, T (23, November, 2014) The Rapid eLearning Blog—Practical Real-World Tips for eLearning Success.

References

Leban, W., & Zulauf, C. (2004). Linking emotional intelligence abilities and transformational leadership styles. *Leadership and Organization Development Journal, 25*(7), 554–564.
Maslow, A. H. (1943). A theory of human motivation. *Psychological Review, 50*(4), 370.
Schön, D. A. (1983). *The reflective practitioner: How professionals think in action* (vol. 5126). New York: Basic books.

Building an e-Learning Center from the Ground Up: The Challenges and Lessons Learned

Amy Thornton and Japheth Koech

Abstract e-Learning has become an essential component of the academic strategy at many institutions. As a result, institutions are challenged by the decisions they must make as to where distance education or e-learning fits within their current organizational structure. This chapter will help readers make decisions as to the best approach to establishing an e-learning center "from the ground up." The topics discussed will illustrate the challenges in creating an e-learning center and offer practical guidance from leaders in the field on how to overcome those challenges. This chapter will cover topics ranging from decisions to establish an e-learning center, assigning roles and services to the center, organizational development, administration and management, and infrastructure and resources. The goal is to provide concrete examples from practitioners that can be applied to numerous institutions.

Keywords e-Learning center • e-Learning division • e-Learning department • e-Learning administration • e-Learning implementation

What You Need to Know

As we are highlighting our experience of establishing an e-learning center in a higher education environment, we are sharing the following definition for an e-learning center. We adopted this definition from E-LEN, a project funded by the European Union that was designed to create a network of e-learning centers and lead organizations in the field of learning technologies.

An e-learning center is established for serving the learning needs of students, faculty, and staff of an educational/training organization, for the deployment of innovative curriculum pedagogy and state-of-the-art learning technology in real

A. Thornton (✉) • J. Koech
Columbus State University, Columbus, GA, USA
e-mail: thornton_amy1@columbusstate.edu; koech_japheth@columbusstate.edu

© Association for Educational Communications and Technology 2018   73
A.A. Piña et al. (eds.), *Leading and Managing e-Learning*, Educational Communications and Technology: Issues and Innovations,
https://doi.org/10.1007/978-3-319-61780-0_6

courses, and for the development of new learning technologies guided by theory and validated by observation of practice. (E-LEN, 2004).Insert heading called

Decision Making Guidance

This chapter will help you make decisions about:

- Establishing an e-learning center
- Overcoming challenges in creating an e-learning center
- Assigning roles and services to the center
- Organizational development
- Administration and management
- Infrastructure and resources

Decision to Establish a Center

There are various reasons for establishing an e-learning center, division, or department. In this section, we will discuss the reasons we have been involved directly in as well as taken the opportunity to revisit the literature from the field and highlight what others have experienced, seen, learned, or suggested during their implementation of e-learning centers. We hope that by sharing this information, your decisions to implement an e-learning center will be better informed.

In our experience e-learning at many higher education institutions begins organically with 1 or 2 faculty or departments making the decision to branch out into offering a few online courses or a fully online program. Typically when this happens the institution has not had the opportunity to consider what support and infrastructure are needed to support these ventures. Faculty are left on their own to figure out how to design a course, teach online, and support the students. From our experience this has been one of the major reasons for forming an e-learning center. Faculty find themselves overwhelmed taking on these extra responsibilities, which in turn affects the quality of the instruction being delivered and ultimately impacts student success. To meet the training needs, improve performance, and create a learning culture throughout an organization, establishing an e-learning center can fill these gaps (Malone, 2012).

For many institutions e-learning has become a part of their overall mission and strategic plan. When developing a strategic plan for e-learning it should include strategies for growth, support, marketing and recruitment, faculty development, change management, a funding model, and organizational development. This creates a need to establish an e-learning center as a central point of providing organized support to achieve a successful implementation of a system-wide and sustainable e-learning strategy at the university level (Softić & Bekić, 2008).

We have worked with many faculty who struggle with the idea of teaching online because they feel it will take away from their teaching style or struggle with admitting that they need help in learning new ways to facilitate the teaching and learning process. For some it's a matter of moving away from the traditional teaching model of standing in front of a classroom to deliver information through lecture. This requires a change of mindset. Faculty need help from instructional designers, instructional technologists, and course developers who have the expertise to help them transform teaching and learning through the provision of access and high quality education for all (Softić & Bekić, 2008). An e-learning center with expert instructional staff can help educators develop necessary skills to implement these powerful pedagogies (Repetto & Trentin, 2011). An e-learning center can also include the support to innovate, research, explore, and promote excellence in teaching and learning with diverse technologies (Repetto & Trentin, 2011).

What You Can Do

At this point you may be asking yourself, "What can I do to establish an e-learning center?" From our experience, we believe that there are many questions that should be answered before making this decision. The answers to these questions are different depending on the culture of your campus, faculty buy-in, administration buy-in, funding, and need. Many campuses have some form of support for e-learning even if it's just providing the technology support for the learning management system. Often, this starts in the information technology department. When schools embark on their e-learning journeys, the first thoughts are typically about the technology infrastructure. Who is going to make it work? Though this is important, it can also be short sighted because there are so many more things to think about (e.g., course design, faculty development, course review, student development, student services, state authorization). The list of roles, duties, and functions of an e-learning center, from our perspective, is long. These are things that have to be discussed. That list should drive the decisions about the technology infrastructure and decision to establish your center.

There can be many paths to the creation of a center. We have experienced scenarios on opposite ends of the spectrum, but at the heart of both, in terms of their success, was academic oversight. e-Learning is a medium for education, not the education itself. One of the authors once worked with a department leader who held the view that the learning objectives for an online course should be different than the learning objectives for a face-to-face course. e-Learning doesn't change learning objectives; rather, it just changes the methods by which those objectives are achieved. It's important to remind naysayers of this when proposing changes. An e-learning center should be focused on the academic side of e-learning, providing the voice of reason from an academic perspective, not IT perspective, of what e-learning is, why it's important, and to be the voice of reason for those who can't see past the "cool" bells and whistles associated with technology.

One of the most frequent questions asked, especially by slow adopters, is related to why a center needs to be created now. Sometimes, the decision comes because of a directive from an outside agency. For one of the authors, the institution's accrediting body, the Southern Association of Colleges and Schools (SACS) had some real issues with the way e-learning was being handled on the campus (i.e., lack of academic oversight). There is not necessarily one best way to ensure quality assurance, but examination of the e-learning infrastructure and face-to-face learning to make certain that there are equivalencies are important in making certain that institutions are asking the correct questions. Who is making decisions about e-learning? Are the information technology or other department faculty/staff involved in making those decisions? Are there inputs from faculty, students, Academic Affairs, and other constituents? What is driving decisions for your e-learning center—technology or instructional needs? Even if accreditation bodies have not presented you with mandates, their standards can provide wise guidance when evaluating what your needs are in terms of infrastructure to support online learning in your e-learning center. Another good resource we encourage you to explore is the Online Learning Consortium's Quality Scorecard. This can provide a framework for you to ensure the inclusion of components necessary for a quality online learning program within your e-learning center.

From our experience, unless an external force such as an accreditation body is involved, institutions should take the time to get all of the stakeholders at the table. Each institution is different, but stakeholders could include representatives from academic affairs units, information technology, college/department faculty, student services, enrollment services, disability services, recruitment, and the registrar. All of these departments/constituents have an impact on e-learning at an institution. Getting the support from these areas is critical as the new center will most likely be taking over some of the duties performed by one or more of these areas as well as taking some of their personnel. Without buy-in from these groups, the journey will not be smooth. Pulling all of the stakeholders together provides e-learning center creators opportunities to solidify the institutional goals for e-learning and ensure unanimity in supporting center goals. Any new center is doomed to failure if needed support from campus partners is missing.

Another big question that needs to be answered when starting a center is related to the source(s) of funding. Typically a scarce commodity, funding has to be pulled from some other place to fund a new center unless special allocations are available. Money is always a sensitive subject and can cause a lot of resentment, especially from an area whose funding is negatively impacted. We recommend an analysis of the revenue stream created by offering e-learning. For the sake of online students, consideration should be given to whether online tuition and fees are being used to serve online students rather than on services not utilized (e.g., athletics and the student recreation center fees). Issues related to services not used by online students should be explored to determine the feasibility of expanding services that assist online students, such as 24/7 help desk, online tutoring, or an online orientation.

The maturity in e-learning involves seven factors, including policy and governance, ongoing training evaluation, priority, outcomes assessment, readiness, and investment in faculty and staff (Bichsel, 2013). Other factors that need to be addressed when developing an e-learning strategy include (a) a clear vision of desired outcome, (b) an understanding of current capacity and attitudes of the relevant staff, and (c) a coherent set of steps to move from the current situation to the desired outcome (MacKeogh & Fox, 2009) as well as the use of benchmarking to assist institutions comparing their own practices with other similar institution's practices (McNaught, Lam, & Kwok, 2012).

Challenges of Establishing a Center

Funding: It should be noted that there can be numerous challenges when undertaking the task and process of implementing an e-learning center. The biggest challenge we have faced is identifying the funding source as noted in the previous section. Without proper funding it makes it very difficult to build the staffing necessary to provide effective services and support. This is supported by others who have cited some of the challenges including inadequacy of staff, the technological know-how of faculty (Bichsel, 2013) and the challenge of tight funding and competing priorities (MacKeogh & Fox, 2009).

Growth in e-Learning: Another challenge that we've run into is the exponential growth of e-learning. This has been a challenge in particular when there isn't a strategic plan in place to manage that growth. This can also lead you back to your funding source. If a funding source that is tied to e-learning has not been identified, it can make it very difficult to grow your support services adequately to ensure quality support.

Regular Review of Needs and Change Implementation: A challenge for administrators and faculty is the need for regular review of institutional e-learning strategies because of the ever-changing educational technologies, policies, and laws (Stoltenkamp, Kies, & Njenga, 2007). Technology changes so rapidly which requires the change of teaching and learning pedagogies to constantly be reviewed and changed as well. It takes an investment of funds and human resources to ensure faculty have access to the most up-to-date tools and training to effectively integrate them into their course design.

Compliance with Laws: One of the most recent challenges for many institutions is the new laws and guidelines regarding compliance with the federal Section 508 guidelines. Section 508 was an amendment added in 1998 to the Rehabilitation Act of 1973 that specifies the need for electronic content to be made accessible from the point of creation, which includes online courses. The Higher Education Opportunity Act also includes language regarding the accessibility of educational resources. Although this amendment was added over 15 years ago, it has received more attention of late due to the notable higher education lawsuits. Like many institutions we are dealing with the challenge of addressing this issue and ensuring our online courses are in compliance. These requirements have required our department to update our skills to incorporate universal design techniques and the integration of these accessibility standards in our design process to share with the faculty we work with. We are also working on an accessibility plan to ensure the compliance of our online courses moving forward.

Where to "Fit" the e-Learning Center: Organizational development has been a challenge we have encountered at every institution we've been. e-Learning does not usually fit into the mold of existing higher education, so for administrators it presents the challenge of deciding where to put us. For example, our current department has been under IT, under the library, and under Academic Affairs. At a previous institution they couldn't decide how centralized they wanted us to be, so struggled with deciding whether to include marking and recruitment in our department as well as certain student services.

Depending on your institutional culture you could run into any number of challenges including the issues of funding, lack of synergy, lack of clear position, and the active role of the university (Schneckenberg, 2008). It is very important that institutional e-learning strategy be complementary to institutional strategies for teaching, learning, and assessment (E-LEN, 2004). Being aware and well informed of all the challenges will assist you in formulating a strategy to address the challenges you may face before, during, and after your e-learning implementation.

Organizational Development

Once you have made the decision to establish a center for e-learning it is very important to consider where within the organization this center best fits. To do this, think about what the mission and goals of the center are going to be. Are they going to be focused on faculty development, student services, technology support, administration (e.g., state authorization, proctoring, online program development), some combination, or all of these? This should serve as a guide in your decision-making process when thinking about where a center fits. In our organization, ultimately Academic Affairs seemed to offer the best alignment but this may differ, depending on your institutional structure.

Once you've determined your mission and goals for the center, you can begin identifying the types of personnel that will be needed, and this will depend on the focus of the center. If you will be focusing on faculty development, you will need instructional designers and trainers; if focusing on technology support, you will need a learning management system administrator; if focusing on state authorization and other administrative areas, you will need personnel who have experience in those areas. Unfortunately, there is no one-size-fits-all solution. Your correct decisions depend on the answers to questions previously proposed. You must also consider whether there will be funds for hiring new personnel or if you will need to use existing personnel in other departments and provide support through education or training for them to fill the needed roles. Both scenarios can be expensive propositions. We have found that a combination of both is often used.

The e-learning project at the University of Rijeka provides a good example of a successful development of an e-learning center within a university. This development project was highly successful, including the achievement of efficiency and efficacy of teaching and learning by students, improvement of teaching practices by educators, easier course and student management, improved educator's time management, and improved e-learning literacy (Lučin, Mikac, Nemčanin, Nebić, & Žuvić-Butorac, 2011).

There are three approaches to realizing and managing change in higher education: top-down, bottom-up, and middle-out (Cummings, Phillips, Tilbrook, & Lowe, 2005). Answering more questions will help you determine the best approach for your institution. Where will your decision to establish an e-learning center, division, or department come from? How would it be accomplished? Is it from the top leadership (top-down)? Is it from middle-management (middle-out)? Is the decision based on the needs of stakeholders, requiring a bottom-up approach? The most important thing to remember is to find the approach that works best for your institution and use that approach to implement your e-learning center (Khan & Badii, 2012).

Part of a successful organizational development plan is change management. Most campuses have their own unique culture and political hurdles. Six proposed characteristics of change management include leadership, champions, planning, purpose, institutional culture, and support (Cummings et al., 2005). One of the authors once worked at an institution where they formed a Change Management Taskforce as part of the e-learning strategic plan. The taskforce was made up of representatives from different colleges and divisions at the institution and their task was to be the champions within their divisions promoting the changes and selling their colleagues on the benefits of moving in this direction. They were also the ears to the ground to bring back potential obstacles that could prevent the implementation from being successful.

Roles, Functions, and Services of an e-Learning Center

Depending on the setup and implementation of an e-learning center, there are numerous roles, duties, and services that can be accomplished by the center. The e-learning center may be staffed by various educational professionals (e.g., administrators, media, technology specialists, and faculty support specialists). These professionals also include instructional designers who provide training and support of educators by providing effective engagement with e-learning tools and the enhancement of teaching and learning processes (Stoltenkamp et al., 2007).

Other members of an e-learning center may also include the digital media team who provide training to educators on enhancing teaching and learning through the provision of skills related to the use of digital media content (Stoltenkamp et al., 2007). As a service or support role, an e-learning center can provide services and activities such as supporting, filtering, coordinating, advising, assisting, evaluating, promoting, and training (E-LEN, 2004).

A true e-learning strategy must address issues of culture, leadership, justification, organization, and change as illustrated by the study of a network of e-learning centers (E-LEN, 2004). The services that a department includes are largely dependent on decisions made during the process of establishing the center. Some centers are very centralized and support every aspect of online learning. Typically, these are identified as campus- or college-wide services. They would operate much like a campus or college with a Dean or Vice President overseeing the operations and providing academic oversight. These organizational patterns are most often seen in larger institutions that can support a separate infrastructure or in institutions where online learning is a significant part of the institution's enrollment. Centers like this have their own marketing, student services, and technology teams to support every aspect of students' online experiences. A benefit of this structure is that online students receive services that are geared to their specific needs, and there is typically more emphasis put on ensuring that all institutional services are equivalent for this population of students. A disadvantage of this type of structure is that students are isolated as either online or traditional students, and this can present its own challenges. Though a larger investment is required for infrastructure and overhead, finances may be more easily tracked and attributed to the two alternatives.

On the opposite end of the spectrum, there are e-learning centers that do little more than provide technical support. They support the learning management system through training. This might even be a function of the institution's faculty development center or teaching and learning center or the IT department. The main focus in these centers is typically training the faculty to use the technology for teaching online.

These examples provide two extremes. Midway between the two are endless combinations of services. Potential services that might be included are: proctoring, state authorization, LMS admin, training, instructional design, course development, multimedia development, marketing and recruitment, online program development, course accessibility, course and program evaluation, administration of grants or faculty stipends, facilitation of policy and enforcement, student services, and enrollment services. Each of these areas comes with its own benefits and challenges. What must be remembered is that there is a lot more than just supporting technology that goes into having a successful online learning program. Due to a shift in the last few years in the enforcement of state laws, it is more important than ever for an institution to have centralized units that can manage the data collection and reporting to ensure compliance for accreditation and compliance and offering online learning across state lines.

Administration and Management of the Center

Successful administration of an e-learning center requires strong leadership so as to lead the implementation as well as articulate the mission, vision, and goals in an educational setting (Keengwe, Kidd, & Kyei-Blankson, 2009). A challenge in the administration of an e-learning center includes rapidly evolving technology and relationship building with stakeholders (Chow, 2013). This requires leaders and technology administrators to also evolve to remain current with the changes.

From our experience, choosing the leadership for a new center is one of the most important decisions to be made. It is essential that whoever fills a leadership role be supportive of the mission and goals of the institution and be prepared to align center goals with those of the institution. If a new department is being formed, whoever takes the leadership role will be responsible for hiring all of the staff and providing the overall direction for the new e-learning center. Personnel new to the institution will need to be able to build relationships with existing administration and faculty and learn the culture of the institution. Many centers grow organically, starting as a small department with one or two staff members, adding staff as the need grows or as functions in other departments that would be a better fit in this new center are transferred. Based on our experience, it is indeed rare to begin with all the needed funds to establish all of the positions and services envisioned over the long term. It is possible that it can happen very quickly though. We went front a department of 1 full-time staff to a department with 7 full-time staff and 4 student workers in less than 4 years time. Managing the growth and change was definitely a challenge. Every position had to have a job description written from scratch since we were hiring positions that had not existed at our institution before and as every manager knows scheduling and conducting interviews is an extremely time-consuming task especially while trying to establish new relationships and services for an entire campus. Setting priorities and communicating those priorities to your stakeholders becomes very important to ensuring success.

There are a lot of logistical decisions that must be made in any new department. For example, where will the new department be housed physically? Desirable space is usually a scarce commodity on campus, and many times the new department will be placed wherever there is space available. If there are options available, consider who you will be serving and which space is going to be closest and most accessible to your customers.

Administration considerations for provisions of e-learning include such issues as, stakeholder objectives, milestone progress and reporting, current and future learner content requirements, support tools for learners, integration of components, learning management system (LMS) usability, management of professional development objectives, platform support for administrators, and security of the system (Anaraki & Director, 2004). Strategic planning should be used to align an e-learning center with the institutional goals and vision and to play a critical role across the entire institution (Softić & Bekić, 2008). A strategic approach is necessary to ensure that the e-learning center has the best possible chance to succeed.

Infrastructure and Resources

As has been noted, when establishing any new department, funding is always an issue. From our experience, many institutions that offer online learning programs or courses assess some type of fee (i.e., a convenience fee) or establish a different online tuition rate. Students are usually willing to pay this extra fee for the flexibility and convenience of taking courses online. Institutions new to online learning might decide to assess a higher online tuition rate or an online learning fee, which could provide direct funding for the e-learning center. This would result in growth and funding directly linked to enrollment—advantageous in some respects but lacking in security/stability of the unit's budget. If, however, the e-learning center is being established on a campus already engaged in online learning, extra tuition or fees for online learning are likely to have already been claimed by other areas. Once a funding source has been claimed, it is very difficult to reassign it to another area. In this situation, we recommend that center leaders propose a long-term plan for how money could be redirected in phases.

When building the infrastructure after online learning already exists at your institution, particularly when it has grown significantly, it is important to take into consideration the needs of your already existing online faculty and students. You will need buy-in from these groups to support the creation of an e-learning center and the redirection of resources. Some areas of support that are often needed include the learning management system, multimedia, and educational technologies to enhance the learning experience (Stoltenkamp et al., 2007). Other services that are typically of need are equipment, training, and course or curriculum support (Arabasz & Baker, 2003). For a successful implementation of e-learning infrastructure, resources such as technical support for all stakeholders should be planned and committed (O'Neill, Singh, & O'Donoghue, 2004).

The eventual success or failure of online learning is due to factors that have always been central to the provision of a quality online experience (Trang, Kwan, & Fox, 2006). e-Learning stakeholders include students, instructors, educational institutions, content providers, technology providers, and accreditation bodies (Khan & Badii, 2012). For the success of e-learning initiatives within institutions, leaders should be motivating, guiding, and directing the users of e-learning delivery formats, because the success of e-learning in higher education is a shared responsibility of all stakeholders involved (Wagner, Hassanein, & Head, 2008; Stoltenkamp et al., 2007).

Conclusion

As illustrated, there are many questions to consider when building an e-learning center. It should not be something that is done haphazardly. The important thing to remember is that it should align with institutional goals and priorities. Challenges include finding a funding source for the center, identifying roles and duties of the center, obtaining buy-in from all stakeholders, and gaining the support of your administration. Also, the identification and formation of a review and oversight team must be addressed at the inception phase so as to have a smooth formation and implementation of the center.

If e-learning is not a priority for your institution right now, it may not be the right time to create an e-learning center. Although, if your institution offers any type of e-learning, it is important to take the time to ensure the quality of the design and delivery of the courses and ensure that the institution is meeting required accreditation standards and state regulations.

Keep in mind that the results from creating a center can take time; lag time or incubation period is needed before results can be seen (Lučin et al., 2011). After the center has been established, a regular review and assessment of institutional e-learning strategies and policies are warranted because of the ever-changing educational technologies (Stoltenkamp et al., 2007) and a regular review and assessment give the e-learning center administration an opportunity to align its goals and services. This realignment of goals and services are needed to address issues such as selecting e-learning technologies that are reliable, secured by student data, easy for both faculty and students to use, and be effective (Bichsel, 2013).

Close collaboration of different support units within the university is an example of a successful e-learning strategy, as mentioned by Schneckenberg (2008), in implementing e-learning innovations. The ability of the center to adapt to current social relations within the university, as per Goodfellow and Lea (2008), is another example of factors that lead to successful implementation of e-learning centers.

Finally, in making the decision to implement an e-learning center and for it to be successfully implemented, a workable funding source must be identified, and an offer of incentives for training and productivity for faculty as well as the needs of all e-learning stakeholders such as administrators, educators, and students must be in place (Orozco, Fowlkes, Jerzak, & Musgrove, 2012). It must also have the support of top institution management through policy, budget, and directional support (Lučin et al., 2011).

For More Information

Following is a table of reading resources that may be instructive in establishing an e-learning center, division, or department. The selection criteria for the reading resources were based on how closely they relate to the creation of an e-learning center. Some of these readings offer excellent examples of setting up the centers, lessons learned during the implementation as well as other related experiences in the area of e-learning (Table 1).

Table 1 Further reading resources

Author(s)	Descriptive keyword	Type
King, Nugent, Russell, Eich, and Lacy (2000)	e-Learning Policy Framework	Article
McGrath (2009)	Departmental e-Learning Policies	Article
E-LEN and a network of e-learning centers (2004)	Implementing e-Learning Center	Article
Khan (2005)	e-Learning Management	Book
Malone (2012)	Setting Up Corporate e-Learning Center	Book
Miller et al. (2013)	Leading e-Learning Transformation in higher education	Book
Stoltenkamp et al. (2007)	Lesson learn from institutionalizing e-Learning division	Article
Lučin et al. (2011)	Experience from framework Implementation for e-Learning	Article
Orozco et al. (2012)	Forming an e-Learning center in 108 days	Article

References

Anaraki, F., & Director, N. O. C. (2004). Developing an effective and efficient e-learning platform. *International Journal of the computer, the internet and management, 12*(2), 57–63.

Arabasz, P., & Baker, M. B. (2003). Evolving campus support models for e-learning courses. *Educause Center for Applied Research Bulletin*, 1–9, Retrieved from http://www.educause. edu/ir/library/pdf/ecar_so/ers/ERS0303/EKF0303.pdf.

Bichsel, J. (2013). *The state of e-learning in higher education: An eye toward growth and increased access*. Louisville, CO: EDUCASE Center for Analysis and Research.

Chow, A. S. (2013). One educational technology colleague's journey from dotcom leadership to university e-learning systems leadership: Merging design principles, systemic change and leadership thinking. *TechTrends, 57*(5), 64–73.

Cummings, R., Phillips, R., Tilbrook, R., & Lowe, K. (2005). Middle-out approaches to reform of university teaching and learning: Champions striding between the top-down and bottom-up approaches. *The International Review of Research in Open and Distributed Learning, 6*(1), 1–18.

E-LEN: a network of e-learning centres. (2004). *Implementing an institutional e-learning centre: Guiding notes and patterns*. Retrieved from http://www2.tisip.no/E-LEN/documents/ ELENDeliverables/Guidelines_for_ELEN_centers.pdf.

Goodfellow, R., & Lea, M. R. (2008). *Challenging e-learning in the university: A literacies perspective*. Buckingham, GBR: Open University Press.

Keengwe, J., Kidd, T., & Kyei-Blankson, L. (2009). Faculty and technology: Implications for faculty training and technology leadership. *Journal of Science Education and Technology, 18*(1), 23–28.

Khan, B. H. (2005). *Managing E-learning: Design, delivery, implementation, and evaluation*. Hershey, PA: Information Science.

Khan, K. U., & Badii, A. (2012). Impact of e-learning on higher education: Development of an e-learning framework. *Life Science Journal, 9*(4), 4073–4082.

King, J. W., Nugent, G. C., Russell, E. B., Eich, J., & Lacy, D. D. (2000). Policy frameworks for distance education: Implications for decision makers. *Online Journal of Distance Learning Administration, 3*(2), 1–5.

Lučin, P., Mikac, T., Nemčanin, D., Nebić, Z., & Žuvić-Butorac, M. (2011). Establishing an institutional framework for an e-learning implementation–experiences from the University of Rijeka, Croatia. *Journal of Information Technology Education, 10*(IIP), 043–056.

MacKeogh, K., & Fox, S. (2009). Strategies for embedding eLearning in traditional universities: Drivers and barriers. *Electronic Journal of e-Learning, 7*(2), 147–154.

Malone, S. A. M. (2012). *How to set up and manage a corporate learning centre*. Abingdon, GB: Gower.

McGrath, L. (2009). *Developing eLearning policies at the department level*. Kennesaw, GA: DigitalCommons@ Kennesaw State University.

McNaught, C., Lam, P., & Kwok, M. (2012). *Using eLearning benchmarking as a strategy to foster institutional eLearning strategic planning*. Retrieved from http://www.academia.edu/2848054/Using_ELearning_Benchmarking_as_a_Strategy_to_Foster_Institutional_ELearning_Strategic_Planning.

Miller, G., Benke, M., Chaloux, B., Ragan, L., Schroeder, R., Smutz, W., & Swan, K. (2013). *Leading the e-learning transformation in higher education: Meeting the challenges of technology and distance education*. Herndon, VA: Stylus.

O'Neill, K., Singh, G., & O'Donoghue, J. (2004). Implementing elearning programmes for higher education: A review of the literature. *Journal of Information Technology Education: Research, 3*(1), 313–323.

Orozco, M., Fowlkes, J., Jerzak, P., & Musgrove, A. (2012). Zero to sixty plus in 108 days: Launching a central elearning unit and its first faculty development program. *Journal of Asynchronous Learning Networks, 16*(2), 177–192.

Repetto, M., & Trentin, G. (2011). *Faculty training for web enhanced learning*. Hauppauge, NY: Nova.

Schneckenberg, D. (2008). *Educating tomorrow's knowledge workers: The concept of ecompetence and its application in international higher education*. Delft, The Netherlands: Eburon Academic.

Softić, S. K., & Bekić, Z. (2008). *Organizational aspects of supporting e-learning at university level*. Paper presented at the Information Technology Interfaces, 2008. ITI. 30th International Conference.

Stoltenkamp, J., Kies, C., & Njenga, J. (2007). Institutionalising the elearning division at the University of the Western Cape (UWC): Lessons learnt. *International Journal of Education and Development using ICT, 3*(4), 143–152.

Trang, P., Kwan, R., & Fox, R. (Eds.). (2006). *Enhancing learning through technology*. River Edge, SG: WSPC.

Wagner, N., Hassanein, K., & Head, M. (2008). Who is responsible for e-learning success in higher education? A stakeholders' analysis. *Journal of Educational Technology & Society, 11*(3), 26–36.

Distance Education and Technology Infrastructure: Strategies and Opportunities

Robert L. Moore and Brian P. Fodrey

Abstract Distance education provides a wealth of opportunities and areas for innovation, but it also presents unique challenges for implementation and eventual success. To mitigate these challenges, this chapter will present four critical components—systems, objectives, evaluation, and personnel—that combine into one to create a technology infrastructure that can support distance delivery. Through this chapter, e-learning leaders will gain the knowledge to not only identify key features of tools used for distance delivery, but also understand and appreciate the correlation between a holistic infrastructure approach and quality distance delivery. The absence of one of these critical components will likely result in an unsuccessful technology integration. To aid in the explanation of these critical components, the chapter will focus on three main distance education delivery forms—webinars, classroom captures, and e-learning modules. The chapter will provide an overview of the types of questions and elements that should go into consideration of any distance education tool, and will aid in the effective assessment and evaluation of these tools, as well as personnel considerations that should be taken into account.

Keywords Technology infrastructure • Web conferencing • Webinars • e-Learning modules • Instructional design • Distance education • Evaluation • Classroom capture • Interaction

Decision-Making Guidance

This chapter will help you make decisions about developing your institution's IT infrastructure, and after reading the chapter you will be able to:

- Understand the relationship between software tools and systems as it relates to distance delivery

R.L. Moore (✉) • B.P. Fodrey
University of North Carolina at Chapel Hill,
Knapp-Sanders Bldg, CB 3330, Chapel Hill, NC 27599, USA
e-mail: rob@mindofaninnovator.com; fodrey@sog.unc.edu

© Association for Educational Communications and Technology 2018
A.A. Piña et al. (eds.), *Leading and Managing e-Learning*, Educational
Communications and Technology: Issues and Innovations,
https://doi.org/10.1007/978-3-319-61780-0_7

- Identify the key features of tools for distance education content creation
- Evaluate and select the most appropriate software and systems for distance delivery

What You Need to Know

Distance education is a rapidly growing segment of higher education as more and more students are pursuing degrees, training, and certifications in this format. Ozkan and Koseler (2009) identify this tremendous growth and the "trend towards location-independent education and individualization [as a motivation for] universities to invest their resources on developing online programs" (p. 1286). Previously, distance education was seen as a peripheral alternative or one that was not the focal point of many of our more traditional universities, but that too has changed. Simonson, Smaldino, and Zvacek (2015) explain that distance education is seen as a viable option for many learners and is actually the preferred method of receiving instruction for many of them. This is further evidenced by the most recent enrollment numbers provided by the National Center for Education Statistics. They report that in fall 2013 over 5.5 students were enrolled in distance education courses at degree-granting postsecondary institutions. In that same year, over 2.6 million, or 15.1%, of undergraduates enrolled at degree-granting postsecondary institutions took at least one distance education course, and almost 2 million, or 11.3%, did a fully online program (National Center for Education Statistics, 2016). As more data becomes available, one would expect to see the number of students taking fully online programs to continue to increase along with the number of students who take at least one online course during their postsecondary careers.

However, the quality of instruction cannot suffer, and instructional designers are often faced with the challenge of providing support for faculty while simultaneously managing new content delivery tools. At the management level, administrators are tasked with aligning institution resources to the most effective and efficient models for distance education delivery. But with so many options, it can be a challenge to identify exactly which is the best fit for an institution. Administrators need to understand that distance education is more than simply posting a copy of a PowerPoint presentation online; students want interaction both with their peers and with the instruction. Students also look for rich educational experiences from the location of their choosing.

A Model for Technology Infrastructure

Just as interest and enrollment in distance education courses has grown exponentially, a similar growth has been seen on the technological side. Two areas—mobile and e-learning in particular—have direct implications for distance education (Balch,

Fig. 1 Four critical
components for technology
infrastructure

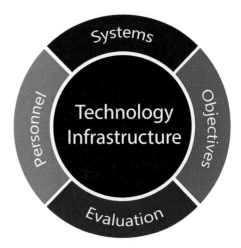

2014). Bosch, Hartenberger Toby, and Alkhomsi (2015) point out that these innovations now have "educators trying to find any channel possible that can deliver quality education and interactions to people at a distance" (p. 137). In meeting this demand, e-learning leaders must determine the most effective and efficient ways to deliver their instructional content. As these leaders seek to meet needs, they need to manage multiple stakeholders and interests. Paul and Cochran (2013) identify the four components of institution, student, faculty, and technology as essential for distance education. Taken individually, these components are critical, but "the larger risks and rewards for online education occur where these components intersect" (Paul & Cochran, 2013, p. 50). These components provide a useful framework for an institution-wide view of distance education. But within the information technology (IT) divisions that are tasked with supporting distance education initiatives, there is a need for an effective way to identify, evaluate, and implement tools that can support distance education and the organization's instructional mission. Alsabawy, Cater-Steel, and Soar (2013) explain that "IT infrastructure services [are] a critical factor which affects the [institution's] activities [as it relates to distance education]" (p. 431). This IT division-level framework is what will be referred to in this chapter as the technology infrastructure, the four components of which are displayed in Fig. 1.

Each of these components are required for any distance education technology infrastructure, and the absence of one component will likely result in a less effective implementation of distance education services. There is not a specific order for this model which aligns with how projects may be initiated. For instance, a faculty member may express an interest in using GoToMeeting, a web-based video conferencing tool, which would be in the *systems* part of the model. The IT Division would next need to find out the faculty member's learning objectives, determine how or if GoToMeeting is able to meet those needs, and evaluate how it will work within the enterprise environment of the institution. Finally, the division will need to determine if it has the personnel who can support this new tool, both in terms of training

Table 1 Overview of different delivery options

	Webinar	Classroom captures	e-Learning module
Synchronous	Yes	Yes	No
Asynchronous	Yes	Yes	Yes
Student interaction	Yes	Yes	Yes
Student to student interaction	Yes	No	No
Student to faculty interaction	Yes	Yes	Limited
Real-time polling	Yes	Yes	No
Real-time question and answer	Yes	Yes	No
Typical length (in minutes)	60–90	Varies	15–35

the faculty member but also potentially for live-event support (if that is required). This is just one of many examples of ways that this model can work within the IT Division.

Systems. There are two aspects of interest within the systems component. The first is what format or delivery method you are using to create your instructional content, and the second is what platform or tool you will use to deliver this content. We begin with the first aspect, which is the format and delivery method. Although there are many permutations and definitions of distance education delivery methods, we will focus on webinars, classroom or lecture captures, and e-learning modules (Table 1).

In this chapter, the term *webinar* will be used to refer to a synchronous recording that features some level of direct interaction with the instructor and students and which can be recorded and archived for on-demand access by students. These synchronous recordings are delivered using a web platform and originate from the presenter's laptop or desktop. They will include audio and visuals (typically in the form of PowerPoint slides), and may also include video of the presenter. Students will view these real-time recordings using their laptop or desktop computer. The instructor may decide to leverage small groups, usually termed a *breakout room*, to allow students to have more student-to-student interactions during the webinar. In the live event, students will be able to answer any poll questions posed by the instructor providing immediate feedback to the instructor and also ask questions of the presenter using text-based chat. Typically, a webinar will run from 60 to 90 min.

Classroom or lecture captures are meant to be exactly what their name implies— a digital representation of what happened in the classroom. They are meant to capture what information was transmitted via the teacher in a classroom setting but will not feature many of the collaborative elements of a face-to-face classroom such as small group work. Similar to a webinar, a classroom capture offers the opportunity for a synchronous session that can also be recorded and archived and later provided to students for asynchronous viewing. Capturing a lecture for students is a helpful study and review tool. These captures can be accessed by students interested in studying or reviewing their own notes after the class session. The length of a classroom capture will vary, but can be understood for the purposes of this chapter as being a full class session—from 45 min to 3 h. It would be presented to students as one long recording, similar to what their experience would be within the classroom. Instructors will be able to offer polling during the synchronous version but should be aware that if video is being used there may be a latency issue or delay in transmission, which makes real-time polling difficult.

Of the three delivery options, e-learning modules are typically the most labor-intensive option for faculty to create and deliver. This is often due to the fact that an e-learning module is self-paced and is meant to provide not only instruction, but also opportunities for student interaction. This can take the form of quizzes or interaction with the content on the slide, such as clicking on boxes to reveal information. With e-learning modules, the feedback is instant, whether that is from a quiz being marked correct or incorrect and receiving additional feedback or by having to use a drag and drop exercise to correctly position a list or objects. The modules will have a customized look and feel to match the subject matter and will have engaging content including animations and audio. These modules do not have a real-time component, and the interaction will be designed by the instructor, with students completing it at their own pace and time. The results of the quizzes may be reported to a learning management system (LMS) if SCORM or some other type of tracking (http://scorm.com/scorm-explained/) has been enabled and is supported by the LMS. For more information about LMSs, refer to the LMS chapter within this book. In these e-learning modules, students will receive their instruction using a web-enabled device that may include their laptop or mobile device such as a tablet or iPad. Since these are self-paced instructional materials, students will be interacting indirectly with their instructor. The instructor may include quiz questions with immediate feedback provided, but there will not be opportunities for real-time question and answer or polling such as with classroom captures and webinars. Typically, these modules will take between 15 and 35 min to complete.

The second aspect for systems is how the content is being delivered, and this is where the specific tools come into play. Many of these tools you may already be familiar with, including Adobe Connect, GoToMeeting, or WebEx. Preset and Andrews (2015) provide what they call the "magic quadrant for web conferencing" (Fig. 2), which organizes the various tools into four quadrants of leaders, challengers, visionaries, and niche players.

Present and Andrews define leaders as those who "have achieved significant market share relative to their competitors … [and] have robust, scaled products with a wide range of features," and they continue to explain that these leaders "are doing well today and are prepared for the future" (p. 16). Cisco, Adobe, Microsoft, IBM, Citrix, and AT&T are all found in this leader's category. Challengers are defined as being companies which "are characterized by operational excellence and good standing in the market … but do not have long-term roadmaps or their products lack some features" (p. 16). Interestingly, Google falls into this category according to Preset and Andrews. The visionaries quadrant, which includes companies such as Zoom, Fuze, Vidyo, PGi, and West Unified Communications Services, is defined by companies that "have important, unique and/or well-developed technical capabilities, and provide key innovations that illustrate the future of the market … [but] have not yet developed the sales and support capabilities to address or influence the

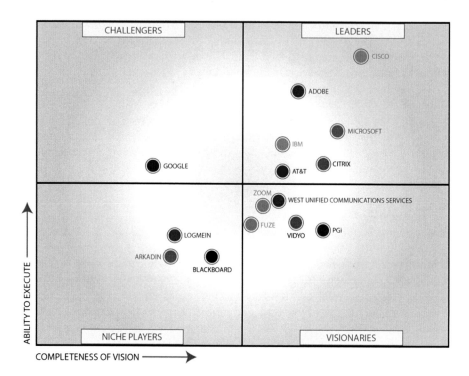

Fig. 2 Magic quadrant. Adapted from Preset and Andrews (2015)

whole market" (p. 16). Finally, the fourth quadrant is for niche players which are defined as "[having] good technology, but are limited by their service, breadth of product line … [and] some have chosen a niche strategy" (p. 17). Companies within this quadrant include LogMeIn, Arkadin, and Blackboard.

Objectives. Moore (2014) states that it is imperative that technology supports instruction. Too often, a fun or new technology tool is added to a course before it has been carefully reviewed and vetted. This can often lead to frustration from both the students and instructor. It is critical to establish clear learning objectives and to align these with the technology tools that are selected and implemented. It will also be easier to evaluate the tools if you understand what you are trying to accomplish. For instance, an instructor may feel that students need a solid foundation in specific concepts before they can move on to higher levels of application and critical think-ing. In order to meet this need, an e-learning module may be developed that covers these fundamental concepts, and it may then be published and distributed to stu-dents using Adobe Connect. Within the module, there would be knowledge check quizzes, and the instructor could link these scores to the LMS. This would allow for an effective evaluation of the e-learning module. Conversely, if the instructor was given a tool that is suited for classroom capture to develop this e-learning module, it would fail to meet the learning objectives. Thus, it is important to properly align the technology to the learning objective.

Evaluation. There are two parts to evaluation within this model. There is the initial evaluation of the particular tool or service that is going to be used for the distance education option. Furthermore, there is also the continuous evaluation that must happen after the implementation. Ozkan and Koseler (2009) explain that "assessment has become an essential requirement of a feedback loop for continuous improvement but often this is overlooked by the IT division" (p. 1286). In many scenarios, the tool or service is deployed to the institution and then the IT division moves on to the next project. In this scenario, the IT division fails to develop a mechanism for evaluating if this solution is continuing to meet the needs of the institution. The evaluation that IT should be responsible for is how the technology is meeting the stated objectives for the course. This may require engaging with the faculty members to provide instructional objective feedback to compare with the technical evaluation and assessment that the IT team can provide. Together, this feedback loop will make sure that the technology is meeting the instructional needs. The rapid advances in technology make it critical that solutions and tools are under constant review and consideration. Preset and Andrews' magic quadrants demonstrate that there is quite a bit of fluidity between the levels, and while one may have chosen a tool from the leader's quadrant, a challenger or visionary company may actually be able to better meet the needs of the institution in the future.

Personnel. Personnel is an important requirement for technology infrastructure. Higher education institutions are driven by providing instruction. One of the ways to help align technology with instruction is through the hiring of an instructional designer. This instructional designer can serve multiple purposes. First, they will be able to work with faculty on integrating technology into their instruction and aligning technology to learning objectives. Just as faculty are subject matter experts in their field, an instructional designer is a subject matter expert in integrating technology into instruction. For some faculty who are not as experienced with technology, this support will be beneficial; for other faculty, the instructional designer can help them think of new ways to be innovative in the classroom. Additionally, the instructional designer will be able to interface with the technical personnel within the IT Division. Consider an LMS. There is the actual installation and maintenance of the LMS—things such as backups, updates, and patching—that is well suited for a LMS administrator. But that LMS administrator may not know which of the forum tools is best suited for instructors and students, or may not know how quizzes should be delivered within the actual course. These pedagogical decisions that are technology based are best addressed by the instructional designer. Having these two skill sets within the same IT division team allows for a more holistic support structure and will make the technology infrastructure more sustainable. It will also feed into the learning objectives and evaluation components as it will provide the people through which to accomplish these two critical steps.

What You Can Do

Now that you have been furnished with a model for technology infrastructure and understand the terminology, it is time to discuss how to actually evaluate the various tools that are available for use. We could provide specific tools and an evaluation of those tools, but that is a limiting exercise. Each institution will have different needs and factors that will influence these decisions. Therefore, we will discuss what things to look for when evaluating different tools. By focusing on the *process* of the evaluation, it will make this more applicable to a wider audience. These are merely suggestions informed by the experiences of the authors in building technology infrastructures and best practices from other practitioners. These are meant more as guideposts to get you started on developing your own institution-specific evaluation that will cater to those needs. We will focus again on the three delivery options previously defined—webinars, classroom or lecture capture, and e-learning modules. The following sections provide guiding questions for each delivery option that will help make the selections.

Webinars

When evaluating options for webinars, there are six key questions that you will want to answer.

1. How Does the Solution Handle PowerPoint or Keynote Animations?

PowerPoint is the tool most faculty are familiar with, and typically how they will organize their content. For those using Mac-based computers, they may be using Keynote, which offers similar presentation functionality to PowerPoint. During the webinar, the faculty will want to present their content and have the participants be able to follow along. Although there are many options for how to deliver your webinar, from a Google Hangout to a GoToMeeting session to Adobe Connect, a key distinction will be in how animations are handled. Adobe Connect will be able to handle PowerPoint animations, but other tools, such as Blackboard Collaborate or WebEx, will create static images of each slide that will not allow for animations, such as bullet points appearing on mouse click. These tools can provide a work-around in allowing the instructor to share their screen which is running PowerPoint on the local machine, but this can present latency issues.

2. What Type of Participant Interaction is Needed?

We have all sat through a webinar that was nothing more than a talking head and know how painful that experience was as a participant. Good instructional practices mean that there will be participant interaction during the webinar and the different tools will handle this differently, if at all. Here is where the learning objectives come into play. If the instructor attempts to employ webinars as a means of doing a review session, they may have different needs than if they are trying to use webinars as a way to replace a face-to-face class session. The way that the participants interface with the instructor and each other may differ. At the time of this publication, some tools, such as GoToMeeting or WebEx, did not provide comparable polling features to ones offered by other tools, such as Blackboard Collaborate and Adobe Connect. Another part of participant interaction are breakout rooms. Some tools allow for a session's participants to be moved into their own virtual breakout rooms where they can collaborate and have private discussions similar to how a face-to-face class may have small group work; other tools do not have this component.

3. How Much Customization Can Be Done for the Layout?

Some tools provide a default layout that has a space for the participant list and text-based chat and then the display of either a shared desktop screen, whiteboard area, or PowerPoint slides. This may meet the needs for most faculty, but others may want the ability to change layouts and add in different components such as video files or other multimedia components that can help engage the learners.

4. Can You Save Your Room Configurations?

For instructors who are looking to do webinars on a regular basis, such as replacing a weekly face-to-face class session or teaching a fully online course synchronously, being able to save their room configurations is a huge benefit. This connects with the previous question on customizations. If the room can be customized to have the widgets and tools that are needed, but it cannot later be saved and the faculty member must do this setup before each meeting, this will be frustrating and inefficient for the faculty member. The additional setup time may dissuade them from either using these additional components that could better engage learners or not want to use the tool at all.

5. How Many Learners Can Connect?

Most webinar solutions are based on *connections* to the room. These connections may be referred to as users, learners, or participants, but these all mean the same thing. It will be important to look at what the average class or session size and use that to determine which package to select. Each class meeting would be considered a session, and you will want to check how many connections are allowed per session. For example, if these webinars are for online courses that have an enrollment cap of 25 students, there is no need to pay for a room that allows for 100 connections as this can become cost-prohibitive when you try to scale up to support more online instruction. It is important to distinguish between how many people are connecting to the webinar versus how many are actually going to be watching it. If each student is signing in from their own computer, those are many individual connections. However, if students or participants may be meeting in groups and using a projector in a conference room to project the webinar, you would only be counting that single connection, not everyone that was in the room.

For licenses, vendors typically do not place limits on the number of times you can use an existing room during the license terms. In other words, if you pay for a 50 seat room, you would be able to use that room as many times as you wanted to. The limitations are typically in concurrency of usage. This means that while you may reuse your room URL as many times as you want, you can only host one meeting at a time per room URL. When recording is an option, most solutions will create a new URL for just the on-demand version which is different from the original room URL. At the author's institution, Adobe Connect is used for webinars and instructors use one main room for all of their webinars. The webinar room has a standard configuration for questions, polling, and other features, and then each webinar's slides are loaded into the middle area. After recording the meeting, a new on-demand link is automatically created by the system allowing viewers to see the on-demand version and the reuse of the original room URL.

6. Do You Have the Ability to Host or Store Content?

Some of the webinar tools do not provide long-term storage options or have storage as an additional expense in addition to the fee to use the webinar tool itself. If content is being created for a course, this may be an important factor. Some tools, such as Adobe Connect, provide unlimited storage of content during the length of the contract. You will also want to consider what type of export options you will have for recorded content in case you need to move services or want long-term storage. Some tools, such as Blackboard Collaborate and Adobe Connect, provide included export of recordings but may require specific playback players or have a loss in quality on these downloads. Thinking about what you want to do with the content after you have recorded it as part of your tool evaluation process will help avoid potential mismatches between needs and expectations with faculty. The last thing you want is for a faculty member to expect the content to be available for an entire semester but your tool only allows for 30 days of storage.

The licensing agreement that you have with your host provider will address many of these issues. Most vendors will offer annualized pricing that is cheaper than paying per month. It is important to check with your system office or central IT to find out if there are any preexisting web conferencing contracts. If not, each vendor should offer a higher education pricing that is different from the normal price points. Verifying the storage parameters and also how to export and move information from the host server to a local or different server are all things to look at when evaluating potential third-party service providers.

Classroom or Lecture Capture

Many of the same questions for webinars will also be applicable for evaluating classroom or lecture capture tools, but there are a couple that are specific to this delivery medium.

1. Is There Specific Hardware Required in Addition to the Capture Hardware?

For some tools, such as MediaSite, you may need to have a physical, vendor-specific recording appliance that simultaneously captures the video of the presenter and the PowerPoint slides. Other tools or solutions may capture the video using a simple webcam and software running from the presenter's computer. There are pros and cons to both approaches and associated costs that will help narrow down the options based on your specific needs.

2. Is There a Livestream Option?

For some tools, learners can watch a livestream or webcast version of the presentation which can be helpful if students are not able to physically convene in the same location. However, there may be some latency issues with the livestream which limit the ability to use interactive features such as polling. With MediaSite, the authors have observed as much as an 8 s latency delay between a livestream and what is actually happening in the classroom; such a large latency period makes polling with livestream attendees impossible. Another factor to consider will be the network connectivity of those watching the livestream. If they are on slower connections, the latency period could be much higher and may impact their satisfaction with the livestream; if students are not able to reliably watch the classes, they will not be able to actively participate in the class and learning will suffer.

3. How Easily Can You Export Content and Use It In Different Locations?

All of the tools will offer a playback player that will show the recorded content, but many will not export the content in a format that would be supported by another application. Thus, moving from a tool such as Echo360 to MediaSite could be incredibly difficult.

e-Learning Modules

For e-learning modules, there are three questions that you should answer in evaluating options.

1. How Will Modules Be Created?

In some situations, faculty may be the ones creating the modules on their own without the use of an instructional designer. In this case, you will want to have a tool that has a low barrier of entry in terms of costs and learning curve for using the tool. However, if your situation has faculty working closely with an instructional designer on developing the module, you can consider one of the more expensive e-learning development tools such as Adobe Captivate, Adobe Presenter, or Articulate Storyline. These rapid e-learning development tools have steep learning curves but your instructional designer should be experienced with at least one, if not all, of these tools. Their experience with the tools will likely be working with subject matter experts to organize and develop the content through these tools.

2. How Will You Deliver the Content? How Will Students Access the Content?

You will want to consider how you will be sharing the content that is being developed as e-learning modules. The authors are currently leveraging Adobe Connect to both host their e-learning content as well as using Adobe Connect for webinars. Since there is unlimited storage as part of the contract for the webinar rooms, the storage for the e-learning modules is not an additional cost. Files created with Articulate Storyline can also be uploaded and shared using Adobe Connect, although it cannot be published directly from Storyline to the Connect server as you can with Captivate and Presenter files. Modules created with one of these tools can be exported as zip files which can then be uploaded to a web server or within an LMS, such as Blackboard, Moodle, or Sakai, or distributed and viewed locally on students' devices.

3. Will You Be Using SCORM or Some Other Standard?

SCORM is a standard that allows for the tracking of student progress and scores on quizzes and is typically reported and managed through an LMS. If this is something that your faculty are looking for, it is important to pick a tool that will allow for the publishing of files in a format that will work within your LMS. Most commercially available e-learning development tools (e.g., Captivate, Presenter, and Storyline) can publish to SCORM, however, they may not be able to publish to other formats. It will be important to make sure the LMS and software are able to communicate correctly.

Conclusion

Over the last decade, we have seen a shift from distance education being an exception to gradually becoming an accepted norm for instruction. Public perception has changed to be more accepting of distance education. The previous perception was that it was not possible to receive high-quality online education, but that perception has waned over the years. Additionally, in the past, students shied away from distance education out of concerns about the quality of the instructional experience, but we are also seeing these feelings shift. The authors have observed a significant increase not only in demand from students for distance education offerings but also in interest from faculty in providing more distance education offerings. These two needs present a rich justification for developing a long-term infrastructure plan that is able to meet the needs of the institution, faculty, and students as well as allow for flexibility to evolve and adjust as technology changes.

One of the limitations of this chapter is that it cannot possibly provide the answers for all situations because each institution will have a specific enterprise infrastructure available. Additionally, each institution will have unique needs from the size of the student population to the percentage of online course offerings or overall course objectives. The challenge for e-learning leaders is fully understanding the underlying concepts and needs for a technology infrastructure plan and then adapting and applying it to their specific environment. This chapter aids in that process by providing background information about webinars, classroom captures, and e-learning modules and some guiding questions to consider when evaluating each of these tools.

For More Information

- Gartner technology research: http://www.gartner.com/technology/home.jsp
- Indiana University Adobe Connect resources: https://kb.iu.edu/d/bfnl
- University of Colorado Boulder Zoom FAQs:: https://oit.colorado.edu/services/conferencing-services/web-conferencing-zoom/faq
- Web Conferencing Tools Matrix (UNC-Chapel Hill): http://its.unc.edu/resource/web-conferencing-tools-matrix/

References

National Center for Education Studies. (2016). *Digest of Education Statistics, 2014 (NCES 2016-006)*. Retrieved from http://nces.ed.gov/fastfacts/display.asp?id=80.

Alsabawy, A. Y., Cater-Steel, A., & Soar, J. (2013). IT infrastructure services as a requirement for e-learning system success. *Computers & Education, 69*, 431–451.doi:10.1016/j.compedu.2013.07.035

Balch, O. (2014, April 13). Four mobile-based tools that can bring education to millions. *The Guardian*. Retrieved from http://www.theguardian.com/sustainable-business/2014/aug/20/mobile-phones-smartphone-education-teaching.

Bosch, A., Hartenberger Toby, L., & Alkhomsi, A. R. (2015). In a world of explofing possibilities in distance learning, don't forget about the light bulb. *The Quarterly Review of Distance Education, 16*(2), 129–138.

Moore, R. L. (2014). Importance of developing community in distance education courses. *TechTrends, 58*(2), 20–24.

Ozkan, S., & Koseler, R. (2009). Multi-dimensional students' evaluation of e-learning systems in the higher education context: An empirical investigation. *Computers & Education, 53*(4), 1285–1296. doi:10.1016/j.compedu.2009.06.011

Paul, J.A & Cochran, J.D. (2013). Key interactions for online programs between faculty, students, technologies, and educational institutions: A holistic framework. The *Quarterly Review of Distance Education, 14(1)*, 49–62.

Preset, A., & Andrews, W. (2015, December 28). *Magic quadrant for web conferencing*. Retrieved from http://www.gartner.com/document/3181419?ref=lib.

Simonson, M., Smaldino, S., & Zvacek, S. (Eds.). (2015). *Teaching and learning at a distance: Foundations of distance education* (6th ed.). Charlotte, NC: Information Age.

An Educational Leader's View of Learning Management Systems

Anthony A. Piña

Abstract The Learning Management System (LMS) is a technology success story. While many educational technology applications over the years have failed to take hold, the LMS has reached an extraordinary level of adoption at higher education institutions. In 2002, the Campus Computing Project estimated that three-quarters of all colleges and universities in the USA had adopted an LMS, with approximately 20% of all courses being delivered via the LMS (The 2002 campus computing report, Encino, CA, 2002). By 2014, the EDUCAUSE Center for Analysis and Research (ECAR) reported that—according to its survey of more than 92,000 higher education faculty and students and nearly 800 institutions—99% of colleges and universities had an LMS in place and that the systems were being used by 85% of faculty and 83% of students (The current ecosystem of learning management systems in higher education: Student, faculty, and IT perspectives, Louisville, CO, 2014).

Although it is critical for those who teach fully or partially online courses to become competent in the use of their institution's LMS, it is also critical that those called upon to lead e-learning to have a basic knowledge of these systems and the issues surrounding them. This chapter is designed to introduce leaders to relevant LMS information and issues.

Keywords Learning Management Systems • Course Management Systems • Virtual Learning Environments • Distance education • Administration

Decision Making Guidance

This chapter will help you make decisions about:

- Selecting a learning management system
- Determining the organizational structure for a learning management system
- Formulating policies related to learning management systems

A.A. Piña (✉)
Sullivan University, 2100 Gardiner Lane, Suite #301, Louisville, KY 40205, USA
e-mail: apina@sullivan.edu

© Association for Educational Communications and Technology 2018   101
A.A. Piña et al. (eds.), *Leading and Managing e-Learning*, Educational Communications and Technology: Issues and Innovations,
https://doi.org/10.1007/978-3-319-61780-0_8

What You Need to Know

Definitions

It is usually helpful to establish some definitions to assure that there is a common understanding when certain terms are used. The following terms are used throughout this chapter:

- **Hybrid Course**: Also known as *Blended Course*. A course which contains a combination of in-class and online class sessions. The percentage of in-class versus online sessions can vary among or within institutions.
- **Learning Management System (LMS)**: Also known as a *Virtual Learning Environment, Personal Learning Environment,* or *Course Management System.* A software system that interfaces with one or more databases and provides a secure environment to facilitate delivery, interaction, assessment, and management of online, hybrid, and web-enhanced instruction via the Internet.
- **Online Course**: A course in which all or nearly all of the instruction is delivered online, most commonly by means of an LMS.
- **Web-Enhanced Course**: A course in which all class sessions are held in-class (i.e., face to face/classrooms), but which utilizes the LMS for required outside-of-class work.

Higher Education LMS Market Share

Which learning management systems are most widely used in higher education? At the time of this chapter's publication (2017), Wikipedia's LMS list included 60 different platforms. (https://en.wikipedia.org/wiki/List_of_learning_management_systems). However, Fig. 1 provides a much less diverse view of the LMS higher education market. In 2016, only six systems accounted for over 90% of LMS adoption by colleges and universities. These include (in order of market share) Blackboard, Moodle, Canvas (Instructure), Brightspace (Desire2Learn), Sakai, and LearningStudio (Pearson). LearningStudio—formerly eCollege—which has hovered between 2 and 5% of the market since being purchased by Pearson in 2007, is scheduled to be discontinued as a product by 2018 (Nagel, 2007; Straumsheim, 2016).

LMS Features

Walker, Lindner, Murphrey, and Dooley (2016) classified the basic features of an LMS as Interface, Gradebook, Assessment Tools, Course Materials (content collection management), Communication Tools, and Administration. Many systems also include products that extend the basic capabilities of the LMS.

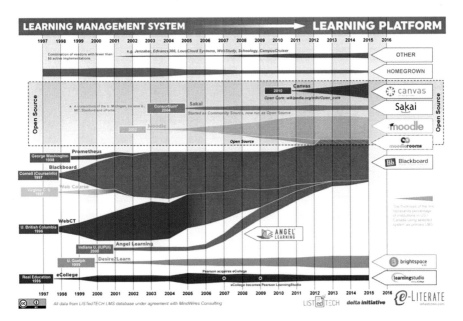

Fig. 1 LMS Market Share for US and Canadian Higher Ed Institutions—Spring 2016. Attribution: LMS_MarketShare_20160316 licensed under Creative Commons by Phil Hill

Interface refers to the ease of use of the LMS, rather than to a specific tool or function of the system (Walker et al., 2016). Interface features include intuitiveness of navigating courses, placement of course menus (e.g., on the left or right margins, embedded within course modules), where and how course settings can be modified or customized and whether instructors can view courses as students. The way a course is designed can also facilitate or hinder the user experience.

Gradebook is often the most widely used component by both instructors and students. For instructors, the gradebook provides a spreadsheet-like tool to record student grades and progress and to provide feedback for student assignments. The gradebook also displays grades and feedback for student view. A full-featured LMS will include the capability to display submitted student papers inside the gradebook (without having to download the paper onto the instructor's computer) and will include annotation tools allowing the instructor to highlight text, strike out text, draw, add marginal comments, or type text directly into students' papers. Many gradebooks include the ability for instructors to create and utilize rubrics for grading and for students to view rubrics. While instructor feedback to students within the gradebook has been primarily through typed text, the increased storage capacity of a cloud-based LMS is providing instructors with the ability to offer audio- or video-based feedback.

Assessment Tools provide instructors with a number of ways to test, survey, and track student achievement and activity in the course. Common tools include a test/assessment manager for creating and deploying exams, a generator for creating different types of questions (multiple choice, true/false, essay, short answer, matching, etc.) and question pools or test banks to store questions that can be used for multiple exams. Questions in an exam (and choices in a multiple-choice question) can be randomized and can be displayed one-at-a-time or all at once. Instructors can give a time limit for exams and can specify the type and amount of feedback that students receive for correct and incorrect answers. Exams can be graded, ungraded, or delivered as anonymous surveys with aggregated results (Piña, 2013, p. 3).

Course Materials (content collection management) allow instructors to generate course content within an embedded text/HTML editor or to upload documents, spreadsheets, presentations, images, animations, audio, or video into the LMS. Hyperlinks can point to websites or documents residing outside LMS. Assignments or drop boxes provide a place for students to submit assigned materials to their instructors for grading and feedback. Instructors can organize content into folders and subfolders and can use the content release feature to display or hide folders and individual content items, thereby giving the instructor control over when content is viewable by students (Piña, 2013, p. 2).

Communication Tools allow instructors to incorporate student–instructor and student–student interaction into the course. Asynchronous (non-real-time) tools include course announcements, student web pages, e-mail to instructors and class members, threaded discussion boards, wikis, blogs, and file sharing (Piña, 2013, p. 3). Synchronous (real-time) tools found in an LMS can range from text chat and a sharable whiteboard to full-featured videoconferencing, including multiple video streams, polling, and sharing of presenters' desktops, applications and files to all participants.

Administrative Tools for instructors include control panels with the ability to manage the settings for the content creation, communication and assessment tools, customize the look of the course, make tools, content and resources available or unavailable to users, manage files and move or copy content. Administrative tools for LMS system administrators allow them to manage the creation of user accounts and courses, enrollment of instructors and students into courses, enabling and disabling of accounts and courses, and tracking activity in the system (Piña, 2013, p. 3).

Extensions to LMS

e-Portfolios enable students to compile and share representative samples of their work in a format that may resemble a course, but that can be made available to instructors or to the public. An e-portfolio may be thought of as similar to a digital resume or curriculum vita, except with actual examples of one's work. The e-portfolio allows students to archive the assignments and projects created in their courses (often referred to as "artifacts") for use in later courses, for meeting graduation requirements, or for perusal by potential employers (Piña, 2013, p. 3).

Learning object repositories are digital storage facilities within the LMS that allows content to be stored outside of individual courses. They are analogous to a personal network drive or USB flash drive. A personal learning object repository permits an instructor to save content apart from a particular course and then import the content into one or more other courses. Many learning object repositories also allow instructors the option to link to items inside the repository, rather than having to copy the item each time into their courses. The advantage to this is that if the instructor wishes to edit or modify the item residing in the repository, the linked items within the courses will also be changed (Piña, 2013, p. 3).

Web meeting/conferencing tools are increasing becoming integrated or bundled with LMSs to expand the (primarily) asynchronous nature of LMSs with more robust synchronous capabilities. These include integrations of BigBlueButton into Canvas, YouSeeU into Brightspace, and Collaborate into Blackboard. These tools allow instructors to conduct virtual office hours, meetings with individual or groups of students, host guest lecturers, or to record sessions for later viewing by students.

Analytics and outcomes assessment systems work in tandem with the LMS and other campus systems to pull learning outcomes data across all courses and track student outcomes and improvement according to institutional objectives and standards. Some vendors, such as Blackboard, have separate systems for student learning outcomes and for institutional analytics. These systems address increasing calls for accountability and measurable outcomes by state and federal regulatory agencies and by accrediting bodies (Piña, 2013, p. 4).

Self- or Vendor-Hosted

One of the early decisions to be made by institutional leadership is regarding the physical location, maintenance, and configuration of the LMS hardware and software. An LMS can be hosted and maintained on the institution's own servers or the choice can be made to contract with an outside vendor to provide hosting and maintenance through an application service provider (ASP) agreement. Self-hosting allows institutions to retain a greater level of control over the operation, storage size, timeline, upgrades, and maintenance of the system and will usually result in significantly lower fees paid to the vendor. This option is most desirable for organizations with sufficient in-house application, database administration, SQL or other database language programming and server expertise and staff and where the IT culture of the institution places a high priority on supporting instructional technologies. However, when trouble occurs or it is time to upgrade the LMS version, self-hosted institutions often find themselves paying premium fees to the vendor for upgrading help and technical assistance (Piña, 2013, p. 8).

An ASP-hosted arrangement may be a more feasible solution for many organizations, since the annual fee paid to the vendor is usually far less than the cost of periodic servicing of hardware and hiring of full-time technical personnel to manage and maintain the LMS servers, program the database, run reports, etc.. Other reasons to consider ASP hosting is that the LMS would not have to compete with other campus entities for limited technology resources, personnel, support, and bandwidth. Most ASP vendors provide 24/7 technical support—something that educational organizations typically cannot afford to do. A disadvantage of not hosting the LMS in-house is the lack of control of the "back end" of the system, since most vendor-hosted clients do not have "root level" administrative rights to the LMS server. ASP hosting and support can be provided by an LMS vendor or by an outside technology support company (Piña, 2013, p. 8).

Commercial or Open Source

In an open source environment, the source code of the product is made available to the user without charge. Software licensing fees, which can be substantial, are eliminated. Open source software may free the user from a contractual agreement with a specific vendor. A program or system based on open source software may be customized and branded according to a user or institution's needs and desires—rather than to a vendor's current priorities. In the case of learning management systems, there exists a vibrant and active community of developers for Moodle and Sakai, the two most popular systems, and for several other open source LMSs (Piña, 2013, p. 8).

While it is true that the source code of an open source LMS is free, the implementation of an open source LMS may involve a substantial investment in infrastructure. This would include server hardware and software, server administration, database administration, programming, and technical support that would otherwise be supplied by the vendor of a commercial system. In order to leverage the advantages of being able to customize the LMS (a primary "selling" point for open source software), an institution running Moodle would require in-house expertise in MySQL and PHP programming, while Sakai would require Java programmers (Piña, 2013, p. 9).

Operating a customized and institution-specific LMS has its own potential pitfalls. The "closed" nature of commercial learning management systems limits internal modifications and provides a cadre of users whose systems operate more or less the same. An open source LMS that has been heavily customized by local programmers and developers (for whom the LMS may be one of many competing duties) might be quite unlike those at other institutions and users may find themselves alone if a customization goes awry. Open source code carries no guarantee or warranty. Many of the above issues could be mitigated by contracting with an emerging cottage industry of third-party open source support vendors. These provide hosting, custom programming, and support services for open source learning management systems. This type of arrangement mirrors the ASP relationships that institutions have with commercial LMS vendors and include many of the same advantages. However, it is also true that an ASP relationship means that the institution may have merely switch one commercial company for another and could be locked into using that company's version of the open source LMS (Piña, 2013, p. 9).

LMS Integration

Three important administrative functions of an LMS are the creation and management of user accounts; the creation and management of course shells; and the enrollment of students and instructors into their courses. These functions can be performed using a standalone or integrated LMS strategy. In a standalone setup, the LMS does not have a direct interface with other campus administrative or academic systems (Piña, 2013). In a standalone system, the creation and enrollment functions are either done manually (i.e., creating each course individually and enrolling each instructor and student) or by extracting batch text files from the institution's student information system (SIS) or enterprise resource planning system (ERP), editing the files into a format compatible with the .LMS and uploading the files into the system (Piña, 2013).

A much more efficient approach is to integrate the LMS with the institution's SIS or ERP. In an integrated system, the files for user accounts, course creation, student enrollment, and instructor assignment are fed directly from the SIS or ERP system into the LMS. Integrating the LMS with campus administrative systems eliminates time-consuming data entry or manual uploading of multiple text files. Another advantage is that instructors do not have to manually enroll or drop students into their online courses. Students who drop or who have an academic hold placed on their accounts are made invisible to the instructor (i.e., they disappear from the class roster). When the hold is lifted, the students' accounts are automatically enabled—without having lost their previous assignments or grades. The main disadvantages of integrated systems are the extra costs involved in programming the systems to work together (Piña, 2013, p. 7).

Server-Based or Cloud-Based

Historically, an LMS was provided to the client on a dedicated server with a relatively limited amount of storage space—particularly for vendor-hosted installations. It was not uncommon for an institution's LMS to be allotted as little as 20 GB in total storage, precluding the inclusion of audio, video, or animation in courses, unless the files were streamed from an external server. The advent of cloud computing as allowed LMS vendors to provide multiple terabytes of space to their clients for very little cost (Piña, 2013, p. 8). Software-as-a-Service (SAAS) allows vendors to run a single version of an LMS for multiple users and perform updates to the product to all users at the same time. Some vendors are now offering their LMS only as a cloud-based SAAS solution, while others offer a choice between SAAS and dedicated server versions. The advantages of a cloud-based solution include potentially lower cost and greater memory and space for multimedia content. A disadvantage is that a SAAS solution usually eliminates the option to self-host the LMS.

The LMS Is a Technology for Learning

Perhaps the most important thing that leaders need to know about their LMS is the difference between an LMS and other institutional technologies, such as payroll, accounting, and student information systems (SIS). The fundamental difference lies in the concepts of **information technology**, which emphasizes the management and use of hardware and software system for the storage, retrieval, and communication of information, and **instructional technology**, which focuses upon how people learn and the methods, processes, and tools to facilitate learning. The training, expertise, and priorities of information technology and instructional technology professionals tend to differ markedly from one another.

Leaders who view their learning management system primarily as an information technology, akin to the SIS, will often house the LMS within the institution's information technology department, reporting to the "business side" of the institution. This is particularly common when the institution administers the LMS servers "in house." Since the LMS is, essentially, a database with an interactive front-end interface, information technology professionals trained in database administration, SQL programming, and reporting tools can customize the system to the institution's needs and engage in sophisticated reporting.

The leader who considers the LMS to be, first and foremost, an educational or instructional technology will often place the development and administration of the LMS in a unit reporting to the institution's "academic side." This is a common occurrence when the LMS is hosted in an ASP (managed) hosting agreement with the LMS company or another third party solution provider who specializes in learning management systems. In this view, the LMS is not merely another system of data entry and retrieval, but is a dynamic and changing environment where instruction, communication, assessment, and interaction (student–instructor, student–student and student–content) occur in ways very distinct from the systems and technologies in which information technology professionals are trained.

What You Can Do

Having provided a primer on what you should know about learning management systems, we'll switch from third-person to second-person and discuss some recommendations will assist you in the selection and deployment of your institution's LMS. The critical nature of the LMS to e-learning makes this an important area of attention for those who oversee online, blended/hybrid, or web-enhanced learning.

Centralizing LMS Operations and Functions

While large research-based universities may have a "silo" culture in which individual colleges, schools, or departments wish to run their own separate online/distance learning programs. Thus may include the desire to run multiple learning management systems within a single institution. This often results in greater institutional costs and inefficiencies, due to multiple LMS vendor contracts, technical inconsistencies between platforms, differing integrations with student information systems, multiple licenses and differing technologies for SIS and third party systems, redundant personnel or inconsistent staffing and lack of consistency in course development, course quality, training and support. Whenever possible, centralizing institutional LMS functions is preferred.

Determining Where the LMS Resides

As more learning management systems move to cloud-based hosting and management, the number of in-house hosted systems will most likely decrease. Analytical tools within the LMS are becoming more sophisticated and easier to use—thus negating the need for information technology professionals specializing in SQL queries, Crystal Reports, and other such tools. If your institution is using an open source LMS with heavy local customization and your institution has a robust I.T. department with the staffing to maintain professionals specializing in instructional technology—and who are not distracted with other systems—there may be a good argument to maintain an information technology-centric view towards the LMS.

However, if your intention is to grow or scale your institution's e-learning programs or offer fully online degrees or large number of online programs, you should seriously consider housing the LMS in a unit reporting to the academic side of the house. This is particularly true if the server hardware is hosted and maintained by the vendor (e.g., cloud/SAAS-based), who can offer 24/7/365 server maintenance and user support (something that most college and university I.T. department do not have the staff to do). This will bring the LMS closer to the institution's teaching and learning facilitates course development, training, and support of students and faculty. It also assures that the LMS will not have to compete with other systems for the attention, priority and limited personnel and resources of the I.T. department.

Selecting and Adopting an LMS

It is likely that—at some point—you will be involved in the selection and adoption of a new LMS. During the past decade, LMS technology had advanced and the market has become volatile, resulting in discontinuance of a number of popular systems, including WebCT, ANGEL, and Learning Studio (eCollege). There are many examples in the literature of case studies of institutions that have gone through the LMS selection and adoption process and the guidelines and lessons learned from the process (e.g., Benson & Whitworth, 2014; Kats, 2013). An entire chapter can be dedicated to this one topic, so the following ideas can be used as a starting place:

- *Just because your colleagues choose a certain LMS does not necessarily mean that it is the best one for you.* A college that offers only blended/hybrid courses or a limited number of online courses for its geographically resident students may require a different LMS than one that offers a large number of fully online programs to a national or global population. You should conduct an institutional needs analysis to determine where the LMS fits into your institution's current and future online, hybrid, web-enhanced present and future.
- *On the other hand, seeking outside expertise and experience can be beneficial.* Current users of the LMS platforms that you are considering can be a source of "behind-the-scenes" data that you will not receive from the LMS vendors themselves. Take advantage of your professional network and those of your faculty and I.T. staff.
- *Consider the LMS features listed above* (interface, grade book, assessment tools, course materials tools, communication tools, and administration tools) as areas for comparison between different LMS platforms.
- *Include relevant constituencies.* It seems intuitive to seek faculty and student input when selecting an LMS, as these individuals are most affected by the systems. However many other individuals and groups are also influenced by an LMS, including instructional designers, librarians, network security and database administrators, registrars and student and faculty support personnel. These should be consulted during the institutional needs analysis and during the LMS evaluation process.
- *Assess your infrastructure and capacity.* Your institutional needs analysis should include an assessment of your institution's network infrastructure, including sufficient bandwidth, user-friendly on-campus and off-campus access, ability to integrate the SIS with the LMS and adequate staffing or external partnerships to be able to provide 24/7/365 support for faculty and students.
- *Conducting field tests.* While demonstrations from LMS vendors can be very useful, so can arranging for "sandbox" courses and a "test instance" of the LMS, to allow you and your staff to try before you buy. Be sure to include the uploading and conversion of a number of existing courses, as the results and ease of conversion are not the same for all systems.
- *Provide resources for migration.* Despite claims from most vendors regarding the ease of adopting their systems, moving from one LMS to another can be a difficult, complex, and time-consuming process. Oftentimes features and capabilities of the prior LMS will not migrate well into the new LMS, causing modifications to be made in some or all courses. Tests, rubrics, and other assessment

tool, in particular, may need to be reset or rebuilt. You should assign a project manager and steering committee to oversee the LMS conversion and make sure that all aspect of the conversion (course triage and clean-up, SIS and other technical interfaces, user and administrator training, job aids, etc.).

Formulating Policies

Institutional policies can either facilitate or impede the effective usage and operation of an LMS. Therefore, one of the most important tasks that you can perform is the formulation of sound policies and procedures. Below are items and issues commonly addressed in LMS policy. The actual wording of the policy will depend largely on your institution's needs and culture. As a general rule, it is easier to start with more restrictive policies and then relax them at a later date than it is to have relaxed policies that need to be made more restrictive.

- Who has administrative access to the LMS
- Access and system rights of administrators, faculty, support staff, and students
- How LMS user accounts are created and who can create them
- Which information about users will and will not be placed in the LMS
- Integration of the LMS with the SIS
- How courses are created in the LMS and who can create them
- Whether content from sections of the same course (e.g., ENG 101) is pulled from a common master course or whether sections of the same course are allowed to differ from each other
- How much freedom do faculty have to edit or modify courses that they teach in the LMS
- How course content is copied from term to term
- How long courses remain in the LMS
- How students are enrolled into courses and who can enroll them
- How long student information remains in the LMS

Empowering Your People

Finally, the most important resources that you have for your LMS are the people that administer, support, and teach in it. The technology evolves continuously and there is every increasing features and best practices. By supporting training and development activities to allow your team to become expert in the LMS and develop related skills in instruction, support, and administration, your students, faculty, and institution will benefit greatly.

Conclusion

Online learning continues to be the most steadily growing area of higher education (Allen, Seaman, Poulin, & Straut, 2016; Campus Computing, 2002; Dahlstrom, Brooks & Bichsel, 2015). The e-learning leader plays a critical role in the successful selection, adoption, implementation, and continued operation of the institution's learning management system.

For More Information

Benson, A. D. & Whitworth, A. (2014). *Research on course management systems in higher education.* Charlotte, NC: Information Age Publishing.

Kats, Y. (2013). *Learning management systems and instructional design: Best practices in online education.* Hershey, PA: Information Science Reference.

LMS companies and products

Blackboard	eFront	Moodle
www.blackboard.com	www.efrontlearning.net	www.moodle.org
BrainHoney	Edvance 360	Moodlerooms
www.brainhoney.com	www.edvance360.com	www.moodlerooms.com
Claroline	Element K	OLAT
www.claroline.net	www.elementk.com	www.olat.org/
ClassRunner	Haiku	Rsmart
www.classrunner.com	www.haikulearning.com	www.rsmart.com
CourseMill	HotChalk	Saba Software
www.trivantis.com	www.hotchalk.com	www.saba.com
Desire2Learn	ILIAS	Sakai Foundation
www.desire2learn.com	www.ilias.de	www.sakaiproject.org
DialogEDU	Instructure (Canvas)	SAP Enterprise Learning
http://dialogedu.com/	www.instructure.com	http://www.sap.com
Docebo	ItsLearning	Schoology
www.docebo.com/doceboCms/	www.itslearning.net	www.schoolology.com
Dokeos e-learning	JoomlaLMS	Sclipo
www.dokeos.com	www.joomlalms.com	www.sclipo.com
Edmodo	Kewton	SkillSoft
www.edmodo.com	www.knewton.com	www.skillsoft.com
EDU 2.0	LoudCloud,	SumTotal Systems
www.edu20.org	www.loudcloudsystems.com	www.sumtotalsystems.com

References

Allen, I. E., Seaman, J., Poulin, R., & Straut, T. T. (2016). *Online report card: Tracking online education in the United States.* Babson Park, MA: Babson Survey Research Group and Quahog Research Group.

Campus Computing. (2002). *The 2002 campus computing report.* Encino, CA: The Campus Computing Project.

Dahlstrom, E., Brooks, D. C., & Bichsel, J. (2015). *The current ecosystem of learning management systems in higher education: Student, faculty, and IT perspectives.* Louisville, CO: EDUCAUSE Center for Analysis and Research.

Nagel, D. (2007). Pearson to acquire eCollege. *Campus Technology May 14, 2007.* Retrieved from https://campustechnology.com/articles/2007/05/pearson-to-acquire-ecollege.aspx.

Piña, A. A. (2013). Learning management systems: A look at the big picture. In Y. Kats (Ed.), *Learning management systems and instructional design: Metrics, standards and applications* (pp. 1–19). Hershey, PA: Information Science Research.

Straumsheim, C. (2016). Pearson narrows focus. *Inside Higher Ed. February 3, 2016.* Retrieved from https://www.insidehighered.com/news/2016/02/03/pearson-leave-learning-management-system-market-2018.

Walker, D. S., Lindner, J. R., Murphrey, T. P., & Dooley, K. (2016). Learning management system usage: Perspectives from university instructors. *Quarterly Review of Distance Education, 17*(2), 41–50.

Diffusing Change: Implementing a University-Wide Learning Management System Transition at a Public University

Christi Boggs and Meg Van Baalen-Wood

Abstract In July 2012, the University of Wyoming's (UW) Office of Academic Affairs appointed a Learning Management System (LMS) review committee to lead an open, university-wide review of LMS products and services. The transition would not only effect a substantial change in technology, it would lead to a wholesale cultural shift. Two years after the committee's inception, the university had completed a full-scale transition to a single learning management system.

In this chapter, we discuss how UW designed and enacted a university-wide change in essential technology from selection to implementation. In contrast to the widespread technical and social anxiety we anticipated, the LMS transition was virtually painless; in fact, it significantly increased buy-in and satisfaction among students, faculty, and administrators. Moreover, the transition catalyzed interest and participation in faculty development programs for face-to-face, distance, and adjunct instructors. It also launched many new initiatives, both related and unrelated to the LMS. The LMS committee continues to oversee daily operations of the LMS as well as several spin-off projects using the new platform.

Keywords LMS • Learning Management System • Instructional design • Instructional technology • Faculty training • Faculty support • Technology adoption • LMS transition • LMS migration

Decision-Making Guidance

This chapter will help e-Learning leaders make decisions about how to design and implement an effective LMS transition with minimal disruption to administrators, users, and support personnel. We will be focusing on managing the cultural, affective shift required to facilitate institution-wide adoption of a new technology, rather

C. Boggs (✉) • M. Van Baalen-Wood
University of Wyoming, 1000 E. University Ave., Laramie, WY 82071, USA
e-mail: CBoggs@uwyo.edu; MegW@uwyo.edu

© Association for Educational Communications and Technology 2018
A.A. Piña et al. (eds.), *Leading and Managing e-Learning*, Educational Communications and Technology: Issues and Innovations, https://doi.org/10.1007/978-3-319-61780-0_9

than only addressing technical selection, implementation, and deployment of the LMS. After reading the chapter, e-Learning leaders will be able to

- Design a strategy to select the best LMS for an institution/organization
- Assemble effective transition, implementation, and support teams
- Create a process that values stakeholder input
- Implement a seamless LMS transition

Our aim is **not** to provide a *blueprint*—we believe there are too many variables to do so when working in the human/affective domain. Prior to each section, however, we provide suggestions for successfully implementing an institution-wide, technology transition. This process is equally applicable to other similar large-scale technology initiatives.

What You Need to Know

In July 2012, the University of Wyoming's (UW) Office of Academic Affairs appointed a Learning Management System (LMS) review committee to lead an open, university-wide review of LMS products and services. Two years after the committee's inception, the university had completed a full-scale transition to a single learning management system.

In contrast to the widespread technical and social anxiety we anticipated, the LMS transition was nearly painless; in fact, it significantly increased buy-in and satisfaction among students, faculty, and administrators. Moreover, the transition catalyzed interest and participation in faculty development programs for face-to-face, distance, and adjunct instructors. It also launched many new initiatives, both related and unrelated to the LMS.

The Landscape: Situating the Transition

Strategies for success:

- Analyze your institutional culture and the broader regional, national, or international context in which you operate
- Identify key stakeholders in the transition
- Determine your support/training infrastructure capacity
- Evaluate how these elements will impact your technology implementation process

The University of Wyoming (UW) is a public, land-grant university with an enrollment of roughly 13,000 graduate and undergraduate students combined ("Points of Pride", n.d.). As the only public, 4-year university in Wyoming, UW values the autonomy and the expertise of instructors teaching face-to-face classes as well as online.

Building upon this premise, the university's instructional support model is based on the belief that faculty should control both their course content and course shells. Instructional designers train, consult, and support instructors in designing course shells that will realize their specific pedagogical objectives. This philosophy under-girds instructional designers' approach to support and training: we neither coerce faculty to participate in training nor require them to use the LMS. Individual departments and colleges oversee course quality, and faculty participation in professional development or support programs is completely voluntary. Nevertheless, as many faculty work to improve teaching and learning, they actively seek out professional development opportunities.

Like any technology transition, UW's transition took place within both our unique institutional context and the broad landscape. Specifically, according to a 2014 Educause Center for Analysis and Research study (Dahlstrom, Brooks, & Bichsel, 2014), in 2013 99% of the 800 participating higher education institutions had an LMS in place. While most LMSs had been in place for only 8 years, roughly 15% of institutions were planning to replace them within the next 3 years. Like UW's, the "main motivations for updating these systems [were] to upgrade functions (71%), replace legacy systems (44%), and reduce costs (18%)" (p. 6).

When LMS transitions are not managed carefully, they can disrupt teaching and learning as well as systems administration, resulting in widespread frustration. Faculty legitimately worry they will spend valuable hours migrating materials and learning new systems, often without any additional compensation (Smart & Meyer, 2005; Ryan, Toye, Charron, & Park, 2012). Moreover, while these transitions are often "framed by technology system requirements" (Hannon, Hirst, & Riddle, 2011, p. 558), by themselves, technical knowledge and expertise do not ensure effective LMS transitions. Indeed, as Straub (2009) argues, "technology adoption is innately social, influenced by peers, change agents, organizational pressure, and societal norms" (Section Discussion, para. 2).

What You Can Do

Armed with the above information, the UW review committee recognized that in order to effect a successful LMS transition, we would need to create a collaborative team, foster stakeholder buy-in, and provide robust and on-going guidance and support for faculty, staff, and students. Two overarching guidelines framed the transition and implementation process: (1) Invite multiple groups across campus into the conversation. These groups represented three broad areas: administration, support, and training; users (i.e., faculty, staff, and students); and upper administration. The first group, administration, support, and training, included Outreach Credit Programs (OCP), the Ellbogen Center for Teaching and Learning (ECTL), and the Division of Information Technology (IT). LMS users also needed to have a strong voice in the selection process. Finally, to ensure financial and university support, it was essential to involve upper administration in the process. (2) Communicate extensively with all stakeholders throughout the transition and implementation process.

In this section, we discuss how the above framework informed the transition process from selection through implementation, training, and support. The crux of our goal was to adopt an LMS that would meet the needs of both distance and face-to-face faculty. To accomplish this, at each phase we convened multiple subcommittees to include stakeholders throughout the campus community. In order to assure coherence, a four-member, interdepartmental committee oversaw each subcommittee.

Below, we briefly identify the collaborative team that drove the process. Next, we provide an overview of each phase of the transition: LMS selection, transition and implementation, training, and support.

Getting Started: The Collaborative Team(s)

Strategies for success:

- Establish a small (4–6 person) leadership team comprised of representatives from each of the key stakeholder units
- Identify institutional change agents, including both expert and non-expert, technical, and academic representatives
- Leveraging the above personnel, create a suite of cross-institutional, collaborative committees focusing on discrete aspects of the technology/transition

In contrast to previous LMS searches, the review committee was intentionally designed to include personnel from key units *across* campus. The interdisciplinary committee comprised four members: the authors, Christi Boggs, an instructional designer from OCP and Meg Van Baalen-Wood, an instructional designer from the ECTL; the LMS administrator from OCP; and the director of application and database services for IT. Van Baalen-Wood and Boggs also taught (and continue to teach) both face-to-face and online.

Like the review committee, every subcommittee was intentionally designed to reflect the breadth of stakeholders. Instructional subcommittees included online and face-to-face faculty from diverse disciplines. Technical subcommittees included administrators and technical personnel from all strata of the university. Students contributed their voices through meetings with ASUW, our student governing body, as well as participation in the vendor demonstrations (discussed below).

LMS Selection

Strategies for success:

- Conduct a thorough needs analysis that leverages the experiences of comparable institutions and solicits input from all stakeholders

- Locate example requests for proposals and evaluation matrixes; adapt examples to meet your specific needs and context
- Host public, on-site vendor demonstrations and meetings
- Provide multiple avenues for feedback
- Accept the rule of 80/20: You won't be able to please everyone; aim for meeting the needs of 80% of your user base

The selection process spanned several phases: First, the review committee completed a needs analysis to determine the needs of all stakeholders. Building on the work of a precursor committee that focused on LMS needs for face-to-face courses, the review committee began by conducting extensive Internet research and reviewing several similar institutions' requests for LMS proposals. In addition, the committee met with instructional designers and administrators from other colleges and universities that had recently migrated to new a LMS.

Next, the committee convened three subcommittees. A survey committee, comprised of faculty from diverse departments, Boggs, and Van Baalen-Wood, created an online survey informed by the information gleaned through the above research. While the survey committee developed and administered this survey, the IT director, technical personnel, and a group of administrators evaluated LMS maintenance, support, and integration with the University's existing human resources and student information systems. Although the committee sought primarily a course delivery and management tool, this group also considered potential secondary applications of the LMS. We discuss some of these applications in the conclusion.

Needs analyses completed, the review committee developed a request for proposals (RFP) and again convened proposal review subcommittees representing the stakeholder groups defined above. After identifying the proposals that best met the RFP criteria, we hosted open vendor presentations. Each vendor led three distinct presentations, one for each of the above audiences. Finally, the review committee reconvened the faculty, administrator, and technical groups to make a final selection.

Several key aspects of the LMS selection process were crucial to the transition's relative seamlessness and ultimate success. Below, we discuss the online faculty survey, the RFP evaluation process, and the vendor presentations:

- Faculty survey: The faculty survey's express objective was to obtain information about faculty's LMS usage, needs, and expectations. At the time, however, we did not appreciate the role the survey would play in gaining faculty buy-in. Indeed, in retrospect we believe the survey, developed by and for faculty, marked the first step in an implementation process intentionally crafted to maximize faculty involvement. In an effort to get as much faculty input as possible, as well as to make sure faculty felt included, the committee advertised the survey heavily through email and campus mailings. To our surprise, although at the time only 25% of the courses at UW used the LMS, roughly 26% of the faculty responded to the survey.
- RFP evaluation: In keeping with the structure we used for the needs analysis phase, the committee again enlisted three groups of evaluators: instructional,

technical, and administrative. The University Disability Support Services office also evaluated the proposals for evidence of each system's ADA compliance.

- Vendor presentations: The vendor demonstrations were pivotal to gaining stakeholder buy-in. Each vendor presented to three different audiences: faculty/staff, students, and technical/administrators. The committee marketed the demonstrations extensively, through email, campus mailings, posters, and, of course, word of mouth and solicited feedback via a brief survey at the conclusion of each demonstration. The faculty and technical demonstrations were well attended, and while few students attended, the students who did attend provided thoughtful feedback.

Transition and Implementation

Strategies for success:

- Provide multiple informational/introductory sessions situated across campus and online
- Recruit early adopters and mentors to pilot the system and beta-test best practices; these early adopters will become your champions, mentors, and change leaders
- Develop a two-pronged migration strategy: (1) frame preliminary trainings around content migration, and (2) provide migration services for users who need them

On July 1, 2013, the LMS review committee presented its findings and recommendation to the Office of Academic Affairs. On July 9, Academic Affairs accepted the recommendation and executed a contract. With the LMS search successfully concluded, the review committee was repurposed and renamed the LMS steering committee. On August 1, 2013, transition to the new LMS, branded WyoCourses, began. Figure 1 illustrates the LMS adoption trends throughout the transition from fall 2012 through spring 2016. During the spring 2014 transition, or opt-out semester, WyoCourses housed roughly ½ of the 1051 course shells. (The legacy LMS housed the remaining course shells.) Moreover, while total course offerings remained stable throughout the transition, WyoCourses usage increased from 1366 course shells in fall 2014 (the first semester after full phase out of the legacy LMS) to 1553 in spring 2016. This widespread adoption marked a significant cultural shift at the University of Wyoming.

Three factors were key to the transition's success:

- The pilot project and mentor development
- Extensive and ongoing communication
- Support for migration of course content

Anticipating the upcoming transition, in early summer 2013, Van Baalen-Wood and Boggs recruited a pilot group of volunteers to teach with the new LMS in the

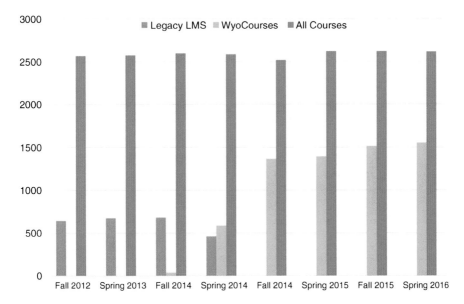

Fig. 1 LMS adoption trends

fall semester. The pilot group comprised 30 well-respected faculty—representing a breadth of disciplines, teaching styles, and class sizes, both online and face-to-face; three graduate teaching assistants; and over 1000 unwitting students! Due to our short adoption timeline, the courageous pilot instructors had about 2 weeks to learn to navigate the platform, create course content, and instruct their students in the use of the platform. The pilot had three chief objectives:

- Learning and sharing the intricacies of the new system: Van Baalen-Wood and Boggs had experimented with the new LMS throughout the selection process. Since the contract was signed just weeks before the fall semester began, however, we had not received any formal training. When the pilot began, no one at UW had any real expertise with the new platform.
- Fostering change leaders: Knowing we would need well-respected leaders to champion an innovation of this size, we deliberately recruited instructors who were highly regarded throughout the campus community to participate in the pilot. This group included both self-avowed technical innovators and senior faculty with multiple teaching awards.
- Training mentors: Recognizing that by themselves, two instructional designers would not be able to effectively train and assist the university's 1000+ faculty and graduate teaching assistants (GTAs), Boggs and Van Baalen-Wood recruited 22 members of the pilot group to serve as mentors in the spring semester of 2014. Drawing from startup funds provided by the Office of Academic Affairs and the Outreach School, the steering committee paid each mentor's department to relieve him or her from teaching one class. In exchange, mentors fulfilled the following responsibilities:

Table 1 Legacy LMS usage

Class type	Spring 2013	Fall 2013	Spring 2014
Fully online	212	207	230
Hybrid courses	75	74	80
Face-to-face courses	387	402	153

- Attending several work sessions the week before the Fall 2013 semester began
- Attending weekly work sessions to learn and share their experiences
- Testing WyoCourses to help develop best practices
- Assisting with LMS trainings and workshops in spring and summer 2014
- Helping colleagues in their home departments and colleges learn WyoCourses
- Championing WyoCourses

Throughout the pilot, the technical team worked to integrate the new LMS with the existing student information system. Through this integration, for the first time in UW history, spring 2014 course shells were automatically created and students automatically enrolled in every course being offered. For this one semester, however, instructors could opt out and continue using the then existing, or legacy, LMS.

Table 1 illustrates legacy system usage for three semesters: the semester prior to the transition (spring 2013), the WyoCourses pilot semester (fall 2013), and the opt-out semester (spring 2014). Notably, while face-to-face usage of the legacy LMS declined dramatically during the opt-out semester, the number of fully online and hybrid courses increased.

As the pilot group vetted WyoCourses, the steering committee launched a university-wide communication campaign. The campaign included two prongs: First, multiple targeted emails and print mailings alerted instructors about the upcoming transition, trainings, and resources for help. Committee members also met with numerous university representatives, committees, and departments to overview the transition and implementation timeline and demonstrate WyoCourses' benefits.

Second, in late spring 2014, the steering committee launched what we affectionately dubbed "the traveling roadshow." We designed the two-tiered roadshow to reach as many stakeholders as possible, from the upper administration to the department level. First the steering committee developed interactive presentations for the university's leadership teams (the Executive Council, the Deans and Directors Council, Faculty Senate, and the student governing body, ASUW). The leadership presentations focused on the following elements of the transition: the rationale for transitioning, the timeline and key events calendar, and information about support and training resources.

Van Baalen-Wood and Boggs led the second tier of support, which focused at the department and program levels. Here, we contacted college deans and department heads and offered to provide a 10-min informational session about the LMS at one of the department/program's already scheduled meetings. At each session, we gave a brief presentation and then invited participants' questions. Although we did not meet with all departments/programs, these sessions effectively disseminated the transition, training, and support plans throughout the colleges.

Third, while the steering committee viewed the transition as an opportunity for instructors to redesign, reimagine, and replan their courses, we recognized the substantial time investment required to migrate course content. Because the legacy LMS did not include any export functionality, content would have to be migrated from the legacy LMS to WyoCourses manually. To address this concern, UW contracted with the WyoCourses vendor to migrate 500 courses from the legacy LMS to WyoCourses. A team of graduate assistants in OCP and ECTL assisted with course content migrations. Although the committee gave online instructors priority access to content migration, we also migrated content for numerous face-to-face instructors who had developed deep, complex course shells. Assisting with content migration did not just minimize potential anxiety; it also encouraged faculty to evaluate the design of their courses. Moreover, the content migration process created a new wave of enthusiastic WyoCourses adopters.

Training

Strategies for success:

- Create multifaceted training programs, including basic and advanced skills, stand-alone sessions and series, and foundational and targeted workshops
- Offer custom workshops and sessions in users' home departments
- Develop a digital training repository

If cross-departmental integration was essential to successful LMS selection and transition, it was equally crucial to training. To assure that all faculty received sufficient and comparable training and support, Boggs and Van Baalen-Wood developed a suite of trainings shared by the ECTL and OCP. The training phase kicked off in November 2013 with 2 days of workshops led by the WyoCourses provider. We advertised these workshops widely to faculty and GA instructors. Following the vendor trainings, Van Baalen-Wood and Boggs developed and delivered several workshops series. We tested a variety of models throughout the process, from biweekly workshops during the opt-out semester to the diverse suite of services that is currently in place. Figure 2 illustrates the evolution of the training model.

Through trial and error, we developed the following four-pronged approach to training. To serve off-campus faculty, we hosted training webinars and posted recordings of live trainings to a website devoted to the new LMS.

- Two hour, hands-on Rapid Course Design workshops guide novice instructors through basic WyoCourses design and configuration. Participants receive hands-on assistance setting up the basic functionality for an existing or upcoming course, including the syllabus, course modules, discussions, announcements,

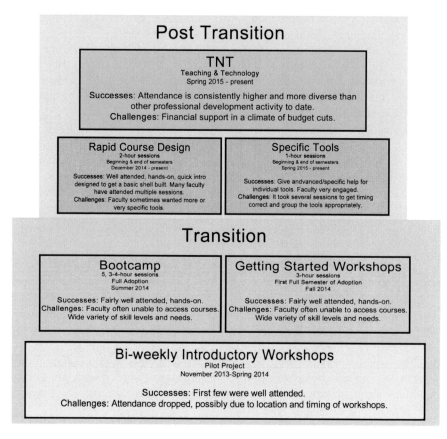

Fig. 2 Evolution of training

assignments, and so forth. We offer 2–3 Rapid Course Design sessions at the
beginning and end of every fall and spring semester.
- Focused on using specific tools and functions to achieve pedagogical goals,
  WyoCourses mini workshops, build on the foundations developed in Rapid
  Course Design workshops. We offer 4–6 mini WyoCourses workshops every fall
  and spring semester.
- In summer 2014, we offered the first WyoCourses boot camp, starting in late May
  (shortly after the spring semester ended) and ending in August. Participants chose to
  attend any or all of the five full-day boot camp sessions. The first two sessions (May
  and June) were identical: On day one, participants designed and created a robust
  WyoCourses shell for an upcoming course. Day one's focus was primarily technical. Day two repeated day one. Privileging pedagogy over technology, days three,
  four, and five delved into the platform's advanced capabilities. Throughout the boot
  camp, we interspersed formal sessions with hands-on "play" time. Building on the
  framework created in summer 2014, the summer 2015 and 2016 boot camps delved
  further into WyoCourses' basic and advanced tools.

As our training model evolved, we learned that careful attention to scheduling and location are crucial to attendance. Most of our classrooms and faculty offices are located on our central campus. The early workshop location, however, required most participants to trek roughly ½ mile across campus. This location dissuaded many instructors from attending the workshops. We now hold workshops in the centrally located main campus library or in the Business building next door. Similarly, we have learned that workshop attendance dwindles significantly 6 weeks after the beginning of each semester and resumes 2–3 weeks before the semester ends. Instead of scheduling formal workshops in the intervening weeks, we direct instructors' questions to bi-weekly instructor drop-in sessions (called TOUCH) or meet with instructors individually. We discuss TOUCH below.

Support

Strategies for success:

- Assemble a multifaceted support team that includes the vendor, IT, and instructional support personnel
- Provide access to robust 24/7 support through a range of media, e.g., Help pages; training videos; online, telephone, and email support
- Offer regularly scheduled drop-in hands-on assistance and support

Even prior to the transition, our fragmented support model had proven dysfunctional. Again, an integrated model for both technical and instructional support was a cornerstone of the steering committee's implementation plan.

Three separate entities comprise the support team: the vendor, UW IT, and the UW instructional support team.

- The first line of technical support, the LMS vendor, provides Tier 1 support to the entire university community, including both online and face-to-face instructors, staff, and students. Vendor support focuses on the LMS platform and tools, browser functionality, and limited computer support as it pertains directly to WyoCourses. The vendor's support structure is extremely robust: Users can access support personnel 24/7 by telephone, email, and/or chat.
- UW's IT department serves as our second line of support. UW IT supports technical issues directly related to university systems, e.g., issues with usernames and passwords, enrollment issues, and integration with existing systems. In addition, IT provides services to enable faculty to add graduate and teaching assistants, supplemental instructors, guest instructors, and other enrollments that are configured outside the standard processes.
- An instructional support team, led by Boggs and Van Baalen-Wood, serves as the third line of support. The instructional support team includes one additional instructional designer from OCP, two instructional technology educational specialists (one each from OCP and ECTL), two graduate assistants, and a distance

education librarian. This team provides the majority of instructional support for both online and face-to-face faculty.

Although the UW technical and instructional support teams are geographically dispersed, it is crucial for them to work closely together. To ensure prompt and seamless support for all constituents, in August 2013, the steering committee created two group email addresses, one for each support team. Respondents copy the group email address to indicate when a question has been answered. This process assures all members of the team are aware of the questions users are asking. Moreover, the process serves as a mechanism for team members to learn from one another as new questions arise and are successfully resolved. When technical team members receive requests for instructional support, they forward them to the instructional team, and vice versa. Any questions that are directed to either technical or instructional support staff's individual emails are forwarded to the person who is best equipped to respond, both promptly and accurately. This support model has alleviated much of the frustration LMS users experienced prior to the introduction of WyoCourses.

Bi-weekly, open drop-in sessions for instructors, called TOUCH, augment the above support structure. Three to five instructional support team members staff every 2-h TOUCH session, with increased staffing around peak periods in the semester. Instructors can attend TOUCH face-to-face, by phone, or via a web conferencing tool. Questions about WyoCourses, instructional technology, course design, and/or any aspect of pedagogy are welcome. No appointment is required. However, many instructors schedule appointments during TOUCH sessions with specific instructional support consultants or about specific questions.

The TOUCH model is both efficient and effective. During the 2015–2016 school year, over 200 faculty and staff attended TOUCH sessions with questions ranging from course design and pedagogy to detailed strategies for using individual instructional tools. TOUCH focuses many of the ad hoc questions the instructional design team would field through email and/or individual consultations into 4 h each week when we are staffed to respond. Feedback from TOUCH attendees is overwhelmingly positive. Ironically, even instructors who do not attend TOUCH regularly (or at all) tell us they value the program's existence.

Conclusion

Two years after the LMS review committee's inception, the university had completed a full-scale transition to a single learning management system that serves all faculty and students. The LMS steering committee continues to oversee integration, training, and support for WyoCourses as well as several spin-off projects. The first spin-off, WyoGroups, leverages WyoCourses for use by non-academic groups. Any

WyoCourses user can request a WyoGroup to use for collaboration, both within and outside UW. A second project, due to launch in fall 2016, will create WyoCourses shells for student advising purposes. Every primary, secondary, and tertiary student advisor will automatically receive a WyoAdvising shell for communicating with his/her advisees. The advising shells will also consolidate often hard to find resources for both advisors and advisees. The third, and perhaps most powerful of these spin-offs is an assessment project. In collaboration with the vendor, the steering committee designed a tool that leverages WyoCourses' native assessment features to conduct systematic, institution-wide assessment of student learning. This tool is scheduled to launch in summer 2016.

The transition also catalyzed faculty, staff, and administrators' interest in pedagogical development and related instructional technologies. In response to this interest, in spring 2014, Van Baalen-Wood and Boggs developed a semi-weekly, Teaching and Technology (TnT) series to showcase instructors' innovative pedagogies. Each fall and spring semester, we accept presentation proposals from 4 to 5 faculty and/or graduate students from diverse disciplines. Focusing on active and engaged learning, presenters lead interactive, 90-min sessions that both discuss and model their pedagogies. The TnT series has sparked enthusiastic interest in professional development and excellence in teaching and learning among a broad range of instructors.

Preliminary student feedback indicates that students want instructors to use WyoCourses and to use it more effectively. In fall 2016, the LMS steering committee will resurrect the traveling road show to provide updates about WyoCourses' usage as well as resources for training and support. This renewed roadshow is an opportunity to celebrate the successful WyoCourses transition, showcase its capabilities, and expand LMS adoption and usage.

For More Information

- Transition Timeline: http://bit.ly/wyotimeline
- Announcement of LMS Review: http://bit.ly/wyolmsannounce
- LMS Review Phases: http://bit.ly/wyophases
- Online Faculty Survey: http://bit.ly/wyofacultysurvey
- Faculty Needs Assessment results: http://bit.ly/wyoneeds
- ADA Requirements Rubric: http://bit.ly/wyoada
- Instructional Requirements Rubric: http://bit.ly/wyoinstruc
- Administrative Requirements: http://bit.ly/wyoadmin
- Learning Management System Product Presentations: http://www.uwyo.edu/lmsreview
- Faculty Pilot Invitation: http://bit.ly/wyopilotinvite

References

Dahlstrom, E., Brooks, D. C., & Bichsel, J. (2014). *The current ecosystem of learning management systems in higher education: Student, faculty, and IT perspectives. (Rep.).* Louisville, CO: ECAR.

Hannon, J., Hirst, D., & Riddle, M. (2011). Implementing e-learning: A migration story. In *Ascilite 2011: Changing demands, changing directions: Wrest Point, Hobart, Tasmania, Australia, 4–7 December 2011: Proceedings* (pp. 557–561).

Points of Pride. (n.d.). In *University of Wyoming.* Retrieved from http://www.uwyo.edu/uw/aboutuw/points-of-pride.html.

Ryan, T. G., Toye, M., Charron, K., & Park, G. (2012). Learning management system migration: An analysis of stakeholder perspectives. *International Review of Research in Open and Distance Learning, 13*(1), 220–237.

Smart, K. A., & Meyer, K. A. (2005). Changing course management systems: Lessons learned. *EDUCAUSE Quarterly, 28*(2), 68–70.

Straub, E. T. (2009). Understanding technology adoption: Theory and future directions for informal learning. *Review of Educational Research, 79*(2), 625–649. Retrieved from http://libproxy.uwyo.edu/login/?url=http://search.proquest.com/docview/214121884?accountid=14793.

Weaving Information Literacy Instruction into the Fabric of Your e-Learning Program

Mary Kickham-Samy and Sandra C. McCarthy

Abstract e-Learning leaders can promote student success and increase retention by enriching the educational experience of their students and their instructors with a robust library presence in their programs in four ways. First, the e-learning leader should encourage teamwork amongst the librarians, the instructional designers, and the subject-matter teaching faculty. Second, the e-learning leader should support the design and development of self-instructional, online library tutorials. Third, the e-learning leader should encourage the enhancement of instruction in information literacy through virtual reference (VR) via sophisticated collaborations that provide 24/7 service or more limited, but less expensive stand-alone, in-house chat services. Fourth, e-learning leaders should support the acquisition of a remotely accessible collection of electronic books and journal databases for students and instructors. For those K-12 students and corporate trainees who do not have authentication privileges to proprietary materials, the e-learning leader should provide guidance via VR services to open access e-books and journal articles that are freely available on the Internet or that are available through state-supported portals funded by state tax dollars. The presence of library instruction and library resources enhances e-learning environments by empowering the learner with the lifelong learning skills and with the knowledge needed to identify an information need, as well as find, evaluate, and use information.

Keywords Information literacy • Virtual reference • Open access • Proprietary databases • Electronic books • Embedded librarian • Embedded tutorials • Screen capturing • Life-long learning

M. Kickham-Samy, PhD, MLIS, MA (✉)
McDonough Geschke Library, Marygrove College, Detroit, MI 48221, USA
e-mail: mkickham@marygrove.edu

S.C. McCarthy, MSLS, MA
Bailey Library, Washtenaw Community College, Ann Arbor, MI 48105, USA
e-mail: mccarthy@wccnet.edu

© Association for Educational Communications and Technology 2018
A.A. Piña et al. (eds.), *Leading and Managing e-Learning*, Educational Communications and Technology: Issues and Innovations,
https://doi.org/10.1007/978-3-319-61780-0_10

Decision-Making Guidance

This chapter will help you make decisions about how to:

1. Include librarians as part of your instructional design team
2. Choose the right content and sequencing for the information literacy component of your e-learning program
3. Promote and support virtual reference collaborations
4. Incorporate freely available resources into your e-learning program

What You Need to Know

When considering what library resources and services to incorporate into an e-learning program, e-learning leaders need to be familiar with the culture of the librarian who will facilitate library support for their programs. Librarians are great collaborators and they have a strong public service ethic. Librarians network not only with colleagues within their own library circles but also with colleagues from other educational institutions, government agencies, nonprofit organizations, and corporations. Therefore, they are great blog readers and creators. They are listserv users and conference goers. They form and join overlapping consortia and cooperatives. Librarians know that in order to fulfill their mission to provide high-quality low or no cost information services to all their patrons, whether in e-learning or traditional face-to-face environments, they must collaborate.

Team Building for Student Retention: Librarians, Instructional Designers, and Subject-Matter Specialists

A library component within an e-learning program can enhance the experience of not only the student, but the instructor as well. The richness of a constructive collaboration between an experienced, well-qualified librarian inspires teaching faculty to create more challenging content for their courses and for their assignments. The influence of a librarian has the subtle effect of bringing critical thinking components to assignments. The guidance of a librarian gives the teaching faculty new ideas with which to develop assignments that are viable and challenging for their students. As for the students, they are also inspired and encouraged by the librarian-faculty collaboration. Students drop out of academic programs for many reasons, but of those that are connected to academic issues, there are two main ones. Students drop out because they are either under or over challenged. Enhancing the critical thinking component of a course with a library research paper, project or presentation can excite a student with the thrill of the pursuit of information and knowledge. When there are librarians or library resources guiding the way, the less academically prepared student feels empowered with the enabling skills needed to find and evaluate information. For these reasons, information literacy instruction positively impacts student retention in e-learning programs.

Information Literacy: A Criterion for Accreditation

It is also important for the e-learning leader to know that colleges and universities are required to offer information literacy instruction or library programs for their students for purposes of accreditation. The Association of College and Research Libraries (ACRL), a division of the American Library Association (ALA), lists six accrediting agencies that either mention information literacy specifically, or access to library resources and instruction, more generally, as a criterion for accreditation. These agencies are the Middle States Association of Colleges and Schools, North Central Association of Colleges and Schools, New England Association of Schools and Colleges, Southern Association of Colleges and Schools Commission on Colleges, and Western Association of Schools and Colleges (2011) (Association of College and Research Libraries, 2011).

Information Literacy: Competency Standards and Their Framework

In 2000, ACRL approved a set of Information Literacy Competency Standards for Higher Education. Concisely stated, these standards define the information literate person as one who knows what information is needed, when to seek it, and how to find it (Association of College and Research Libraries, 2000). The information literate person knows how to evaluate and use information efficiently, effectively, and ethically. In 2015, ACRL introduced a new, more constructivist perspective to the Standards in its formulation of the "Framework for Information Literacy for Higher Education" (Association of College and Research Libraries, 2015). The emergence of the Framework document created a paradigm shift. For librarians, the measure of an information literate person became less a static checklist of learning outcomes and more as a dynamic interactional learning process where the source of authority is questioned, where research is recognized as an iterative process, where the student researcher is not only a consumer of information but a producer as well. The research process does not just reveal existing knowledge but creates new knowledge. This new knowledge can take many different forms and can be displayed in different formats.

Access Entitlement Principle

In 2008, ACRL approved and in 2016 revised a set of standards for distance learning library services, at the core of which is the "access entitlement principle," which states that all students, whether they are studying face-to-face or remotely, whether they are traditional or nontraditional students, whether full-time or part-time, whether in a credit or noncredit program have a right to an equivalent library experience (Association of College and Research Libraries, 2008). Librarians must work to provide all of their patrons with instruction in information literacy skills though the mode of delivery for the e-learning students may necessarily be different from that of the traditional, face-to-face student. One ubiquitous service that librarians use to instruct and guide the e-learning student is virtual reference.

Virtual Reference (VR) Services and Collaborations

VR is a library reference service conducted via digital communications technology that includes chat, videoconferencing, Voice-over-IP, email, instant messaging, and texting or a combination of several options. Librarians maintain these e-reference services through the use of chat software that is a freely available resource on the web. There are also commercially available products that include support services and enhanced features.

To increase the hours of availability of VR and to share cost and human resources, some librarians have formed complex collaborations, within which librarians work together to provide their students with library instruction via synchronous online chat, 24 h a day, 7 days a week. Membership in these collaborations is often fee based through annual subscriptions. QuestionPoint, an OCLC product, provides the most sophisticated VR collaboration available globally. When subscribing to QuestionPoint, a library can be a stand-alone institution with limited hours of operation, part of a regional or affiliation-based collaboration with limited hours of operation, or part of a 24/7/365 global cooperative. Recently, QuestionPooint lost its position as the only entity that provided a 24/7 virtual reference service. Now, LibraryH3lp and RefChatter also provide this service. The 24/7 virtual reference services cost more and require more advanced training, but the benefit is around-the-clock research assistance for your e-learners.

Free Library Resources

When incorporating information literacy into an e-learning program, e-learning leaders need to know what their institution's library has to offer in term of resources and services. Libraries provide free access to high-quality information. Librarians assist students in finding and accessing this information. They also instruct students in how to critically evaluate and properly use information. The e-learning leader needs to know that these services are available for free as enhancements to their e-learning courses and programs. However, not all libraries are equal fiscally, so all libraries provide free resources, but libraries with large budgets provide more of these free resources than those with small budgets.

However, budgetary considerations are not the only factor. The mission of the library also has an impact on the library collection. Library collections support the needs of their primary patrons. Therefore, to support the research needs of their students, academic libraries subscribe to a greater number of expensive proprietary databases than public libraries and K-12 school libraries. Large research universities and small medical libraries have a greater number of scholarly science database subscriptions than community colleges and 4-year college libraries.

Most scholarly databases are proprietary and require authentication for access. Students enrolled in K-12 schools and employees in corporate or industrial settings do not have permissions to view valuable databases available to students enrolled in colleges and universities. Community college and university students access proprietary materials for the duration of their studies but lose this benefit once they graduate or leave their respective institutions. Therefore, an e-learning program should incorporate instruction in how to find open access (OA) materials and/or proprietary information through state-funded, public library channels. In this way, the e-learning program is empowering the learner to engage in life-long learning opportunities.

Electronic Book Collections

Each library has its own policy regarding print vs. electronic book collections. Some libraries still consider print books the foundation of their collection. So, they allocate more funds to print that to electronic books. Other libraries have a more balanced policy. When possible, these libraries order a print and an electronic copy of each item, or alternatively, spend an equal amount of their budget on e-books as they do on print books. An emerging policy is to favor the selection of electronic books over print ones.

The e-book vendors also influence collection development policy. Some vendor contract agreements allow many students to use ("check out") the same e-book at one time. Other agreements allow only three students to use a particular e-book at one time and others only allow one student at a time. e-Book vendors have introduced a "patron-driven" book acquisition system where e-books are added to the library collection as the patron requests them. This system has proven to be popular because it eliminates the situation where a librarian has selected and paid for an e-book that no one ever uses.

However, the expansion in the acquisition of e-books poses a threat to the permanence of a library collection because the library does not truly own e-books it pays for. Depending on the licensing agreement, once the library discontinues its contract with a given e-book vendor, it may lose access to all the e-books that it has selected. Equally disruptive to service is the vendors' restrictions on use through digital rights management (DRM) practices, such as the contractual prohibition of printing, copying, or downloading that is enforced through technological blocking mechanisms.

Librarians are beginning to push back on these restrictive contracts. In November 2015, at a conference at North Carolina University, the Charlotte Initiative was launched which advocates for changes in the way e-book vendors control the access and use of e-books. Proposed at the conference were three guiding principles: "irrevocable perpetual access and archival rights, unlimited simultaneous users, and freedom from any digital rights management" (Ivins, 2015).

What You Can Do

Welcome Librarians as Part of the Instructional Design Team

It is important to remember that librarians are great collaborators. To take advantage of this human resource, we recommend that you include librarians as an integral part of your instructional design teams. Librarians can play the role of design consultant or teacher. They can function as a facilitator in the development of discipline-specific courses or as a subject-matter expert in the field of information literacy.

Introduce Librarians to Your Teaching Faculty as Consultants

As research experts, librarians can help classroom professors or teachers describe their research assignments with greater clarity and precision. Librarians are skillful in finding flaws in the way research assignments are explained to students. Occasionally, faculty assign topics for which the library has few directly related sources. Librarians can alert faculty to this paucity of information on a topic and advise the instructor in ways to guide the student in how to overcome this obstacle. Another common path to unnecessary confusion for the student is the definition of certain words. To illustrate, consider the word "Internet." When professors tell their students they cannot use sources from the Internet, usually the professors actually mean that they want their students to use scholarly materials, not websites, especially not commercial websites. The librarian can help the faculty member avoid these potential landmines in the wording of their research paper assignments with suggestions for more precise, less ambiguous vocabulary.

Introduce Librarians to Your Teaching Faculty as Teachers and Colleagues

As mentioned earlier in this chapter, access to library resources and instruction in information literacy is a criterion for many accrediting agencies. Accreditation agencies value competency in information literacy for college and university students so it is advisable to incorporate this kind of critical thinking instruction into your e-learning programs.

The Embedded Librarian

One tested approach to incorporating information literacy instruction into an e-learning program is to embed a librarian into a subject-specific online course through the course management software (CMS), such as Blackboard or Canvas. With this approach, librarians respond to student questions via e-mail and through participation on the discussion board of the CMS.

Some librarians who have embedded themselves in a faculty member's course report that this approach is time-consuming and unsustainable. The model of one librarian per course is not viable. There are simply too many courses, too many students, and too few librarians. The emergence of MOOCs has put further stress on an already collapsing instructional model. Therefore, a major challenge to incorporating information literacy instruction into an e-learning program is scalability.

The Embedded On-line Tutorials

In response to this reality, librarians are now making prerecorded instructional presentations and embedding these tutorials into the online course within the CMS. Keeping pace with this trend, software companies, such as TechSmith and Panopto, are developing sophisticated, user-friendly, screen capturing software for different instructional purposes and e-learning environments. TechSmith developed Jing and Snagit, screen capturing software products, which are suitable for quick, temporary solutions for single users or small groups. For an instructional problem that needs a more permanent solution, TechSmith developed Camtasia, a software product that allows the editing of recordings. It also has a zoom feature to focus the student's attention on a particular part of the screen, and a feature with which the instructional design team can generate quizzes. For ADA compliance, Camtasia supports open and closed captioning.

The Information Literacy Course

We recommend that the e-learning leaders make available to their students a comprehensive course in information literacy within their e-learning programs so that students who complete their programs are equipped with the research and critical-thinking skills needed to become life-long learners. Curriculum committees are increasingly approving petitions for courses in information literacy for undergraduate college students. These courses are sometimes required and sometimes not, sometimes for credit and sometimes not. Sometimes, they are a semester long and sometimes less. More times than not, these courses are web-based, largely self-instructional and often self-paced.

Choose the Right Content for the Information Literacy Component of Your e-Learning Program

The content of your information literacy component should incorporate the ACRL approved Information Literacy Competency Standards as they are informed by the Framework for Information Literacy of Higher Education, and they should adhere to college and university national accreditation standards. Typically, the content of a course in information literacy instructs students in how to locate print books on the library shelf, and how to access electronic books and journal articles from proprietary databases. More in-depth courses include strategies for evaluating sources and discussions regarding the ethical use of information and intellectual property laws. Required and/or for-credit information literacy courses can take the form of a blended or completely online course with sequential or nonsequential units.

Choose the Right Sequencing of the Course Content

Stand-alone courses in information literacy can consist of instructional modules arranged in a fixed sequence, where the student must complete one module before continuing to the next. These courses can be embedded in the platform of a CMS, such as Blackboard or Canvas. This option allows librarians' access to CMS analytics with which they can monitor such student activity as the number of clicks on material, time spent on task, scores on self-assessment, and other assessment tools.

Alternatively, a stand-alone course in information literacy can consist of modules that have no fixed sequence. The student can choose to complete only those modules that are relevant to the completion of a specific assignment. The platform for these modules can be a webpage on the library website or an open source product, such as Drupal or WordPress.

It is an emerging practice for instructional librarians to embed their information literacy instructional modules into the library's LibGuides, a ubiquitous commercial product of Springshare. LibGuides offers an easy way for librarians to create websites with links to tutorials, books, websites, RSS feeds, images, videos, surveys, and much more (Yelinek, Neyer, Bressler, Coffta, & Magolis, 2010). There are many examples of information literacy tutorials using LibGuides as the delivery platform. LibGuides also allows a librarian from one library to request permission from a librarian at another library to copy and modify an entire LibGuide. This sharing protocol provides a quick and easy way for a library to provide quality online information literacy tutorials for both students and faculty.

Discipline-specific teaching faculty can play an important role in making these information literacy instructional modules accessible to students. In consultation with the department liaison librarian, the faculty can review the information literacy modules, and then, select, in an á la carte fashion, those that align with their course assignments. In addition, faculty can give librarians access to their CMS so that the librarians might guide and assist students in completing the information literacy modules. However, this "one-librarian-to-one-course" model is not the most efficient approach. A better way is to integrate a collaboration of virtual reference librarians into your e-learning program.

Promote and Support Virtual Reference Collaborations

The latest research has shown that at least 75% of academic libraries offer some form of a virtual reference service to their students, either via in-house programs or collaborations. Although a large majority of libraries provide VR, the literature states that the majority of academic librarians prefer to offer in-house staffing over joining a collaboration (Yang & Dalal, 2015). This reluctance may be due to the librarians' perception that they can service their own students better than a librarian from another institution can and that they are less able to help a student from another institution than that student's own librarian. To counter this hesitancy, e-learning leaders should try to influence librarians at their respective institutions to join virtual reference collaborations because these associations enrich the librarians' knowledge of the resources and practices of librarians at other institutions while providing a robust service to their combined student populations.

The virtual reference marketplace offers a wide range of products from the completely free to the relatively high priced, from the most basic to the very complex. Examples of free chat software are Google Chat/Talk, Aim, and Yahoo Messenger, to name a few. This free software allows librarians to provide a basic service. Software features are minimal and planning is simple. Librarians usually monitor these free services at the reference desk.

One of the more expensive products on the market is OCLC's QuestionPoint. QuestionPoint, a leader in the industry, has achieved a global client base. With its broad world-wide reach, it is able to provide its members with a robust global 24/7/365 collaborative service. It also provides training opportunities and assistance in quality control.

Recently, the market has witnessed a growth in relatively low-cost, but comparatively robust virtual reference software, such as LibraryH3lp, Mosio/TextaLibrarian, RefChatter, and LibAnswers (Springshare). With these moderately priced products, librarians are able to provide the users with many of the same services that the more expensive products provide. For example, librarians are able to push pages to a student, create personalized scripts, and generate reports. With these features, librarians are able to instruct students in how to find the information they need rather than simply transferring it to them. The software also allows follow-up with the user after the chat session has ended.

However, these low-cost, but complex types of software require the librarian to engage in more planning and organizing for quality assurance. Very importantly, although some of these products, namely LibraryH3lp and RefChatter, provide a 24/7 backup service, they do not coordinate collaborative arrangements. Librarians must work together with their colleagues to coordinate their own collaborations. In addition, librarians need practical training in how to use this more complex software. In general, the added complexity of working within a virtual reference collaboration requires that the librarians monitor the virtual reference service in a secluded location away from the reference desk, where they can focus on the e-learning student's needs.

Use Your Library Book Budget to Support Your e-Learning Programs

Consider including librarians in meetings where educational resources are discussed. Librarians are skilled at forming library consortia for the purpose of buying products and services at a reduced cost. Your e-learning program may be able to benefit from these cost-saving relationships. In addition, very often libraries, especially academic libraries, have their own budget with which they allocate funds to pay for books, subscribe to journal titles, and provide services for the purpose of supporting the programs of the institutions they serve.

Most libraries have a collection development policy that gives priority to patron requested materials. In general, librarians prefer the collection to be patron-driven. Often, librarians will keep funds aside for those unanticipated end of the fiscal year requests from patrons. Therefore, remember to request whatever materials you need for your e-learning program whenever you need them.

Lobby for a Stronger Collection of e-Resources and for Document Delivery

Managers, directors, and deans of libraries usually have a standing library advisory committee. Be sure to get on this committee in order to influence collection development policy so that more funds might be allocated to electronic resources in support of your online programs. Find out if your library has an interlibrary loan and document delivery program that provides courier delivery of print books. Your remote learners in your e-learning programs have the same right to benefit from the print collection as your local learners.

A Note Regarding e-Learners in K-12 Schools and in the Industrial World: A Shared Challenge

Of all the e-learners, the K-12 student needs the most scaffolding and guided support. At the same time, K-12 programs have the least funding for libraries and staffing. For help in providing library instruction, resources, and services for their students, K-12 teachers are relying more and more on assistance from their colleagues in the public and community college libraries. The e-learning leader should promote and nurture collaboration among librarians and teachers within and outside their institution.

e-Learners in the workplace of the corporate and industrial worlds can benefit from instruction in information literacy, especially from the self-instructional and self-paced materials that provide just-in-time and just-in-case research support. The older professional worker is usually a more independent learner, one who needs less scaffolding than the K-12 student. The more mature e-learners are often more disciplined and motivated than their younger K-12 counterparts. However, both the K-12 and the corporate e-learners share a common challenge.

The K-12 students and the e-learners from the industrial workplace may not have access to as many library resources as the community college and university students do. Therefore, information literacy instruction for these e-learners should focus on freely available, high-quality resources, both scholarly and popular. It is essential that all e-learners should be aware of the free resources available to them, either Open Access (OA) resources or resources provided by their state libraries, funded by their tax dollars.

Conclusion

Libraries can provide your e-learning programs with a vast amount of free, high-quality scholarly and popular print and electronic books, and journal databases. At no cost to your e-learning student, your librarians can demonstrate how to access expensive proprietary materials that are available through your local public libraries, as well as your county and state libraries. Librarians can instruct your students in how to find and evaluate open access journal articles. Librarians can partner with your instructional design team as consultants to your teaching faculty. They can also participate in your e-learning programs as instructors in information literacy. Library resources and librarian expertise can make your programs more rigorous by engaging your students in critical thinking exercises through a robust information literacy component. Give your e-learning students the opportunity to take a whole course in information literacy and give them further exposure by embedding short, stand-alone, self-instructional modules into your courses. Librarians, as natural collaborators and service-oriented academics, can make highly constructive contributions to your e-learning programs.

For More Information

Bernnard, D., Bobish, G, Bullis, D. Hecker, J, Holden, I. Hosier… & Loney, T. (2014). The information literacy user's guide: An open, online textbook. D. Bobish & T. Jacobson (Eds.). Minneapolis, MN: Center for Open. Retrieved from Education.https://open.umn.edu/opentextbooks/BookDetail.aspx?bookId=190.

The American Library Association (2012). Welcome to VRC! Retrieved from http://www.ala.org/rusa/vrc.

Mudd, A., Summey, T. & Upson, M. (2015). It takes a village to design a course: Embedding a librarian in course design. *Journal of Library & Information Services in Distance Learning, 9*: DOI: 10.1080/1533290X.2014.946349.

Mune, C., Goldman, C., Higgins, S., Eby, L., Chan, E. K., & Crotty, L. (2015). Developing adaptable online information literacy modules for a learning management system. *Journal of Library & Information Services in Distance Learning, 9*(1–2), 101–118. DOI: 10.1080/1533290X.2014.946351.

References

Association of College and Research Libraries. (2000). *Information literacy competency standards for higher education.* Retrieved from http://www.ala.org/acrl/standards/informationliteracycompetency.

Association of College and Research Libraries. (2008). *Standards for distance learning library services.* Retrieved from. www.ala.org/acrl/standards/guidelinesdistancelearning.

Association of College and Research Libraries. (2011). *Accreditation.* Retrieved from http://www.ala.org/acrl/issues/infolit/standards/accred/accreditation.

Association of College and Research Libraries. (2015). *Framework for information literacy for higher education.* Retrieved from http://www.ala.org/acrl/standards/ilframework.

Ivins, O. (2015). *The Charlotte initiative for permanent library acquisitions of ebooks. [PowerPoint slides].* Retrieved from http://www.slideshare.net/CharlestonConference/the-charlotte-initiative-on-ebook-principles-a-mellon-funded-project.

Yang, S. Q., & Dalal, H. A. (2015, May). Virtual reference: Where do academic libraries stand? In spite of the types and sizes, academic libraries must find ways to cope with the shortage of staff and budget cuts, while still providing their best service against all odds. *Computers in Libraries, 35*(4), 4+. Retrieved from http://www.infotoday.com/cilmag/.

Yelinek, K., Neyer, L., Bressler, D., Coffta, M., & Magolis, D. (2010). Using LibGuides for an information literacy tutorial. *College & Research Library News, 71*(7), 352–355. Retrieved from http://crln.acrl.org/content/71/7/352.full.

Information Policy and e-Learning

Dian Walster

Abstract Information policies effect all aspects of the e-learning environment from privacy and security to creation, access and use of intellectual property through backup, storage and destruction of data and creative works. This chapter provides a working definition of information policy for e-leaders, discusses particularly relevant types of information policies, and considers areas for decision-making. Action steps to inventory, evaluate, and recommend information policies are included in the second part of the chapter. Through considering the ideas presented e-learning leaders will be more effective in managing the information policy environment in their organization.

Keywords Information policy • Copyright • Intellectual property • Information security • FERPA

Decision-Making Guidance

This chapter will help make decisions about information policies which can impact the effective management and efficient functioning of e-learning programs of study through:

- Considering how information policies, both those already existing and those which are locally created, affect the operation of e-learning environments.
- Identifying federal, state, and corporate information policies which impact the e-learning environment in your organization.
- Differentiating among information policies applicable to administrative, instructional, and student roles regarding e-learning.
- Analyzing how information policies may interact to create complex decision-making within the local e-learning environment.

D. Walster (✉)
Wayne State University, Detroit, MI 48202, USA
e-mail: ah1984@wayne.edu

© Association for Educational Communications and Technology 2018   141
A.A. Piña et al. (eds.), *Leading and Managing e-Learning*, Educational
Communications and Technology: Issues and Innovations,
https://doi.org/10.1007/978-3-319-61780-0_11

What You Need to Know

This chapter addresses information policies affecting the administration of e-learning programs, the instructional environment for e-learning, and the individual rights and responsibilities of e-learners. Implications regarding a number of universally encountered information policies will be examined along with a selection of lesser known aspects of information policy. These policies may have a profound effect on e-learning beyond typical privacy and security issues. Information policies can affect decision-making within e-learning from complex areas such as choosing an e-learning platform to the more mundane such as creating information policies which ensure legal guidelines for the use of copyrighted materials are followed.

In this section three aspects of information policy which directly affect decision-making for e-learning in all organizations will be explored:

- An overview of information policy as an area of study including general definitions of information policy and a definition of information policy which drives the foundational concepts in this chapter.
- A review of types of information policies which affect the administration of e-learning programs, the delivery of instruction within e-learning environments, and the roles and responsibilities of e-learning students.
- An examination of selected examples demonstrating the intricacies of how information policies interrelate to create complexity for decision-makers. A discussion of why local information policies may be needed to bridge gaps in relationships among disparate information polices will also be addressed.

The next section, "What You Can Do" provides specific ideas and actions to identify, support, and integrate information policies into the e-learning environment in your organization.

Overview of Information Policy

Information policy is becoming an interdisciplinary arena which draws upon scholarship in communications, information science, law, and other subject areas (Braman, 2011, pp. 1–2). According to Hernon and Relyea (2010) the area might more appropriately be called "information policies" because they "... tend to address specific issues and, at times, to be fragmented, overlapping and contradictory." (p. 2504) Within this chapter whether addressed in the singular or the plural, the general context is meant to be the information life cycle and how it is managed through both formal and informal means. A more specific, applied definition that will be used for the purposes of this chapter is discussed next.

Definitions of information policy vary depending upon whom is developing the definition and the functions or situation within which the definition will be used.

Classical definitions are more formal in nature and scope. They try to provide a theoretical or conceptual understanding of the breadth of the information policy environment. However, one of the "catches" of all of the definitions is that information is often not defined at all. A classic definition would be:

"The set of rules, formal and informal, that directly restrict, encourage, or otherwise shape flows of information" (Daniel, 1999, p. 1).

Part of the difficulty in deciding upon a definition for information policy is considering the use to which the definition will be put. If one is looking to encapsulate an academic area, then the definition of information policy might look quite different than if one is trying to come up with a way of identifying those policies which affect the creation, access, flow, dissemination, transformation, destruction, etc. of information for a particular purpose such as the functions of information within an e-learning environment. In this case the definition of what constitutes information in a practical sense becomes an absolutely critical component of the overall definition. In one regard everything can be considered information but doing so will not provide the limitations necessary for decision-making in an environment such as e-learning.

Therefore, for the purposes of this chapter, information policy will be defined and limited in the following ways to provide guidance for decision-making related to essential information processes that affect e-learning environments:

- Information is data which can be collected, created, accessed, retrieved, transformed, disseminated, curated, preserved, and destroyed.
- The types of data which are most relevant to administering the e-learning environment include personal information regarding individuals, instructional information which is transmitted through the e-learning environment, data which is collected, created, disseminated, or destroyed as a result of the e-learning process, and creative works or intellectual property that is accessed or used through the e-learning system. While there are many other potential types of information, this chapter will provide a focus on those listed here.
- Formal policies are those which are written and made widely available. For example, there are information privacy statements provided by a social media website. Informal policies are those which affect information decisions but are considered to be so widely accepted or "common sense" they do not need to be codified. An example of an informal information policy within e-learning might be the general belief that all e-mail communications should be answered promptly.

Within the framework proposed above: Information policies are those laws, rules, regulations, and guidelines, both formal and informal, that affect the way individuals and organizations collect, create, access, retrieve, disseminate, transform, curate, preserve, and destroy information. This chapter will discuss and address the most common information policies with which e-learning administrators will want to become familiar. It will also look at how organizations may wish to consolidate, coordinate, or consider the information policies the organization has written or wishes to write. In general there are four types of information policy to consider:

- Those written by external agencies (federal, state, local) which have legal weight and must be adhered to or considered by the e-learning organization (e.g. Federal Communication Commission, 2016; U.S. Copyright Office; U.S. Department of Education, 2015).
- Those written by the organization which effect the e-learning environment. These occur throughout an organization from top governance to individuals (e.g. Texas Higher Education Coordinating Board, 2017).
- Those on behalf of the companies which provide access and services related to e-learning. This can include both formally contracted services and those commonly used by e-learners such as browsers, cloud storage (e.g., He & Cernusca, 2011), and email.
- Personal information policies (usually informal) by which individuals make their own decisions within the e-learning environment (e.g., how much personal information they are willing to share, their expectations regarding storage and destruction of their personal information, what level of security risk they are willing to accept)

In addition, the complexities of the information policy environment for e-learning include being able to navigate, coordinate, and keep up with not only the currently existing policies but also the changes, revisions, and updating which occur. Changes may be minor but in some areas regular oversight is necessary to avoid legal entanglements or unexpected problems.

Examples of Information Policies by Type of Information

There are many information policies which have significance across the board for all types of e-learning environments. Whether it is in public schools, post-secondary education, corporate training and development, or any other area where e-learning occurs, the following are examples of policies which can affect the flow and use of information:

Policies regarding the privacy and security of personal information. For students in organizations that receive funds under an applicable program in the U.S. Department of Education, the Family Educational Rights and Privacy Act (FERPA) protects the privacy of students' educational information. Until a student is 18 this act gives rights to parents. After 18 the rights transfer to the student. Therefore, even though FERPA is a uniform act it may be applied differentially in K-12 education and post-secondary education. e-Leaders will need to know how this act affects their students in their organization.

Policies regarding copyright and intellectual property. In the United States it is not only U.S. Copyright law which must be considered but a series of additional acts and rulings that can change the landscape at any time. Often educational institutions work within the guidelines related to "Fair Use" but when something considered fair use is challenged in court a new ruling can change what is now fair. In addition, the Digital Millenium Copyright Act (DMCA) added language regarding digital products and the Office is consistently working on a series of active policies studies to look at specific issues such as visual materials or the software in everyday items. If the educational organization works beyond the USA, then international or foreign regulations must be considered.

Policies regarding who can or should have access to information and under what conditions. The Children's Internet Protection Act (CIPA) imposes requirements on schools and libraries that receive E-rate discounts for internet access. These requirements limit who can access what information. The American's with Disabilities Act (ADA) provides reasonable accommodations for students with identified educational disabilities. This includes modifying or changing information and class materials into alternative forms to improve access and use.

Policies regarding proprietary information which cannot or should not be shared. Learning management systems, primary vendors, and third party vendors may have differing policies regarding how many copies of software may be distributed or how many users may access the software or information, such as an e-textbook (e.g., Bossaller & Kammer, 2014), at any one time. The variations in these policies will need to be known and transmitted to all who are impacted.

Policies regarding information storage, backup, and destruction. Depending on the systems, networks, servers, and storage facilities, information can be stored and searchable forever, backed up only irregularly and/or partially and destroyed or deactivated on different schedules. Where e-leaders function within an organization will affect their relationships to the information life cycle. There most likely will be local servers and networks, off-site backup and storage and cloud servers and third party storage and backup. The policies of all of these information gatherers and managers need to be known and coordinated.

Examples of Information Policies by Function: Administration, Instruction, and Learners

Another way to look at information policies is not by the content of the policy but by which part of the e-learning function is most affected by the policies: Administration, instruction, or learners.

Information policies which impact administration of e-learning environments. Administratively focused information policies are typically policies which originate at the government or corporate level and influence the overall functioning of e-learning initiatives. Personal information privacy and security is affected by policies such as FERPA at the government level. The learning management systems (LMS) privacy and security policies regarding personal information also involve the overall administration of e-learning programs. There is another policy issue regarding differences among information policy requirements for government and corporate entities. Government agencies must have and must conform to federal guidelines regarding information policies related to information privacy. Corporate entities are under no such obligation. They are not required to have information policies related to privacy. However, if they do have them, they must follow their own policies.

Information policies which influence the design and delivery of instruction. Examples of information policies which impact the design and development of materials for e-learning (e.g., Waterhouse & Rogers, 2004) include areas such as copyright guidelines (e.g., Aufderheide, Milosevic, & Bello, 2015), intellectual freedom, academic freedom, and library policies (e.g., Butler, 2012). Examples of information policies which affect the delivery of instruction include such issues as proprietary systems restrictions, user registrations, password protections, and privacy and security of personal information.

Information policies which affect learners. Learners are impacted by information policies in differently. They have little input into the choice of learning management system, the way information policies are implemented, or how information policy is written for their organization. However, they should be made aware of not only their rights but also their responsibilities. This can mean an organization needs to write information policies or procedures to inform students of those policies which will affect them from privacy and security to intellectual property to communication, access, and retrieval. For example:

- There are risks and benefits to students when their personal information needs as regards privacy and security are in conflict with the educational resources they must use within and e-learning environment.
- Administrative choices of e-learning platforms affect student privacy and security of personal information depending upon the policies of the vendor chosen.
- There can be potentially conflicting information policies within an e-learning environment that affect student responsibilities. For example, departmental policies may not be in alignment with university policies. Also consider library policies regarding fair use that are more restrictive or less restrictive than the U.S. Copyright Office guidelines.

Relationships Among Information Policies and Decision-Making

This section addresses three common examples of how different levels of an organization delivering e-learning may need to consider coordinated efforts to avoid conflicts at the administrative, instructional, and learner levels.

Typically FERPA guidelines are considered at the upper administrative levels of an organization. Guidelines are put into place to ensure that FERPA statements are placed prominently on organizational websites, that individuals who work with student information on a regular basis sign FERPA contracts, and that some type of FERPA training is made available at least to registrar's offices. However, FERPA regulations also apply to the design and delivery of instruction if, for example, private student information is made available on unprotected sites used for the development of class materials.

Often different levels of an organization develop their own interpretations regarding copyright guidelines and fair use. The library systems may provide a written explanation on their website of what they can provide within their understanding of copyright, while the individuals in charge of a learning management system may offer their rules regarding how instructors are to follow copyright guidelines. Students may be given an entirely different set of instructions or no instructions at all as relates to what they are allowed to create for educational products that fall within copyright guidelines.

There are factors to balance in e-learning environments regarding information privacy and security. For example, some government agencies require employees not to provide personal information including work details, pictures, addresses, or other identifying information in electronic forums. However instructional situations often require students to share this information with their peers and their instructors. This is sometimes on secure sites and sometimes not. Student disabilities offices provide the instructor with guidelines regarding how accommodations for individuals need to be made but when students are working in a group setting, what of this can and should be shared with the group can be unclear.

In this section an overview of information policy was presented and a functional definition of information policies used in this chapter was described. Further descriptions of types of information policies and the relationships among administrative, instructional, and learner components of e-learning were explored. At the end of this chapter the "For More Information" section has additional resources toward learning more about information policy.

What You Can Do

This section discusses some actions that can be taken and initiatives that can be employed to identify, manage, and interpret the various aspects of information policies which were discussed earlier in the chapter. These are samples of possible activities and actions. They should not be taken as legal guidance or all-encompassing formulas. Each organization and e-leader will have a unique situation. Actions, decisions, and procedures will be tailored to meet the requirements of your organization, your instructional situation, and your students. Three types of actions that e-learning leaders can begin with are outlined and discussed in this section:

- *Inventory:* Conduct an environmental scan regarding federal, state (e.g., Reindl, 2013; Texas Higher Education Board, n.d.), organizational, and corporate/business information policies which impact the e-learning environment in your organization. Different types of organizations and different kinds of e-learning delivery systems will be affected by different information policies.

- *Evaluate:* Careful review of how your organization disseminates information regarding legally applicable rules, regulations, and guidelines. This will include looking across all levels of the organization and examining administrative, instructional, and student-related materials.

- *Recommend:* Decision-making regarding what types of policies and or guidelines need to be written or referred to specifically related to the aspects of e-learning for which you are responsible. Your place within the overall organization will affect this component of your relationship with information policies. For example, a Chief Information Officer or a District e-learning Coordinator will have a wider range of responsibilities for creating organization information policy than a department head. The department head would have more responsibility for knowing and appropriately applying organizational information policies.

Create an Information Policies Inventory Using an Environmental Scan

One of the first things to do is an environmental scan to identify all of the information policies that affect the e-learning environment for your organization and then create an inventory or chart (see Table 1). The first two levels (governmental and organizational) will be the most critical to begin. As an e-learning leader you will need to identify what type of organization you are working for and then find the information policies which specifically relate to that type of organization. There are different laws, rules, and guidelines in effect. Some such as copyright guidelines apply across the board no matter the type of organization that is under consideration. "Fair Use" guidelines within the copyright legislation may apply differentially depending on the profit or nonprofit function of the materials created and used.

Governmental information policies will differ depending on the type of organization you are working within. K-12 schools have different policies (e.g., Abilock & Abilock, 2016), particularly as regards students, because, for example, most students are minors and their personal information must be guarded more securely and with more caution than higher education. Post-secondary institutions (e.g., public institutions or those which receive governmental support of some type) are subject to FERPA provisions for example. Corporate entities which provide e-learning environments may have less need to worry about the privacy of individual information from governmental regulations but may be subject to more scrutiny regarding use of intellectual property and creative works.

Organizational information policies can exist at any level and within any part of the organization. There will be board or university or district policies that affect all

Table 1 Chart for developing an information policies inventory

Type of Information	Governmental policies	Organizational policies	Third party policies	Individual policies (e.g., students)
Personal information (name, address, transcript, email address, etc.)	FERPA	How FERPA is implemented	Learning Management System privacy policy	Personal policies related to work or legal requirements (e.g., restraining orders)
Instructional materials	ADA	University policies regarding copyright and works for hire and intellectual property (e.g., Cate, Drooz, Hohenberg, & Schulz, 2007)		Informal student policies regarding their preferences for textual, visual, auditory, etc. materials
Creative works	U.S. Copyright Law DMCA	Library policies interpreting copyright and fair use	Policies regarding who owns materials stored on their systems (e.g., pictures, videos)	Informal policies regarding instructor's believing they own the copyright for everything they create
e-learning data (data created by processing information entered into an e-learning system)	Human Subjects guidelines for use of data created by e-learning system and used for research	Policies regarding creation, backup, storage, and destruction of reports based on system created data	Policies regarding who owns data created by the learning management system	

parts of the organization. There will be specific areas of the organization such as the information technology (IT) department or the library or office of summer programs which have information policies related to their specific needs and information processes. There will be college or school, departmental and instructor policies that may be consistent or may clash with each other. As an e-leader the scope of your responsibilities will be determined by your role and position within the organization. Gathering information from all parts of an organization will be useful, no matter what your role or responsibility level.

An example of a chart (see Table 1) to fill in types of information policies is provided. The grid has been partially completed to show examples for public post-secondary education e-learning program. This is by no means everything that could be on a grid of this type. It is merely an illustration of how to begin to collect examples of information policies.

You may want to consider constructing a grid such as this for the different types of e-learning delivery systems your organization works with. For example, MOOCs may be subject to different information policy requirements than courses offered through password protected learning management systems. Hybrid courses may have different privacy issues than completely online courses.

e-Leaders need to be up to date on legislation regarding the information policy environment for e-learning. A process for scanning upcoming legislation, court cases, and rule changes should be part of the keeping the inventory up to date. Consider:

- Federal, state, local laws, regulations, and guidelines that must be adhered to as regards information in e-learning
- The need to think about not just information use but creation, access, dissemination, transformation, and disposal and what laws, regulations, and rules may be considered as new technologies and e-learning platforms evolve. For example, the 2015 ruling on MOOCs and Fair Use (Decherny, 2015).
- Not only educational needs but also how the e-learning environment uses information for educational purposes that may have different laws than using information for commercial purposes.

Evaluating Local Information Policies

Once an inventory of existing information policies is created, then an evaluation of their goodness of fit, coherence, and quality can be undertaken. Processes for how they are disseminated, who is responsible for keeping up to date on changes and how they will be explained or implemented across the organization will be considered as part of this evaluation. A strategy that can help in organizing this material is a concept map or graphic organizer. A visual representation of information policies, where they are located in the organization and which ones affect which levels of the organization can be extremely useful in identifying strengths, gaps, and missing policies.

One aspect of evaluation relates to the types of questions you may wish to ask yourself regarding the effectiveness and usefulness of the information policies your organization has written and that have accreted over time:

- Organizations and individuals may be affected in different ways by information policies or different information policies may be in effect if you are an organization or an individual. How do e-leaders balance the needs of individuals with the requirements of the organization? In evaluating your local information policies will you evaluate them both on the basis of organizational needs and individual needs or will organizational requirements take precedence?
- What and how much are you required to make available to students? What is the organizations responsibility and what is individual responsibility in terms of

understanding information policies? What do you do when student need is in conflict with organizational goals?

- How will the information components of ADA play out in your organization? Is there an ADA office which will make the needed accommodations regarding transforming information into different formats or will each individual instructor be responsible?
- With e-learning and online delivery are their some jobs that require extra measures to ensure both employee and student privacy? For example, if students share papers as part of a class or learn about each other's grades, do they need to sign FERPA waivers?
- Information policies often indicate age as a factor in information privacy, access and retrieval especially. Are there safeguards in place not only for minors but also allowing adults access to which they are entitled?

The evaluation of local information policies is not a one-time occurrence but rather, like the environmental scan, should occur on a regular basis. Creating a work team or committee responsible for this process as part of their regularly scheduled duties would be one option to consider. Representatives from all parts of the organization and areas affected by e-learning would also help to keep evaluations balanced, cohesive, and coordinated.

Recommending Information Policies for the Organization to Revise or Write

Creating an inventory of information policies also means identifying areas where may be gaps. Evaluating information policies will also bring to light policies which need rewriting or revision. Figuring out who will write policies, how they will be reviewed, and what process will be used for approving, implementing instruction if necessary, and then disseminating the policies are actions related to the overall process of writing information policy.

There a number of types of policies that might need to be undertaken:

1. Policies that need to be rewritten so as to be more up to date. For example, at one time there were copyright guidelines specifically called the TEACH Act. These guidelines are now simply part of chapter "Keeping FIRRST Things First: The Delicate Dance of Leading Online Innovation at Your Institution" of the copyright law (110 (2) to be exact). If you go looking for the TEACH Act within the Copyright Office, it is impossible to find anything but an out-of-date reference. If your organization has data related to the TEACH Act, it may be time to update the language.
2. Policies that need to be consolidated across the organization so there is more cohesion in interpretations or implementation guidelines.
3. Policies that do not exist and need writing such as:

(a) A consolidating or guiding policy indicating which policy takes precedence if there are discrepancies or contradictions among information policies at various levels of the organization. For example, if a department website says it is acceptable to email the pdf files of journal articles as long as it is for educational purposes and the University policy, indicates that under no conditions can pdf files of journal articles be emailed which would take precedence? This problem is not actually as simple as it might appear at first glance. Perhaps the department is talking about pdf files of journal articles from faculty in the department who own the copyright and who have put them in a "creative commons" type depository and in fact emailing these pdf files is perfectly acceptable. While perhaps the University policy relates to journal holdings purchased by the University Library and subject to all features of copyright law in which case emailing is not acceptable. Policies or guidelines need to be written to help these contradictions and inconsistencies be worked through and consolidated or explained appropriately.

(b) Informative and comprehensive information should be provided for students regarding how their personal and class created information is backed up, stored, accessed, retrieved, made available to other parties, secured, and destroyed. This includes all forms of information such as audio, video, text, chat and pictures or visual materials. If there is differential treatment based on format, it should be indicated. Guidelines also include what recourse students have to request information be removed from systems and the necessary procedures.

(c) Descriptive interpretations of issues and problems associated with privacy and security related to social media platforms. This would help both full-time and adjunct faculty understand what they can and cannot do regarding additions to e-learning environments beyond those provided for and approved by the organization. This also includes what they can and cannot require their students to create, share, produce, use, or demonstrate with external social media platforms.

This section has reviewed three action steps which can be taken toward improving the information policy environment: (1) Inventorying the information policies related to the e-learning environment in your organization. (2) Evaluating the quality, consistency, and coherence of the information policies affecting e-learning. (3) Improving the information policies through keeping up to date with changes, revising, and coordinating policies when needed and writing new policy when necessary.

Conclusion

In summary, the scope of information policy is well beyond the level of privacy and security of personal information which can be the first and sometimes the only consideration when one thinks about information policy. Braman (2011) has said that information policy "... creates conditions under which all other decision making takes place." (p. 2) The types of information policies which affect decisions for e-learning include both those with legal implications for the e-learning administrator and those which may expose ethical or values based decisions for instructors and learners.

In writing this chapter I uncovered many different organizational schemes for identifying types of information that should be considered when writing information policies, strategies for identifying information policies of relevance and ideas regarding writing information policies. However, none of them were explicitly designed for application by e-leaders in e-learning environments. The categories of information policies, kinds of information of relevance, and examples were specifically chosen as most appropriate to e-learning. These choices were based on my own experiences as an instructor of information policy, as an administrator responsible for online learning initiatives, and as an e-learning instructor.

For More Information

Jaeger, P. et al. (2015). Teaching information policy in the digital age. *Journal of Education for Library and Information Science*, *56*(3), 175–189. Doi: 10.12783/issn.2328-2967/56/3/1.

Journal of Information Policy. http://www.jip-online.org/.

Information Policy series from MIT Press. https://mitpress.mit.edu/books/series/information-policy.

References

Abilock, R., & Abilock, D. (2016). I agree, but do I know? Privacy and student data. *Knowledge Quest*, *44*(4), 10–17.

Aufderheide, P., Milosevic, T., & Bello, B. (2015). Impact of copyright permissions culture on the US visual arts community: The consequences of fear of fair use. *New Media & Society*, *18*(9) 1–16.

Bossaller, J., & Kammer, J. (2014). Faculty views of eTextbooks: A narrative study. *College Teaching*, *62*(2), 68–75.

Braman, S. (2011). Defining information policy. *Journal of Information Policy*, *1*, 1–5.

Butler, B. (2012). *Massive open online courses: Legal and policy issues for research libraries*. Association of Research Libraries. Retrieved from http://ssrn.com/abstract=2412817.

Cate, B., Drooz, D., Hohenberg, P., & Schulz, K. (2007). *Creating intellectual property policies and current issues in administering online courses*. San Diego: National Association of College and University Attorneys.

Daniel, E. (1999). *What is information policy?* Retrieved March 7, 2016, from http://ils.unc.edu/daniel/InfoPolicy/policy.html.

Decherny, P. (2015). Fair use, MOOCs and the Digital Millenium Copyright Act. *Federal Register*, *80*(208), 65962.

Federal Communication Commission. (2016). *Children's Internet Protection Act.* https://www.fcc. gov/consumers/guides/childrens-internet-protection-act.

He, W., & Cernusca, D. (2011). Exploring cloud computing for distance learning. *Online Journal of Distance Learning Administration, 14*(3), n.p.

Hernon, P., & Relyea, H. C. (2010). Information policy: United States. In *Encyclopedia of library and information sciences* (3rd ed.pp. 2504–2518). New York: Marcel Dekker. doi:10.1081/E-ELIS3-120009040

Reindl, T. (2013). *Regulating online postsecondary education: State issues and options.* Washington, DC: National Governor's Association.

Texas Higher Education Coordinating Board (2017). *Distance Education Policies, Procedures and Forms.* Retrieved from http://www.thecb.state.tx.us/index. cfm?objectid=A5A152AC-D29D-334F-872625E9E77B3B37.

U. S. Copyright Office. (n.d.). http://www.copyright.gov/.

U.S. Department of Education. (2015). *Family Educational Rights and Protection Act.* http:// www2.ed.gov/policy/gen/guid/fpco/ferpa/index.html; http://familypolicy.ed.gov.

Waterhouse, S., & Rogers, R. O. (2004). Importance of policies in e-learning instruction. *EDUCAUSE Quarterly, 3,* 28–39.

Can I Use This? Developing Open Literacies or Understanding the Basics and Implications of Copyright, Fair Use, and Open Licensing for e-Learning

Olga Belikov and Royce Kimmons

Abstract Open educational resources (OER) have garnered increased attention in recent years as a means for driving down educational costs, addressing differentiation and adaptability needs, improving accuracy and quality of materials, and supporting collaboration in the design of digital coursework. Perhaps one of the greatest identified barriers in the adoption of OER has been a lack of literacy regarding copyright, fair use, and open licensing. These concepts are commonly misunderstood in educational institutions. Many instructors and educational leaders struggle with understanding what is copyrighted, when it is copyrighted, what it means if it is copyrighted, and what *open* means. This leads educational leaders and their programs to either improperly use these materials (i.e., illegally or unethically) or to be fearful when using them in legitimate, allowable ways. Through this chapter, we seek to provide educational leaders with an understanding of what is necessary to make full and safe use of both copyrighted and open educational resources.

Keywords Copyright • Fair use • Creative commons • Public domain • Open educational resources • OER • Open literacies

Decision-Making Guidance

This chapter will help you make decisions about:

- The use of copyrighted and open materials in your institutions' courses.
- How to release your own materials under an open license.
- The additional copyright questions you must ask of legal counsel for your specific context.

O. Belikov • R. Kimmons (✉)
Brigham Young University, 150J MCKB BYU, Provo, UT 84602, USA
e-mail: olgambelikov@byu.edu; royceKimmons@gmail.com; roycekimmons@byu.edu

© Association for Educational Communications and Technology 2018
A.A. Piña et al. (eds.), *Leading and Managing e-Learning*, Educational Communications and Technology: Issues and Innovations,
https://doi.org/10.1007/978-3-319-61780-0_12

What You Need to Know

Copyright and related issues (such as fair use, public domain, and open licensing) are widely misunderstood by educators and e-learning professionals. This leads to situations in which potentially viable educational materials are often underutilized or in which copyright laws are flagrantly disregarded. In this chapter, we hope to provide e-learning professionals with a basic understanding of copyright, public domain, fair use, and open licensing that will help them to better understand the laws regulating the use of educational materials and what options are available to them for course creation. We also hope to provide guidance for the role of the e-learning leader as they advise professionals at their institutions on best practices of copyright, public domain, fair use, and open licensing. Copyright in particular is a complicated legal landscape to navigate, so the contents of this chapter should not be perceived as legal advice in particular cases. Also, this chapter deals entirely with the United States context. Copyright law varies from nation to nation, but given the complexity and multiplicity of these laws, we can only deal with a single context in this chapter. As the authors of this chapter, we are also educators trying to navigate copyright and related issues and we are providing our perspective on these issues, but are not lawyers. We hope you find the resources and information we share to be useful as you may face similar questions, conundrums, and frustrations as we have faced when creating and sharing our own resources. We hope that our perspectives will help you to recognize the right questions to ask as you continually seek to approach e-learning in a legal, ethical, and open manner.

Copyright

Copyright in the United States originated with the U.S. Constitution, and its purpose is to ensure that authors of creative works have legal support that will allow them to profit from their works, thereby allowing them to make a living as creative artists, authors, and scholars. The goal of copyright is to benefit society and increase the diffusion of knowledge by safeguarding the rights of those who generate creative works and to allow authors to enjoy the security necessary to continue to create for a lifetime. In the USA, copyright applies to any creative work including printed works (e.g., books, essays, journals, sheet music) and digital works (e.g., e-books, plays, musical performances, movies).

The goal of understanding copyright for the e-learning leader is to be able to ensure that their professionals are not violating copyright laws at their institution. e-Learning leaders should also be able to point professionals to those who are well versed in copyright, such as librarians and other campus professionals, should in-depth questions arise. Some of the artifacts that e-learning professionals deal with regularly that are subject to copyright include books, book chapters, journals, journal articles, images, music, video, syllabi, and any other physical or digital works that were created by a person. In order for copyright to apply to a work, the work must exist in a fixed medium and cannot merely be conceptual. For this reason, facts, equations, and ideas are not copyrighted, though the works in which those concepts may be expressed, such as a textbook, equation reference guide, or instructional video, would be subject to copyright.

One of the biggest misconceptions about copyright regards when copyright begins or what action is needed to make a work copyrighted. This misconception likely rises out of the evolving history of copyright law and confusion with patent law, which has a different legal framework intended to protect inventions. In patent law, patents must be applied for, reviewed, and granted by a federal agency. Copyright operates differently in that it is automatically granted to any creative work as soon as it is created, without application or review. This means that as soon as a teacher creates a syllabus, that syllabus is copyrighted, or as soon as a photographer snaps a photo, that photograph is copyrighted. The creator of the work does not need to do anything to establish copyright; it is applied automatically, and the work is regarded as the intellectual property of the creator. After the work is created, copyright owners do have the option of registering their copyright on a particular work through the U.S. copyright office, but this is only required if the author will need to pursue legal action against someone who violates their copyright.

Another misconception is that in order to be copyrighted a work must have the copyright symbol on it. The copyright symbol is used as a signifier or reminder of copyright, but it actually has relatively little value as an indicator of copyright, because many copyrighted works will not have the symbol and many works that have the symbol may no longer be copyrighted. Thus, the symbol serves as a reminder or potential warning against infringement, but it carries no legal status with it.

For these reasons, before including any creative works in electronic coursework, e-learning professionals should assume that materials are copyrighted and subject to legal protection unless they have strong reason to believe otherwise or that the intended use is allowable without permission from the copyright holder, which we will discuss below. If a work is copyrighted, then e-learning professionals need permission (often in the form of a limited use license) to use the work in their courses.

In short, if a work is copyrighted, then the creator of that work is the only person who has the right to profit from it, to make copies of it, to store it, to change it, and to share it, and no one else has this right unless they are explicitly granted it by the copyright holder. Thus, if you are creating an online course, you must have permission from the copyright holder to use any copyrighted work in that course, and you must assume that every image, journal article, book chapter, blog post, or music track you hope to use in your course is copyrighted, because it was created by someone.

In light of these realizations, e-learning professionals may rightfully feel overwhelmed and wonder: what are we to do? After all, if you cannot use any copyrighted works without first seeking permission, then you would be seriously inhibited in your ability to efficiently create and distribute meaningful online coursework, and in many cases you likely might not be able to gain legal permission to use materials in the desired educational manner (e.g., sharing an article for purposes of critique). Thankfully, U.S. copyright law has two considerations that provide great benefit to e-learning professionals (and everyone else): public domain and fair use.

Public Domain

The first consideration is that copyright is not intended to be applied to creative works for an infinite amount of time and that not all creative works are subject to copyright. The applicable length of copyright law has changed over time. Currently in the USA, copyright only applies to creative works for the life of the author plus 70 years. This means that as soon as an author dies, a countdown timer begins on the author's creative works, and once the copyright expires, the work moves into what is called the public domain.

The public domain is an often misused legal term that applies to a group of creative works that are not subject to copyright. Due to age, older creative works such as Shakespeare's sonnets or Herman Melville's *Moby Dick* are no longer subject to copyright and can be freely copied, changed, sold, and adapted without permission of the copyright holder or an estate. There are many internet resources that catalog and provide access to public domain works. These collections include classical texts, images, video, and music that can be freely used without any copyright restrictions.

In addition to old works, there are other resources that are available in the public domain. These works all operate on the premise that even though copyright is granted as soon as a work is created, the author or owner has the power to give up copyright and to allow it to pass into the public domain for unrestricted public use. Thus, a photographer can take a picture, post it to an online repository like Flickr, and mark it as being in the public domain, which would allow anyone to use that picture however they would like without permission. Some organizations require their employees to release their work into the public domain. For example, since public domain is intended to support the U.S. public, the federal government requires many of its employees to release their works to the public. Thus, pictures taken by active duty military members, park rangers, and others may be found without copyright restriction on sites like the U.S. Army website and the U.S. Fish and Wildlife Digital Library.

It is the role of the e-learning leader to ensure that resources be considered from the public domain when appropriate. e-Learning leaders are also in a position to advise professionals on where to find these resources and how to use them appropriately. For the e-learning professional, the public domain represents a vast collection of resources that can be meaningfully leveraged for constructing course materials on subjects such as history, literature, and biology. Pertinent resources that are in the public domain can be used without any restriction and without the need of permission or even a citation.

Despite the great benefits offered by public domain, there are at least three limitations that e-learning professionals should be aware of. First, works are subject to the copyright law that was in existence when the work was created, and for this reason, it may sometimes be difficult to decipher whether a work is in the public domain, because U.S. copyright law has changed many times since its inception. Second, many types of courses require the use of modern educational resources, such as contemporary literature, modern scientific illustrations, and recent cinema, which will likely not be found in the public domain. Third, if someone creates a work that they would like to share with others, releasing the work into the public domain precludes that author from gaining exclusive monetary value from the work or in controlling how it is used. So, if an e-learning professional creates a course and wants to share it with others, releasing it to the public domain may not be a good way to share, because it would allow others to profit from the work and allow it to be used in ways that the author may not approve of. For these reasons, public domain works can be of great value to e-learning professionals, but this value may be highly contextual to specific subject areas.

Fair Use

Recognizing that copyright could become a mechanism for rigidity of thought and prevention of the free flow of ideas, copyright law was also constructed with a second consideration that allowed for particular exceptional uses of copyrighted materials without permission under the fair use clause. Fair use is also commonly misunderstood by educators because many believe that fair use means that any copyrighted work may be used in any way as long as it is meeting an educational objective. Though fair use does allow e-learning professionals to use some copyrighted materials without permission, there are important guidelines for determining what constitutes fair use and what does not.

Fair use is intended to allow people to make use of copyrighted materials for educational and other purposes, but fair use is intentionally ill-defined in copyright law, and it is often very difficult to determine what constitutes acceptable fair use. The only way to determine if a particular use is fair is for a judge to make a ruling on that particular case in a court of law. In making a ruling on fair use, a judge will consider the four factors of fair use that are written into law. These factors include the following:

1. The purpose and character of the use.
2. The nature of the copyrighted work.
3. The amount and substantiality of the portion taken.
4. The effect of the use upon the market.

We will now explain each of these four factors in more detail.

First, in determining fair use, a judge will consider whether the use of the copyrighted material is a transformative use or whether it aligns with the author's intended purpose. Fair use favors transformative use of copyrighted materials, or the use of a creative work in a way that it was not intended to be used. For instance, if you are creating a course on comparative literature and you would like to include an excerpt of J. K. Rowling's Harry Potter for students to analyze and deconstruct, this could be a transformative use of that work, because the author created the book for the purpose of entertainment and you would be using it as a subject of academic analysis. If, on the other hand, you chose to include an excerpt from a comparative literature textbook in the same course, this would likely not be transformative use, because you would be using the textbook in the same way that the author intended it to be used. Thus, the first example would lean more toward fair use and would be looked upon more favorably in a court of law.

Second, a judge would then consider the nature of the copyrighted work and whether it was factual or creative (e.g., fictional) in nature. Fair use exists to support the dissemination of knowledge, and for that reason uses of copyrighted material that utilize factual information will be more closely aligned to fair use than will be works of a fictional nature. Thus, excerpts from a biography about an historical figure used in a course would align more with fair use than would excerpts from a novel.

Third, a judge would consider how much of the creative work you are using and whether this amount is justified given what you are trying to accomplish. For instance, including a one-page excerpt from a physics journal will be looked upon very differently than including multiple articles. However, even if you only take a short excerpt of a work, the substantiality of the excerpt also comes into play if it is considered to be "the heart of the work." For instance, including the first page of a mystery novel would be looked upon very differently than including the page where the murderer is revealed. Generally, the heart or most memorable part of a work is provided more protection than other parts of the work and is less likely to be allowable as fair use.

Fourth, a judge would consider whether your use of the copyrighted material negatively impacts the author's ability to profit from the work. For instance, if you include a page from a textbook in an online course, it is unlikely that this would affect the author's ability to profit from that textbook, because students would not have bought the textbook for that single page. If, however, instead of requiring students to purchase a textbook, you include the heart of that textbook or so much of the textbook that students are no longer purchasing it to access the material that they need for class, then this would not be considered fair use, because you have used the author's copyrighted work in a way that disadvantages the author and prevents them from profiting from textbook sales.

Considering these four factors together, a judge would try to weigh what she feels to be the most important factors in the case and make a ruling on whether or not a specific case of use was fair. As these guidelines illustrate, however, there are no clear rules for the use of copyrighted material in a manner that ensures fair use compliance. Fair use is contextual and subjective and must be determined by a judge. Many institutions will adopt their own standards of fair use that are intended to prevent personnel from engaging in practices that would likely constitute violations, such as limiting the percentage of a book that can be copied to 10%, but these standards are not based in law and are rather institutional interpretations of law that may or may not hold up in a particular court case.

Examples of recent fair use cases may be found on Copyright.gov (n.d.), and summaries of these cases reveal that court rulings operate explicitly by the four factors of fair use mentioned above but that sometimes fair use must be determined by counterbalancing factors against one another. We will provide two examples to illustrate: Penguin Grp. (USA), Inc. v. Am. Buddha (2015) and TCA Television Corp. v. McCollum (2015).

In the first example, the publisher Penguin Group brought a lawsuit against the American Buddha website for making complete digitized copies of four of its books (with minor formatting changes) and sharing these copies on its website. The court found that this was not an example of fair use, because (1) the minor formatting changes were not sufficient to justify that the use was transformative, (2) the work was creative (not factual) in nature, (3) the books were copied in their entirety, and (4) it was believed that the distribution of the books on the website would adversely impact the publisher's ability to sell their books. In this case, all four factors strongly weighed against fair use and were used to support the subsequent ruling against the American Buddha website.

In the second example, TCA Television, which owns the copyright on Abbott and Costello's famous "Who's on First?" comedy routine, brought a lawsuit against McCollum, who was the producer of a newer comedy "Hand to God," because the latter included a scene wherein over 1 min of the "Who's on First?" routine was quoted verbatim by a character through a sock puppet. The court found that the case favored fair use in the first and fourth factors, because (1) the use was funny for different reasons than the original, thereby making it transformative, and (4) the use would not negatively impact the copyright holder's ability to profit from the original (and might even introduce new audiences to the original). However, the court also found that the case shied away from fair use in the other two factors, because (2) the work was creative (not factual) in nature, and (3) the newer comedy used the heart of the original work. In the end, the court ruled that the considerations in favor of fair use outweighed those against, and the use was determined to be fair.

As you can tell from these cases, the four factors are explicitly used for determining fair use, but it is not always clear whether a judge will interpret factors the same way that plaintiffs or defendants might, and judges must sometimes decide which factors are most important, weighing factors against one another in particular cases. Overall, e-learning professionals should use these examples to recognize that the four factors are indeed important to consider when utilizing copyrighted materials but that interpretation of the factors and their comparative weights to one another may be very subjective and may vary between the copyright holder, the e-learning professional, and a judge. e-Learning leaders are to be particularly judicious of fair use of resources at their institution and ensure that professionals at their institutions are abiding within legal parameters when claiming fair use of copyrighted materials.

Open Licensing

Copyright is an essential legal framework for supporting the ongoing creation of knowledge and free exchange of ideas. However, sometimes the rigidity of copyright law, the fuzziness of fair use, and the assumptions that copyright makes about content creators and their intentions are not appropriate and may actually limit the free exchange of ideas. For instance, a teacher might create a lesson plan and put it online specifically because she wants others to benefit from it by using it in their own classrooms or changing it and adapting it to their needs, but copyright would prohibit other teachers from doing so (without permission). Given the fuzziness of fair use, it is often difficult for educators and others to know how they can use resources even when those resources seem to be provided for the express purpose of being used. For this reason, it is necessary and helpful for content creators to expressly indicate the copyright status of the content they create and how they are permitting others to use it. Since copyright is automatically applied to a creative work, any work created is instantly protected by all the restrictions that copyright law allows. If an author wants to ease some of these restrictions in a way that preserves ownership of the work, they have the power to do so through open licensing.

The concept of open licensing took hold in the software development community a few decades ago as developers were trying to understand how they could share their projects in ways that would allow others to build upon them without continually seeking permission. The open source and free software movements created licenses that software creators could apply to their work so that anyone that wanted to use the software would know exactly what they could and could not do with it, thereby alleviating many of the unnecessary or unwanted restrictions that copyright placed on the work by default. This same principle has more recently been applied to other types of creative works such as books, videos, music, and educational resources, and there are many types of licenses to help content creators articulate their own expectations for the way their content can be used without permission.

These materials released under various open licenses are commonly known as open educational resources (OER). The sharing of these materials reflects a movement of openness which seeks to encourage educators, content experts, and others to disseminate knowledge for the benefit of others rather than for financial gain. OER however, not only provide low or no cost materials to educators and encourage the free exchange of knowledge and ideas, but also provide a variety of pedagogical benefits. Those who adopt or create OER are encouraged to retain, reuse, revise, remix, and redistribute the materials they use in their courses. The revision of the resources allows e-learning professionals to adapt these materials in ways that build upon instruction and allow others to benefit from the revisions made, thereby perpetuating the dissemination of knowledge and openness of resources.

Open software licenses, like the MIT and GNU-GPL licenses, are sometimes applied to other types of creative works, but the unique nature of software does not always make this the most suitable choice. In response, Creative Commons licenses have arisen as a means for authors to choose how and in what ways their other types of creative works, such as images, movies, and blog posts, can be shared. To be clear, openly licensed works are still copyrighted, but the adoption of an open license provides preemptive permission to others to know how the author allows the copyrighted work to be used without permission.

Creative Commons is a nonprofit organization that provides and articulates seven different licenses that a content creator can apply to their creative work to denote some level of openness or copyright permission. To understand these licenses, we must first understand four principles upon which they are based:

attribution, share-alike, noncommercial use, and non-derivative use. We will now explain each of these in turn and then illustrate how they are used to construct the seven Creative Commons licenses.

First, attribution means that if a work is going to be used without permission, then the user of that work needs to attribute authorship to the original author by including the author's name, a link to the original resource, and other information. This consideration ensures that authors can still receive prestige and credit for their efforts even if their works are freely used or adapted by others.

Second, share-alike means that if someone is going to use an author's copyrighted work in their own work, then the new author must share their new work under a similar license as the previous work. Thus, if you were to use an image in your course with the share-alike requirement, then it would be expected that you would share your course with the share-alike expectation also. The purpose of the share-alike consideration is to ensure that openly licensed works promote ongoing sharing rather than just being used or consumed in new works that are not open themselves.

Third, noncommercial use simply means that the work cannot be used for direct commercial benefit. Creative Commons defines "commercial benefit" as a use "primarily intended for commercial advantage or monetary compensation" (CC BY-NC). For instance, if you used noncommercial OER to create a textbook, you would not be able to sell that textbook and therefore profit from the work of others. The intent of the noncommercial concept is to ensure that authors who provide resources freely to the community can still gain commercial benefit themselves from their resources without having to compete against others who have adapted their resources for new use, thereby essentially competing against themselves.

And fourth, non-derivative means that a work cannot be adapted or changed in subsequent works. Placing an image in an online course would be an example of non-derivative use, because the image itself is not changed. If, however, you applied filters to, cropped, or otherwise altered an image before including it in your course, then this would be considered a derivative work. Non-derivation is intended to ensure authors that their work will continue to be used in the way that they initially provided it to the community, thereby preventing it from being used in ways that the author might believe to be artistically, morally, or professionally inappropriate or displeasing.

When considering whether to release a work to the public, authors should ask themselves whether they want to require attribution, to require users to share their own work in similar ways, to restrict commercial use of their work, or to restrict others from changing their work. Based on answers to these questions, authors may adopt the appropriate Creative Commons license that articulates the freedoms and restrictions that they want to be applied to their own work (cf. Table 1). These licenses reference the four considerations above in short form as follows: Attribution (BY), Noncommercial (NC), Share-Alike (SA), and Non-derivative (ND). When considered together, these considerations are used to create the seven Creative Commons licenses: CC0 (no copyright restrictions are maintained; public domain), CC BY (attribution), CC BY-SA (attribution and share-alike), CC BY-ND (attribution and non-derivative), CC BY-NC (attribution and noncommercial), CC BY-NC-SA (attribution, noncommercial, and share-alike), and CC BY-NC-ND (attribution, noncommercial, and non-derivative).

Table 1 Logic model for selecting an appropriate Creative Commons license for your work

Step	Question	Yes	No
0	Do you want to require people to seek your permission before using your copyrighted material in any way?	Retain all copyright restrictions	Go to step 1
1	Do you want to allow anyone anywhere to use the work however they want without giving you credit?	Public domain or CC0	Go to step 2
2	Do you want to make sure that anyone who uses your work also shares their work in the same way?	Go to step 3	Go to step 4
3	Do you want to prevent others from profiting from your work?	CC BY-NC-SA	CC BY-SA
4	Do you want to prevent people from changing your work?	Go to step 5	Go to step 6
5	Do you want to prevent others from profiting from your work?	CC BY-NC-ND	CC BY-ND
6	Do you want to prevent others from profiting from your work?	CC BY-NC	CC BY

By adopting one of these seven licenses, an author can make explicit to any potential user exactly how the work can be used without permission. If a user violates the license (e.g., uses a CC BY image without providing attribution), then this is a copyright violation just as if the resource had not been shared under an open license. In this way, Creative Commons licenses do not replace or supplant copyright, but they build upon it to ensure that created works are able to be freely used in a manner that is permitted by the author. e-Learning leaders should be able to advise professionals at their institution on open licensing considerations, as well as assist professionals in adopting and adapting OER appropriately should the professionals make the decision to do so in their teaching and learning setting.

What You Can Do

There are a variety of best practices and risks involved with using copyrighted and variously licensed creative works. Copyright may be difficult to navigate, but that should not discourage e-learning professionals from using resources appropriately. e-Learning leaders are in a position to assist e-learning professionals in navigating copyright. Understanding copyright, public domain, fair use, and open licensing will allow e-learning leaders to both aid professionals in working within copyright parameters, and connect their professionals with others on and off campus who are well versed in these legal constraints. There are materials released under a variety of licenses that can be used in conjunction with an appropriate understanding of the restrictions placed upon them. It is important to note that there is a degree of legal risk in any non-permitted use of a copyrighted work, and purchasing a work does not automatically grant unfettered ownership over the material encompassed within a work, as it typically only grants a license for limited personal use. Copyright will restrict how and where you can use the work, your ability to distribute the work to students, and whether you can modify the work.

It is the role of the e-learning leader to advise and provide resources to e-learning professionals on best copyright practices. For e-learning professionals, copyright can be a double-edged sword: it protects you as a content creator while simultaneously limiting you as a content remixer or adapter. As a content creator, you can develop coursework and materials with certainty that your products cannot legally be reused or shared without your permission. However, you must afford other creators the same protections you enjoy and cannot, therefore, ignore copyright as you utilize their works.

If you want to use copyrighted material in a manner that is not covered by the license, you can always request permission from the copyright owner. Sometimes copyright holders will be willing to allow your desired use, while at other times, they may require you to pay a licensing fee in order to use the material in the desired manner. Asking for permission is never a bad idea; it just takes time and may be a fruitless endeavor. The e-learning leader should also promote the understanding and use of items in the public domain.

Public Domain

Public domain is useful to educators, but identifying whether or not something is in the public domain can be extremely difficult. The e-learning leader must be in a position to advise on matters of public domain and point professionals to public domain resources. If something is identified as in the public domain, the use of this material is straightforward and limited in legal implications. Those resources within the public domain are free to be used without restriction, and without the need of citation. There are a variety of repositories that can be explored to select public domain materials. Some of the most prominent public domain collections include Archive.org and Wikimedia Commons. Although materials that exist within the public domain are limited and often old, they can be a safe set of resources from which e-learning professionals can legally compile course content. Should you choose to release a resource into the public domain, it should be understood that the copyright has been relinquished and this material can be used by anyone without permission or restriction.

Because U.S. copyright law has periodically changed, especially throughout the twentieth century, and a work's copyright status is generally determined by the law at the time it was created, it is sometimes difficult to know if a work is in the public domain or to even project when a specific work will pass into the public domain. If a work was published before 1923, then it is fairly safe to assume that it is now in the public domain, but if it has been published since that time (or was never published), then determining copyright expiration may be difficult and require the aid of legal counsel. Some works that you might anticipate to be in the public domain, such as Disney's *Steamboat Willie* (1928), are still copyrighted, while others that would not be expected to be found in the public domain, such as the 1963 film *McLintock!* starring John Wayne and Maureen O'Hare and which was determined to be in the public domain as early as 1994, can be used freely.

For some educational contexts, public domain can be very useful. Courses on classical literature, for instance, can draw upon centuries of creative works from resources like Project Gutenberg or Librivox without concern for copyright or licensing. However, this same freedom is not available to fields that rely upon more modern creative works. Thus, e-learning professionals should recognize differences between the fields they serve and consider how public domain works may be a tenable solution for some.

Fair Use

If you must use others' copyrighted materials in your own e-learning products, the safest solution is to seek written permission from the copyright holder and (if necessary) to pay required licensing fees for using them. An e-learning leader's responsibility is to ensure that those are their institution are abiding by appropriate fair use principles. If your intended use prevents this from being a viable solution, then you must consider how your intended use aligns with the four criteria of fair use. You should also consider the risks and benefits of including the materials, because even if your intended use aligns well with fair use requirements, this does not prevent the copyright holder from taking legal action against you. In the end, fair use in specific cases can only be determined by a judge, so the best you can do is to make sure that you have a strong case for fair use and limit your risks.

While the legal implications of violating fair use are serious, there is a safeguard for nonprofit organizations. If nonprofit organizations are sued for copyright infringement and are found to be guilty, they are not responsible for financial damages to the copyright holder *if and only if* they had reasonable grounds for believing their use was fair (U.S. Code Title 17 504(c)2). This means that nonprofit organizations and their employees have protection against financial copyright-related damages if they reasonably and intentionally apply the four factors of fair use. For this reason, before using copyrighted materials without permission, e-learning professionals in nonprofit institutions should document why they believe their use should be considered fair (under the four criteria) as reasonable justification. If, however, these same individuals and institutions blatantly violate copyright knowing that their use would not reasonably be considered fair, then this protection would not apply.

As stated at the outset, the purpose and scope of this chapter is not to provide legal advice, as the authors are not qualified to do so. Rather, for clarification and guidance, e-learning professionals should seek counsel from a competent professional, especially when using materials under the fair use clause. The information provided in this chapter merely gives e-learning professionals a baseline of knowledge necessary for recognizing the importance of these issues and helping them to understand which questions to ask. If you are employed by an institution, you should follow the institutional policies provided to you related to fair use, because such policies are often put into place to ensure that a reasonable defense can be made if a lawsuit were filed. Ultimately, if you are going to be sued for copyright infringement, you want your institution to be on your side, and one way to ensure this is by abiding by the guidelines that institutional legal counsel provides.

Open Licensing

When using materials that have been openly licensed, it is essential to abide by provided restrictions. After all, even openly licensed works are still copyrighted. If specified, works must be shared-alike or attributed to the author. There are times when works may not be used for commercial purposes or derivatives of the works may be restricted. Failure to abide by these restrictions constitutes copyright violation. There can be a litigious risk in using these resources if they are misused. Although legal implications in these cases are not as clearly defined as traditional violations of copyright, there is a contractual obligation to abide by license specifications when using any resources released under a Creative Commons or other open license. e-Learning leaders are in a position to both advise proper use of openly licensed resources, and to aid those at their institution should they decide to use open licenses on their own work, when and if appropriate.

In addition, a valuable way to contribute to the body of knowledge and to perpetuate the ongoing creation of knowledge and free exchange of ideas is to release the resources that you create under open licenses as well. Releasing a resource to the community under a Creative Commons license can allow your materials to easily be shared and improve accessibility to a wide variety of educators. This provides great pedagogical and administrative benefits to other e-learning professionals, because it makes their job of seeking copyright permission and determining fair use much easier. Additionally, time and cost savings arising from the use of OER can be reallocated to supporting educators and e-learning professionals in the process of adapting and remixing resources, making them perfectly suited for their specific contexts. e-Learning leaders can encourage those at their institutions to use Creative Commons licenses on the works they release to others, as well as advise on best practices and license choices should those they are working with decide that an open license is appropriate for them.

Conclusion

All the nuances of copyright, fair use, public domain, and open licensing may be difficult for the e-learning professional to understand. As educators, we wrote this chapter as a means for giving voice to our own navigation of various legal and ethical requirements while making recommendations for effective practice to others. The contents of this chapter are not meant to be taken as legal advice but rather as suggested areas for further exploration, because understanding copyright is necessary for those working with educational resources, especially for those working primarily online. The constraints of copyright exist to ensure the livelihood of those creating original works. By automatically applying copyright, those who are creating resources that we often use for teaching and learning are motivated to continue disseminating knowledge through their works. The life of copyright is not exhaustive and after appropriate time has passed, creative works fall into the public domain, and these resources can be used without restriction. Some individuals or entities may even choose to release their materials into the public domain and relinquish copyright before the life of the work has expired. There are times as well, when copyrighted materials may be used for educational purposes under the allowance of fair use. Fair use is ill-defined, and considerations need to be made regarding whether or not the work is truly being used fairly. A way to avoid some of the legal complexities of copyright is the use and release of materials under open licenses. Through Creative Commons licenses, e-learning professionals can select and release resources that may be widely disseminated with only a few restrictions. By understanding these various concepts at a foundational level, we hope that e-learning professionals can approach the creation and dissemination of course materials in a manner that is legal, ethical, and open to sharing, thereby realizing the promise and purpose of copyright and ensuring the ongoing growth and dissemination of knowledge.

For More Information

Creative Commons Legal Code. (n.d.). Retrieved April 15, 2016, from https://creativecommons.org/licenses/by-nc/4.0/legalcode

Harper, G. K. (2007). Copyright crash course. Retrieved from http://copyright.lib.utexas.edu/

Kimmons, R. (2015). Copyright crash course for teachers. Retrieved from http://iptla.byu.edu/courses/copyright_crash_course_for_teachers

References

Penguin Group (USA) Inc. v. American Buddha, 4:13-cv-02075-JGZ (D. Ariz). (2015).

TCA Television Corp. et al v. McCollum et al., 1:2015cv04325 1 (S.D. N.Y.) (2015).

U.S. Copyright Office. (n.d.). Retrieved April 15, 2016, from http://www.copyright.gov/.

A Framework for Aligning Campus Data with Accreditation Requirements

Cheryl A. Murphy

Abstract As an e-learning leader you are responsible for gathering and presenting data that demonstrate your online activities meet or exceed accreditation standards. However, understanding what evidence is needed and locating information that satisfies accreditation requirements can be challenging. This chapter provides assistance by offering a framework to guide and align your data gathering efforts with key accreditor concerns. Within the data framework eight core categories are identified (context, policies, infrastructure, resources, support, curriculum, faculty, and students), each broken into subcomponents. Information that is of highest interest to accreditors or that receives more intense reviewer scrutiny is presented within each subcomponent section, providing you with the information needed to focus and prioritize your data gathering efforts. This information is then used within the data framework to illustrate specific questions that can be asked and identify potential data sources you may consider within each core area. Thus, after reading this chapter you should be more familiar with key accreditation concerns, which will improve your ability to align your campus data gathering efforts with accreditor expectations and requirements.

Keywords E-learning leader • Higher education • Accreditation • Data framework

Decision-Making Guidance

This chapter examines components relative to distance education that must be understood by higher education leadership to effectively prepare for accreditation reviews. It will help you make decisions about how to organize, prioritize, and gather data associated with the many components of online learning on your campus. This will allow you and your campus to address accreditation requirements in a more informed, thorough, and strategic manner. More specifically, after reading this chapter you should be able to:

C.A. Murphy (✉)
University of Arkansas, Fayetteville, AR 72701, USA
e-mail: cmurphy@uark.edu

© Association for Educational Communications and Technology 2018   169
A.A. Piña et al. (eds.), *Leading and Managing e-Learning*, Educational
Communications and Technology: Issues and Innovations,
https://doi.org/10.1007/978-3-319-61780-0_13

- Organize the components of online efforts on your campus into one of eight key framework areas: context, policies, infrastructure, resources, support, curriculum, faculty, and students
- Recognize what accreditors are most interested in knowing relative to each of the eight framework areas
- Identify specific data questions and sources on your campus that can be used to address key accreditor concerns

What You Need to Know

Jung and Latchem (2012) state the obvious when they assert that accreditation is not the most engaging of subjects, and some in academe consider it to be nothing more than a necessary evil (CHEA, 2007). As a result of these views many administrators face accreditation with trepidation, but much of that fear and anxiety stems from "the unknown." The more familiar you are with the expectations associated with the accreditation process, the easier it is to demonstrate to evaluators that your institution is effectively meeting requirements. However, it can be time consuming and confusing attempting to decipher accreditation regulations as they apply to online academic programming. "Numerous standards, criteria, guidelines, and benchmarks have been developed by accrediting bodies, institutes, consortiums, and trade associations at the national, regional, and state levels for distance learning in higher education" (Southard & Mooney, 2015, p. 56), and weeding through them to determine the data your campus should gather can be a challenge.

If you struggle to understand the relationship between accreditation regulations and your online initiatives, you are not alone. In attempts to provide clarity, researchers have recently completed extensive reviews of accreditation requirements and standards related to distance learning. Keil and Brown's (2014) work specifically examines accreditation policies relative to distance education, while Southard and Mooney's (2015) research focuses on a compilation of quality assurance standards for online learning. Both of these publications, as well as previous significant works by Jung and Latchem (2012), O'Brien (2013), Seok (2007), and Shelton and Saltsman (2005), identify key online activities that are evaluated during accreditation reviews.

While the aforementioned works do a great job of clarifying accreditation requirements and quality standards, what they fail to provide is a meaningful framework that can be used by e-learning administrators to guide specific data gathering activities. This chapter fills this gap by distilling findings from these extensive reviews into a general "data framework" consisting of eight core data gathering categories: context, policies, infrastructure, resources, support, curriculum, faculty, and students. These core areas are prevalent throughout the previous research reviews, and all are critical to the successful implementation of your online learning initiatives. Therefore it should not be surprising that these eight areas are of keen interest to accreditors, and each category will be addressed in this chapter.

To facilitate your understanding of this data framework and how it can support your accreditation efforts, each of the eight core areas are broadly introduced below, then broken into appropriate subcomponent sections. A brief description of key accreditation considerations as well as areas that fall under more intense scrutiny are provided for each section. This is followed by tables that offer suggestions on questions to ask and potential data sources for each section, which can assist in your data gathering efforts. Please note that this chapter and framework is not meant to be an exhaustive list of all possible data considerations for accreditation. Rather, its purpose is to provide you, an e-learning leader, with a general structure (i.e., data framework) by which you can organize your thinking and prioritize your data gathering efforts relative to accreditation and your online learning activities. With that caveat let's begin our exploration of the data framework.

Context

The first component within the data framework involves consideration of the broad and overarching context of your campus. Accreditors will examine your distance learning activities from a macro level, seeking to confirm that your online activities fit within the institutional context, mission, vision, and purpose (Keil & Brown, 2014). You must be able to demonstrate that your online learning initiatives are appropriate to the context of your campus, support the mission, and help the institution fulfil its intended purpose. At a minimum accreditors want to see direct connections between your online endeavors and the institutional mission, but they will also look for evidence of involvement in core mission-centric activities such as campus planning and governance.

Mission

While it is not necessary that the mission statement for your campus mention distance or online education specifically, it is critical that you are able to articulate to accreditors how your online efforts support the mission and purpose of your institution. To do this you must have a firm understanding of the online programs and services you offer, and the role these online activities play in moving the campus forward. Period. As the e-learning advocate and leader for your campus you should be able to articulate this with little need for supporting data.

Planning

In addition to showing that your online activities support the mission and purpose, institutional recognition of the importance of and support for distance education should also be presented to accreditors. This can be accomplished by demonstrating that your online efforts are embedded within the campus planning processes and guiding documents for your institution. In particular, accreditors are interested in seeing evidence that online activities are mentioned in things such as strategic plans, multi-year budgets, and infrastructure or facilities plans. In other words, it is important to show reviewers that distance education is integrated into the core planning processes of your campus, not an "add-on" or afterthought.

Governance

Another way to illustrate that online activities are embedded within the context and culture of a campus is through participation in governance structures. Evaluators expect to see an appropriate level of oversight of online activities, including the appointment of an e-learning leader such as yourself. Participation of that e-learning leader and his/her staff in various levels of governance lets accreditors know that the campus values, respects, and understands the contributions of online learning activities to the institution.

Policies

We will continue our exploration of the data framework with a discussion of policies. Policies of all sorts are of great interest to accreditors; they want to see that institutions offer distance education programs that are well maintained, staffed, and supported, and they expect administrators to create policies that ensure this occurs (Southard & Mooney, 2015). They are also required to confirm that your institution abides by federal and state regulations as part of their accreditation responsibilities. Consequently, they are eager to see evidence that (1) you are in compliance with all relevant external policies, and (2) the institution has created and abides by appropriate internal policies. Specific policy data that are of most interest to accreditors are explored below, but be forewarned: Although this is the longest section presented within this chapter, even with its current length it does not represent a comprehensive list of the many policies that should be considered by the e-learning leader.

External

The key thing an e-learning leader must understand relative to external policies is that these are not optional data areas; evidence must be presented to accreditors that demonstrates your adherence to all federal and state regulations. Noncompliance or a lack of data can lead to fines, loss of Title IV funding or accreditation, lawsuits, and other unpleasant repercussions that you want to avoid at all costs. Thus, it is crucial that data are collected to confirm your campus is in compliance with all policies applicable to distance education.

External policies that apply to distance education occur at the state and federal levels. At the state level you must provide records illustrating your online degree programs have been approved by your state higher education board. You must also show procurement of state authorizations to provide academic programming within each state in which you enroll online students, either through individual state approvals or via agreements such as the State Authorization Reciprocity Agreements (SARA). Rest assured that accreditors will ask you to provide evidence of your state authorizations, so be prepared with data in this area.

A bit more encompassing than state policies, federal policies that must be followed include everything from Family Educational Rights and Privacy Act (FERPA) compliance to how your institution assigns credit hours. While space limitations prevent an in-depth review of each federal regulation, there are a few policy areas that will garner more attention than others during an accreditation visit. Due to increased federal scrutiny, reviewers will pay close attention to your credit hour calculations, student verification processes, transfer policies, contractual/consortial partnerships, and default rates. Also, because Title IV funds are involved, accreditors will want to see proof that there are distinctions within your online distance and correspondence courses as required by the Electronic Code of Federal Regulations Definition 600.2. Again, you must demonstrate that you are in compliance with all federal policies, but those listed above will receive closer examination by accreditors than others. It is also recommended that you or someone you appoint diligently monitor federal regulations, as the issues and rules do change.

Internal

As indicated above, external compliance is critical and mandatory. As a result, accreditors will expect to see an alignment between your internal policies and the aforementioned external requirements. In other words, evaluators will seek to verify that your internal policies related to areas such as copyright, credit transfer, and credit hour assignments both support and promote adherence to the external regulations.

Internal policies that support external regulations are often easy for an e-learning leader to locate and share with accreditors because they are published in documents such as the catalog of studies and student handbook. Conversely, other internal policies that directly impact online learning endeavors, such as faculty workloads or compensation for teaching online courses, can be more difficult to find. Campus policies must be published, but colleges, departments, and programs can adopt policies relative to online learning that may or may not get circulated. This means you will need to communicate with programs, departments, and colleges to identify all existing internal policies that relate to online activities.

Once you identify all existing internal policies applicable to online learning, you may find that there are multiple or conflicting policies across campus, between colleges, and amongst departments and programs. The goal is to identify all internal policies so you may begin to address inconsistencies, conflicts, and gaps before an accreditation evaluator identifies them for you. As a potential guidepost, areas where accreditors tend to look for and find inconsistencies include policies associated with faculty issues such as tenure/promotion, faculty workload, teaching compensation, faculty training requirements; student issues such as satisfactory academic progress, complaint processes, and attendance policies; and curriculum issues related to course development, curriculum approvals, and course scheduling. Through this policy review process you will not only gather a list of all internal policies you can share with accreditors, but you also afford yourself the opportunity to review your policies for alignment and consistency.

Infrastructure

The next area for consideration within the data framework is a category identified as "infrastructure." While this term can mean many things, for the purposes of this chapter infrastructure is defined as the technologies and electronic systems needed to support online learning. McCarthy and Samors (2009) note that online learning programs need consistent and sufficient technological resources to succeed, and accreditors will want to see evidence that you have such systems and resources in place. The paramount and overarching component of all infrastructure areas is security, but other features such as capacity, functionality, compatibility, stability, availability, and integration are also examined during accreditation reviews. As an e-learning leader you will want to establish that all of your systems are secure, and that all technologies effectively support your online initiatives. This includes your network and learning management system (LMS), student information system (SIS), and instructional hardware and software.

Network and LMS

The most important things to consider relative to the network and LMS include security, capacity, reliability, and stability. First and foremost, both the network and the LMS must be secure such that access to either of these tools can only be obtained through appropriate institutional approvals. Keeping data within the network and the LMS secure is critical, and although this may be the purview of your information technology (IT) office, accreditors will want assurance that data pathways and systems used in your online endeavors are secure. Beyond security, evaluators will want to know that these core components are both reliable and stable, and may ask to view statistics on down time to confirm that these critical elements are available when needed. Lastly, the capacity of these systems must not only meet the needs of current online efforts, but should also be scalable so that they can effectively support these efforts over time.

Student Information System

Another system that must also be both scalable and secure is the SIS. Data security is of the upmost importance for this system, but other areas of consideration that may be explored by reviewers include systems integration, data sharing, and reporting capabilities. Depending on the scale of your online learning activities, integration between your SIS, LMS, and other core technology resources such as retention, advising, scheduling, and financial software can be critical. As such, accreditors may inquire into the ability of the campus SIS to share information with other systems in a manner that effectively supports your online efforts.

Hardware and Software

Unlike the broad systems listed above, the hardware and software used within online programs or activities can differ. Because of this, areas that evaluators want to learn more about include the availability, accessibility, and compatibility of the hardware and software required of students. This can include everything from course-specific software to the use of electronic textbooks. More specifically, of recent concern to accreditors and the federal government are the student costs associated with degree completion. As an e-learning leader you will want to have an understanding of what is currently required of students within your online offerings, and demonstrate to evaluators that you and your campus are working to ensure online student costs for hardware and software are reasonable and appropriate.

Resources

The next important area of consideration within the data framework relates to institutional costs, and includes an examination of both the financial and human resources needed to effectively support online learning. As respondents in McCarthy and Samors's (2009) report indicate, administrators are consistently seeking more reliable and stable revenue models to sustain online endeavors; accreditors will be interested in knowing how your online activities are financed. Similarly, they will want to know that the institution is providing sufficient human resources to support all facets of your online efforts.

Financial

The value an institution places on any initiative can be assessed with the examination of one document: the budget. Allocation of financial resources in multi-year budgets is the clearest indicator an institution can provide that online initiatives are viewed as a vital activity. Additionally, implementation of an appropriate funding model is also critical in demonstrating the financial stability of online activities. The key is to demonstrate to accreditors that the model in use at your institution has the ability to support current and sustain future online endeavors. In this regard, of particular interest to evaluators will be current and predicted revenues and costs, as well as information regarding cost sharing or contractual/consortial partnerships that may impact revenue allocations.

Human

In addition to demonstrating that finances are sufficient to support online initiatives the e-learning leader must also show that the campus is appropriately staffed to support online activities. This can include obvious contributors such as instructional designers or marketers who are dedicated full time to online learning endeavors, but it also includes campus personnel who contribute a half, quarter, or even an eighth of their work day to support online learning. As examples, staff from accounting, financial aid, and the registrar's office aid online students with administrative tasks, while personnel in the testing office, counseling services, and the library offer various levels of support to online students. Exactly who contributes to your online endeavors, how much, and in what ways are things that accreditors will seek to understand, and you should be prepared to share that information.

Support

The fifth data framework area is derived from the financial and human resources mentioned in the previous section. These items work together to provide specific support services to both students and faculty. These supports can include academic, administrative, technical, and pedagogical assistance, and Southard and Mooney (2015) identify support for students and faculty as vital to the success of online activities. This is echoed in various distance learning guidelines where the incorporation of support for students and faculty is labeled a necessity (C-RAC, 2011; Shelton & Saltsman, 2005). Thus, the e-learning leader must consider what student and faculty support services are offered to ensure online students and faculty have the assistance needed to be successful.

Student

As with on-campus students, online students need to be supported in numerous ways. Your institution should provide them administrative assistance with admissions, financial aid, and registration, while academically they should have access to a plethora of resources including but not limited to the library, tutoring, advising, counseling, proctoring, and technical assistance. There are too many student support services to mention, but as a general rule of thumb you should consider the support that is traditionally provided to on-campus students (i.e., bookstore, financial counselors, time management workshops) and work to demonstrate to accreditors that you offer those same supports to your online students.

Faculty

Just as online students need support, so too do faculty who teach online. While some of these supports mirror student necessities, such as the need for technical assistance and library access, other areas are unique to faculty. Specifically, faculty members who teach online should be provided with support and training related to pedagogy, media development, instructional design, and assessment. Demonstrating to reviewers that faculty assistance is supplied in these areas will work to assure evaluators that faculty have the help they need during the design and delivery of online instruction.

Curriculum

The next important area of consideration within the data framework is labeled "curriculum," but actually involves broad oversight of online academic programs. The integrity of online programs is paramount and institutions must demonstrate that they systematically evaluate online academic programs in relation to curriculum, rigor, learning goals, and student outcomes (O'Brien, 2013). This means that the e-learning leader must have a firm grasp of the types of academic offerings provided, the requirements associated with these offerings, and the assessments that are incorporated to demonstrate the success of these online courses and programs.

Offerings

Any e-learning leader should be able to identify which online degree programs, certifications, and courses are offered within his or her institution, but sharing this information with accreditors will not be enough. Evaluators will also be interested in knowing more about your targeted online offerings, particularly if they include dual or concurrent credit courses which have come under close scrutiny of late. Likewise, they will want assurance that students who graduate from your certificate programs meet the federal requirements for gainful employment, which is a relatively new regulation. Lastly, anticipate that the length of your online courses will be examined. In particular, accelerated courses will be closely inspected. As the e-learning leader you will want to ensure that you have data to show you are in compliance with dual/concurrent credit regulations, can satisfy gainful employment requirements, and can clearly demonstrate that students within accelerated courses achieve the same outcomes as those in more traditional 8, 10, or 16-week courses.

Requirements

Similar to ensuring accelerated classes are appropriate, the e-learning leader must demonstrate that degree requirements for all online programs are suitable and have been approved by the proper academic units via a program approval process. This is particularly important to accreditors if curricular materials are purchased or generated outside of the institution. Other critical areas of concern include documenting credit or clock hours in a manner that is fitting for the degrees awarded, and demonstrating that suitable transfer policies are in place. Because both of these items relate to federal compliance, they will be closely reviewed by evaluators. An additional Title IV federal regulation of importance to accreditors involves confirmation that your "distance" courses include substantial interaction. Reviewers will seek to verify that your online courses adhere to the federal definitions of distance and correspondence courses, so you should be prepared to offer data that illustrate compliance with this key regulation.

Assessment

It is not enough to demonstrate that your online programs have obtained appropriate academic approvals and comply with federal requirements; accreditors will also expect to see evidence that illustrates students within these online programs are successfully achieving the intended academic outcomes. This means that your online courses and degree programs should have clearly articulated outcomes, and these outcomes must be measured in an appropriate manner. At the program level this may involve obtainment of specialized accreditations or participation in internal program review processes, either of which can provide evidence that students are meeting the program goals. At the online course level this can include traditional assessment methods, but may also involve alternative assessments such as competency-based or direct assessment practices. Because regulations surrounding alternative assessments are changing rapidly, specific suggestions to meet these requirements are not offered within this chapter. However, you should be prepared to demonstrate both how and why these alternative assessments are appropriate if your institution decides to tie one of these non-traditional assessment paths to the awarding of course credits.

Faculty

The seventh component within the data framework considers the faculty who design and deliver online instruction. It can be difficult to remain abreast of the demographics, credentials, and employment status for all faculty within your online courses and programs. However, federal regulations and an intense renewed focus by regional accrediting agencies on faculty qualifications make it essential that the e-learning leader track each of these areas closely.

Demographics

Affirmative action requires institutions to recruit and advance diverse faculty based on race, gender, and disabilities. As an e-learning leader you must be able to report to evaluators how your institution complies with this regulation. Additionally, reviewers may be interested in knowing the level of diversity you have within your faculty regarding academic rank (assistant, associate, full professor) and years of experience. The demographics of your online faculty can speak volumes to evaluators, not only in relation to diversity but also with regard to the stability the faculty bring to the online programs in which they teach.

Credentials

In addition to diversity, accreditors need assurance that faculty are appropriately credentialed to teach their assigned online courses. Recent changes to regulations have placed this particular faculty area under extreme scrutiny, particularly for faculty who teach in concurrent or dual enrollment online programs. The gist is that you should be prepared to present data that prove all faculty who teach online are credentialed (academically or experientially), and they are teaching in a subject area appropriate to their credentials.

Employment Status

In addition to tracking credentials, knowing how much faculty teach has also become critical. Reviewers will be interested in seeing that your institution is maintaining an acceptable balance between full time and part-time faculty, and that their workloads are appropriate. However, they will be more interested in confirming your institution abides by the Affordable Care Act. This federal regulation requires institutions to provide benefits to employees, including part-time or adjunct faculty, who work 30 h or more per week. Meeting this requirement is not an option, and evaluators will look for evidence of compliance throughout your campus and within your online activities.

Students

The final data framework component that should be considered involves students. In addition to understanding the demographics of enrolled online students, the e-learning leader needs to know about the processes utilized by your campus that serve to attract, monitor, and support students from first contact through successful degree completion. As well, the e-learning leader should be able to demonstrate that student integrity permeates each of these stages. Due to recent federal scrutiny, accreditors will be particularly interested in hearing about the recruitment, admissions, and retention processes that touch students from the initial point of contact through successful degree completion.

Recruitment and Admissions

Concerning the recruitment and admission of students into your online programs, a key duty of evaluators is to confirm that your advertising and marketing materials contain complete, up-to-date, and accurate program information. Similarly, you should be able to demonstrate that recruitment personnel are well versed in academic program requirements and trained on the regulations regarding misrepresentation found in the Program Integrity Rules passed in 2010. In addition to demonstrating that your recruitment practices are appropriate, you also want to show that proper admissions practices are followed. This can include sharing your admissions policies with accreditors, but data validating that the processes are followed will also be desired. Thus, you should be prepared to demonstrate that all admitted online students went through your admissions process, and are appropriately qualified per your institution's stated admission requirements.

Demographics

Once students are admitted, tracking them throughout the system is critical. It is important to have a firm grasp of the demographics of your online students. As expected, this includes consideration of the student population relative to gender, race, socioeconomic status, and age which can serve to answer diversity questions that reviewers may ask. However, also of importance to accreditors is seeing student enrollment patterns within and across academic programs, and by state locations (i.e., state authorization). Provision of this information offers reviewers a better understanding of the breadth, depth, and overall dispersion of students within your online degree programs.

Integrity

Regulators look to maintain the integrity of online education by curtailing online student fraud. More specifically, higher levels of scrutiny regarding both Title IV funds and academic integrity are of keen interest to accreditors and the government. Regulators assert that stronger oversight is needed to deter fraud rings that illegally obtain Title IV funds via distance education programs (U.S. Department of Education, Office of the Inspector General, 2014), and changes to federal regulation 602.17 (g) requires institutions to ensure that the student who enrolls is the same student who completes the work and receives academic credit. Because of intense federal scrutiny in both of these areas, accreditors will pay particular attention to the processes you use to prevent Title IV fraud and verify student identities. These are federal regulations that must be met, so data gathering in these two student-related areas is a necessity for you and your campus.

Success

As you work to gather information, do not overlook data associated with student success. Federal requirements mandate the public reporting of student success data such as graduation rates, retention rates, and gainful employment statistics. They also require each institution to offer students a formal complaint process by which students can report issues that may be impeding his or her success. You should assume that evaluators will examine the aforementioned rates and statistics, and in many cases accreditors will also request to view the student complaint log. Be prepared with data in all of these areas.

What You Can Do

As McCarthy and Samors (2009) have recognized, one of the issues in examining online learning is that it is not a "siloed" endeavor. Multiple units and entities are typically involved, which can make gathering the data needed to demonstrate the effectiveness of your efforts extremely difficult. Now that you have a framework that outlines key areas of interest to accreditors, you can begin formulating a plan to gather the data they are interested in reviewing. Vital to your plan will be understanding what questions to ask and whom to ask. While this process is contextual and will differ for each e-learning leader, the tables presented within this section are organized according to the data framework and offer general suggestions on where you may begin your data search within your campus.

Context

Data to address this particular area of the framework will primarily reside in campus-wide documents, plans, and committees. Specific questions that can serve as data prompts as well as potential data sources are presented in Table 1.

Policies

Ensuring you abide by external policies is critical, and there are serious ramifications for non-compliance. Similarly, internal policies are important as they demonstrate how the quality and effectiveness of online learning are maintained on your campus. Specific questions that can serve as policy data prompts as well as potential data sources are presented in Table 2.

Infrastructure

Consistent and sufficient technological infrastructure is critical, and data to demonstrate the adequacy of your infrastructure will primarily be located within IT services. Specific questions that can serve as data prompts as well as potential data sources are presented in Table 3.

Resources

Accreditors want to know that institutions have adequate financial and human resources to support online endeavors. Specific questions that can serve as data prompts as well as potential data sources for these resource areas are presented in Table 4.

Table 1 Data questions and potential sources related to context

Context	Questions to ask	Potential data sources
Mission	• In what ways do online endeavors support the campus mission?	• Published mission • List of all online endeavors
Planning	• Are online activities reflected in plans and budgets for campus, colleges, and programs?	• Strategic plans • Facilities plans • Multi-year budgets
Governance	• Is there adequate representation on key governance committees?	• Committee member lists • Meeting notes

Table 2 Data questions and potential sources related to policies

Policies	Questions to ask	Potential data sources
External (state)	• Who obtains state academic program approvals; how many programs are currently approved or in process? • Who handles our state authorization requests and where are we approved? • Are we a member of SARA or the State Authorization Network (SAN)? • How/where do we inform constituents of above approvals?	• Provost, Vice Provost for Academics, Deans, or Academic Programs office • Legal or compliance office • Listed on state websites • SARA website • SAN website • Student handbook, websites, recruitment materials
External (federal)	• Who is in charge of federal compliance? • How do we adhere to FERPA? • What student verification processes do we use? • How are we addressing ADA requirements? • Who handles copyright issues and education? • How do we calculate credit hours for online courses? • How do we ensure courses are correctly identified (distance vs. correspondence)?	• Legal or compliance office • SIS personnel • IT services experts • LMS administrator • Testing services • Director for ADA office • Library • Vice Provost for academics • Institutional research office • Registrar • Instructional designers • Definition or policy series
Internal	• What campus online learning policies support external policies? • What policies are unique to our campus? • Do colleges have individual policies? • Do departments have individual policies?	• Campus policy series • Student/faculty handbooks • Online learning policy series • Deans • Department and program heads

Table 3 Data questions and potential sources related to infrastructure

Infrastructure	Questions to ask	Potential data sources
Network and Learning Management System (LMS)	• How secure are the network and LMS? • What is the capacity of both, and are they scalable as we grow? • Are we nearing capacity? • How stable and reliable are both?	• IT services • Network administrator • LMS administrator • Usage data and network/LMS status reports
Student Information System (SIS)	• How secure is our SIS? • Does the SIS interface with the LMS? • What data can/does the SIS share? • What data reports can be generated?	• IT services • LMS administrator • SIS administrator • Institutional research
Hardware and Software	• What hardware and software are required of online students? • What are the extra costs to students?	• Faculty • Instructional designers • IT services

Table 4 Data questions and potential sources related to resources

Resources	Questions to ask	Potential data sources
Financial	• How are online initiatives integrated into the institutional budget? • What are the operational costs and revenues for all online activities? • How does our financial model support current and future activities? • Do we participate in any cost sharing? • Do we have any contractual or consortial agreements?	• Chief financial officer • Institutional budget • Budget office • Yearly financial reports • Multi-year budget for online • Strategic plan • Deans • Legal office • Memorandums (MOU's)
Human	• How many employees work specifically to support online efforts? • What campus areas provide staff support to online activities? • How much support do those staff member provide to online learning?	• E-learning leader • Human resources office • Provost's office • Organizational chart • Directors of support services • Supporting staff members

Table 5 Data questions and potential sources related to support

Support	Questions to ask	Potential data sources
Student	• What services related to admissions, financial aid, and registration are offered to online students? • What library support is offered? • What tutoring support is offered? • How are online students advised? • How are ADA accommodations handled for online students? • What technical support is offered? • What is the judicial process for online students?	• Admissions office • Financial aid office • Registrar • Library staff • Director of student support • Program coordinators • Director for ADA office • Compliance office • IT services or LMS support • Dean of students • Department heads or chairs
Faculty	• What pedagogical support is offered? • What faculty training is provided? • Who provides media development? • What instructional design support is given? • What assessment support is offered?	• Teaching support center • Training logs or certificates • Media services • Instructional designers • Faculty • Testing/proctoring services

Support

Online students and faculty must be supported by a wide array of administrative and academic resources. Specific questions that can serve as data prompts as well as potential data sources to help identify these resources are presented in Table 5.

Curriculum

The e-learning leader should understand the curricular requirements and assessments associated with approved online academic programs. Specific questions that can serve as curriculum data prompts as well as potential data sources are presented in Table 6.

Faculty

Remaining aware of the demographics, credentials, and workload of your online faculty is imperative. Specific questions that can serve as data prompts as well as potential data sources in each of these areas are presented in Table 7.

Students

It is important to know and understand your students and the processes utilized by your campus that serve to attract, monitor, and support them. Specific questions that can act as data prompts as well as potential data sources concerning these forms of student data are presented in Table 8.

Table 6 Data questions and potential sources related to curriculum

Curriculum	Questions to ask	Potential data sources
Offerings	• What online degree programs, certifications, and courses do we offer? • Do we offer dual enrollment or concurrent credit online courses? • What employment information do we gather on certificate students? • Do shorter duration courses require the same outcomes as longer counterparts?	• Catalog of studies • Provost • Outreach office • Enrollment reports • Graduate surveys • Foundations/alumni database • Instructional designers • Faculty
Requirements	• What approval process was used for our online degree programs? • What is our credit hour definition and how is this calculated? • What are our transfer policies? • How do we ensure substantial interaction occurs in online courses?	• Academic policy series • Course/programs committee • Vice provost for academics • Institutional research • Catalog of studies • Instructional designers • Faculty
Assessment	• Where are our program outcomes listed? • What accreditations or program reviews have our programs completed? • What course assessment practices do we use?	• Catalog of studies • Vice provost for academics • Deans/Associate Deans • Instructional designers • Faculty

Table 7 Data questions and potential sources related to faculty

Faculty	Questions to ask	Potential data sources
Demographics	• What are our faculty recruitment and hiring processes? • What is the diversity of our faculty in relation to Affirmative Action groups? • What are the faculty breakdowns relative to rank and experience?	• Provost and Deans • Human resources office • Diversity office • Affirmative action office • Institutional research office • Fact book or yearly reports
Credentials	• What faculty credentials do we require within our online programs? • What are the current credential levels of all online faculty?	• Human resources office • Deans/Associate Deans • Institutional research office • Vice provost of academics
Employment status	• What are the faculty breakdowns relative to full time and part-time? • What are our faculty workload policies and current workload assignments? • How do we prevent part-time faculty from working 30 or more hours weekly?	• Institutional research office • Deans/Associate Deans • Faculty handbook • Department heads or chairs • Human resources office • Employment policies

Table 8 Data questions and potential sources related to students

Students	Questions to ask	Potential data sources
Recruitment and admissions	• Who ensures our recruitment/marketing materials are accurate and complete? • Are recruiters trained on federal regulations? • What are our admissions requirements, policies, and processes? • What is the admissions process? • What are the admissions numbers for online programs?	• Marketing office • Recruitment office • Compliance office • Training office • Catalog of studies • Student handbook • Admissions office • Director/Dean of admissions • Institutional research office
Demographics	• What are the demographics of online students relative to race, gender, age? • What % of students get financial aid? • What is the pattern of online student enrollment by program over time? • What is the pattern of online student enrollment by location (state) over time?	• Institutional research office • Diversity office • Financial aid office • Enrollment reports • Program chairs • Enrollment office • Compliance office
Integrity	• What are our financial aid processes and how do we prevent fraud? • What student verification processes do we use campus-wide? • What verification processes do we use within courses?	• Financial aid office • Treasurer's office • IT services experts • LMS administrator • Faculty • Instructional designers
Success	• What are graduation rates (online, all)? • What are retention rates (online, all)? • What are we doing to improve our rates? • How are we tracking and reporting gainful employment data?	• Fact book or yearly reports • Graduation/retention office • Provost's office • Compliance office • Deans/Program chairs

Conclusion

As the e-learning leader for your campus you want and need accurate reporting. Having data relative to your online learning activities allows you to quickly illustrate that your online endeavors meet or exceed the expectations of accreditors. However, the data needed to satisfy accreditor concerns can be difficult to identify, let alone locate. This chapter has provided a general framework for this data gathering by first identifying eight core component areas, then breaking each area into subcomponents to further delineate and describe the types of information that is of highest interest to most accreditors. Once these areas were described, specific questions to ask in each area and potential data sources were provided. It is the hope of this author that the information and data framework provided within this chapter serves you well as you work to align your campus data gathering efforts with accreditor expectations and requirements.

For More Information

The accreditation information presented in this chapter is not inclusive of every area in which e-learning leaders need to gather data. However, it does offer a general framework, guiding questions, and potential data sources from which data gathering activities can begin. In addition to the data framework presented here, there are numerous websites and guides that can assist in the understanding of various accreditation requirements. A few of the most recognized non-accreditor sources of information are presented below.

Websites

American Council on Education (ACE) website: http://www.acenet.edu/Pages/default.aspx

Council for Higher Education Accreditation (CHEA) website: http://www.chea.org/default.asp

Higher Education Compliance Alliance (HECA) website: http://www.highered-compliance.org/matrix/

National Council for State Authorization Reciprocity Agreements (NC-SARA) website: http://nc-sara.org/

Western Cooperative for Educational Telecommunication (WCET) website: http://wcet.wiche.edu/

References

Council for Higher Education Accreditation (CHEA). (2007). Preparing for the self-study: The president's role. Retrieved from http://www.chea.org/pdf/Presidential_Guidelines_3.pdf

Council of Regional Accrediting Commissions (C-RAC). (2011). Interregional guidelines for the evaluation of distance education programs (online learning). Retrieved from http://www.msche.org/publications/Guidelines-for-the-Evaluation-of-Distance-Education-Programs.pdf

Jung, I., & Latchem, C. (2012). *Quality assurance and accreditation in distance education: Models, policies and research*. New York, NY: Routledge.

Keil, S., & Brown, A. (2014). Distance education policy standards: A review of current regional and national accrediting organizations in the United States. *Online Journal of Distance Learning Administration, 17*(3). Retrieved from https://www.westga.edu/~distance/ojdla/fall173/keil_brown173.html.

McCarthy, S. A., & Samors, R. J. (2009). *Online learning as a strategic asset, vol. 1: A resource for campus leaders*. Washington, DC: Association of Public and Land-grant Universities.

O'Brien, P. M. (2013). Accreditation: Assuring quality and fostering improvement. In M. G. Moore (Ed.), *Handbook of distance education* (pp. 481–492). New York, NY: Routledge.

Seok, S. (2007). Standards, accreditation, benchmarks, and guidelines in distance education. *Quarterly Review of Distance Education, 8*(4), 387–398.

Shelton, K., & Saltsman, G. (2005). *An administrator's guide to online education*. Greenwich, CT: Information Age Publishing.

Southard, S., & Mooney, M. (2015). A comparative analysis of distance education quality assurance standards. *Quarterly Review of Distance Education, 16*(1), 55–68.

U.S. Department of Education, Office of the Inspector General. (2014). *Semiannual Report to Congress, No. 68*. Washington, DC: U.S. Department of Education. Retrieved from https://www2.ed.gov/about/offices/list/oig/semiann/sar68.pdf.

Motivating Instructors and Administrators to Adopt e-Learning

Lauren Cifuentes, Rinki Suryavanshi, and Alexandra Janney

Abstract We submit here that by strategically identifying motivating tactics, higher education administrators can turn avoidance motivators into adoption motivators. University presidents, provosts, and deans who want to motivate instructors and other administrators on their campuses to adopt e-learning are well advised to be informed and vigilant regarding the beliefs and circumstances that interfere with adoption as well as motivations among those who adopt online offerings over time. We focus here on how instructors' motivation to provide students with online learning opportunities develops and why motivation changes for both instructors and administrators. Identifying what motivates instructors as well as administrators to either avoid or adopt e-learning provides us with the information we need to identify strategies that higher education leaders might employ to encourage campus-wide adoption.

Motivational tactics that leaders are advised to implement on their campuses are described below based upon literature review and experience in one regional university campus. If they hope to offer online programming, then leaders need to manage both avoidance of e-learning while encouraging adoption. Below we review the literature and our research findings regarding avoidance and adoption motivators for instructors and administrators. We provide separate toolkits of motivational tactics for instructors and administrators.

Keywords Administrator motivation for e-learning • Avoidance of e-learning • Barriers to e-learning • Continuity of learning • Distance learning strategies • e-Learning in higher education • Instructor readiness for e-learning • Instructor motivation for e-learning • Motivational strategies • Professional development • Systematic motivational design • Toolkits for e-learning

L. Cifuentes (✉) • R. Suryavanshi • A. Janney
Texas A&M University–Corpus Christi,
6300 Ocean Drive, Unit 5779, Corpus Christi, TX 78412, USA
e-mail: Lauren.cifuentes@tamucc.edu; rinki.suryavanshi@tamucc.edu;
alexandra.janney@tamucc.edu

© Association for Educational Communications and Technology 2018   189
A.A. Piña et al. (eds.), *Leading and Managing e-Learning*, Educational
Communications and Technology: Issues and Innovations,
https://doi.org/10.1007/978-3-319-61780-0_14

Decision-Making Guidance

This chapter will help you make decisions about:

- Tactics for motivating instructors in higher education to adopt e-learning
- Tactics for motivating administrators in higher education to adopt e-learning
- Strategic plans for e-learning

What You Need to Know

The primary purpose of this chapter is to help you implement a systematic motivational design process for e-learning adoption. Many university strategic plans include the mission that instructors are able to teach online from off campus. This mission is particularly important when a university campus' geographic location makes it vulnerable to hurricanes, earthquakes, or other disasters that might require mandated evacuation (Meyer & Wilson, 2011). Although online education has long been a possibility and continues to grow in demand, many universities have failed to tap its full potential to address continuity of learning in the event of campus closure (Schneckenberg, 2010). Along with addressing natural disasters, university administrators are recognizing the potential of e-learning to save campus space, grow enrollment, and address the need for affordable and sustainable approaches for students to obtain learning experiences and degrees (Beckem & Watkins, 2012).

However, a persistent barrier to adoption of e-learning is instructors' and administrators' beliefs that online delivery of instruction is not in the best interest of their students (Kowalczyk, 2014). Administrators who impact adoption include marketing officers, chief financial officers, chief information officers, vice presidents for research, vice presidents for compliance, deans, and department chairs across disciplines. We have found this belief to be the most significant obstacle to integration of online learning at both the course and program levels. Overcoming this avoidance motivator is an administrator's critical task if they want to successfully implement e-learning on their campuses.

The ARCS model of motivation for learning and performance (Keller, 2010) frames our suggestion to more deeply understand motivation for using online learning technologies among instructors and for supporting online learning among higher education administrators. Although there are several scholarly motivation theories in the literature, our literature review identifies John Keller's (2010) theory to be most useful when trying to identify ways to motivate educators to adopt e-learning. The guru of motivational instructional design, Keller identifies four key categories of measurable motivators: attention, relevance, confidence, and satisfaction. Gaining attention involves making e-learning stimulating and interesting. Perceived relevance involves instilling the belief that e-learning is valuable for the institution's success. Instilling confidence involves supporting stakeholders so that they believe they will succeed. And, instructor and administrator satisfaction is derived from both internal and external rewards. Keller asks, "How can we determine what motivational tactics to use and when to use them?" (p. vii). We also ask this question on our regional campus and use the ARCS model for categorizing both avoidance and adoption motivators.

Keller's theory provides guidance in the form of motivational design processes for diagnosing specific motivational problems and proposes that those who want to motivate others should take a systematic approach. "Motivation refers broadly to what people desire, what they choose to do, and what they commit to do," (p. 3). Instructors' and administrators' choices to adopt e-learning depend upon their expectations that online courses and programs can facilitate student success and that e-learning is a valuable solution to problems in higher education, such as limited access and ability to serve underrepresented populations. Such positive expectations and values are prerequisites for commitment to adopt e-learning. However, adoption of e-learning is not simply attitudinal; it involves time commitment and formulating a concrete plan as to when and how to accomplish the goal of building e-learning programs.

The systematic approach to instilling value in instructors for e-learning involves deeply understanding their attachment to instructional strategies in their current mode of face–face delivery. Given the instructional strategies to which they are so attached, a change agent can administer professional development (PD) in how e-learning might provide, and even improve upon, their instructional strategies. The systematic approach to instilling value in administrators involves identifying management strategies that they have adopted for institutional effectiveness. A change agent can provide suggestions for applying those strategies to address the mission of moving instructors online for increased effectiveness.

Turner and Patrick (2008) suggest that the most useful explanations regarding motivation are derived from a focus on how motivation develops and why it changes. We summarize our findings along with findings of other researchers to compile avoidance motivators and adoption motivators in order to identify catalytic tactics that we recommend to facilitate adoption of e-learning on your campuses. Ours is an Hispanic-serving institution in a large state system with approximately 12,000 students. The threat of hurricanes is an adoption motivator that no one should ignore. However, avoidance motivators exert their power, requiring systematic and systemic attention. Our goal is to provide you with tactics that we have applied or plan to apply that we believe can close the gap between the way things are and the way you would like for them to be regarding e-learning adoption on your campus.

Avoidance Motivators

A long line of literature describing barriers to e-learning adoption includes Muilenburg and Berge's (2001) identification of ten barriers to distance education. Subsequent research has validated their findings indicating that, although shifts toward adoption are in place and some barriers are less powerful than they were over a decade ago, avoidance motivators are still prevalent on campuses (Berge, 2013, Chen, 2009; Gutman, 2012; Loogma, Kruusvall & Ümarik, 2012; Neben, 2016; Wickersham & McElhany, 2010). The first barrier is administrative structure and policy. Lack of agreement regarding costs, tuition and fees, distribution of revenue, and scheduling among units within an institution can be problematic. The second barrier is slow organizational change. When processes are not in place, each step of the way takes time, from choosing which courses go online, to approval from regional accrediting agencies. The third barrier is lack of technical expertise, support, and infrastructure required for designing, developing, teaching, and implementing online courses and programs. The fourth barrier is concern that online courses lack sufficient social interaction and programs lack sufficient quality to support and sustain student success. This along with a fifth barrier identified by Muilenburg and Berge, evaluation/effectiveness, were the dominant avoidance motivators to be overcome for our campus to move forward with e-learning. A sixth barrier, lack of faculty compensation and time, is the avoidance motivator most commonly identified in the literature. It includes instructors' concern that developing and teaching online courses takes time away from research, thereby interfering with progress toward tenure and promotion. A seventh barrier, the threat of technology, has become a more significant barrier as instructors fear that MOOCS and master courses might supplant their courses. Some feel that their teaching competence, authority, and job security are threatened. Legal issues such as copyright, accessibility, use of open educational resources, intellectual property rights, and academic integrity provide an eighth barrier. A ninth barrier, access, has become less of a concern as learning technologies become more pervasive, particularly for instructors. However, given the goal of reaching underrepresented learners, access is still an issue for those in society's margins. The last and tenth barrier is student-support services that do not equal those for on-campus students.

Another relevant body of literature describes instructor beliefs that impact adoption of learning technologies. Most seminal is the work of Ertmer and Ottenbreit-Leftwich (2010) who explore the "necessary characteristics, or qualities, that enable instructors to leverage technology resources as meaningful pedagogical tools" (p. 255). They identify the following areas to be addressed through professional development: knowledge and skills, self-efficacy, pedagogical beliefs, and school/discipline culture.

To gain insight into the avoidance and adoption motivators on our campus we surveyed instructors ($n = 169/634$; 27%) and interviewed 29 administrators including the president, provost, vice presidents, deans, and department chairs. We applied the constant comparative method to qualitative findings and established descriptive statistics for the quantitative data. Table 1 briefly summarizes the avoidance motivators that saturated the qualitative findings categorized according to the ARCS. In the current higher education environment, e-learning has instructors' attention. They know how significant it is. However, sense of irrelevance, lack of confidence, and dissatisfaction interfere with their adoption. We find that instructors who avoid offering courses online believe that it is less effective for students and too difficult

Table 1 Beliefs and concerns expressed on our campus that interfere with adoption (avoidance motivators)

	Avoidance
Attention	None indicated
Relevance	I would prefer teaching face–face than teaching online
Confidence	Online teaching is harder than face–face teaching
	Web-conferences are difficult to implement
	Teaching blended or fully online is more difficult than I would like it to be
	Some of Blackboard's features are difficult to implement
	Students can cheat more easily in online classes than face–face classes
Satisfaction	I am not sufficiently compensated for online teaching (release time, student help, stipend, etc.)
	Using online tools in my teaching will not improve my chances for getting tenure and promotion

for them. They also feel that they will not be sufficiently compensated for their effort should they choose to develop or teach online.

Interviews with administrators reveal that avoidance motivators include instructors' perceptions that e-learning takes too much time and that they are not adequately compensated. However, administrators often do not have enough resources to positively address instructors' wishes for compensation. In addition, administrators do not know where funds might come from for recruitment and marketing once programs are developed. Many believe that although online instruction is widely adopted elsewhere, it does not meet the needs of our particular students who benefit most from a great deal of face-to-face instruction.

Adoption Motivators

Motivation to adopt e-learning on a campus develops in administrators as they see that their institution will have a broader reach, increase enrollment, be better prepared for continuity of business, and increase income as online offerings increase. Adoption of e-learning is dictated by numerous factors such as organizational support, adequate infrastructure, and perceived ease and usefulness of technology, to name a few. Among these factors, studies assert that instructors will continue to play a vital role in campus readiness for e-learning (Volery & Lord, 2000). Change theorists such as Fullan (1993) recommend that adoption can be encouraged through instructor advocacy by actively engaging faculty in the change process. Rogers (2003) emphasizes that for positive change to occur instructors have to perceive a relative advantage; they have to see that e-learning might be an improvement over face–face delivery. They also have to perceive that e-learning aligns with their current values and needs, is easy to use, and can be adopted on a trial basis and be easily rejected or adopted based on that trial experience. Most significantly on our campus, and in line with Roger's recommendations, we have found that when instructors experience or observe positive results with e-learning they feel comfortable adopting. Positive experience is the ultimate catalyst for change.

In a meta-analysis of motivators to teach in distance education, Gannon-Cook et al. (2009) report that findings in three studies provide evidence that faculty are inherently motivated to teach online. A fourth study indicated that while faculty members are committed to helping students, they want their own needs to be met through incentives provided by administrators. Gannon-Cook's (2010) two overarching recommendations for motivating e-learning adoption on campuses are: "establishment of project teams that involve a variety of campus support professionals" and "authentic administrative participation" (p. 157).

As stated before, instructors on our campus report that e-learning has gained their attention. In their surveys, means of Likert scale questions established that, as a whole, they agree with the following statements: "Teaching online is concrete enough to keep my attention on it"; "Online teaching is interesting and appealing"; "Online learning tools such as discussion boards and online assessments catch my eye and interest me"; "I hear so much about distance education that the subject has my attention"; "I am curious and want to learn more about online teaching"; and "Being able to teach online interests me."

They also find e-learning to be relevant: "Students can learn as much in online classes as in face–face classes"; "Fully online teaching provides ample opportunities for interaction between students and their instructors"; "I feel students are ready to learn in blended or fully online classes"; "Stories and examples about successful blended or fully online courses encourage me to teach online"; "Online teaching is relevant to my interests"; "I listen to stories of how teaching blended or fully online can be important for our students"; "I want to be in step with trends in higher education by teaching a blended or fully online class"; "I believe that teaching online can be a rewarding experience"; and "It is worthwhile knowing how to teach online."

Instructors have confidence in e-learning: "I have time for blended or fully online teaching"; "I have confidence that when I develop a blended or fully online course it will be well evaluated by students"; "I am disciplined about making progress when developing online course materials"; "I am confident that my students will learn from my online instruction"; "I have confidence that when I develop a blended or fully online course, if I submit it for review, it would be well reviewed by administrators"; "I have technological expertise to develop and teach a blended or fully online class"; "I am disciplined about online presence while teaching"; "I can apply what I already know about teaching to develop online courses"; "I have confidence that, given the opportunity, I would teach well online"; and "All the information about well-designed online courses make it easy to remember, pick-out, and include important design features."

And development and teaching online courses provides instructors with satisfaction: "I enjoy teaching online so much that I want to do it more"; "I feel rewarded for my efforts to use online tools in my teaching"; "Fully online teaching provides ample opportunities for interaction among students"; "I enjoy online course development"; "I enjoy teaching online"; "Developing online course materials gives me a feeling of accomplishment"; "Participating in distance education expands my

Table 2 Catalytic tactic to gain instructors' attention

Avoidance motivator	Catalytic tactic	Adoption motivator
Insufficient evidence of student success	Gain instructor buy-in. Provide research findings indicating no significant difference between online and F-F outcomes, superior outcomes from online courses, and design features that lead to student success	Students can be successful in online courses

professional opportunities"; "Teaching a course online successfully is important to me"; "Online course development gives me satisfaction"; and "Teaching online gives me satisfaction."

We find that positive experience is the ultimate catalyst for adoption given that instructors care most about student success. Motivation to teach online develops in instructors as they become convinced through experience that there is added value for students over face-to-face instruction. One instructor reported that "hearing from students" is what convinced him or her to adopt. Another expresses that "I find I have better direct contact with students [in online courses than in face–face courses]." Confidence builds as instructors find that they are "better at giving specific comments regarding assignments and tests online." And they are satisfied that "[online delivery] enables students to engage more fully with course materials, assignments, with [the instructor], and with one another." The ultimate motivator is expressed by one faculty member who reported that "my motivation is related to enhanced-learning." In addition, as instructors gain experience with online teaching, they find that ultimately it can provide them with more convenience and flexibility so that they can conduct research in their fields.

But positive experiences with e-learning do not just happen. They must be strategically planned for by the institution and only happen when faculty are provided with quality professional development, course development support, and ongoing technical and pedagogical support.

What You Can Do

In order to motivate instructors and administrators to participate in or promote e-learning, we have to identify what interferes with positive attention, perceived relevance, confidence, and satisfaction. By identifying such avoidance motivators, distance learning administrators can design tactics to reframe them as adoption motivators. We have identified some avoidance motivators, motivational tactics, and adoption motivators for instructors below (see Tables 2, 3, 4, and 5).

Implementation of the above catalytic tactics to motivate instructors depends upon the buy-in and leadership of administrators. Without such buy-in a campus cannot move forward to offer e-learning. We identify some avoidance motivators,

Table 3 Catalytic tactic to contribute to instructors' sense of relevance

Avoidance motivator	Catalytic tactic	Adoption motivator
Unsuitable for our region's student population	Arrange mentoring relationships among instructors who have designed effective, well-attended, and well-evaluated courses and instructors who doubt the positive impacts of online courses	Online courses provide convenience and flexibility, meeting the needs of our students
Inapplicable for my discipline	Provide positive examples of successful, discipline-specific online courses and instructors	Online courses are applicable for my discipline
Inadequate course and program quality	Provide PD in alignment, instructor presence, interaction, and student engagement	Online courses and programs have high quality
Lack of social interaction with peers or instructors	Provide PD in use of tools and strategies to support learner–interface, learner–content, learner–support, learner–learner, and learner–instructor interactions	Online tools create opportunities for robust interaction
Concerns for academic integrity	Provide PD in campus resources, ways to address authentication, LMS options, site-based and software proctoring; and design solutions such as project-based, problem-based, and case-based learning that lead to unique student products	Online environments support academic integrity
Concerns about time investment	Provide PD in managing instructor workload: how to design a manageable course and provide manageable supports, teaching strategies, and time allocation strategies	Online teaching provides flexibility and allows time for attending conferences, conducting field research, and teaching according to my own schedule
Students lack access	Collect access information in the application process. Provide PD in designing courses for access with mobile devices. Help students identify public, networked computer labs	Students have access
Added expense for students	Provide PD in open educational resources to save on textbook expenses	Less expense for students

motivational tactics, and adoption motivators for administrators below (see Tables 6, 7, 8, and 9).

Conclusion

In summary, given instructor' and administrators' legitimate beliefs and concerns, an e-learning leader needs to know what motivates instructors and administrators to overcome barriers to offering online instruction. e-Learning administrators can turn

Table 4 Catalytic tactic to contribute to instructors' sense of confidence

Avoidance motivator	Catalytic tactic	Adoption motivator
Insufficient technical support	Provide 24/7 helpdesk. Provide for just-in-time support. Offer online tutorials responsive to FAQs	Sufficient technical support
Insufficient institutional student support	Design online supports that correspond to on-campus supports. Inform instructors on how to refer students to services online. Design the campus course template to have information for students regarding services	Sufficient institutional student support
Lack of technical expertise	Disseminate contact information for easy-to-access technical support. Provide continuous PD in LMS, web-conferencing, and other tools	Technical expertise
Lack of design and development expertise	Provide PD in design and development as part of certificate programs. Establish project design and development teams to include an instructional designer. Promote project, problem, and case-based designs	Design and development expertise
Concern for legal issues: copyright, piracy, intellectual property, accessibility, authentication, hackers, and viruses	Require evidence of competence in these areas. Provide PD in each. Involve the library, disability services office, and information security offices. Provide online authentication and proctoring. Review courses for copyright and accessibility and help revise courses for compliance. Consider outsourcing closed-captioning. Clarify institution's guidelines regarding intellectual property and ownership of online courses	Assure compliance
Threat of being replaced by packaged courses	Provide PD in the contribution of instructors to packaged courses. Emphasize the relevance of their shared expertise	Assurance regarding instructors' importance

avoidance motivators into adoption motivators by identifying what triggers avoidance and strategically targeting concerns. A lot is already known about why instructors and administrators avoid or adopt e-learning and we have identified tactics for addressing those avoidance motivators. In addition to using tactics identified here, administrators can keep fingers on the pulse of their campus communities in order to target specific issues raised by instructors and administrators. Naysayers on campuses can provide useful insight into what needs to be addressed. Surveys and interviews can provide valuable insight into the most salient avoidance motivators.

Most important and sustainable are motivators involving immersion in a supportive context where online offerings provide a clear relative advantage over face-to-face offerings. When advantages are evident, e-learning grabs instructors' and administrators' attentions. When, through experience, instructors and administrators see that students are successful in e-learning, it gains relevance; and, when instructors experience success in their teaching and the other aspects of their

Table 5 Catalytic tactic to contribute to instructors' sense of satisfaction

Avoidance motivator	Catalytic tactic	Adoption motivator
Lack of incentives	Recognize accomplishments of instructors through certificates, awards, stipends, travel funds, course release, tenure and promotion, and interinstitutional collaboration	Incentivized
Perception that online teaching is boring	Encourage and incentivize experimentation and innovative teaching practices	Perception that online teaching is interesting
Negative effects on student evaluations	PD in course design for high levels of alignments, presence, interaction, and engagement	Positive student evaluations
Alienation among peers	Share success stories and observation of successful online teaching practices. Discussion among instructors regarding how they use online tools. Create peer-course review and mentoring programs	Community

Table 6 Catalytic tactic to gain administrators' attention

Avoidance motivator	Catalytic tactic	Adoption motivator
Resistance to organizational change	Develop a shared vision and a strategic plan and identify key personnel	Positive change
Loss of student presence and dynamic campus environment	Create online learning communities for students. Encourage blended course designs. Create an active social media presence for students. Create online events	Appreciation for the power of innovative technologies that support informal learning and social presence
Reluctance to enforce online adoption	Gain instructor buy-in. Provide research findings indicating no significant difference between online and F-F outcomes, superior outcomes from online courses, and design features that lead to student success	Mandating online adoption

positions, they become confident. Satisfaction comes from student success, increased enrollments, rising retention, and recognition for excellence. The ARCS model provides a framework for designing such a supportive context.

For More Information

Blog for administrators regarding online adoption: https://onlinelearninginsights.wordpress.com/2014/03/05/why-is-adoption-of-educational-technology-so-challenging-its-complicated/

John Keller's website on motivation: http://www.arcsmodel.com/

Table 7 Catalytic tactic to contribute to administrators' sense of relevance

Avoidance motivator	Catalytic tactic	Adoption motivator
Online instruction does not meet our students' needs	Provide PD and resources to support continuity of learning. Share stories of student success in online learning	Online instruction meets our students' needs
Lack of funds for incentives	Prioritize budget distribution	Adequate funds
Lack of up-front funds for recruitment and marketing	Prioritize budget distribution	Adequate funds
Inadequate reports to accrediting body	Document instructor and student readiness and efforts toward compliance with legal issues. Pull reports from the LMS	Excellent reports to accrediting body
Inadequately assuring student readiness	24/7 helpdesk. Require orientations to online learning. Provide web-based tutorials for just-in-time learning. Provide online tutoring	Assuring student readiness
Inadequately assuring instructor readiness	Adopt a service perspective. Provide certificate award for online course design and development, teaching, and peer mentoring. Consider purchasing online training resources	Adequately assuring instructor readiness
Added expense for students	Build capacity and enrollment in order to reduce fees. Provide credit for prior learning. Provide competency-based programs	Less expense for students

Table 8 Catalytic tactic to contribute to administrators' sense of confidence

Avoidance motivator	Catalytic tactic	Adoption motivator
Inadequate administrative structure	Give adequate authority to key personnel. Hire sufficient support staff to help with technical and pedagogical problems	Supportive administration
Inadequate infrastructure	Create partnerships among different units, find agreement and establish transparency regarding budgets, costs, fees, and distribution of revenue, scheduling, and issuance of credits	Supportive infrastructure
Inadequate course and program quality	Support provision of certificate programs and program evaluation	
Insufficient institutional student support	Ensure that most services available to F-F students are also available to online students	Sufficient institutional student support
Concern for legal issues: copyright, piracy, intellectual property, accessibility, authentication, hackers, and viruses	Develop guidelines for compliance that align with accrediting body. Require evidence of competence in these areas. Provide online authentication and proctoring. Review courses for copyright and accessibility and help revise courses for compliance. Consider outsourcing closed-captioning. Consider creating a position for managing accessibility compliance in online courses. Establish guidelines regarding intellectual property and ownership of online courses	Assure compliance
Concerns about accreditation	Include addressing each accreditation requirement in strategic plans	Meet accreditation requirements
Need for state authorization	Monitor federal, state, and licensure regulations. Join and maintain state reciprocity agreements. Gain authorization from states that are not members of a reciprocity agreement	Comply with state authorization

Table 9 Catalytic tactic to contribute to administrators' sense of satisfaction

Avoidance motivator	Catalytic tactic	Adoption motivator
Fear of decreased enrollment	Recruit and market each online program using the latest web-based approaches as well as traditional recruiting and marketing strategies	Increased enrollment
Fear of decreased retention	Provide orientations to online learning, systematic advising, early alert systems, mentoring, tutoring, and course quality assurance	Increased retention
Poorly recognized programs	Address enrollment and retention as described above	Well-recognized programs

References

Beckem, J. M., & Watkins, M. (2012). Bringing life to learning: Immersive experiential learning simulations for online and blended courses. *Journal of Asynchronous Learning Networks, 16*(5), 61–70.

Berge, Z. L. (2013). Barriers to communication in distance education. *Turkish Online Journal of Distance Education, 14*(1), 374–388.

Chen, B. (2009). Barriers to adoption of technology-mediated distance education in higher-education institutions. *Quarterly Review of Distance Education, 10*(4), 333–338.

Ertmer, P. A., & Ottenbreit-Leftwich, A. T. (2010). Teacher technology change: How knowledge, confidence, beliefs, and culture intersect. *Journal of Research on Technology in Education, 42*(3), 255–284.

Fullan, M. G. (1993). Why teachers must become change agents. *Educational Leadership, 50*, 12.

Gannon-Cook, R. (2010). *What motivates faculty to teach in distance education.* Lanhom, MD: University Press of America.

Gannon-Cook, R. G., Ley, K., Crawford, C., & Warner, A. (2009). Motivators and inhibitors for university faculty in distance and e-learning. *British Journal of Educational Technology, 40*(1), 149–163.

Gutman, D. (2012). Six barriers causing educators to resist teaching online, and how institutions can break them. *Distance Learning, 9*(3), 51.

Keller, J. M. (2010). *Motivational design for learning and performance: The ARCS model approach.* New York, NY: Springer.

Kowalczyk, N. K. (2014). Perceived barriers to online education by radiologic science educators. *Radiologic Technology, 85*(5), 486–493.

Loogma, K., Kruusvall, J., & Ümarik, M. (2012). E-learning as innovation: Exploring innovativeness of the VET teachers' community in Estonia. *Computers & Education, 58*(2), 808–817.

Meyer, K. A., & Wilson, J. L. (2011). The role of online learning in the emergency plans of flagship institutions. *Online Journal of Distance Learning Administration, 14*(1). Retrieved from http://www.westga.edu/~distance/ojdla/spring141/meyer_wilson141.html.

Muilenburg, L. Y., & Berge, Z. L. (2001). Barriers to distance education: A factor-analytic study. *The American Journal of Distance Education., 15*(2), 7–22.

Neben, J. (2016). Attributes and barriers impacting diffusion of online education at the institutional level: Considering faculty perceptions. In A. A. Piña & J. B. Huett (Eds.), *Beyond the online course: Leadership perspectives on e-learning* (pp. 21–34). Charlotte, NC: Information Age Publishing, Inc..

Rogers, E. M. (2003). *Diffusion of innovations* (5th ed.). New York, NY: Free Press.

Schneckenberg, D. (2010). Overcoming barriers for E-learning in universities—Portfolio models for eCompetence development of faculty. *British Journal of Educational Technology, 41*(6), 979–991.

Turner, J. C., & Patrick, H. (2008). How does motivation develop and why does it change? Reframing motivation research. *Educational Psychologist, 43*(3), 119–131.

Volery, T., & Lord, D. (2000). Critical success factors in online education. *International Journal of Educational Management, 14*(5), 216–223.

Wickersham, L. E., & McElhany, J. A. (2010). Bridging the divide. *Quarterly Review of Distance Education, 11*(1), 1–12.

Suggested Readings

Eccles, J. S., & Wigfield, A. (2002). Motivational beliefs, values, and goals. *Annual Review of Psychology, 53*, 109–132.

Elgort, I. (2005). E-learning adoption: Bridging the chasm. In *Proceedings of ASCILITE* (pp. 181–185).

Hall, G. E., & Hord, S. M. (2001). *Implementing change: Patterns, principles, and potholes.* Needham Heights, MA: Allyn and Bacon.

Hramiak, A., & Boulton, H. (2013). Escalating the use of Web 2.0 technology in secondary schools in the United Kingdom: Barriers and enablers beyond teacher training. *Electronic Journal of E-learning, 11*(2), 91–100.

Österåker, M. C. (1999). Measuring motivation in a dynamic organization—A contingency approach. *Strategic Change, 8*(2), 103–109.

Palloff, R. M., & Pratt, K. (2011). *The excellent online instructor: Strategies for professional development.* San Francisco, CA: John Wiley & Sons.

Reigeluth, C. M., & Karnopp, J. R. (2013). *Reinventing schools: It's time to break the mold.* Lanham, MD: Rowan & Littlefield Education.

Schunk, D. H., Pintrich, P. R., & Meece, J. L. (2008). *Motivation in education. Theory, research, and applications* (3rd ed.). Upper Saddle River, NJ: Pearson Education Inc..

Straub, E. T. (2009). Understanding technology adoption: Theory and future directions for informal learning. *Review of Educational Research, 79*, 625–649. Retrieved from http://rer.aera.net.

Touré-Tillery, M., & Fishbach, A. (2014). How to measure motivation: A guide for the experimental social psychologist. *Social and Personality Psychology Compass, 8*(7), 328–341.

Ulrich, T., Marsh, H. W., Nagengast, B., Ludtke, O., Nagy, G., & Jonkmann, K. (2012). Probing for the multiplicative term in modern expectancy-value theory: A latent interaction modeling study. *Journal of Educational Psychology, 104*(3), 763–777.

Leading Faculty Through a Paradigm Shift: Creating and Sustaining a Needs-Based Approach to e-Learning Faculty Development Programs

Michael G. Strawser and Tara Bunag

Abstract e-Learning leaders have a responsibility to train faculty to produce quality online and blended courses. To foster this mandate, this chapter provides e-learning leaders with a framework for faculty development. Specifically, this chapter includes material that reinforces the importance of recruiting qualified e-learning instructors and supporting e-learning faculty in an effort to produce courses that resound with sound pedagogy and high-quality instructional strategy. This chapter also explores e-learning issues and concerns as indicated by faculty and provides answers to common faculty questions. Finally, this chapter will provide a roadmap for the entire e-learning faculty development process: from recruiting faculty participants to designing e-learning faculty development curricula and, finally, assessing the effectiveness of e-learning faculty development initiatives.

Keywords Faculty development • Faculty training • Faculty recruitment • Faculty support • Assessment

Decision-Making Guidance

This chapter will help you make decisions about:

- Designing a systematic approach to recruitment and support of e-learning faculty

M.G. Strawser (✉)
Bellarmine University, 2001 Newburg Road, GBCH 203C, Louisville, KY 40205, USA
e-mail: mstrawser@bellarmine.edu

T. Bunag
University of the Pacific, Stockton, CA, USA
e-mail: tbunag@pacific.edu

© Association for Educational Communications and Technology 2018
A.A. Piña et al. (eds.), *Leading and Managing e-Learning*, Educational Communications and Technology: Issues and Innovations,
https://doi.org/10.1007/978-3-319-61780-0_15

- Answering common faculty challenges and barriers of transitioning courses or programs to e-learning platforms
- Creating and implementing an effective and needs-driven development training plan
- Assessing faculty development programs

What You Need to Know

Maybe this situation has happened to you. A faculty member comes to your office and asks about "teaching online." You explain the process, indicate next steps, and then, you ask, "In an ideal world, if all technology was at your disposal and we could create the perfect e-learning class, what would be your dream design?" Unfortunately, some responses to this question are staggeringly discouraging. Faculty responses may range from, "Well, I would LOVE to have a recurring 2-hour video conference, every Monday from 6:00-8:00 pm" or "Honestly, I only know how to lecture, so is there a way that our Learning Management System (LMS) can handle a two-hour lecture recording every week?" These responses are frustrating for e-learning administrators but, sadly, these ideas are not uncommon in higher education.

As e-learning leaders, you are witnessing nothing less than a paradigm shift. Faculty members, of the "Sage on the Stage" ilk, are frightened because new modalities are fraught with challenges and, for many, confusion. Faculty members have a natural tendency to do what has been done because it either (a) worked or (b) allowed them to score higher on teaching evaluations. Some faculty see e-learning as the great unknown, an abyss where interaction and student learning go to die. Some even view e-learning as a threat to their existence. However, it is important to let faculty know that the modern student is a new breed. Content must be relevant, experiential, and engaging for the twenty-first century learner (Moore, 2007).

Students may appreciate new and innovative modalities but, for faculty, the transition to e-learning is difficult. It is crucial, in any faculty development initiative, that resources and infrastructure are provided to ease faculty anxieties while creating a smoother institutional transition (Behar-Horenstein, Garvan, Catalanotto, & Hudson-Vassell, 2014), but this is particularly important for e-learning courses and programs. Online course instructors need training regarding instructor responsibility and quality assurance in order to maintain high-quality courses (Strawser, Buckner, & Kaufmann, 2015). e-Learning leaders have a responsibility to train faculty to produce quality online and blended courses.

As higher education institutions struggle to address challenges posed by the twenty-first century learner and the trend toward distance learning initiatives, it is imperative that training programs directly address the needs of the faculty (Chisholm, Hayes, LaBrecque, & Smith, 2011; Steinert, 2000). The ability to respond to faculty concerns with a program designed to answer faculty questions can be effective in strengthening faculty skills (teaching and otherwise), improving knowledge, and conducting research (Steinert, 2000). According to Behar-Horenstein et al. (2014), the aim of faculty development is to "impart skills and knowledge that promote growth in regard to institutional and individual vitality, to foster understanding of the science of learning, and to build capacity towards providing state of the art instructional practices" (p. 75). Faculty evaluation systems and faculty development programs are necessary components of a successful campus cultural transformation and no cultural transformation may be more pressing than e-learning.

Managing and leading faculty within e-learning programs includes a number of challenges. In a typical education setting, these challenges are addressed in a reactive manner, instead of through the creation and implementation of a comprehensive, systematic plan. As a counter to this typically reactive process, this chapter will focus on how leaders in e-learning can evaluate their institutional culture and existing infrastructure to develop a systematic approach to recruitment, training, support, and assessment of e-learning faculty. To combat common faculty e-learning challenges, this chapter will specifically explore e-learning issues as indicated by faculty and will provide answers to common faculty questions and concerns. Additionally, this chapter will provide a roadmap for the entire e-learning faculty development process: from recruiting faculty participants to designing e-learning faculty development curricula and, finally, assessing the effectiveness of e-learning faculty development initiatives.

What You Can Do

Evaluating Existing Culture and Infrastructure

Administrative leaders, faculty, and staff must recognize the dramatic shift that occurs when an institution strategically moves into the realm of e-learning or builds a completely online program. New knowledge, skills, support, and faculty development are needed to prepare faculty members to embrace e-learning modalities (Gautreau, 2011). The transition, as difficult as it is, must be framed within a preexisting recognition of the current institutional culture. As Michael Allen (2003) says, e-learning is about success and behavioral change, both individual and organizational. Before transitioning to an e-learning model, e-learning leaders must determine the current organizational climate. As such, you should attempt to perform a thorough needs assessment that focuses on the cultural makeup of your institution (Tobey, 2005). The transition from a traditional "brick and mortar" modality to that of blended or online learning is not just a change in format, but a revision of ideology. However, many institutions are not just transitioning from the more traditional model to e-learning. In fact, institutions may be entirely online or could have never engaged in a traditional model. Ultimately, whether your institution is transitioning from a traditional model to distance learning, or if your institution has always been entirely online, the identification of institutional culture is of primary importance as you engage faculty.

Stakeholders

There are, obviously, many stakeholders (e.g., workforce partners with faculty expectations, accreditation agencies, community partners, professional associations, regents or other higher level groups, or even existing administrative structures within an institution) who have a direct connection to e-learning. One primary stakeholder group, faculty, hold a unique and revered position in higher education. It is crucial that leaders create a current faculty profile, as well as a prescriptive profile for faculty members that may be needed during and after the transition. For instance, some questions that should be answered during a faculty evaluation include:

– Are there established processes and procedures to recruitment, training, support, and assessment of faculty?
– What are the educational backgrounds and pedagogical credentials of existing faculty?
– Are faculty tenure-track, full-time non-tenure track instructors, adjunct, or a mixture?
– What do students expect of faculty members and how are faculty members expected to relate to the student body?
– Do faculty have experience with e-learning and technologies in general?

Gathering this information is vital when crafting an approach to address faculty issues. You would do well to lead a collaborative enterprise with faculty members so they feel that the mandate is not "top-down" and is, instead, something that is community-owned and driven by collaboration. Further, accreditation bodies consider the impact and level of faculty governance at institutions. As an e-learning leader, your role may be viewed in conjunction with faculty. Therefore, defining clear faculty roles in university governance and leadership may be helpful when preparing e-learning initiatives.

Structure

In many instances, the e-learning leader is responsible for unifying the campus around e-learning initiatives. In an effort to craft a holistic campus response to e-learning, it is imperative that administrators explore the current infrastructure and navigate appropriately.

e-Learning initiatives should fit seamlessly within the current university mission and vision. New programs and institutions encounter vastly different challenges in this aspect of planning than established programs and institutions, but both share the need for a clear vision to ensure appropriate institutional support of faculty within programs. Determining current institutional conditions is vital to determining a realistic systematic approach. It is deceptively simple to create a strategic e-learning plan, but the most elegant strategy will not be effective if it does not reflect institutional foundations.

Institutional Strategic Plan

One of the first steps for the e-learning leader when creating a plan for faculty development is to understand the current strategic plan centered around the institutional response to teaching and learning. Some leaders will jump into implementing a particular approach based on an assumption of how the institution will respond. This is a recipe for institutional resistance, or even outright failure. Organizational, or administrative, expectations or timelines may require completing this evaluation quickly, but do not skip it entirely. The more information you can gather before you decide on a new or revised approach to faculty leadership, the better.

Institutional History of e-Learning

While gathering information, leaders should evaluate the overall institutional history of e-learning and try to weave this history into a coherent present faculty program. As the plan is developed, try to comb through the annals of what your institution has tried in the past. If your institution has previously implemented e-learning initiatives, talk to current administrators and faculty members and decipher why the initiative failed or how it could be improved.

One area of concern may be the traditional faculty response to innovation. If your institution has a history of a smaller student–teacher ratio, face-to-face teaching, or lecture-based teaching, faculty may be resistant to a change in modality or course format. The "freedom" to innovate may be met with substantial resistance by the people you count on for quality pedagogy. One way to navigate this challenge is to meet with faculty either one-on-one or in small groups to give faculty members a voice and respond to concerns they may face. In many cases, faculty members need a forum and working with faculty will help alleviate anxiety. It is crucial to continually assess and address faculty issues, and to maintain a focus on quality pedagogy. Policies may be needed to continue to support student–teacher ratios and other faculty interests. Faculty must have clear and realistic expectations.

Institutional Policy Structure

Leaders in e-learning need to determine their appropriate role in drafting or revising documents and policies at an institutional or programmatic level to reflect a focus on e-learning. As you build your e-learning initiatives, you must also reassess and redevelop your policy documents regarding faculty members. For example, you may have to create a new syllabus template with modified learning outcomes, requirements for technology, expectations of course modality, etc. As you are planning your approach, you will need to reexamine your accreditation and create a plan that is appropriate for your accrediting agency. As such, you will need to focus on faculty members who are qualified and diagnose an appropriate policy concerning training structure. These policies cannot be overlooked and it is up to the e-learning leader to make sure the new policies align to the overall vision of the institution, while also setting a trajectory for years to come. As an aside, at some institutions faculty members have a significant role in institutional leadership, while some institutions thrive on a more administrative or top-down model. Regardless of the faculty role in leadership of the institution, they should be included wherever possible in discussions of new policies. Omitting faculty from the process can prove unwise when it comes time to implement the new process.

As you examine current institutional policies, try to, again, take the pulse of necessary stakeholders. Converse with key decision makers to determine how the process can be more collaborative and community-focused. If your institution follows a master course model, faculty may not be as involved in the creation of curriculum. At smaller institutions, faculty and other administrative stakeholders may be heavily involved in the design and implementation of your e-learning initiative. At Bellarmine University, in Louisville, Kentucky, and University of the Pacific, in Stockton, California, for example, each faculty member has significant control over the design and implementation of online and blended courses. Other institutions may craft the framework and institute a university-wide course template requirement. Assess the situation and, depending on your institution, proceed accordingly. One additional policy note that also should be explored as you train faculty how to teach in online or blended environments is the approach your institution takes with students with disabilities. In order to be ADA compliant, courses should be universally accessible and faculty members should be supported in helping students with a variety of disabilities. This challenge is a matter of policy as well as pedagogy and, sadly, is often ignored in university e-learning models.

Recruitment

Institutions may feel pressure to develop courses immediately without examining how e-learning fits into the broader mission of the university, and often this is a mistake. As a substantial stakeholder in the university, faculty must understand and be on board with the university vision for e-learning. Once you have addressed the issues above, it may be time to start recruiting faculty members for programs and courses that are transitioning into an e-learning environment. In established, traditional programs, the recruitment challenge may be in convincing faculty who have only taught in face-to-face settings to try e-learning or to develop methods for recruiting full-time faculty with this interest. In other institutions, the challenge may be in narrowing large pools of applicants to the best qualified, both academically and technically. It is very easy to misread the interested faculty pool, and many interesting programs have languished due to lack of a good recruitment model.

Regardless of context, having clear faculty requirements is essential to ensure adherence to accreditation standards, establish a connection with existing faculty groups, and identify appropriate candidates for positions. Depending on institutional structures, an e-learning leader may have a role in drafting, implementing, or supporting recruitment plans.

Incentives, like stipends or course release time, can encourage faculty participation in new course development. Incentive plans must be strategic and sustainable, while fitting within the existing compensation structure. Some institutions will designate monetary compensation as a means to encourage effective course design. At institutions without a master course model, instructors could receive a stipend to develop the course and then regular pay to teach the course in corresponding quarters or semesters. Be aware that this could cause issues with pay inequality. To avoid issues like pay inequality, course release time may be an appropriate avenue for your institution to reward faculty members for designing and teaching a new online or blended course, or for participating in e-learning training or faculty development.

Monetary incentives may not be realistic for your institution. Instead, try other innovative incentive ideas. Many faculty members, especially tenure-track faculty, have expectations to publish on a regular basis as a means by which they are evaluated. For example, at Mount Saint Mary's University, Los Angeles, the decision to consider Open Educational Resources when evaluating for tenure and promotion helped to support faculty involvement in both OER and e-learning development. Encouraging faculty collaboration through the scholarship of teaching and learning, as it relates to e-learning, may present an initiative for faculty members that has minimal financial burden on the institution. By creating an atmosphere of data-driven and research-based e-learning initiatives, you encourage community collaboration and can serve an important role on the research team. The opportunity to publish articles, books, and other items related to their e-learning experience may be an ideal incentive for faculty members. No matter what incentive plan you use, make sure that it is tied directly to your university mission and fits within preestablished faculty policy or that the existing policy is revised to support new incentives.

Incentivizing e-learning training and instruction may lead to an abundance of potential instructors. As such, make sure you identify characteristics of your "ideal" e-learning faculty member. e-Learning experience is preferred, but not a necessity. We agree with Ko and Rossen (2010) who believe faculty of all ranks who are enthusiastic about the possibilities offered by teaching online [or in other e-learning formats], and who are willing to invest some time in learning new technology and methods for the sake of personal and professional growth, are good candidates for e-learning instructor positions.

Leaders must solidify a concrete application process to ensure equal opportunity, but don't be afraid to encourage certain faculty members to apply. Identifying specific requirements (like training time, faculty development, course evaluation expectations, etc.) of e-learning faculty will create an opportunity to institute specific requirements. This could, in essence, also influence requirements of traditional faculty members. Unionized faculty present unique challenges. As you address the application process, incentives, and instructional requirements, make sure you are in consistent communication with a union representative.

It is important to note that as you decipher how you will select faculty members, you must also determine an appropriate infrastructure for holding faculty members accountable. You, as the e-learning leader, may be responsible for determining if a faculty member is qualified to teach. If so, you must determine standards for instructional effectiveness. Additionally, if you are going to observe instructors throughout their course, or if department chairs or department deans share in this level of accountability, you must create a mandate for effectiveness. How will you determine whether or not a faculty member is creating a classroom climate that is functional? Make sure to specify assessment realities before your e-learning programs launch. Further information on this topic is provided in the assessment section of this chapter.

Training

Developing a comprehensive training model for e-learning faculty depends heavily on existing institutional training models, faculty backgrounds, and training resources. As a general rule, the training model of your institution should align with different faculty staffing and recruitment models and institutional policies ranging from faculty contracts to institutional schedules.

Training programs can be unique to your institution. For example, the University of Central Florida has used a training program called Blendkit. BlendKit is a 5-week course designed in an open, online format specifically for faculty and designers preparing to design and teach blended learning courses. As e-learning leaders you have to determine which department is responsible for training (specific academic departments, faculty development, instructional or academic technology, etc.). The design and development of faculty training programs may differ depending on the institution however, the design and delivery of faculty training, no matter the format, is an e-learning imperative and something leaders should designate as an area of primary concern.

As previously mentioned, one of the most prevalent training issues is the distinction between full-time and adjunct faculty members. Many institutions do not distinguish between full or part-time faculty and, thus, have training requirements that are identical for each population. However, for institutions who recognize the difference between these two groups, it is important to understand that whether a faculty member is full-time or an adjunct, an appropriate training baseline and a solid pedagogical foundation and framework are important. Training faculty members how to engage students in an online environment, crafting interactive and collaborative activities, or simply using the LMS (learning management system) may all constitute areas of need for either full-time or adjunct faculty. Carroll University attempted to overcome faculty technology anxiety by offering faculty Bootcamps to focus on technology adoption of faculty in e-learning modalities (Johnson, Wisniewski, Kuhlemeyer, Isaacs, & Krzykowski, 2012). University of the Pacific held comprehensive workshops, "camps," and outreach to increase faculty acceptance and use of both the new learning management system and e-learning in general. No matter what training format you choose, remember that ineffective training is costly (Allen, 2003), both financially and in terms of time and resources. Therefore, craft training mechanisms are effective and tailored to your faculty audience.

In some institutions all faculty are required to demonstrate specific technical or pedagogical skills before they are hired. If this is the case for your institution, these facets would not need to be addressed to the same depth in the training model. However, you could create mandatory or optional trainings that continue to explore varying technologies and new approaches to e-learning. At an institution where the main criteria for hire is research experience, providing training opportunities for both pedagogy and technology would be essential. Ko and Rossen (2010) identified five important categories for training including software training, facilitative or methods training, course design, personal consultation, and supervised start-up. These five areas are essential but it is also important to assess unique faculty member expertise. No matter what e-learning background faculty may have, continued faculty and professional development are important for success. As you consider training programs suited to your faculty, keep in mind that formatting your training is crucial. Providing an online training may encourage greater participation, as the modality is more flexible, and can provide instructors an e-learning experience and a pedagogy laboratory (Cook & Steinert, 2013), but face-to-face workshops may be necessary if your faculty prefer to meet in person.

Surveying faculty at your institution to determine instructional background and experience level may help you determine whether or not training should be mandatory. There are strengths and weaknesses to each approach. A mandatory training may be approached begrudgingly, especially if it is an administrative mandate and is not faculty owned. However, you have greater control over the content that is distributed to every faculty member. Optional training may be approached more positively by faculty but could be less frequently attended and may not provide a consistency of faculty standards. If your institution does offer faculty training that is not required, there are ways to further enhance or encourage attendance. Training centers can offer free "swag" like pens, university promotional items, or giveaways as a means of motivating attendance. Emphasizing service to the university, especially at institutions with tenure-track faculty members, may provide an additional incentive for attendance.

As an aside, you, as an e-learning leader, can serve as an example for course design by how you design and develop your training. You can provide a variety of training formats beyond the traditional face-to-face modality. Faculty may be more likely to attend a training session if it is available online and can be completed at home or on their own time. When training faculty, it is important to remember that your sessions should include interactive and collaborative activities, facets that are also important in e-learning programs. Faculty may appreciate a gamification of their training as a way to stay engaged. Badging or credentialing systems, that encourage a competency-based progression of e-learning instructional skill, may also stimulate a positive faculty response. No matter what training avenue you choose, a variety of training options will create an environment that is faculty-centered.

If you are overwhelmed by the thought of designing a brand new training package, have no fear. Several training options are available on the open market. Quality Matters (QM), a national organization that specializes in benchmarks for online course development, offers training that centers on becoming a certified QM course reviewer. The Quality Online Learning and Teaching (QOLT) program offers free training for e-learning specialists. Additionally, Magna publications has several videos and training initiatives available for purchase. Even if your institution is not ready to develop in-house training, there are other options available.

No matter the format, training should be faculty-centered. As such, it is important to align training with faculty recruitment, potentially even with the receipt of a course development stipend, and it is crucial that faculty training is relevant for individual skills and needs. Conducting a needs assessment that determines faculty skill level in the e-learning realm can save your institution from requiring redundant training. A tiered training approach, where level one focuses on e-learning essentials and the basics of the context and movement to e-learning, level two focuses on e-learning pedagogy, and level three on innovative assignments, enhanced uses of technology, and other evolving areas of instruction, could be an appropriate strategy depending on the acumen of your faculty population. Bay Path College, and several other institutions, incorporate three distinct areas of faculty training that include an initial training, peer mentoring, and continuing and ongoing faculty support. Peer mentorship, collaborative communities, and one-on-one consistent course consultation can supplement training programs.

Training must be designed appropriately and marketed effectively, beyond email blasts, to inspire or boost attendance. Creative internal marketing endeavors, posters, giveaways, and peer learning or mentor groups can help foster a holistic vision of the importance of faculty development. The institution must communicate the importance of e-learning faculty training and, as such, should establish faculty-led communities of practice that focus on the peer collaboration element. It is also a necessity to recognize and herald faculty members who complete the training. Faculty members who initiate innovation and attend training sessions faithfully should be recognized and praised openly.

Faculty Support

Support models for faculty in e-learning programs vary greatly from nearly no support to extensive support in pedagogy, curriculum development, technology, and services (such as library, bookstore, and student support). Determining how extensive the support needs to be for a particular institutional context can be challenging.

Certain elements of support may cost a surprising amount, and this cost may be unnecessary if faculty will not use the support system. In addition to the financial cost, the time required to implement a support model must be considered. It is rare for faculty to have the time to devote to learning how to access complicated support structures, and those providing support will also need the time to provide assistance. For example, providing face-to-face technical support may be worth the time and expense in an established, single-campus institution that is new to e-learning, but this same support may not be appropriate for a dispersed faculty group.

Faculty Needs for Support

Before creating a university-wide e-learning program make sure you have outlined appropriate support structures for faculty members (Marek, 2009). Even in institutions where good teaching is clearly articulated as part of the core mission, support structures for online teaching need to be examined (Marek, 2009). Institutions generally promote teaching excellence, but without careful examination of the support structures, they may not have an appropriate infrastructure to support effective pedagogy (Marek, 2009). There are both obvious and less obvious areas of support in e-learning programs, and it is important to recognize both.

Technical Support

Technical support is often the first area of support that comes to mind. Faculty in e-learning programs require 24/7 technical support as much as possible, but it is vital to determine what that means. Also, who will provide the support? How will faculty know to contact the right person or people regarding support? How much do faculty currently trust existing support models? Expanding the services provided by a support system the faculty do not trust can be frustrating for struggling faculty.

Hardware Issues

Will your institution provide hardware, such as computers, phones, cameras, and microphones, to faculty, or will they be expected to work on their own devices? Both approaches provide unique support challenges. If the institution provides the hardware, what happens when it breaks? Does your process support geographically distant faculty? If the institution does not supply the hardware, how will you communicate the hardware requirements to faculty? How will this be communicated to potential faculty in the recruitment process?

Software Issues

Consider how your institution adopts software to help determine what type of support may be required. What software will the institution provide to faculty? What type of software support will be available to students, and will faculty be part of that support structure?

Technical Trainings/Workshops

Regardless of the technical support model you decide to use, providing technical trainings or workshops is an important part of providing comprehensive support. Necessary trainings or workshops vary based on the technical requirements of faculty in recruitment. If faculty are required to demonstrate high levels of technical proficiency before they are selected, then the training or workshops provided would be at a different level and depth than if the faculty are new to the technology or if you have a mixed group.

Pedagogical Supports

Often, pedagogical support focuses on workshops and trainings on pedagogy, but it is also beneficial to provide just in time pedagogical support. Who will answer questions when a faculty member is concerned about best practices in the middle of a course?

Also, who will provide support for creating courses within the e-learning environment? Does your institution have an instructional design team or group? How do faculty members request assistance? Is this support required or optional? Part of this will depend on the program's course model. If the courses are based on a master course model, versus a boutique model, this will change the support required. Even if the program involves pre-built, predefined courses, it is still beneficial to provide support to faculty on how they can personalize their courses, support rigor and academic honesty, and respond to unexpected situations.

Library and Bookstore

What support is available for faculty in selecting textbooks and additional readings for their courses? How do the library and bookstore fit? If your institution is promoting lower cost alternatives or open educational resources, at minimum it is best practice to provide information to faculty to help them select these resources.

Other Supports

Consider what other supports are needed for faculty. Examine what support is currently provided for faculty on campus, if applicable. These could include a wide range of support services, such as ADA, Title IX, health and wellness, employee assistance, and trainings. How will these be provided for faculty who may never be physically on your campus?

Coordinating Support

There are a number of support concerns that may bridge the technological and pedagogical realms. Establishing clear lines of communication between individuals and groups answering both types of questions is essential to ensure that all questions are addressed and that they are answered appropriately.

Coordinating support can be particularly complex if the same support structure will be used for both e-learning and face-to-face support. How many of your current support structures require a faculty member to walk into someone's office? How do you track support, and do all individuals who may be involved in tracking support have access to the system(s) used? Tech support is typically comfortable with ticketing systems, but consider both the benefits and drawbacks. A ticketing system can definitely help with tracking if it is used consistently, but it can also decrease the personal touch.

Marketing of Support

Regardless of the types of support provided at your institution, awareness of the support is essential. To market support, use channels faculty will use. For example, if your faculty tend to prefer face-to-face support and training, you will need to provide more physical marketing tools, such as flyers, brochures, and swag, while fully online remote faculty would be more easily reached with email, LMS-based announcements, social media, or teleconferencing.

Assessment

Determining a faculty assessment model for an e-learning program is a process full of internal challenges and external requirements. Balancing the internal requirements and expectations of assessment with the requirements of accreditors and the culture of the institution can be a delicate process, fraught with political challenges.

Institutions with both traditional, face-to-face programs and e-learning programs will need to determine if faculty assessment processes will apply to faculty in all modalities, and if faculty members do not meet expectations in the assessment process, what will be the result?

Expectations of Assessment

Before establishing any faculty assessment process or plan, it is essential to examine the existing faculty assessment plans and attitudes toward assessment. When assessment is viewed as a punishment or a top-down mandate, there can often be resistance to implementing assessment plans. Encouraging a view of assessment as a part of personal and professional development can help to build a more positive attitude toward assessment. Whether the approach is top-down or faculty-driven, the assessment process must be fair and accurate, and it should provide clear, positive areas of improvement.

Types of Assessment

Assessment could include student course evaluations, teaching observations, course design review, and self-review.

Traditional student course evaluations are often used to compare instructors, although there may be issues with the validity of these comparisons (Kalender, 2015). In addition, these evaluations often have little impact on teaching effectiveness (Knol, Dolan, Mellenbergh, & van der Maas, 2016). Selecting a well-tested student evaluation tool is only one component of the process. It has to be implemented effectively, which can be challenging in an e-learning environment. Will students be required to complete evaluations or will they be optional? If they are optional, how will students be encouraged to participate? If faculty are part of that process, what will be the institutional policies regarding making student evaluations part of the course grade? If your current institutional policies require a paper-based evaluation, how will you approach revising these policies?

Observations of e-learning teaching can be a particularly challenging aspect of assessment. First, consider the existing institutional climate toward observations as assessment. Some institutions have a rich history of using observation as a tool to develop faculty, while others have a history of using it against the faculty. These types of histories will deeply impact how you should approach observations.

Regardless of the purpose and history of observations, it is essential to make it clear to faculty why observations are being conducted, how they will be conducted, and what could possibly happen after the observation. Is the observation required or optional? Will the results be used to determine their future employment, or is it solely for professional development? Will faculty be alerted before you look into their e-learning environment? Who will see the observation when it is completed? Consider if your institution mandates the use of particular systems or not. If the institution mandates the use of a specific LMS, official email addresses, and other institution-specific tools, the logistics of gaining access to a particular course will typically be streamlined in comparison to an institution that allows faculty to use other systems, but this can come at a cost in terms of faculty buy-in.

Course design review ensures that e-learning courses are designed appropriately, include the appropriate level of rigor, are easy to navigate, and otherwise clear and appropriate for supporting student learning. If your institution uses Quality Matters (QM) or Quality Online Learning and Teaching (QOLT) for training, then you may want to use them for course design review in either a formal or informal process, since these focus on peer review. It is easy to underestimate the time and resources needed for review. Expecting faculty to review each other's courses without some type of incentive is a recipe for rejection of the process and/or inadequate reviews, even if faculty are initially in favor of this type of approach. Having an instructional designer or course designer evaluate could be an alternative approach, but faculty may be less accepting of feedback from nonfaculty. Ensure that the individuals completing the review fit your institutional culture and expectations.

Self-review can include both review of teaching and design of the course, and it is an often forgotten but essential aspect of assessment. Self-review can be a formal process, requiring submission of reflections on teaching practices or areas of the course that could be improved, or it could be an informal process. For either approach, faculty should be provided with self-review tools, such as checklists or rubrics such as those provided by QM or QOLT, clear guidelines based on faculty requirements, and support for questions about how to conduct a self-review.

Assessments should work together in a meaningful way. For example, if students are asked to evaluate the faculty member's communications through the LMS, any observations or reviews should also look at this. This can be particularly challenging if assessment does not fit the expectations for faculty. In this same example, if faculty have no clear requirements or expectations to communicate with students through the LMS, then faculty may ignore or become resistant to any feedback on this.

Closing the Loop

Any official assessments should, ideally, impact teaching and learning in a positive way, but this is rarely the case (Knol et al., 2016). Make a clear and specific plan on how you will support faculty development based on assessment. Are you able to gather enough information from your student evaluation or other assessment processes to support faculty development? For example, if a faculty member is consistently rated low on responsiveness to student questions, how will you approach this issue? Are there any repercussions for repeated poor evaluations, or alternatively, are there any benefits to improving evaluations over time? Answering these questions will create a clear assessment roadmap for e-learners and prevent potential faculty frustration. This will also highlight areas for improvement for both support and training.

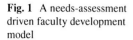

Fig. 1 A needs-assessment driven faculty development model

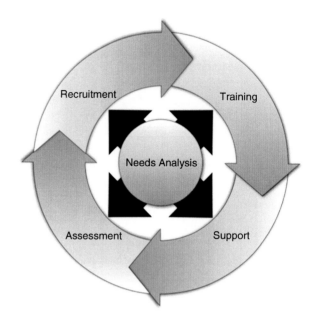

Conclusion

This chapter was an overview created to designate a systematic process for recruiting, training, supporting, and assessing e-learning faculty. Faculty-centered, needs-based training can reinforce key instructional strategy and position your institution as a high-quality twenty-first century leader in the e-learning movement. To further illustrate our emphases, the figure below (Fig. 1) represents a summative diagram to demonstrate the importance of a needs-based faculty recruitment, training, support, and assessment.

As an e-learning leader you have a wonderful opportunity and a magnificent responsibility. Not only can you lead your institution in adopting, transiting to, or continuing high-quality instruction, but you can also serve as a catalyst for e-learning initiatives and a liaison to faculty. While it is true that some faculty members may ask about recording a two-hour lecture as a sole means of e-learning instructional strategy (something we would not recommend), these same faculty members may thrive once provided with the appropriate training and encouragement to pursue additional learning strategies.

For More Information

The Quality Matters Program
Quality Online Learning and Teaching
Education Advisory Board
Magna Publications

References

Allen, M. (2003). *Michael Allen's guide to e-learning*. San Francisco: Pfeiffer.

Behar-Horenstein, L., Garvan, C. W., Catalanotto, F. A., & Hudson-Vassell, C. (2014). The role of needs assessment for faculty development initiatives. *The Journal of Faculty Development, 28*(2), 75–86. Retrieved from http://ezproxy.uky.edu/login?url=http://search.proquest.com/docview/1673849427?accountid=11836.

Chisholm, M., Hayes, E. J., LaBrecque, S., & Smith, D. (2011). The role of faculty evaluation in transformative change. *The Journal of Faculty Development, 25*(1), 36–42. Retrieved from http://ezproxy.uky.edu/login?url=http://search.proquest.com/docview/1095350621?accountid=11836.

Cook, D. A., & Steinert, Y. (2013). Online learning for faculty development: A review of the literature. *Medical Teacher, 35*(11), 930–937. doi:10.3109/0142159X.2013.827328

Gautreau, C. (2011). Motivational factors affecting the integration of a learning management system by faculty. *Journal of Educators Online, 8*(1), 1–25.

Johnson, T., Wisniewski, M. A., Kuhlemeyer, G., Isaacs, G., & Krzykowski, J. (2012). Technology adoption in higher education: Overcoming anxiety through faculty bootcamp. *Journal of Asynchronous Learning Networks, 16*(2), 63–72.

Kalender, İ. (2015). Measurement invariance of student evaluation of teaching across groups defined by course-related variables. *International Online Journal of Educational Sciences, 7*(4), 69–79. doi:10.15345/iojes.2015.04.006

Knol, M. H., Dolan, C. V., Mellenbergh, G. J., & van der Maas, H. J. (2016). Measuring the quality of university lectures: Development and validation of the instructional skills questionnaire (ISQ). *PloS One, 11*(2), 1–21. doi:10.1371/journal.pone.0149163

Ko, S. S., & Rossen, S. (2010). *Teaching online: A practical guide*. New York: Routledge.

Marek, K. (2009). Learning to teach online: Creating a culture of support for faculty. *Journal of Education For Library & Information Science, 50*(4), 275–292.

Moore, M. G. (2007). Learners come in different types. *American Journal of Distance Education, 21*, 1–2. doi:10.1080/08923640701298571

Steinert, Y. (2000). Faculty development in the new millennium: Key challenges and future directions. *Medical Teacher, 22*, 44–50.

Strawser, M. G., Buckner, M. M., & Kaufmann, R. (2015). Design and delivery: Embracing pedagogic responsibility in the online basic communication course. *Florida Communication Journal, 43*(2), 119–125.

Tobey, D. (2005). *Needs assessment basics*. New York: ASTD Press.

e-Learning Instruction: Identifying and Developing the Competencies of Online Instructors

Olysha Magruder and Swapna Kumar

Abstract The rapid growth of online courses and programs in the last decade has been accompanied by a need for quality online instructors who can improve learning effectiveness and student satisfaction. Professional development is an important aspect of online education, as online instruction requires different pedagogical approaches and often requires faculty to transform many teaching practices. Despite calls for online teaching preparation and development, and certificates offered by professional organizations or individual institutions, no consistent approach to faculty development in online teaching from institution to institution has been established, although suggested best practices exist. Each e-learning context is unique, and a standardized training model might not be effective at all institutions and for all disciplines. In this chapter you will learn about the major roles and competencies needed to teach online as synthesized from the literature, and explore the debate on a technology focus versus pedagogy focus in terms of training decisions. Finally, you will learn about a specific faculty development model employed at a state college to encourage adoption of these roles and competencies in online instruction.

Keywords Professional development • Online instruction • Roles and competencies • Student satisfaction • Instructor satisfaction

Decision-Making Guidance

This chapter will help you make decisions about:

- Major online teaching roles and competencies that might be included in professional development for online instructors at your institution

O. Magruder (✉)
Johns Hopkins University, 338 SW 8th Avenue, Gainesville, FL 32601, USA
e-mail: Olysha@jhu.edu

S. Kumar
University of Florida, Gainesville, FL, USA
e-mail: swapnakumar@coe.ufl.edu

© Association for Educational Communications and Technology 2018
A.A. Piña et al. (eds.), *Leading and Managing e-Learning*, Educational Communications and Technology: Issues and Innovations,
https://doi.org/10.1007/978-3-319-61780-0_16

- Strategies to increase proficiency in these roles and competencies through professional development

What You Need to Know

Faculty development and training is an important aspect of e-learning initiatives. Teaching online has been shown to require somewhat different pedagogical approaches and faculty who teach online have needed to transform many teaching practices (Meyer & Murrell, 2014). A report on effective practices by the Online Learning Consortium (OLC, formerly SLOAN-C) discussed the need for faculty preparation for online teaching to improve learning effectiveness and satisfaction (Moore, 2009). Although faculty preparation for online teaching is often recommended, there is no consistent way of training faculty to teach online from institution to institution (Allen & Seaman, 2011). Yet the number of online courses and programs are growing, and so is the need for quality online instructors.

Since training programs for online teaching vary from institution to institution, individual organizations must determine how to prepare faculty to become exceptional online instructors, especially those who have little or no experience teaching online. Leaders at institutions wishing to develop a program to prepare faculty for online teaching must consider how the program will be delivered, but more importantly, what will be expected from the performance of online instructors. Understanding the major roles and competencies that are specific to online instruction is a first step to help pinpoint and define performance expectations of online instructors.

Need for Exposure to Online Pedagogy

An instructor's philosophical perspective and beliefs about learning often inform the choice of learning activity or lesson and more than one perspective is often applied to the learning environment. These perspectives are represented in different ways when designing online instruction or teaching online. Often, it is necessary to help instructors articulate and acknowledge these perspectives during faculty development for e-learning instructors, in order to help them make the transition to teaching online, or to improve their online teaching skills.

Behaviorism

Behaviorism is based on Skinner's operant conditioning theory that focuses on feedback and reinforcement to encourage learning. When a behavioristic approach is adopted, there is a direct map for learning and the assumption is that student learning is predictable and measureable through observation of student performance (Winn, as cited in Duffy & Jonassen, 1992). In an e-learning environment an example of this perspective is when an instructor presents tangible learning goals, posts a lecture focused on these goals, and requires a multiple-choice test on the material to measure learning.

Cognitivism

Cognitivism is focused on the organization of information to gain new meanings, or a change in thought processes. Specifically, Gagné's Conditions of Learning theory, a cognitive-based theory, includes five types of learning levels: intellectual skills, verbal information, cognitive strategies, motor skills, and attitudes (Schuh & Barab, 2007). An e-learning lesson based on this theory might be presented in an organized module that includes an introduction to gain the attention of the learner, a question about the topic to activate prior learning, and a review of definitions and examples. The student is asked to perform tasks based on the information, receives feedback from the instructor, and is given an assessment to measure what was learned. Further remediation might be provided, if necessary.

Constructivism

According to the constructivist perspective, learning has multiple paths since the subject matter contains many meanings and concepts (Duffy & Jonassen, 1992). The constructivist perspective requires a different way of thinking about instruction because the responsibility for learning and meaning-making shifts to the students. This perspective is often more time-consuming and difficult to facilitate, but is used in the e-learning environment to encourage in-depth exploration of a topic. For example, an e-learning instructor might present a problem-based learning lesson in which students work in groups to create multiple solutions to a problem, scenario, or process. There may not be a right or wrong answer, but instead an exploration of the topic and interactions between peers to develop various solutions to the problem.

Based on the discipline and department or teaching culture, instructors might use one of the above approaches more than others both in their on-campus and online courses. Several instructors, albeit experts in their discipline or subject-matter, often do not have prior knowledge of the above perspectives and the different types of activities or assessments they can use in their teaching. They tend to teach the way they were taught, and few faculty members have prior experiences as online learners. Professional development for online instructors thus has to expose instructors to various ways of communicating subject-matter online, different online activities and their benefits for learning processes, and online assessment types. Additionally, professional development can help them acknowledge their own practices as well as use these different approaches online. The delivery of such professional development online or the inclusion of an online component can provide instructors with experiences as online learners.

Major Teaching Roles and Competencies

The previous section explained the need for exposure to online pedagogy. It is important to acknowledge that instructors bring their own assumptions and perspectives to the classroom. In addition to exploring these perspectives in faculty development for e-learning instructors, there are some overarching roles and basic skills that benefit the instructor in the e-learning environment. These include pedagogical role, administrative/managerial role, technical role, evaluation role, active learning role, and instructional design role.

Pedagogical Role

In the seminal work Seven Principles of Undergraduate Education by Chickering and Gamson (1987), the overarching pedagogical role of an instructor includes communicating high expectations, encouraging student–faculty contact, and emphasizing time on tasks, all of which can be applied to the online learning environment. An online instructor additionally takes on a facilitator role that requires a certain set of competencies. These include: identifying student learning goals and outcomes, incorporating opportunities for student motivation and participation, incorporating team or group work, and sharing knowledge within the learning community. An instructor in this role also encourages construction of knowledge through effective learning activities and facilitates social interactions among students to foster and build relationships (Bawane & Spector, 2009; Berge, 1995; Goodyear, Salmon, Spector, Steeples, & Tickner, 2001).

Administrative/Managerial Role

In this role, the online instructor relays and enforces the rules and policies of the classroom (i.e., classroom "netiquette") and the institution (i.e., Federal Education Rights & Privacy Act, or FERPA). In order to do this, online instructors have to provide resources to students and create and adhere to rules and policies themselves. Included in the managerial role is the effective use of time management. Online students benefit from timely feedback through email correspondence, interaction with peers and the instructor in discussion boards, grades, and other student–instructor interactions. Further, an accessible online environment for all learners is an important consideration. Accessibility in an online classroom environment includes things like closed captioning for course lecture videos, preparing documents to be accessible for screen readers, and applying universal design for learning (UDL) when creating course materials. Many institutions have specific policies and guidelines for students with special needs; these need to be shared with online instructors.

Technical Role

Online instructors have to be technically proficient order to assume a pedagogical and administrative role in the online environment. It is inevitable that technical difficulties will occur and competencies such as flexibility and level-headedness are important in the online learning environment. If a student has problems using materials or technologies during the course, e.g., a faulty microphone or web camera during a synchronous session, the online instructor may need to help the student, or know whom to contact for technical support.

Evaluation Role

In general, the evaluator/proctor role includes assessment of student learning and enforcement of policies dealing with grades and ethical considerations (such as plagiarism). In this role an online instructor assesses learning outcomes, monitors originality of student work, and manages grades. An instructor may need to use assessment tools and techniques that are unique to the online environment (e.g., online proctored testing and plagiarism detection tools) when necessary. As mentioned in the pedagogical role, online instructors can evaluate students by providing consistent and frequent feedback to students (i.e., grades and comments on student work) since this is the most frequent type of student-to-instructor interaction that will likely occur.

Active Learning Facilitator Role

Active learning in an online environment includes activities like group and teamwork, student-to-student interactions, and project-based learning. An online instructor acts as the facilitator of active learning by managing cooperative groups, managing student interactions, and encouraging meaningful and interactive discussions. These behaviors relate closely to one of the Chickering and Gamson's (1987) Principles of active learning, which involves the students in their learning such as being engaged in conversations, writing about the learning material, and relating the learning material to their own lives.

Instructional Design Role

Online instructors at many institutions have the benefit of working directly with an instructional designer to design and develop an online course. Through this collaboration, they are able to gain many instructional design skills. Instructional design skills include knowledge and application of educational theory and educational technology. However, many institutions do not have the instructional design support for all unique course developments. In either scenario, an online instructor benefits from exploring educational theory (e.g., behaviorism, cognitivism, and constructivism as explained in the previous section) that influence e-learning instruction. Additionally, online instructors need support with graphic design and Internet and web skills, and if such support is not available, they need to acquire these skills. Collaboration and teamwork skills are also necessary in this role since online course development and delivery often involves a team of individuals such as instructional designers and multimedia experts.

Instructional Design, Technology, and Pedagogy

A fundamental decision to be made when designing professional development for faculty who will or are teaching online is to what extent they will need instructional design, technical and pedagogical skills to be able to develop, teach, and manage their courses. Some institutions invest in teams of instructional designers, multimedia experts, and programmers who support course development while others might not have a beginning budget that allows them to do so. The amount of instructional design knowledge needed by instructors embarking on online teaching depends on the level of instructional design support available at their institution. Thus, in designing faculty development for teaching online, a basic consideration is to what extent instructors will have to design their own courses. In this chapter we share an example of a professional development program for online instructors where instructional design support is provided at the institution, as this is increasingly the case in recent years with the growth of online education.

Often, a second consideration when designing professional development is whether online instructors participating in such a program will teach courses that they develop, revise, and maintain or teach online courses that have been developed by others. We assert that in either case, the roles defined above are important to online teaching, and online instructors have to be skilled in both technology and pedagogy, regardless of the amount of instructional design support they may receive. Discussions when identifying instructors competent to teach online often revolve around the importance of technology or pedagogy when teaching online, with some suggesting that a technology-savvy instructor with little teaching experience is a better online instructor and others arguing that a seasoned instructor with greater knowledge of learning theory and pedagogy is better suited for online instruction.

We maintain that knowledge and skills in both pedagogy and technology are needed to succeed in the online teaching environment.

Without a solid foundation in both pedagogy and technology, the instructor may struggle to navigate the online learning environment. For example, an instructor who is up to date on the latest technology tools but who has little experience facilitating online interactions and evaluating student work may struggle when interacting with students and providing constructive feedback. Likewise, an experienced instructor in the face-to-face classroom who is not technically competent and transitions to the online environment may feel overwhelmed by the myriad of tools and options and limit themselves in the ways in which they interact or which tools they choose to use, thereby potentially hindering learning and limiting students' access to each other and valuable resources.

The main consideration for e-learning leaders is how faculty development can be structured for all types of instructors, e.g., those who are technically-savvy but lacking in pedagogical knowledge, those with extensive teaching experience but low technical skills, those who are new to the academy or to teaching online, and those who have earlier experimented with other technologies or teaching online. The experienced instructor will benefit from learning practical technology tips and exploring the differences between a face-to-face classroom and an online classroom. The technology-savvy instructor may find pedagogical approaches such as evaluation methods and communication strategies useful. A brand-new instructor will benefit from both pedagogical and technological training as well as an introduction to institutional support and resources. In any of these scenarios, providing faculty with opportunities to learn in an environment similar to the one in which they will teach has been found to be valuable. e-Learning leaders aiming to offer faculty development to online instructors should ensure that the program or course offered simulates the technical and pedagogical environment in which they will teach and emulates online teaching practices expected of those online instructors. In the next section we describe how one institution approached faculty development for online instructors to model expectations of online teaching at that institution and to include all types of faculty.

What You Can Do

Implementing Professional Development in Online Instruction

In this section, we provide an example of professional development for online faculty based on a program that was offered at a state college for online instructors. We describe the learning outcomes and activities included in the program. We then discuss the design considerations that e-learning leaders can adapt and use for specific institutional needs. At the end of this section we briefly discuss the benefits and challenges of the presented approach and factors that e-learning leaders should consider when implementing such an approach.

Example of an e-Learning Faculty Development Model

The roles and competencies covered earlier in this chapter were evaluated and used as a guide to create learning objectives, activities, and assessments for an 8-week faculty development program in online teaching. The target audience included both full-time and adjunct faculty who were already teaching or planning to teach online in the future. The faculty represented varying ages, backgrounds, and disciplines, and included those new to the academy and those some nearing retirement. Previously, there had been a lot of emphasis on training instructors in the technical knowledge needed to teach online (e.g., use of the learning management system and other technologies used in online learning environments), but training with a focus on online teaching practices had not been offered at the college. This program focused on the pedagogical and active learning roles of an online instructor with an emphasis on developing skills to create social presence among students, increase communication with students, and provide meaningful feedback to students. It was hosted in the institutional LMS, and offered as a combination of online modules and online synchronous sessions, with flexibility for the instructors to meet instructional designers on-campus or online, in order to accommodate the needs of both adjunct and full-time faculty members. Briefly, the program had the following learning goals:

1. Identify and describe individual online teaching philosophy
2. Reflect upon current teaching practices
3. Identify and describe several theories and practices of online teaching and learning
4. Discuss and debate various topics related to current research on online teaching and learning
5. Participate in and facilitate synchronous, online sessions
6. Apply research-based principles to online courses by creating and implementing a new technique or strategy in an online class
7. Develop a community of practice with other online instructors
8. Collaborate and share tools and ideas with other online instructors
9. Enhance an online course with meaningful use of available technology tools
10. Develop strategies to increase communication and feedback into online courses

Learning Activities

Each learning outcome was paired with specific learning activities, assessments, instructional materials and tools in order to model best practices. For example, the course included exploring the roles and competencies of online instructors (see Table 1, Week 3: What do online teachers do?). The instructors were asked to read

Table 1 Topics, subtopics, tools, and modeled strategies of each module in the program

Module topic and subtopics	Tools and modeled strategies
Week 1, Modules 1–2: Introduction/ Canvas LMS 101 • Community building—intro discussion • Course mechanics • Introduction to course and facilitators	Discussion board (video) introduction with Active Learning (AL) technique Quiz
Week 2, Module 3: Underlying principles of online teaching and learning • Introduction to theories of online teaching and learning • Moore's three types of interaction: student–student, student–instructor, student–content • Community of inquiry • Seven principles of undergraduate education	Lesson Discussion board—online teaching philosophy Reading in text Reflection assignment
Week 3, Module 4: What do online teachers do? • What are the researched roles and competencies of online instructors? • Implementing the seven principles online • Hot topic—is online learning as good as face-to-face?	Lesson Discussion—hot topic Group Project: Group discussion and each group will research a role and/or competency and present to class via synchronous conference
Week 4, Module 5: Strategies for facilitation and communication • Instructor presence, communication, feedback • Discussion—case scenario	Lesson Discussion Web tools to encourage type of teaching method Provide feedback in various ways throughout course Case scenario to model problem-based learning
Week 5, Module 6: Online active teaching and learning strategies • Cooperative and collaborative • Problem based/project based • Discovery and adventure learning • Discussion—how would you do it?	Groups Collaborations Begin final project Project based on active teaching methods and utilizing tools to encourage the method—models PBL (project)

(continued)

Table 1 (continued)

Module topic and subtopics	Tools and modeled strategies
Week 6, Module 7: Strategies to build social presence • Review of main points • First days • Cooperative learning • Groups • Collaborations • Reflections	Lesson Assignment and projects Discussion Group activity Synchronous/asynchronous meeting tools
Module 8, Putting it to practice: applying the strategies—Final project • Final project applying a technique in course or incorporating a technique into future course	Synchronous meeting tool Student-led project

about this topic through the provided resources and lecture pages in the module. They were given a "hot topic" discussion prompt debating the efficacy of online learning versus face-to-face learning. Finally, they were assigned a group project in which they worked collaboratively to research a role and/or competency that they later presented to the other learners during a synchronous meeting.

Design Considerations

As mentioned, each institution has its own culture and context that must be considered before taking on an initiative like faculty development for e-learning. Some things to consider when embarking upon such an initiative include what the purpose and goal of a program will be and what skills and knowledge the faculty will gain from a program. In order to figure out the purpose and goal of the program, it is wise to obtain feedback from all stakeholders in the program, including department chairs and other relevant administration, through conversations about what is most important to include in the professional development. A needs assessment can be sent to the faculty body to determine what the faculty already know, want to know, and don't yet know. The roles and competencies described in this chapter is a starting point for this type of needs assessment. Conversations with stakeholders and a needs assessment will provide a solid foundation for the design of a program like the one described in this chapter.

Benefits and Challenges

The faculty development model described in this chapter benefited the college and faculty in many ways. First, the program laid a foundation for future faculty development initiatives at the college. The program established a precedent for faculty development devoted to e-learning instruction focusing on the best practices of using technology and pedagogy. Many of the participants promoted the program within their departments and to other colleagues across the campus.

Further, instructors who went through the program were able to explore the LMS and other e-learning tools from a student's perspective. Several instructors in the program discussed how it was the first time they were exposed to the use of the technological tools and learning activities from the student perspective. Specifically, the instructors were given an opportunity to interact with peer learners through the debate and group project. The facilitators of the professional development program demonstrated how to manage a group project that explored the subject matter. Finally, the faculty were able to use the synchronous meeting tool firsthand as well as a demonstration on how to host a synchronous session. See Table 1 for more details on each module of the program.

The voluntary nature of faculty development at the college presented another challenge. Instructors are not required but encouraged to take faculty development before teaching online. Thus, those that went through the first iterations of the program were intrinsically motivated to participate. The longer-term program presented another challenge. The time investment was significant for the participants since it was offered as a course one might take as a student. Those who aren't intrinsically motivated to participate in voluntary faculty development may not see the benefit of a long-term program. The question becomes, how do we encourage more faculty to participate in faculty development, especially longer-term programs, without being required to do so? One consideration might be to include veteran e-learning instructors in the design and development and/or facilitation of the program. Faculty who are skeptical or uncertain about the faculty development may feel more comfortable exploring these topics with a veteran e-learning instructor.

Some colleges and universities provide program-specific training and support whereas other institutions work from a central office to provide these services. This is something to consider when deciding what kind of faculty development initiative will be explored at an institution. Nonetheless, the roles and competencies that we suggest in this chapter are relevant to all online instructors. Further, faculty interest and support for professional development is important to acknowledge. An ideal place to start implementation of an initiative is with a group of faculty who already are interested and motivated to participate in these efforts. These initial participants can become the champions of an initiative that is supportive of e-learning instruction.

In addition to a formal professional development course of this nature, e-learning leaders might consider brown bag sharing sessions where faculty share their initial experiences with teaching online, e.g., something that has worked very well for them. This was received very positively by faculty at a large private institution, with faculty sharing resources, practices, templates for activities, and proposing new topics (e.g., writing good online discussion questions) by the end of the academic year. The creation of an online portal where faculty share questions, resources, and concerns in a closed environment can also be helpful, for instance, within a small department. Institutional investment is taken for granted for formal courses and modules, but is also essential for informal professional development of this nature.

Conclusion

Each institution approaches the support of e-learning instruction differently. Some institutions require faculty development for those who teach online while others leave development decisions up to the instructors. Some institutions are decentralized and individual colleges within the institution make decisions about how instructors are trained and how online courses are taught. Other institutions implement broad initiatives for online course development and training. Some institutions provide instructional design support at the individual course level and provide one-on-one support to faculty members as they embark upon online course development and teaching. The authors of this chapter have witnessed all types of institutions as described. We understand that each institution has a unique context and culture that must be considered before implementing faculty development. However, we assert that regardless of the unique characteristics of each institution, the major roles and competencies of online instructors must be explored in order to support e-learning instructors.

In this chapter we discussed several key considerations for identifying and developing these competencies for online instructors. We established the major philosophical perspectives that inform instruction and examples of these in e-learning environments. We then explored the major roles and competencies needed to teach online and what this looks like for online instructors. We presented the debate regarding technology and pedagogy and posit that instructors with strength in one or the other benefit from a faculty development program that allows e-learning instructors to personalize their own learning path. Finally, we presented an example of a faculty development program offered at a state college that explores the roles and competencies while encouraging faculty to apply and adopt these roles and competencies. We discussed the benefits and challenges of the program, both institutionally and for the instructors participating in the program.

For More Information

Palloff, R. M., & Pratt, K. (2011). *The excellent online instructor: Strategies for professional development.* San Francisco, CA: Jossey-Bass.

Rosenberg, P., & Riedinger, B. (2006). Uniting technology and pedagogy: The evolution of an online teaching certification course. *EDUCAUSE Review.* Retrieved from http://er.educause.edu/articles/2006/1/uniting-technology-and-pedagogy-the-evolution-of-an-online-teaching-certification-course

Sibley, K., & Whitaker, R. (2015). Engaging faculty in online education. *EDUCAUSE Review.* Retrieved from http://er.educause.edu/articles/2015/3/engaging-faculty-in-online-education

References

Allen, I. E., & Seaman, J. (2011). *Going the distance: Online education in the United States, 2011.* Newburyport, MA, The Sloan Consortium.

Bawane, J., & Spector, J. M. (2009). Prioritization of online instructor roles: Implications for competency-based teacher education programs. *Distance Education, 30*(3), 383–397. doi:10.1080/01587910903236536

Berge, Z. L. (1995). Facilitating computer conferencing: Recommendations from the field. *Educational Technology, 35*(1), 22–30.

Chickering, A. W., & Gamson, Z. F. (1987, March). Seven principles for good practice in undergraduate education. *AAHE Bulletin, 39*(7), 3–7.

Duffy, T. M., & Jonassen, D. H. (1992). *Constructivism and the technology of instruction: A conversation.* Mahwah, NJ: Lawrence Erlbaum Assoc. Inc.

Goodyear, P., Salmon, G., Spector, J. M., Steeples, C., & Tickner, S. (2001). Competencies for online teaching: A special report. *Educational Technology Research and Development, 49*(1), 65–72. doi:10.1007/BF02504508

Meyer, K. & Murrell, V. (2014) A National study of training content and activities for faculty development for online teaching. Journal of Asynchronous Networks, (18)1.

Moore, J. (2009). A synthesis of SLOAN-C effective practices. *Journal of Asynchronous Learning Networks, 13*(4), 74–91.

Schuh, K. L., & Barab, S. A. (2007). Philosophical perspectives. In J. M. Spector, M. D. Merrill, J. Van Merrienboer, & M. P. Driscoll (Eds.), *Handbook of research on educational communications and technology* (3rd ed.pp. 21–28). New York, NY: Routledge/Taylor & Francis Group.

The eLearning Leader's Toolkit for Evaluating Online Teaching

Thomas J. Tobin

Abstract College and university administrators who are tasked with leading distance-education programs can rely on several strengths: program and curriculum development expertise, knowledge of trends and needs among employers, budgeting skills, and experience in navigating the various regulations and accreditation requirements for new programs. Many of us in leadership positions have not, however, taught online courses ourselves, having left the classroom to become administrators before the "wave" of online teaching reached our institutions.

Although some department chairs and deans have taught online courses themselves (and thus have a feel for the challenges and flow of online teaching), many more administrators conducted their teaching careers exclusively in the face-to-face classroom. Especially for those administrators who moved away from teaching in the early 2000s, they are likely not to have developed or taught courses in a mode other than face-to-face. This chapter is designed to provide eLearning leaders three sets of tools for creating, implementing, and operating an evaluation program for online teaching at your campus.

Keywords Administration • Assessment • Bias • Employment • Evaluation • Formative • Measurement • Observation • Quality • Rubric • Summative • Teaching

Decision-Making Guidance

This chapter will help you make decisions about:

- What criteria should be used in evaluating online-teaching performance
- Who should be involved in the online-teaching observation itself
- When (and for how long) the observation of online teaching should take place
- What biases should be designed out of the evaluation process

T.J. Tobin (✉)
Tobin Consulting, 127 Presidents Drive, State College, PA 16803, USA
e-mail: dr.tobin@att.net

© Association for Educational Communications and Technology 2018
A.A. Piña et al. (eds.), *Leading and Managing e-Learning*, Educational
Communications and Technology: Issues and Innovations,
https://doi.org/10.1007/978-3-319-61780-0_17

235

- How to use evaluation measures to promote and re-hire the best online faculty members

What You Need to Know

Starting in the late 1990s, distance-education transformed into eLearning. This has meant significant shifts for campus leaders and students alike in three areas. Let's look at how things used to be. First, "traditional" distance education provided access to learning for students who were geographically distant from our campuses, but they faced obstacles to their learning, such as having to watch a cable-access TV channel at a particular time in order to see course lectures, or needing to communicate with their professors via slow or clunky mechanisms like using the postal service or attending scheduled phone calls. Second, traditional distance learning programs were modeled on the best practices from the face-to-face classroom, so that students and instructors often relied on lecture and recall as the primary ways to share information and measure student progress. Third, traditional distance learning was predicated on the assumption that students would be, for the most part, self-directed and independent learners. They had to be: there was little interaction with the instructor and with other students designed into the model.

Fast forward to today, where online courses allow students to be both geographically and temporally different from our institutions and instructors. Students need not be available for learning in the same place or at the same time as we are. We also now have a robust body of research demonstrating that best practices for the face-to-face classroom are different from best practices for asynchronous eLearning. There are even entire scholarly journals (e.g., the *Journal of Interactive Online Learning*, *JIOL*) and professional organizations (e.g., the Professional and Organizational Development [POD] Network) dedicated to nothing but the best practices in online learning. We are no longer tied to lecture and recall as the teaching model. Finally, these days, we expect that every class, no matter whether it's being offered face-to-face or online, has some elements for collaboration and interaction between students and the materials, students and classmates, and students and instructors.

Why We Aren't Observing and Evaluating Much Online Teaching Now

The majority of instructors in higher education in North America today teach at least one course in an online or hybrid mode (Allen, Seaman, Lederman, & Jachik, 2012). In fact, more than 10% of the sections we offer in colleges and universities are now online courses, attended by nearly a third of all students (Allen, Seaman,

Poulin, & Straut, 2016, p. 43). One of the challenges facing eLearning leaders is that the people on whom we rely to evaluate the teaching happening in our eLearning courses are often ill prepared to perform those evaluations—or they simply don't. Based on conversations at more than 50 colleges and universities across North America, a significant number of instructors have never had their online teaching evaluated in any summative way (Buller, 2012). Typically, for instructors teaching online, either they are observed only in their face-to-face courses, they are never observed by peers or supervisors, or—the most common scenario—their online teaching is assessed based solely on student end-of-course ratings. Why might our instructors who teach online courses receive poor (or no) scrutiny of their teaching when it takes place online?

Think for a minute about the last time you taught. Most administrators' teaching careers before they became campus leaders didn't include teaching in modes outside of the face-to-face classroom (McCarthy & Samors, 2009). This is changing slowly, as newer administrators with online-teaching or teaching-with-technology experience are joining our ranks. Perhaps you're one of them.

In any case, you probably know at least one administrator at your institution who fits the "never taught online" description, and that's why this chapter is designed to give you the skills to be a kind of "secret evangelist" for the best practices in evaluating online teaching. After reading this chapter, you will be able to define a set of seven measurable and actionable online-teaching practices; create a rubric-based system of observation and evaluation for teaching in online courses; link the outputs of your online-teaching observations to your institution's existing promotion, tenure, and retention measures; and train other leaders on your campus to adopt and implement the online-teaching evaluation system outlined in this chapter.

What You Can Do

College and university administrators who are tasked with leading eLearning programs can rely on several strengths: we have program and curriculum development expertise, knowledge of trends and needs among employers, budgeting skills, and experience in navigating the various regulations and accreditation requirements for our programs. We can add three "toolkits" for creating, implementing, and operating an evaluation program for online teaching at our institutions.

Toolkit 1: Creating the Process   There are purposes for evaluating online teaching that are largely apolitical: we evaluate our online teaching practices so that we can improve our teaching methods, retain students, and best support students in accomplishing their educational goals. Student ratings, self-evaluations, and peer evaluations—especially informal ones—fall into this category.

Conversely, when administrators and their proxies observe and evaluate online teaching, we typically do so in order to determine whether the instructor is re-hired for the following semester (in the case of contingent faculty) or whether the instructor progresses through the promotion-and-tenure process (for tenure-line faculty).

Because the purpose of administrative review is so narrowly conceived, many institutions have already created or adopted an administrator-observation instrument that is separate from peer-evaluation and student-rating instruments. Administrative evaluators for face-to-face courses seldom receive (or need) guidance about

- Determining the people with whom it is appropriate to conduct the review session
- Differentiating between teaching behaviors and course materials
- Determining the length of the observation period

The existence of separate administrator-observation instruments—however open-ended—is an opportunity for opening the conversation about what behaviors constitute good teaching practices, what evidence of those behaviors can be observed, and how those behaviors can be quantified and evaluated (rather than merely noted as existing or not).

Toolkit 2: Implementing the Procedure   Before we can create instruments to evaluate teaching behaviors toward retention and promotion, we must confront several myths about the observable qualities of good teaching. The administrative-observation instruments developed for face-to-face teaching typically share some common observational biases, which are invisible until we start thinking about shifting the modality of teaching from face-to-face to online. We will uncover six biases that may favor face-to-face instructional methods, and one bias that favors online teaching methods.

Toolkit 3: Operating the Program   Instead of looking for specific behaviors or affective elements of the instructor (such as "speaks clearly" or "maintains the interest of students"), administrative observers can find modality-neutral, measurable evaluation criteria by focusing on the effects of instructor behavior. For example, "the instructor communicates in a way that students respond to throughout the range of observation." By observing the behaviors of instructors for what those behaviors elicit from the learners, administrative evaluators can make yes-no determinations and further assign measurable values to the behaviors.

Toolkit 1: Creating the Process

Especially when administrative observation of teaching occurs for the purpose of determining whether to re-hire or promote an instructor, the overarching goal is to make the observation process as standardized as possible: to observe each instructor under conditions as similar as possible to those used to observe his or her peers and to evaluate instructors using a common set of criteria. It is tempting to create a table of equivalences between face-to-face and online course delivery. If one observes 90 min of a face-to-face course, where (and to what extent) should one look in an online course environment to see the same amount of teaching happening?

Part of the confusion about observing face-to-face and online versions of the same course has to do with the visibility of the content and behaviors observed. For a face-to-face class, we do not typically come to the instructor's office hours to observe one-on-one interactions with students, nor do we review samples of the instructor's class notes or e-mails to students.

We have access to all of these elements, and often more, in online courses. We can see the course syllabus, lecture content and multimedia for every unit, students' posts to the discussion forums, student assignments and instructor feedback on them, as well as the instructor's e-gradebook.

Because of these differences in visibility and access between face-to-face and online courses, we should think of what actions administrators can take that other reviewers cannot. For example, a department chair can

- e-mail current students to follow-up on the observation
- Look up past-performance data on current students' previous courses
- Compare observation data from the instructor's previous offerings
- Recommend (and often enforce) instructor remediation actions for noted challenges
- Provide incentives for improved teaching practices, retention, and student satisfaction

All of these actions take place outside of the observation itself, and administrative observers are in a unique position to be able to integrate the observation of online teaching practices into an overall program of feedback to the instructor. Thus, when administrators are the observers, we should employ the process that follows.

Instead of looking for affective instructor behaviors (such as "speaks clearly" or "maintains the interest of students"), we can use modality-neutral, measurable criteria for evaluation by focusing on the effects of those instructor behaviors. For example, "the instructor communicates in a way that students respond to throughout the range of observation." By observing instructors for what their behaviors elicit from the learners, we can assign measurable values to the behaviors. In their seminal article, "Principles for Good Practice in Undergraduate Education," Chickering and Gamson (1987) analyzed a wealth of research on good teaching in colleges and universities. They revealed seven core principles of effective teaching practice that are themselves modality-independent:

1. Encourage student–faculty contact.
2. Develop reciprocity and cooperation among students.
3. Use active learning techniques.
4. Give prompt feedback.
5. Emphasize time-on-task.
6. Communicate high expectations.
7. Respect diverse talents and ways of learning.

By seeking instructor behaviors that help to meet each of these core areas, administrative observers can tailor their observations to the tools and methods being used, regardless of the course-offering modality. For online courses, especially, focusing on Chickering and Gamson's principles allows administrators who may not have taught online themselves to look for evidence of effective teaching interactions throughout the online environment: everything that is not an interaction can be seen as a piece of content.

To answer an earlier question, there is no online equivalent to a 90-minute face-to-face observation. Time and place are the "givens" of face-to-face observation. Online givens are not time or location (both vary), but the online environment itself. To create the process for observing online courses, we should agree on five key factors.

Definition of Teaching Practices

There are many analogues to face-to-face teaching practices that may not be considered "teaching" for the online course. Face-to-face lecturing is a key teaching practice. Videos and lecture notes in online courses are part of the course media, and are not themselves direct evidence of teaching behaviors—especially if the person who developed the lecture notes or videos is not the person facilitating the class.

One strategy for making clear what counts as a teaching practice in an online course is to examine those elements that lead directly to interaction among the students and/or instructor. For example, a set of lecture notes that is presented as a single web page, and which presents information—in the manner of a textbook or article—is part of the course design, and would not be considered in an administrative observation of the online course. Likewise, videos, audio podcasts, and the like are also as part of an online course's materials, and do not "count" as observable teaching behaviors. However, if an instructor responds to student questions in an online-course discussion by posting a mini-lecture or video to explain a concept, that certainly "counts" as an observed teaching behavior, because the content is created or shared as a result of interaction between the learner and the instructor.

Agreement on which elements of the online course represent teaching practices is often the most contentious discussion on a campus, since many elements may be considered either part of the course design or teaching practices, depending on their structure and function, as seen in the example of lecture content above. Create a core agreement that identifies elements of online courses

- That are *always* counted as teaching practices (e.g., discussion forums, feedback on student assignments)
- That *may* be counted as teaching practices, depending on structure and interactivity (e.g., spontaneous "mini lectures," news/announcement items)
- That are *never* counted as teaching practices (e.g., pre-constructed lecture content, assignment directions, content created by third parties like textbook publishers)

The overall question to apply is one of information presentation versus interaction. As a final caveat, items that were created by a person other than the course instructor should never be counted toward administrative observation of online courses. This leads to the second area needing agreement: communication.

Communication Between Observer and Observed

Prior to observing face-to-face teaching, we let instructors know that they will be observed on a given day and time. Perhaps we ask for the syllabus or any handouts. There is little communication between us and instructors during the actual observation.

For online courses, we must still notify the instructor that observation will take place. Instructors should share where they want us to focus, and what is unique about the instruction, especially if there are interactions that go beyond the usual places where interaction occurs. Clarifying and directional questions are often beneficial during the online observation. For example, we may want to see supplemental content that is released to students only after they accomplish various course tasks (and which we cannot unlock). This brings up the next area where agreement is needed: the extent of the observation.

Scope of the Observation

Instructors perform teaching actions outside of formal instruction. Both face-to-face and online instructors engage in student consultations via office hours, e-mail, and telephone calls. Face-to-face, such contact, although it definitely meets the definition of "teaching," is not counted toward administrative observation because it is not readily visible and measurable to observers.

Online, these interactions may or may not be visible, depending on our institution's technological setup. Where the learning management system (LMS) includes real-time text chat, faculty "office hours" may be stored in logs accessible to us as observers. Many instructors have "Q&A" forums in their online discussions that are intended for general questions about the course.

So, where may we look? Face-to-face, the boundary is the classroom itself. Interactions that take place outside the classroom, including office-hour consultations, phone calls, and e-mail messages, are not counted toward our observations. Consider excluding those same types of outside-of-formal-instruction communications from the observation and evaluation process for online teaching, as well.

A last word about scope: the best practice is to allow administrative observers student-level access to online courses, unless there is a compelling reason for access to an instructor-only area of the course. Agreement on this point, and a process for making the request to see instructor-access parts of a course, are best made in advance of the observation. Such agreement helps to keep the focus of the observation on the interactions accessible to students.

Duration of the Observation

We typically observe one face-to-face class meeting: 50–90 min watching the class unfold in real time. Our time spent observing the online environment does not correlate directly to that face-to-face class covering the same scope of ideas and content. First, conduct observations after the course is completed, so that there will be a rich set of interactions to evaluate. If observations take place early in the course, there may not yet be a lot of teaching behaviors in evidence.

We should allow access to the online course environment over a set period of days, and to communicate time-spent expectations up front (e.g., spend no more than 2 total hours observing). This helps observers to know how much attention and detail is required for completing a thorough observation, allows us to focus on the must-observe areas of the course environment, and offers an opportunity to look at other areas of the course environment to determine whether they contain evidence of interaction.

Assistance Available to the Observer

Face-to-face observation requires little technical skill. We arrive at the classroom and take notes about the class. For online courses, administrative observers may not be skilled at navigating the online course environment or may need technical help in observing various elements in the online course. Agreement about the availability, extent, and role of technical staff is needed prior to the observation.

If we require guides who will "drive" during the online observation process, first determine from what area(s) of the institution such technical assistants should come. For instance, tenure and promotion observations may be facilitated by staff members from the teaching-and-learning center, who should draw a "bright line" about answering only process-related questions, leaving the domain of "what to observe" squarely in the hands of the administrative observers.

Further, define the role of the technical assistant. The continuum of assistance can range from fully embedded (where the assistant is at the keyboard all the time, and takes direction from the administrative observer) to consultative (where the administrative observer is at the computer and the assistant offers verbal help) to on-call (where the assistant is not initially involved in the observation, and is brought in only if the observer requests help).

Any assistance offered must be facilitative and not evaluative. For instance, a technical assistant may show an evaluator an online course's discussion forums and may mention that the instructor appears to be responding at the rate of about one message per ten student messages. The assistant should not, however, provide evaluative or comparative advice during the observation, such as saying that a good benchmark for instructor postings is to post between 10 and 20% of the total number of messages in online discussions. This can be challenging for assistants who are, outside of the observation setting, resources for the institution on precisely these kinds of issues. In institutions where teaching-center staff members train administrators in the process of observing online courses, it is a good practice to source the pool of technical assistants from another campus unit, such as the information-technology area, to avoid potential conflicts regarding who is providing the evaluative response in an observation.

Toolkit 2: Implementing the Procedure

To assist us in implementing our evaluations of online teaching behaviors toward retention and promotion, we must confront several myths about the observable qualities of good teaching. The administrative-observation procedures and instruments developed for face-to-face teaching typically share some common observational biases, which are invisible until we start thinking about shifting the modality of teaching from face-to-face to online.

Bias 1: Good Teaching is Embodied

Based on our experiences teaching face-to-face, we can worry that, online, "students can't see the professor or hear his voice:" a bias that body language and voice inflection are integral to effective teaching. While it is true that varied voice inflection and open body language help to keep face-to-face learners engaged (Betts, 2013), such indicators are not the only means of demonstrating instructor involvement.

Likewise, evaluators may observe online video content in the same way we would observe a face-to-face lecture. We may be swayed by professional-style, longer lecture-style videos and disappointed by brief "bare bones" videos of instructors discussing course concepts. Flashy presentation skills can mask a lack of instructor subject knowledge, and chunking of video content is an established best practice for course-related multimedia regardless of the course-offering modality.

By expanding beyond the bias, we see that communication between the instructor and the learners is the key measurement, especially with regard to its frequency, nature, and quality. Think of all of the signals that face-to-face instructors send, and look for similar signals in online courses, such as the frequency of instructor discussion posts and the regularity of follow-up communication with learners about posted video content.

Bias 2: Good Teaching Is Intuitive

The evaluation of face-to-face teaching is often based on the subjective feelings of the administrative observer. Even where there are score sheets, rubrics, or other observation instruments, the questions asked sometimes do not lend themselves to quantifiable responses. Using "I know it when I see it" as an observation criterion exposes a bias for the observer's own learning preferences. Administrators who themselves learned best in lecture courses will rate lecturers as more competent teachers than instructors who favor other teaching practices.

The impact of the bias is magnified when observing online courses: A department chair's concern that "the students can't see the professor or hear his voice" is also a coded way of saying that he can't see the professor or hear his voice, either. To expand beyond this bias, shift your thinking away from charismatic traits (e.g., ability to hold students' attention, strong classroom "presence") and toward their support-behavior analogues (e.g., providing multiple ways for students to consume course content, reaching out to every student with a personal communication at least once per unit).

Bias 3: Good Teaching Happens in Real Time

There is a strong bias toward synchronicity as a hallmark of effective teaching. While online teaching can happen in real time, most eLearning is asynchronous: any time, any place. Real-time conversations allow instructors and students to have immediate feedback, but in face-to-face classrooms, it is often the instructor and a small core of students—between five and ten students, regardless of class size— who are engaged in the class discussion at any given time (Weaver & Qi, 2005). Many students remain silent throughout the entire class.

We can move beyond this bias by focusing on the instructor's ability to engage students through ad-hoc interactions. In fact, engaging one-on-one with learners asynchronously is a uniquely online teaching behavior. Look for evidence of teaching practices that invite learners and instructors to share and shape the conversation through discussions, collaborative group work, and the like.

Bias 4: Good Teaching Appears Effortless

Remember the very first time you taught? Many of us first entered the classroom with a legal pad filled with information and notes, or with a PowerPoint presentation bristling with notations and resource links—reminders of the things we did not want to forget to talk about with the class. Over time, that legal pad got put aside in favor of index cards with a few bullet points to remember. Some of us now rely solely on our experience and memory in order to facilitate each face-to-face class session.

Theatricality, or the appearance of effortlessness, is the most common mental shortcut that we observers use to stand in for "effectiveness" in face-to-face teaching. We are often biased toward the faculty member who can "wing it" from memory. In eLearning, however, instructors are brought back to "legal-pad mode:" much of what instructors typically speak and perform in face-to-face classes ends up as documentation in the online environment—and is thus not observed as an online teaching practice.

Further complicating this bias is the situation that in online courses, the people who design the course outline, lecture content, assessments, videos, and initial discussion prompts may not be the people teaching the course. To the biased eye, this suggests that all that is needed to teach online is a warm body, one who can occasionally answer student questions, grade the tests and quizzes, and report on student achievement at the end of the course.

To work against the sage-on-the-stage bias, avoid confusing information delivery with teaching behaviors. Define ahead of time what behaviors are to be evaluated as online teaching practices. One of the most common forms of face-to-face information sharing, even today, is lecturing. In an online environment, lecture content is information delivery, akin to the textbook readings in a face-to-face course: it's a piece of media to be consumed by the learners in their own time, rather than an interaction to be shared with the class. While it is important that media elements in online courses be expertly created, it is the delivery of the online course—the "teaching"—that is key to administrative reviews conducted for staffing and promotion decisions.

Bias 5: Quantity Bias

There is one factor in administrative evaluation of online teaching that is not typically encountered in observation of face-to-face classes, and which deserves separate consideration: quantity bias. Especially for those of us who have not taught online ourselves, it can be tempting to equate "more things" with greater quality of the online course experience for students—such as the amount of content in the online course, the amount of multimedia used in the course, or the number of communications from the instructor.

To avoid quantity bias, focus exclusively on the interactions among the students and instructor. It is safest to evaluate only the "spontaneous" aspects of the course and not the "canned" materials at all. Instructors might not have authored the content of the course and might have inherited the structural aspects of the course, too. By focusing on just the interactions between students and instructor, as well as on the instructor's facilitation of student-to-student interactions, evaluators can get a true sense of how well online courses are being taught. This points to two take-away lessons for implementing the observation and evaluation process.

First, consider student interaction load. Estimate the amount of effort being asked of learners in the unit or week under evaluation. In a 3-credit course during a 15-week semester, the total effort asked of students typically ranges between 6 and 10 h, including in- and out-of-class work (SACS COC, 2012). Give higher evaluative credit to instructors who interact more often with students as part of the student workload. For example, instructors may ask students to report on assignment progress, provide feedback on collaborative student work, and take an active part in guiding course discussion threads.

Second, look for a balance of planned and just-in-time communication. Provide higher ratings to online courses where the instructor posts regular communications, such as unit introductions, milestone-achievement messages, and roundup/review messages. In addition, look for just-in-time communications that respond to student requests for assistance and provide praise and correction for individual students. It is possible to have an entire online course "in the can" and post only pre-written messages—the equivalent of the same-lectures-every-semester professor who reads from 15-year-old notes. Evaluate the quality of instructor feedback on student work using Chickering and Gamson's principles (e.g., the instructor communicates high expectations, gives prompt and meaningful feedback, and respects diverse talents and ways of learning).

Especially in online courses, it can be tempting to equate greater quantities of interaction with better course experiences. Be sure to take into account the number of students in the course when evaluating the number of instances of interaction seen in the online course environment, as well.

Toolkit 3: Operating the Program

By categorizing elements of online courses as either content or interactions, we can make more fine-grained determinations about which parts of online courses are actually examples of teaching behaviors. Table 1 illustrates one way to match teaching principles against commonly observed teaching behaviors in online courses.

Five Places to Look

Consistent instructor presence is one of the most important components of online teaching practice, helping students feel less isolated and more supported in their learning. In fact, instructor presence supports each of Chickering and Gamson's seven principles. In online instruction, where another course or even institution is just a click away, instructor presence goes a long way toward student retention, academic success, and building a sense of community.

Piña and Bohn (2014) identify specific behaviors unique to the online environment that administrators perceive as effective indicators of teaching quality.

> Our desire was to identify a set of criteria that would yield objective data easily examined by supervisors and peers during an online course observation and serve as a balance to the more subjective data gathered from student surveys. This study focused upon quantitative measures of instructor actions and behaviors that could be readily observed in the online course and/or collected using the reporting tools of the learning management system:

- Has the instructor logged in at least an average of every other day?
- Has the instructor posted a biography of at least a paragraph, in addition to contact info?
- Has the instructor posted announcements at least weekly?
- Is there evidence that the instructor answers student inquiries in 2 days or less?

Table 1 Online teaching behaviors that exemplify teaching principles

Teaching principle	Common online teaching behaviors
Encourage student–faculty contact	Set regular online "office hours" Adhere to a maximum response time for communications Facilitate regular course discussions Post course news updates on a regular basis
Develop reciprocity and cooperation among students	Assign group or dyad projects Require discussion responses to peers Offer encouragement via the public discussion forum, and criticism in private grade-tool feedback
Use active learning techniques	Ask students to summarize and propose next steps Assign "butts out of seats" tasks away from the keyboard (e.g., interview experts); ask students to report back to the class Have students create and post study guides
Give prompt feedback	Respond to each student at least once per graded discussion topic Keep to turn-around time expectations for instructor grading Give students encouragement, reflection, and correction feedback
Emphasize time-on-task	Give students estimates of how long assignments wills take Communicate progress of the whole class toward week/unit goals Provide individual-progress milestones for graded work
Communicate high expectations	Give preview, status, and review communications Provide samples of good practice on assignments and discussion Spotlight students who do good work or improve their efforts
Respect diverse talents and ways of learning	Provide multiple ways for students to respond to assignments (e.g., write an essay, record an audio response, create a video) Allow students to respond to discussions using a variety of media Present materials to allow for a range of possible learning paths

- Does the instructor participate in discussion forums where appropriate?
- Does the instructor provide feedback on assignments?

Piña and Bohn's categorizations provide us with criteria to apply across our evaluation programs. This leads us to the last part of the evaluation program: where to look to find evidence of teaching behaviors. There are five places to look in any LMS to see, count, measure, and assess the interactions of online teaching.

News/Announcements

Every LMS has a feature that allows instructors to post messages that display when learners enter the course. In evaluating instructors, look for frequent, brief messages posted throughout each unit, rather than few lengthy posts. Quality instructors focus their news items on students' progress through the course, include reminders to keep students on task, and include feedback to demonstrate that they are listening to student needs. Advanced-level online instructors create announcements that are audience-specific (e.g., students who earned passing scores see a different announcement than students who need remediation) and that use the personalization features of the LMS (e.g., using "replace strings" to address students by name).

Grades

Unlike in face-to-face evaluation, observers can have access to instructors' gradebook feedback. Look for timely feedback (compare actual turn-around time to promised turn-around), both numerical and text-based feedback, feedback that focuses on learner skills and opportunities for improvement, and use of rubrics to guide feedback and minimize grading inconsistency. Advanced online instructors will send back a separate file to students with comments and feedback (often a marked-up version of the student's own submission file), and they will also personalize feedback as much as possible.

Dropbox

Every LMS has a tool that allows students to send and receive files with their instructors. Look in the dropbox for timely feedback (measured against promised limits) that refers to student expectations. Like with grade-tool feedback, look for instructors to accept diversity of learner responses within the limits of the subject, and for rubric use in providing feedback. Advanced online instructors provide dropbox feedback with an active-learning focus on what student can do with their performance and learning, and they also personalize feedback where possible.

Discussions

The heart of measurable teaching behaviors in most online courses is the asynchronous discussion tool. Competent online instructors are active in the conversation (a good rule of thumb is to look for activity on one more day per week than students are required to participate), challenge their learners to develop the conversation beyond the initial prompt, and provide quality responses to learners (responding to each student in a high-quality way at least once per unit). Good online instructors post messages within or near the "golden ratio" of 10–15% of the total messages posted by the class (cf. Cranney, Wallace, Alexander, & Alfano, 2011; Mandernach, Gonzales, & Garrett, 2006). Advanced online instructors adopt a discussion stance of guiding student examination, and they provide clear expectations for student behavior and for their own behavior, as well.

Surveys

Most LMSes have tools that allow instructors to create anonymous surveys to solicit formative feedback from their students. The surveys themselves may not be evidence of online teaching behaviors; they can be part of the pre-loaded content in online courses. Competent online instructors tell their students that they wish to receive formative feedback throughout the course (at least at mid-term), act on student responses, monitor feedback from students, and feed-forward by making changes to their teaching in response to student needs and requests. Observers should look for advanced behaviors such as sharing all responses received and instructors who adapt the rules and/or pace of the course in response to ongoing learner feedback.

Conclusion

Each of these toolkits helps eLearning leaders to define the measurable teaching behaviors that can be observed in online courses. By treating the evaluation of online course content and the evaluation of online teaching separately, we can ensure that we are assigning praise and corrective feedback to the right people—that we are promoting faculty members along the promotion and tenure line and asking adjunct faculty members to teach again for us, based on measurable and defensible criteria. Especially because evaluation by administrators counts toward job-related decisions, it is imperative that we are consistent and balanced in observing and evaluating our instructors, regardless of the mode in which they teach for our institutions.

By addressing potential biases, creating processes for observation and evaluation of online teaching, and teaching campus leaders where and how to look for evidence of good teaching in the online environment, we create consistency. On many campuses, the greater detail available to evaluators of online courses leads them to reexamine their methods, instruments, and level of detail for face-to-face observations, as well. As a final thought exercise, call to mind the people at your institution who are tasked with administrative observations and evaluations for employment purposes. Are they well prepared to evaluate online teaching? If not, who can help them to get the core skills for observing and evaluating online teaching behaviors? Those people are your core change agents; share Toolkits 1, 2, and 3 with them, and begin bringing your online-teaching evaluation processes into the life cycle of your whole institution's evaluation efforts.

For More Information

The administrative evaluation of online teaching is still a relatively new field. To keep up with the latest research in the field, eLearning leaders should read the *Online Journal of Distance Learning Administration* at http://www.westga. edu/~distance/ojdla/. Key recent resources in the field include

- *Effective Evaluation of Teaching: A Guide for Faculty and Administrators:* this includes several chapters on evaluating online teaching (see Drouin, 2012 and Ismail, Buskist, & Groccia, 2012).
- *Evaluating Online Teaching: Implementing Best Practices* (Tobin, Mandernach, & Taylor, 2015).
- The *Faculty Development* web site at the John A. Dutton e-Education Institute at Penn State University (http://facdev.e-education.psu.edu/) contains many resources such as the peer review of online teaching rubric/process and a list of faculty online-teaching competencies.

Acknowledgments The author is grateful to Wiley for permission to base the "Toolkit 1" and "Toolkit 2" sections of this chapter on Chap. 6, "Administrative Evaluation of Online Teaching" in Tobin, Mandernach, & Taylor, *Evaluating Online Teaching: Implementing Best Practices* (© 2015 John Wiley & Sons, Inc. All rights reserved).

References

Allen, I. E., Seaman, J., Lederman, D., & Jachik, S. (2012). Conflicted: Faculty and online education, 2012. Babson Survey Research Group and Inside Higher Ed. Retrieved from https://www.insidehighered.com/sites/default/server_files/survey/conflicted.html.

Allen, I. E., Seaman, J., Poulin, R., & Straut, T. T. (2016). Online report card: Tracking online education in the United States. Babson Survey Research Group and Quahog Research Group. Retrieved from http://onlinelearningsurvey.com/reports/onlinereportcard.pdf.

Betts, K. (2013). Lost in translation: Importance of effective communication in online education. Online Journal of Distance Learning Administration, 16(2). Retrieved from http://www.westga.edu/~distance/ojdla/summer122/betts122.html.

Buller, J. (2012). *Best practices in faculty evaluation*. San Francisco, CA: Jossey-Bass.

Chickering, A. and Gamson, Z. (1987). Principles for good practice in undergraduate education. *The Wingspread Journal* (Special insert, n.p., June). Racine, WI: Johnson Foundation.

Cranney, M., Wallace, L., Alexander, J. L., & Alfano, L. (2011). Instructor's discussion forum effort: Is it worth it? MERLOT Journal of Online Learning and Teaching, 7(3). Retrieved from http://jolt.merlot.org/vol7no3/cranney_0911.pdf.

Drouin, M. (2012). What's the story on evaluations of online teaching? In M. E. Kite (Ed.), *Effective evaluation of teaching: A guide for faculty and administrators* (pp. 60–70). Washington, DC: Society for the Teaching of Psychology. Retrieved from http://www.teachpsych.org/Resources/Documents/ebooks/evals2012.pdf.

Ismail, E., Buskist, W., & Groccia, J. E. (2012). Peer review of teaching. In M. E. Kite (Ed.), *Effective evaluation of teaching: A guide for faculty and administrators* (pp. 79–91). Washington, DC: Society for the Teaching of Psychology. Retrieved from http://www.teachpsych.org/Resources/Documents/ebooks/evals2012.pdf.

Mandernach, B. J., Gonzales, R. M., & Garrett, A. L. (2006). An examination of online instructor presence via threaded discussion participation. MERLOT Journal of Online Learning and Teaching, 2(4). Retrieved from http://jolt.merlot.org/vol2no4/mandernach.pdf.

McCarthy, S. and Samors, R. (2009). Online learning as a strategic asset. 2 vols. APLU-Sloan National Commission on Online Learning. Retrieved from http://sloanconsortium.org/publications/survey/APLU_Reports.

Piña, A., & Bohn, L. (2014). Assessing online faculty: More than student surveys and design rubrics. *Quarterly Review of Distance Education*, *15*(4), 25–34.

Southern Association of Colleges and Schools Commission on Colleges (SACS COC). (2012). Credit hours: Policy statement. Retrieved from http://www.sacscoc.org/subchg/policy/CreditHours.pdf.

Tobin, T. J., Mandernach, B. J., & Taylor, A. H. (2015). *Evaluating online teaching: Implementing best practices*. San Francisco: Jossey-Bass.

Weaver, R. R., & Qi, J. (2005). Classroom organization and participation: College students' perceptions. *Journal of Higher Education*, *76*(5), 570–601.

Collaborative Management of the eLearning Design and Development Process

Deborah S. Slaughter and Megan C. Murtaugh

Abstract The eLearning design and development process is often one that is overlooked in the planning stages of online programs. In order to deliver effective instructional environments to your learner, collaboration amongst all stakeholders needs to be considered from the inception of the program. This chapter will guide you in creating and managing a streamlined, effective, and collaborative design process for working with subject matter experts. The information presented will assist you with making decisions that are crucial to a successful design and development process. These decisions include selecting an instructional design model, identifying a design and development timeline, creating a course development template to expedite the design and development of courses, choosing collaboration tools for working with and reporting progress to stakeholders, orienting the subject matter expert, and finally by evaluating the development process and courses created as a result of the process.

Keywords Instructional design • Development template • Collaboration • eLearning management • Design process • Subject-matter experts • Process evaluation

Decision-Making Guidance

This chapter will help you make decisions about:

- Selecting an ID model
- Identifying a design and development timeline
- Creating a course development template (this can be used across programs/ schools)

D.S. Slaughter
Dara-Oak Academic Community, 830 Dunks Road, Sherwood, MI 49089, USA
e-mail: drdebislaughter@gmail.com

M.C. Murtaugh (✉)
Dara-Oak Academic Community, 21100 Lonesome Lane, Alva, FL 33920, USA
e-mail: megancmurtaugh@gmail.com

© Association for Educational Communications and Technology 2018
A.A. Piña et al. (eds.), *Leading and Managing e-Learning*, Educational
Communications and Technology: Issues and Innovations,
https://doi.org/10.1007/978-3-319-61780-0_18

- Choosing collaboration tools (i.e., Google, Microsoft, web conferencing software)
- Orienting the subject matter expert
- Evaluating the development process and courses

What You Need to Know

The eLearning design and development process is often one that is overlooked in the planning stages of online programs. In order to deliver effective instructional environments to your learner, collaboration amongst all stakeholders needs to be considered from the inception of the program. Dependent upon the eLearning environment, some decisions will need to be addressed before the design and development phase commences. These decisions include program development and Learning Management System (LMS) organization.

In regard to program development, department chairs or program managers may map out the curriculum that will encompass a specific degree or certification program prior to engaging the resources of an instructional design team. This includes identifying the individual courses and the learning outcomes associated with the overall program and each individual course. One thing to keep in mind when mapping out the curriculum for a program is to avoid excessive overlap in the courses. Learners will quickly be put off if they feel they are double paying for their learning because they cover the same concepts or content in multiple courses.

Another consideration to entertain prior to beginning the design and development process relates to a predetermination of the layout and organization of the chosen learning management system (LMS). This is an important step in the eLearning program development. Consideration of navigation, standard menu items, and content organization should all be determined before the design and development phase begins. In addition, an outside review of the LMS template is highly recommended. Recommendations for eLearning evaluation entities that could be used for an outside review of the LMS template are presented in the *What You Can Do* section of this chapter.

Once these decisions are completed, eLearning leaders can begin the design and development process by selecting an appropriate instructional design model and identifying subject matter experts. Please note that the process described in this chapter is adaptable across LMS platforms and ID models. The design cycle presented as an example is based on content deliverables using an adapted version of the Wiggins and McTighe instructional design model also known as Backwards Design.

Choosing an ID Model

Depending on the institution or business and the type of learning being designed, an appropriate instructional design model needs to be identified. This is the first step in your design and development process. In Table 1, we have outlined a few models, provided a brief description of each model, and listed possible learning environments in which they can be used.

Design and Development Timeline

Adhering to a schedule for development is essential to the successful completion of designing eLearning courses. Dependent upon the components necessary for creating a course, the timeline could range from weeks to months; the average is about 250 h per course, based on a report from the Center for Educational Innovation at the University of Minnesota (2015). By following the process in this chapter, 24 courses per year can be designed and developed by one instructional designer.

Setting reasonable and flexible deadlines will aid in getting the project completed. The cycle presented here allowed the authors to design and develop 115 courses in 2½ years, an average of four classes per month. These courses were 8-week accelerated online, 3-credit hour classes that reflect the New York State Education Department's current policies for online learning learner time on task (2013). Many of these courses were developed and designed utilizing open educational resources, subject matter expert created materials, and authentic assessments (non-publisher dependent content).

A typical design and development cycle can be completed in 16 weeks. One of the most important aspects is the adherence to the process, as outlined below. It is important to determine the amount of time needed for a subject matter expert to create each content deliverable. The 16-week cycle allows the following timeframes for content deliverables:

- Deliverable #1: Weekly Topics and Objectives (1 week)
- Deliverable #2: Assessments and Rubrics (2 weeks)
- Deliverable #3: Discussions and Activities (2 weeks)
- Deliverable #4: Readings and Resources (3 weeks)
- Deliverable #5: Weekly Overviews and Summaries (1 week)

In Fig. 1, we provide a suggested timeline and the description that follows the figure is a quick overview of the timeline process. Some weeks are not elaborated upon as the steps are repeated for each deliverable.

Weeks 1–3. This is considered prep time for designers and stakeholders. During the first few weeks, the subject matter expert should attend an online instruction training course. This course should cover the basics of the learning management system, best practices in eLearning facilitation, and institutional regulations. This is

Table 1 ID models and applicable learning environments

Suggested ID model	Brief description and application	Applicable learning environments
Dave Meier Accelerated Learning Rapid Instructional Design (RID)[a]	This model allows for creation of rapid strategies and standard master courses that are easily adapted to address changing needs in relation to technology, standards, or learning	eLearning training, certification fields (i.e., Accounting, Tax Law)
Gerlach and Ely[b]	Standard or didactic instructional design model that allows you to determine content and objectives linearly, and allows for pre-assessment of learners to determine where they go next	CBE, adaptive, personalized
John Keller ARCs Model[c]	Based on theories of motivation, this model promotes success and produces motivational rewards along with systematic process integrating motivational factors for specific types of learners	Any environment
The Wiggins and McTighe Model (Backwards Design)[b]	This model is often referred to as Backwards Design as it begins at the end (student goals/objectives) and then works through the learning events via learning experiences relative to the objectives and transference of knowledge needed to allow students to master those goals	PreK-20, CBE, higher education, predetermined goals, or outside standards
Smaldino, Lowther, Russell and Mims (ASSURE)[b]	**A**nalyze learners **S**tate standards and objectives **S**elect strategies, technology, media and materials **U**tilize technology, media and materials **R**equire learner participation **E**valuate and revise	K-12, CBE
Kemp, Morrison, Ross, and Kalman[b]	Systematic approach to design from the learner's perspective that focuses on learners, objectives, methods, and evaluation	Curriculum development, program development, start to finish design
Newby, Stepich, Lehman, and Russell (PIE)[b]	In PIE, there are three main design factors: 1. Planning—Analyzing resources and the learning environment 2. Implementing—Building the learning experience through various methods/media 3. Evaluating—Both the learning events and the effectiveness of the lesson This model is focused on instructional media/technology	Heavy multimedia courses, eLearning/Corporate

(continued)

Table 1 (continued)

Suggested ID model	Brief description and application	Applicable learning environments
Sims and Jones (3PD)[b, d]	This online learning model focuses on scaffolding of activities and evaluations in order to deliver an environment that is both dynamic and easily modified during the actual delivery. It includes three phases: 1. Functionality (predelivery) 2. Enhancement (initial delivery) 3. Maintenance (ongoing)	CBE, personalized learning environments, online learning
Dick, Carey and Carey[b]	Self-directed course that allows for guidance of the learner and engagement with the content. Adapting a more systemic approach to design	Skill based learning, CBE, eLearning/Corporate, procedural learning
Alchemy Design Model[e]	"Flexible and sustainable learning environments that empower the learner to apply knowledge and understanding in the world in which they live" (Sims, 2014, p. 143)	Any environment

Note: The sources for the brief ID model descriptions are indicated as:
[a]Meier (2000)
[b]Branch and Dousay (2015)
[c]Keller (n.d.)
[d]Jones and Sims (2002)
[e]Sims (2014)

particularly important for subject matter experts who may be unfamiliar with the eLearning environment or who have not facilitated eLearning courses before.

The instructional designers will receive their list of courses that they are assigned to for the design and development cycle from the eLearning manager. Once this list is distributed, the designer will begin preparing and gathering the necessary documents for the course(s) being designed and developed. This would include requesting a master syllabus or curriculum plan (i.e., course outcomes, proposed resources, assessment outline) from the program manager or department chair, creating a development timeline with proposed deliverable due dates, and updating any design and development presentations for webinars, such as a Subject Matter Expert Orientation.

During Week 3, the designer will send out a welcome email to the subject matter expert that covers the basics of the development cycle and provides proposed dates for Orientation as well as their contact information. It is highly suggested that the designer requests a return email to ensure that the proper email is on file for the subject matter expert. Thus begins the collaborative endeavor that continues throughout the design and development of the course.

Weeks 4-5. Once the subject matter expert has acknowledged the instructional designer's initial email, an orientation is arranged (see Sect. "Orientation of Subject

Fig. 1 Design and development timeline

Matter Experts"), which will be delivered via web conferencing software (see Sect. "Collaboration Tools and Techniques"). A follow-up email is then sent to the subject matter expert to arrange Collaborative Meeting #1. These meetings will take anywhere between 30 and 90 min, dependent upon the topic of the meeting.

During Collaborative Meeting #1, the designer and subject matter expert review the timeline of deliverables, which is acknowledged in a signed agreement. Any changes to the timeline, due to outside circumstances, are communicated and amended and then signed again by the instructional designer and subject matter expert. Once the timeline is reviewed, the next step is to discuss the first deliverable.

The designer will outline what the first deliverable is and explain to the subject matter expert how to use the course development template. This is also the time to decide how feedback and submissions of the template will be handled. Shared document tools, such as Google Docs, are recommended as revisions can be tracked and it provides a true collaborative environment. If a subject matter expert is not comfortable using an online document tool, Microsoft Word's track changes and comment feature is a good alternative.

Weeks 6-7. While the subject matter expert is working on Deliverable #1, the designer will work in the LMS master course by setting up the main Course Information page and preparing shared LMS elements ready for the build that will begin as deliverables are finalized.

The subject matter expert will complete the first deliverable and submit it to the designer. Once this submission is complete, the designer arranges Collaborative Meeting #2. This should take place during Week 6. The designer will review the submission prior to this meeting and then review the feedback with the subject matter expert during the meeting.

Collaborative Meeting #2 consists of the review and finalization of Deliverable #1, with any revisions being made within a timely manner (usually less than a week). Once this review is completed, Deliverable #2 is discussed and the subject matter expert is tasked with completing the deliverable by the next expected deadline, usually within a 7–10 day period.

This collaborative meeting provides a general theme and often sets the tone for subsequent meetings. A good tip for the designer is to work in the course development template live, via a web conferencing tool that allows for screen sharing, taking notes, and providing feedback based on the experts' comments. By doing this, transactional distance then becomes a moot point and the subject matter expert begins to see how collaboration is key in the creation of the content for the eLearning course. This must be a truly collaborative and joint effort to ensure the effectiveness of the process and the creation of a successful course design.

During the weeks where a collaborative meeting is not being held, the designer and subject matter expert can touch base as needed; some experts will need more interactions, some will need less. The key component here is for the designer to stay in contact with the expert through email, providing reminders and check-ins based on their professional opinion or the expressed needs of the subject matter expert.

Week 8. This week is an important week for the design and development cycle. This is when the first stakeholder collaborative meeting takes place. Stakeholders include, but are not limited to:

- eLearning manager/leader
- Academic leaders
- Program managers/Deans/Chairs
- Faculty liaisons
- Academic advisors
- Learners

You may be surprised that an academic advisor and learner would be considered as stakeholders. However, to sincerely make this process collaborative across the eLearning institution, learner voice should be implemented at some point during the design process. One way this can be accomplished is during the evaluation step of the design and development process by including a quick survey or other task that allows learners to share their experiences taking the courses. Academic advisors often are the first to hear whether learners are having difficulty or are dissatisfied with their learning experience. Therefore, their input is just as valuable in the design and development process.

During this stakeholder meeting, which should be facilitated by the designer, a general overview of the course (or courses) will be presented along with an overview of assessments and overall outcomes. A quick preview of the course can be conducted although if it has not been built in the LMS, this can be skipped. This meeting can also serve a dual purpose if departments are utilizing standard rubrics, syllabi, or eLearning criteria. It is important to have this information before the course is completely designed and developed. Allow questions to be asked at this meeting, but stakeholders should understand that this is a "touching base" style meeting and that certain questions may not have answers yet.

Weeks 9–13. Continued development and collaboration based on the content deliverables timetable will occur during these weeks. The instructional designer can be synchronously building the course in the LMS as each deliverable is finalized. This is important for the Week 14 Stakeholder Meeting #2; as it allows for the stakeholders to see the course in its natural environment.

Week 14. Stakeholder Meeting #2 takes place during Week 14. By this time, at least five deliverables should be finalized. At least 1 week's worth of evaluated and reviewed content built within the LMS should be presented at the stakeholder meeting. Best case scenario is to have the entire course built, although it may not be feasible to have it reviewed at this point. This is also a great time to present any innovative assessments, activities, or content. It is very important to explain how the learners will navigate the course, how they will engage with the content, and how they will be assessed. Stakeholders appreciate this information and should be encouraged to provide feedback and ask questions.

Week 15. During Week 15, the instructional designer will present the course for a quality review. This review should be completed by someone who has not been a part of the design and development of the course to ensure a fresh look at the content. Once the course is reviewed, a final collaborative meeting takes place between the designer and the subject matter expert. During this final meeting, the designer will walk the expert through each week, unit, or module of the course and discuss any changes that may have taken place during the quality review and any further updates that may need to be implemented. It is also at this final collaborative meeting that the designer will introduce the subject matter expert to the Design and Development Evaluation survey (see Sect. "Evaluation of Design and Development Process"). It is important for the expert to complete this survey in a timely manner, preferably by the end of Week 16, so data can be collected and analyzed before the next development cycle begins.

While a quality review is a very important step (learners should never encounter bad links, misspelled words, or bad grammar in an eLearning course; not to mention misalignment of outcomes, objectives, and assessments), it is one that is not covered in great detail within this chapter. Please see the *What You Can Do* section for suggestions on quality reviews.

Week 16. During the last week of the cycle, the designer will implement any updates to the course that are needed, send a request to the subject matter expert for one final review, and then, both the designer and the subject matter expert will sign off on the course and present it to the eLearning manager for delivery to learners.

Development Template

Using a template that is predetermined based on criteria set forth by an institution facilitates the design and development process (Borgemenke, Holt, & Fish, 2013; Huun & Hughes, 2014; Piskurich, 2015). Additionally, providing a template for instructional designers and subject matter experts to compile the necessary content for the online courses they are developing allows for consistency across the design and development cycle. Using a design template also allows for the organization of the course information in a streamlined manner and provides a venue for instructional designers and subject matter experts to communicate about the development of the course.

Creating the template to include the components in the same flow or organization as the learning management system also makes it easier for the designers to expedite the build once the content has been procured by the subject matter expert, undergone a review, and is finalized. An example of what might be included in a template would be sections delineated for an overview or introduction to the content, learning objectives, resources (i.e., textbooks, videos, electronic materials), and assessments (i.e., discussions, papers, projects), and the rubrics used for evaluating the assessments. Another possible content item to consider is a wrap up or summary that ties the learning together for the learners on a week-to-week basis.

At the end of the design and development cycle, a completed design template may be several pages long but it provides documentation for eLearning leaders to refer back to in regard to the (a) process, (b) collaboration, and (c) future updates to the course. It is pertinent to note that the eLearning content delivery can be set up on a week-by-week basis or what the authors call a content deliverable basis. In a week-by-week delivery, content for individual weeks is submitted to the designer in the template. In a content deliverable scenario, content is delivered for all weeks in an order that is predetermined by the eLearning leader and their instructional designers. An example utilized by the authors is included in Appendix section title "Example Course Development Template" and can be used for either a Week-by-Week delivery or Content Deliverables.

Collaboration Tools and Techniques

When collaborating with subject matter experts to design online courses, different types of communication can be used. Some situations may offer an opportunity to the instructional designers and subject matter experts to work in the same place at the same time. While in other cases, these individuals need to collaborate remotely, so tools to facilitate communication are necessary. There are many types of tools available for use at minimal or no cost. The most basic tools that you can use for collaborating at a distance are the phone and email. Something to consider, that will help decrease the sense of separation between the collaborating parties, is the use of video conferencing software. There are free (i.e., Zoom, Google Hangout, Skype) or subscription service (Cisco WebEx, BlueJeans, GoToMeeting) video conferencing software to choose from. In order to assemble the content deliverables for collaboration, you will need to identify a document collaboration tool (i.e., Microsoft Word, Google Docs) and a place to store the documents (i.e., OneDrive, Google Drive).

Training for subject matter experts or other stakeholders may be necessary for using the collaboration tools that are selected for use in the collaboration experience. Regular communication should be established between all stakeholders with check-ins prior to deadlines in order to address any problems with the collaboration tools that may arise during the development process.

Orientation of Subject Matter Experts

One of the challenges an instructional designer could face when creating online courses is collaborating with subject matter experts and other stakeholders in higher education. Subject matter experts are knowledgeable about content that will be used to build the online learning experience for learners; however, they may or may not have a background in education. This may impede the development process if the eLearning leader and instructional designer need to communicate the steps in the process and the theory behind it. Subject matter experts should be given a realistic idea of what is entailed in the course development process so that they may make a well-informed decision on whether or not they will have the required time to invest in the project(s) they are recruited to assist with.

Preparing the subject matter expert with a short and streamlined orientation provides them with a means to see how the process will evolve and allows them to ask any questions they may have before the actual design of the course begins. During orientation is the perfect opportunity for the instructional designer to begin building a relationship with the subject matter expert, an important aspect to a successful course development process. In Table 2, we have suggested content that could be included in the development of the orientation training for subject matter experts.

Subject matter expert orientation can be completed on a one-to-one or group basis. If the same process is being used for all courses being developed, it is suggested a group orientation takes place, thus allowing a robust think tank environment where subject matter experts can share prior experiences or ideas with one another and the instructional designer.

Table 2 Subject matter expert orientation content

Roles	What does the designer do? What does the SME do?
Expectations	What are time expectations? Meetings? Contract verification
Timeline Review	Suggested due dates based on a predetermined design and development cycle
Review Development Template	Review each piece of the template with a brief explanation
Deliverable overviews	What is each deliverable and what is the SME expected to complete
Collaboration Tools	An overview of the tools with links to tutorials
Aligning Outcomes and Objectives	Why this is important; provide visual to show how individual week's build off overarching course outcomes (which should be aligned with some industry or outside standard)
First Deliverable Instructions	General overview and kick off for the first deliverable (to be completed within 5–7 days from Orientation)
Questions	Provide at least 15 min for SME's to ask any questions they may have or to just discuss the process

Evaluation of Design and Development Process

The last step in the collaborative management of the design and development process is evaluation of the actual process. One way to do this is to have the subject matter experts who participate in the design and development process complete a survey or exit interview after finishing the project. Information should be gathered on how the process did or did not work for the subject matter experts, whether or not communication between the instructional designer and subject matter expert was effective, what their experience was with using collaboration tools, and whether the amount of time they had to complete tasks was or was not sufficient for the specific deliverables they needed to complete. It may also be helpful to ask the subject matter expert to provide suggestions for future subject matter experts about what they need to know to be successful when collaborating with an instructional designer to design and develop courses.

The following are examples of questions you might want to consider for the subject matter expert survey:

- What did you like about the course development process?
- Were there any requirements that hindered your development progress?
- How would you improve the course development process?
- Had you ever developed this course before for this institution or another institution?
- How many hours per week did you spend on course development?
- Did you develop new and original content for this course?
- Are you interested in developing more courses for us?
- Please provide suggestions for future subject matter experts based on your experiences with the design and development process.

What You Can Do

After digesting all of the information presented in the *What You Need to Know* section, you are probably wondering what else you might need to consider when managing the collaborative efforts of an eLearning design and development process. In this section, we will provide you with some ideas to keep in mind as you manage this collaborative process. Specific tips for aligning and evaluating courses are included to further assist you with setting up a collaborative design and development process at your institution or organization.

Program and Course Alignment

Creating a foundation using outside standards or program outcomes is pertinent to the design and development process as it allows both the instructional designer and subject matter expert to have a general understanding of what the course should deliver. Ideally, you should meet with deans, leaders, and faculty to identify outside standards that align with the program and will be used to guide the development process. If these outcomes are to be determined by the subject matter expert providing additional time in the development cycle is advised. Instructional designers and subject matter experts use these foundational standards or outcomes to align unit objectives and assessments during the process of designing and developing the online course.

Collaborative Evaluation

Once a course is designed and developed, it is important for an outside review to be conducted. This could be by another faculty member in the department or another stakeholder who was not involved in the design and development process. When the course runs for the first time, it is advisable to have the subject matter expert who worked on the design of the course to be the first one to facilitate the delivery of it. This allows for the subject matter expert to identify any discrepancies that may arise when the learners interact with the course. Feedback from the subject matter expert and learners who take the newly designed course should be reviewed and if a pattern is observed, changes should be made to address any concerns. A few suggested eLearning evaluation entities that address course navigation and organization are:

- Quality Matters Higher Education Program Rubric: https://www.qualitymatters.org/rubric
- Quality Online Learning and Teaching Rubric (QOLT) or Rubric for Online Instruction (ROI): http://www.csuchico.edu/eoi/

- ION—Quality Online Course Initiative Rubric: http://www.ion.uillinois.edu/initiatives/qoci/
- Steve Gance's 3D Course Audit Rubric: http://www2.educause.edu/west-southwest-regional-conference/2012/2012/3d-rubric-creating-and-auditing-online-courses-criteria-and-methods-guide-course

Conclusion

Managing an instructional design and development cycle is often not an easy task; add in the eLearning component with participants who may never have experienced learning in this environment before and the task could become harder. With the proper planning and implementation of standard practices, the eLearning leader can create an environment where subject matter experts, instructional designers, and stakeholders collaborate to make this process effective and efficient.

From the choice of a proper instructional design model to the ongoing evaluation of the actual process, true collaboration must take place. Planning a design and development timeline based on the tried and true practices laid out in this chapter and implementing a standardized course development template provides an effective starting point in the cycle. Utilizing collaborative tools and techniques and orienting the subject matter expert to the process alleviates possible time management issues that could arise. When the information provided within this chapter is implemented, the eLearning leader can truly manage a collaborative, effective, and efficient eLearning design and development process.

For More Information

Aleckson, J. D., & Ralston-Berg, P. (2011). *Mindmeld: Micro-collaboration between elearning designers and instructor experts.* Madison, WI: Atwood Publishing.

Dirksen, J. (2016). *Design for how people learn* (2nd ed.). San Francisco, CA: New Riders.

Keppell, M. (2000). Principles at the heart of an instructional designer: Subject matter expert interaction. *Proceedings of the Australasian Society for Computers in Learning in Tertiary Education*, Coffs Harbour, Australia. Retrieved from http://ascilite.org/conferences/coffs00/papers/mike_keppell.pdf

Appendix: Example Course Development Template (1 Week)
Content Deliverable or Week-by-Week

Notes for Subject Matter Expert

Your instructional designer will work from this template; please keep the deadlines in mind for each deliverable.

- *Deliverable #1*—Units #—# Topics and Objectives: INSERT DATE HERE
- *Deliverable #2*—Units #—# Assessments and Rubrics: INSERT DATE HERE
- *Deliverable #3*—Units #—# Discussions and Activities: INSERT DATE HERE
- *Deliverable #4*—Units #—# Resources, including any lectures in document or slide deck format w/detailed notes: INSERT DATE HERE
- *Deliverable #5*—Final Syllabus: INSERT DATE HERE

If you have questions, feel free to contact me at: INSERT CONTACT INFORMATION

All assessments should have a rubric tied to them; an assignment template is available upon request or you may use one that is standard for your department.

This template reflects the environment layout; the content will be placed within the Master Course shell and the information that has been submitted has been reviewed and finalized.

Course Information Page (for reference only)

The following information is the flow and organization of the content that will be seen on the course information page for this course.

Course Description (from catalog/course development document):

- Outcomes (from catalog/course development document):
- Course Introduction Video or Audio Recording
- Syllabus
- Materials
- Course Evaluation (percentage of final grade)

Discussion Rubric and Criteria
Assignment/Project Rubrics
Question and Answer Forum

Deliverable Reminders

- Topics

    - Identify 1–3 Topics/Concepts

- Objectives

  - 2–3 per unit—what will students be able to do, know, demonstrate based on the topics
  - Include ideas about how each can be assessed
  - Utilize Bloom's taxonomy above rote learning

- Assessments/Assignments and Rubrics

  - Provide description, objectives assessed, type of assessment (paper, group work, etc.)
  - Full details and rubric to be provided in separate assignment/rubric document template

- Discussions

  - 1–2 per unit
  - Adhere to effective discussion question characteristics

- Readings and Resources (with Narrative)

  - Group readings, resources, and videos by topics and provide narrative that ties them together.
  - Use library articles or open source resources, industry sites, blogs, etc.
  - Avoid Wikipedia type sources
  - Provide URL or Permalink if from library
  - Note whether material is supplemental
  - Provide URL for Videos

    - Watch entire video to ensure no questionable content
    - Limit to 1–7 min per video

- SME created resource(s) (optional)

  - Supports the hard parts of the unit
  - Do not include any web links
  - Include references for cited material

- Overviews and Summaries

  - Overviews: 1–2 paragraphs overview of the unit: The overview is a short description of topics to be explored, why they are important to study, and how they fit into the grand scheme by tying units together
  - Summaries:

    - Brief summary of what was learned, preparation for next unit
    - Consider adding self-reflective questions, fun activities, tips, etc.
    - Warn students about upcoming *big* assignments

- Instructor Notes

  - Anything that instructors of the course need to be aware of or do during the course.
  - Include answer keys

Week 1 Content Unit 1 Title:
Unit 1 Overview and Topics:
Unit 1 Objectives:

Objective(s)	Possible assessment type
Example: Analyze national and state regulations related to mandated reporting	Case study
.	
.	
.	

Unit 1 Assignment/Assessment:
You will provide separate documents for each assignment at that point in the course development cycle.

Assignment name	Type	Objective(s) assessed	Description (1–2 sentences)
.			
.			
.			

Unit 1 Discussion Questions:

Discussion title	Discussion question	Objective/s assessed
.		
.		

Unit 1 Readings and Resources (Textbook, Articles, Websites, and Videos):
Arrange resources by topics in the order you want students to read/view them. Supplemental Resources will appear at the bottom of the topic content item. Right click and insert row to add new row in table.

Topic subject	Title of resource	URL and est. page numbers	Narrative description	Supplemental Y/N
Example: Regulations	*State of CT ECE Regulations 2015*	http://ece.ct.gov	Describe why the learners must read/view this resource—think about guiding questions you want them to think about as they read the resource	
.				
.				

Unit 1 Wrap Up/Summary:
Unit 1 SME Created Resource(s):
Unit 1 Instructor's Notes:

References

Borgemenke, A. J., Holt, W. C., & Fish, W. W. (2013). Universal course shell template design and implementation to enhance student outcomes in online coursework. *The Quarterly Review of Distance Education, 14*(1), 17–23.

Branch, R. M., & Dousay, T. A. (2015). *Survey of instructional design models* (5th ed.). Bloomington, IN: Association for Educational Communications and Technology.

University of Minnesota, Center for Educational Innovation. (2015, February 15). *Time and cost considerations in developing an online course* [website]. Retrieved from http://cei.umn.edu/support-services/online-learning/time-and-cost-considerations-developing-online-course

California State University, Exemplary Online Instruction. (2014). *Quality Online Learning and Teaching Rubric (QOLT) and Rubric for Online Instruction (ROI)* [website]. Retrieved from http://www.csuchico.edu/eoi/

Gance S. (2012). *A 3D rubric for creating and auditing online courses: Criteria and methods to guide course development efforts.* Poster session presented at the EDUCAUSE West/Southwest Regional Conference 2012, Portland, OR. Retrieved from http://www2.educause.edu/west-southwest-regional-conference/2012/2012/3d-rubric-creating-and-auditing-online-courses-criteria-and-methods-guide-course

Huun, K., & Hughes, L. (2014). Autonomy among thieves: Template course design for student and faculty success. *Journal of Educators Online, 11*(2), 1–30.

University of Illinois, Illinois Online Network. (2006). *Quality online course initiative rubric.* Retrieved from http://www.ion.uillinois.edu/initiatives/qoci/

Jones, D., & Sims, R. (2002). E-learning development in higher education: Maximising efficiency-maintaining quality. In P. Barker & S. Rebelsky (Eds.), *Proceedings of EdMedia: World Conference on Educational Media and Technology 2002* (pp. 890–895). Denver, CO: Association for the Advancement of Computing in Education (AACE). Retrieved from https://www.learntechlib.org/p/10277.

Keller, J. M. (n.d.). *What is the ARCS model?* Retrieved from http://www.arcsmodel.com/#!arcs-model/c1wm1

Meier, D. (2000). *The accelerated learning handbook.* New York: McGraw-Hill.

New York State Education Department, Office of College and University Evaluation (2013). *Policies: Determining time on task in online education.* Retrieved from http://www.highered.nysed.gov/ocue/ded/policies.html

Piskurich, G. M. (2015). *Rapid instructional design: Learning ID fast and right.* Hoboken, NJ: Wiley.

Quality Matters (2014). *Quality Matters Higher Education Program Rubric.* Retrieved from https://www.qualitymatters.org/rubric

Sims, R. (2014). *Design alchemy: Transforming the way we think about learning and teaching.* New York, NY: Springer. doi:10.1007/978-3-31 9-02423-3

Frameworks for Assessing and Evaluating e-Learning Courses and Programs

Florence Martin and Swapna Kumar

Abstract This chapter provides an overview of different frameworks, benchmarks, guidelines, and instruments that exist to assess the quality and effectiveness of e-learning programs. Elements of multiple frameworks and instruments are combined to identify seven quality indicators such as institutional support, technology infrastructure, course design, learner and instructor support, learning effectiveness, faculty and student satisfaction, and course assessment and evaluation in the "What you need to know" section. Key considerations for each of the quality indicators which e-learning leaders can use to make key decisions and implementation considerations are provided in the "What you can do" section. Finally, the chapter also describes the need and the importance of using frameworks to assess and evaluate quality of e-learning courses and programs.

Keywords e-Learning quality • e-Learning frameworks • e-Learning effectiveness • e-Learning indicators • e-Learning evaluation • e-Learning benchmarks • e-Learning implementation

Decision-Making Guidance

This chapter will help you make decisions about assessing the quality and effectiveness of e-learning courses and programs. The chapter provides an overview of different frameworks to assess the quality and effectiveness of e-learning and quality indicators to consider while working on enhancing quality in online learning.

F. Martin (✉)
University of North Carolina Charlotte, Charlotte, NC, USA
e-mail: Florence.Martin@uncc.edu

S. Kumar
University of Florida, Gainesville, FL, USA
e-mail: swapnakumar@coe.ufl.edu

© Association for Educational Communications and Technology 2018
A.A. Piña et al. (eds.), *Leading and Managing e-Learning*, Educational Communications and Technology: Issues and Innovations,
https://doi.org/10.1007/978-3-319-61780-0_19

271

Chapter objectives

e-Learning leaders will be able to

- List the different frameworks that exist to assess the quality and effectiveness of e-learning programs
- Combine elements of multiple frameworks to identify quality indicators that are appropriate for quality assessment in their specific context
- Communicate the importance of using frameworks to assess and evaluate quality of e-learning courses and programs

Need for Assessing and Evaluating Quality in Online Learning

There has been a tremendous growth in online course delivery over the last decade. Allen and Seaman (2015) found that 7.1 million students are participating in at least one online course in higher education institutions in 2013, compared to the 1.6 million in 2002. Perraton (2000) reported that the goal of Distance Education in some countries is to achieve the same level of quality in online learning as that of face-to-face education. This tremendous growth in online learning, competition among institutions offering online courses or degrees, need to offer the same level of quality in online learning in par with face-to-face learning, and continual scrutiny of quality in online courses has established a need for institutions to use quality standards to guide the design and facilitation of online learning.

Quality assurance and accountability for higher education institutions are addressed by accreditation agencies in various countries. e-Learning leaders need to show effectiveness and quality of their online programs to these accrediting agencies, and simultaneously have to market their online programs to a large audience, maintain high quality in their courses, and demonstrate learning outcomes. Also, internally e-learning leaders are expected to continuously improve programs and maintain cost-efficiency. For these various purposes, it is essential for them to be aware of the various frameworks that exist and can assist them in assessing and evaluating quality in their online offerings.

What You Need to Know

Quality Assurance is a systematic approach to check whether online learning meets specific requirements based on a set of standards and frameworks. Several frameworks have been developed by leading organizations in e-learning and online learning and are available as online resources for use by others. Based on their context and needs, e-learning leaders can use these existing frameworks to design and implement online learning in their organization to maintain a desired level of quality. Often, e-learning leaders are only exposed to quality frameworks in their region, or to frameworks that are focused on courses but do not address institutional considerations. We will thus review a wide range of frameworks from across the world that can help assess and evaluate e-learning from an institutional and course perspective in this section. Some of these frameworks include benchmarks and guidelines for online learning that can be adapted, while others provide instruments that can be readily used by e-learning leaders. The frameworks are categorized here according to those that aim to address quality assurance in online learning in general, and those that pertain to programs and courses. Based on the stage in the process of adopting online learning, or the need for quality assessment at various levels in the organizational chain, the general frameworks provide a comprehensive view of all the factors that need to be considered when implementing e-learning. The frameworks for quality in online programs and courses provide measurable indicators or instruments and are often accompanied by descriptions of how these can be used.

Overview of Frameworks, Benchmarks, and Guidelines for Quality Assurance in e-Learning from the USA, Europe, Asia, Africa, and Australia

1. Online Learning Consortium (Formerly Sloan-C) Pillars http://onlinelearning-consortium.org/about/quality-framework-five-pillars/

   The five pillars were proposed by Online Learning Consortium as a framework for measuring and improving online learning (Sloan Consortium, 2002). The five pillars proposed are learning effectiveness, student satisfaction, faculty satisfaction, cost effectiveness, and access (Lorenzo & Moore, 2002). Each organization is able to set their own standard for each of the five pillars on measuring and improving learning effectiveness, student satisfaction, faculty satisfaction, cost effectiveness, and access.

2. CHEA Accreditation and Assuring Quality in Distance Learning
   http://www.chea.org/pdf/mono_1_accred_distance_02.pdf

   The Council for Higher Education Accreditation created the Quality Assurance framework for accreditation of distance education. The framework includes seven key areas that are reviewed when examining quality of distance education. These seven areas include institutional mission, organizational structure, institutional resources, curriculum and instruction, faculty support, student support, and student learning outcomes.

3. Quality on the Line: Benchmarks for Success in Internet Based Distance Education   http://www.ihep.org/sites/default/files/uploads/docs/pubs/quality-ontheline.pdf

   Quality on the Line: Benchmarks for Success in Internet Based Distance Education was developed by the Institute of Higher Education Policy in

Washington DC, USA, with support from Blackboard and National Education Association in 2000. Quality on the Line identifies 24 benchmarks in seven categories essential to ensure excellent in internet based distance education. The seven categories included instructional support, course development, teaching/ learning, course structure, student support, faculty support, and evaluation and assessment benchmarks (Phipps & Merisotis, 2000).

4. Open eQuality Learning Standards (Canada) www.futured.com/documents/ OeQLsMay2004_000.pdf

Open eQuality learning standards was introduced in 2004 and was sponsored by the European Institute for e-Learning (EIfEL) and LIfIA (Learning Innovations Forum d'Innovations d'Apprentissage). This is based on the Canadian Recommended e-Learning Guidelines (CanREGs) which was launched in 2002. These standards can be applied to any e-learning products or services. This includes four sections and 25 standards in the area of Quality Outcomes—Higher Ed, Quality Outcomes—Primary/Secondary, Quality Processes and Practices and Quality Inputs and Resources. http://www.eife-l.org/publications/quality/ oeqls/intro

5. Asian Association of Open Universities (AAOU). Quality Assurance Framework. http://www.aaou.org/ images/fi les/AAOU%20Quality%20Assurance%20 Framework.pdf

The Quality Assurance Framework of the Asian Association of Open Universities (AAOU) includes statements of best practices in ten areas related to quality in distance and open education: policy and planning; internal management; learners and learners' profiles; infrastructure, media, and learning resources; learning assessment and evaluation; research and community services; human resources; learner support; program design and curriculum development; and course design and development.

6. Australasian Council on Open, Distance and e-Learning (2007). ACODE benchmarks for e-learning in universities and guidelines for use.

The Australasian Council on Open, Distance and e-Learning created benchmarks for technology-enhanced learning (TEL) at the institutional level in 2007 with the help of several representatives at member universities. These benchmarks were reviewed and refreshed in 2014 with the goal of supporting continuous quality improvement in TEL. These eight benchmarks constitute institution-wide policy and governance for TEL; planning for institution-wide quality improvement of TEL; information technology systems, services, and support for TEL; the application of technology-enhanced learning services; staff professional development for the effective use of TEL; staff support for the use of TEL; student training for the effective use of TEL; and student support for the use of TEL. Performance indicators and measures are included that make it possible for users to rate these areas on a scale of 1–5.

7. European Association of Distance Teaching Universities (EADTU)

The Quality Assessment for e-Learning: a Benchmarking Approach was published by the European Association of Distance Teaching Universities (EADTU) with an aim to provide a methodology and supporting resources for the quality assurance of e-learning in higher education. The manual contains benchmarks in the areas of strategic management, curriculum design, course design, course delivery, staff support, and student support that were based on E-xcellence projects in the European Union (EU) from 2005 to 2012.

8. The National Association for Distance Education and Open Learning in South Africa

   http://www.nadeosa.org.za/tags/quality-assurance

   Distance higher education programs in a digital era: Good practice guide was published by the Council on Higher Education (CHE) in Pretoria, South Africa, in 2014. It contains conceptualizations of distance education in higher education contexts; good practice guidelines for the application of CHE criteria to program design and development, and teaching and learning in distance education; and key considerations for evaluation. Ideally, it is intended for use along with the Distance higher education programs in a digital era: Program Accreditation Criteria.

Instruments for Quality in Online Courses and Programs

1. Online Learning Consortium Quality Scorecard http://onlinelearningconsortium.org/consult/quality-scorecard/

   The online learning consortium created a scorecard to measure and quantify elements of quality within an online education program based on nine categories, institutional support, technology support, course development/instructional design, course structure, teaching and learning, social and student engagement, faculty support, student support, and evaluations and assessment.

2. Blackboard Exemplary Rubric

   http://www.blackboard.com/getdoc/7deaf501-4674-41b9-b2f2-554441ba099b/2012-blackboard-exemplary-course-rubric.aspx

   The Blackboard Exemplary course program began in 2000 to identify and disseminate high quality online courses. The Exemplary Course Rubric includes 17 key characteristics of high quality online courses within the framework of course design, interaction and collaboration, assessment, and learner support.

3. Quality Matters (QM)

   https://www.qualitymatters.org/rubric

   Quality Matters is a faculty-centered, peer review process designed to certify the quality of online courses. The Quality Matters Higher Education Rubric, Fifth Edition, 2014, includes eight General Standards and 43 Specific Review Standards to evaluate the design of online and blended courses. The eight general standards are course overview and introduction, learning objectives (competencies), assessment and measurement, instructional materials, course activities and learner interaction, course technology, learner support, and accessibility and usability.

Fig. 1 Indicators for institutional online learning quality

4. iNACOL

http://www.inacol.org/

iNACOL designed National Standards for Quality Online Courses in K-12 in 2011 to provide states, districts, online programs, and other organizations with a set of quality guidelines in the areas of online course content, instructional design, technology, student assessment, and course management. This report presents a continuum from "less online learning" to completely online learning. iNACOL previously released the National Standards for Quality Online Programs in 2009 that included institutional, teaching and learning, support, and evaluation standards for K-12 online programs.

What You Can Do

On analyzing these frameworks and standards, some common indicators were identified and listed to provide guidance to e-learning leaders on areas to focus while working on enhancing quality in online learning. The frameworks listed above can be applied at various levels, including country, state, district or county, institution, college, program or course. In this section we will provide key decision and implementation considerations of which e-learning leaders need to be cognizant when assessing quality in online learning in the areas below. These practical considerations are grounded in research on online learning and based on our own experiences as leaders of online programs and prior experience with instructional design and faculty development.

Quality Indicators Derived from Existing Standards, Benchmarks, Frameworks, and Instruments (Fig. 1)

- Institutional Support

- e-Learning leaders are expected to get buy-in from the leadership and administrators to implement online learning. Without the support of the institutional leaders, online learning initiatives are not successful. Therefore, e-learning leaders need to form strategic partnerships with key stakeholders in the implementation of online education. Some of the ways by which the e-learning leaders can facilitate support to online programs are:

  - Advocating budget support in the university's commitment to online programs.
  - Providing course development incentives for faculty who wish to develop quality online courses
  - Fostering understanding and implementation of quality frameworks to support online learning
  - Implementing awards for quality online courses
  - Updating policy statements to reflect university's commitment to online programs.
  - Developing an institutional e-learning strategy
  - Communicating strategic directions of the institution
  - Collaborating with the institutional entities to receive all the appropriate accreditation and support for online programs.

- Technology Infrastructure
- Online learning heavily relies on technology infrastructure. e-Learning leaders have to take decisions on the purchase of technology (both hardware and software), implementation, and services for the institutions online learning needs in the following manner:

  - Ensuring the availability of technology infrastructure and staff to host e-learning initiatives
  - Selecting and hosting the appropriate Learning Management System for the University
  - Aligning student information systems with online learning infrastructure and procedure

- Providing infrastructure for the use of digital resources for both instructors and students (e.g., a video server)
- Selecting and adopting synchronous tools for the university
- Providing a Multimedia studio, technologies, and support staff for faculty development of e-learning materials
- Providing Multimedia software for faculty use

- Course Design
- e-Learning leaders need to be familiar with instruments that measure effective instructional design approaches and pedagogical elements essential for student satisfaction and learning outcomes in online courses. They also have to ensure that their organization or unit

  - Hires and trains instructional designers to assist with course design
  - Is familiar with frameworks that guide course design
  - Provides faculty with professional development opportunities focused on e-learning
  - Is familiar with quality criteria for online course design, including instructional alignment between objectives, assessment and instructional material, measurable goals and objectives and formative and summative assessments for grading
  - Implements quality control procedures before students access online courses
  - Provides accessible and usable instructional material

- Learner and Instructor Support
- Technical, pedagogic, and facilitation support is needed for instructors during the design and delivery of online courses. Technical and administrative support is needed for online learners. Different aspects of course design support for instructors are addressed in the previous section, and faculty incentives for developing online courses are listed above under institutional support. Additionally, e-learning leaders are responsible for ensuring such support structures are in place for instructors and students, in the form of:

  - Academic Technologies Support for instructors
  - Advising and administrative processes (e.g., registration) for students
  - Information literacy support for students
  - A help desk system to support faculty and staff
  - Web resources with FAQs and tutorials to guide faculty and staff
  - Online writing and other academic resources for students

- Course Assessment and Evaluation
- Assessment and evaluation in online learning brings several challenges, including a need for new policies, guidelines, and procedures. e-Learning leaders need to be familiar with various online assessment methodologies.

  - e-Learning leaders need to be familiar with the evaluation techniques to collect variety of data to assist with the evaluation for continual improvement.

- Integration of Student Information System with Learning Management Systems to permit ease of enrollment and reporting grades
- Providing online proctoring support for courses that need it
- Providing plagiarism detecting applications that are integrated with Learning Management Systems
- Establishing peer and student evaluation procedures for online courses
- Ensuring online courses have the same instructional hours as contact hours in face-to-face courses

- Learning effectiveness
- In the end, the main indicator of measuring success is the effectiveness of online learning. e-Learning leaders have to:

  - Ensure collection of assessment and grade data that helps measure effectiveness at various levels at course, program, college, and institution levels
  - Ensure collection of other learning analytics data in an ethical manner that informs of the online learner behavior and participation in the courses
  - Ensure periodic collection of data which assists with student retention
  - Collect data on admissions and completion to identify patterns of growth in various programs

- Faculty and Student Satisfaction

- It is critical that both the online instructor and the online student are satisfied with the online learning experience. e-Learning leaders must be able to choose from different approaches to collect feedback from the instructors and the students and utilize this feedback for continual improvement and increase faculty and student satisfaction. They should:

  - Collect student feedback on instruction, resources, feedback, interaction, support, and accessibility
  - Collect faculty feedback on resources, support, incentives, and appreciation
  - Establish procedures for review and implementation of feedback.

Conclusion

In this chapter we provided (a) a robust overview of the existing frameworks for quality assurance in e-learning or online learning and (b) key considerations among seven quality indicators that e-learning leaders need to consider when implementing quality online learning. Our synthesis of these frameworks and considerations will benefit e-learning leaders who serve in leadership roles at various educational institutions in roles such as directors, coordinators, deans and associate deans, vice-presidents and provosts and have responsibility over e-learning/online learning/distance education in their organizations.

For More Information

Allen, E., & Seaman, J. (2015). Grade level: Tracking online education in the United States (Rep.). Babson Survey Research Group. Retrieved from http://www.online-learningsurvey.com/reports/gradelevel.pdf

Bari, M., & Djouab, R. (2014). Quality frameworks and standards in E-Learning systems. *International Journal of the Computer, the Internet and Management, 22*(3), 1–7.

Bates, A. W. (2000). *Managing technological change: Strategies for college and university leaders*. San Francisco: Jossey-Bass.

Ehlers, U.-D., & Pawlowski, J. M. (2006). *Handbook on quality and standardisation in E-Learning*. Berlin: Springer.

Slimp, M. (2014). *Trends in distance education: What college leaders should consider*. Instructional Technology Council (ITC). Retrieved January 19, 2016, from http://www.itcnetwork.org/attachments/article/1133/TrendsinDistanceEducationNov2014FINALWEBVERSION.pdf

Smithers, M. (2011). *eLearning at universities: A quality assurance free zone?* Retrieved January 19, 2016, from http://www.masmithers.com/2011/02/19/elearning-at-universities-a-quality-assurance-free-zone/

Sun, P. C., Tsai, R. J., Finger, G., Chen, Y. Y., & Yeh, D. (2008). What drives a successful E-Learning? An empirical investigation of the critical factors influencing learner satisfaction. *Computers & Education, 50*(4), 1183–1202.

Shelton, K. (2011). A review of paradigms for evaluating the quality of online education programs. *Online Journal of Distance Learning Administration, 14*(1).

References

Allen, E., & Seaman, J. (2015). *Grade level: Tracking online education in the United States (Rep.)*. Babson Survey Research Group. Retrieved from http://www.onlinelearningsurvey.com/reports/gradelevel.pdf.

Lorenzo, G., & Moore, J. (2002). *The Sloan Consortium report to the nation: Five pillars of quality online education*. Needham, MA: Sloan Center.

Perraton, H. (2000). *Open and distance learning in the developing world*. London: Routledge.

Phipps, R., & Merisotis, J. (2000). *Quality on the line: Benchmarks for success in internet-based distance education* Retrieved from http://eric.ed.gov/?id=ED444407

Sloan Consortium. (2002). *The Sloan Consortium: The 5 pillars*. Retrieved from http://www.sloan-c.org/.

Front-End Evaluation Planning for e-Learning: A Practical Approach

Jacqueline H. Singh

Abstract In educational settings assessment of student learning is among top considerations. Higher education institutions are held accountable for their programs including e-learning and distance education. However, front-end evaluation planning is often overlooked, misunderstood, or ignored. Stakeholders may not differentiate between different types of evaluative inquiry or do not possess necessary competencies to do this work. They may unknowingly conflate evaluation with research and performance measurement. Two dynamic models highlight paradigms of inquiry that intersect and serve as quick references that guide the chapter's structure. Indeed, e-learning leaders will realize the utility of strategic evaluation, beyond end-of-course surveys typically administered across disciplines to inform decision-making. The first model is a Navigational Map that illustrates directional complexities encountered in evaluation. The second model is a Front-end Evaluation Planning Framework. It encourages evaluative thinking and identifies critical areas to consider before taking on any type of evaluation. Basic terms, tools, and approaches associated with evaluability assessment are introduced and described.

Keywords Navigational map • Front-end evaluation planning framework • Conceptualization • Program theory • Logic model • Evaluability assessment • Evaluation questions • Program evaluation • Performance measurement • Assessment

Decision-Making Guidance

This chapter will help you make decisions regarding:

- Evaluation direction and scope
- Clear descriptions and context
- Reasons for evaluation and its purpose

J.H. Singh (✉)
Qualitative Advantage, LLC, PO Box 661, Fishers, IN 46038, USA
e-mail: qualadvant@gmail.com; jacquelinesingh59@gmail.com

© Association for Educational Communications and Technology 2018
A.A. Piña et al. (eds.), *Leading and Managing e-Learning*, Educational Communications and Technology: Issues and Innovations,
https://doi.org/10.1007/978-3-319-61780-0_20

- Practical approaches and tools for conceptualization
- The right evaluation questions
- Choosing an evaluation design

What You Need to Know

Evaluation is usually thought of as an after-the-fact activity. It is meaningful to think of it at the start. Evaluation is formative as much as it is summative or developmental. Indeed, what is of interest may be in development, an innovation, or emerging concept. More importantly, evaluation addresses key purposes, answers stakeholders' questions, and responds to "So what!" Front-end planning saves time in the long run, as it works out conceptualization issues and identifies what evidence to collect. As a by-product, stakeholders make informed decisions, write better grant proposals, contribute to the knowledge base, and respond, in part, to increasing calls for accountability and transparency. Listed below are some basic pointers to consider:

1. Recognize evaluation can be confusing or overwhelming. Some people may even think, "It is a waste of time."
2. Context is everything. It factors into programs at all levels of analysis. Resources are limited and not everything can be evaluated. Program boundaries have to be set and clearly described (e.g., program sub-components, technology, goals, objectives)
3. Primary users of evaluation information should agree upon questions and their purpose—at the beginning. With purpose in mind, the right questions are selected by recognizing what "question types" are asked. Questions reflect an evaluation's purpose that leads to specific designs and plausible approaches that determine what gets asked during data collection. Question development occurs at the front-end and guides evaluation throughout. When addressing normative questions, or aspects of quality, it is important to use criteria (i.e., *Quality Matters Rubric Standards* or *The Sloan-C Quality Framework and The Five Pillars*)
4. There are many theories and approaches to evaluation. Stakeholders may not know where or how to begin. It is important to choose the type of evaluation and approach that can be realistically undertaken. Whether a comprehensive program evaluation or rigorous evaluation research—remember, credible data are gathered that answer the question "As evidenced by what?"

Strategic Evaluation

Evaluation is often seen as a compliance activity, but nothing is further from the truth. Rather it is strategically planned to answer key stakeholders' questions. A review of literature shows that questions asked require different approaches falling into one or more categories:

1. Demonstrate the extent that an intervention supports the organization and its mission
2. Make an intervention's design explicit, so improvements, modifications, or replications can be made
3. Examine the intervention's implementation, processes, outcomes, performance, or impacts
4. Expose successes and/or challenges to stakeholders, collaborators, supporters, and funders
5. Justify costs or discern return on investments
6. Validate or discover effective methods, approaches, and/or applications associated with the intervention
7. Communicate or disseminate information about what works—or, does not

Strategic evaluations use iterative processes to create a cogent evaluation plan that yields meaningful information for intended primary-users.

Terms and Definitions

Much like statistics, logic, and psychometrics, evaluation is transdisciplinary with attributes of a discipline across a range of other disciplines (Mathison, 2005; Scriven, 1991). There is no singular definition of evaluation. Although, it is often defined as a process that determines the merit, value, and worth of someone (e.g., teacher, student, or employee) or something, such as a product, program, policy, procedure, or process (Scriven, 1991). The Joint Committee on Standards for Educational Evaluation offers another definition useful for e-learning and distance education that expands on the meaning of value (i.e., merit, worth, importance, and significance) including:

1. Systematic investigation of the quality of programs, projects, subprograms, subprojects, and/or any other components or elements, together or singularly
2. For purposes of decision-making, judgments, conclusions, findings, new knowledge, organizational development, and capacity building in response to the needs of identified stakeholders
3. Leading to improvements and/or accountability in the users' programs and systems
4. Ultimately, contributing to organizational or social value (Yarbrough, Shulha, Hopson, & Caruthers, 2011)

In the same vein, e-learning terms are used interchangeably (e.g., e-learning, online learning, hybrid/blended learning, web-based learning, and distance learning). e-Learning leaders need to be cautious of terms that represent concepts with subtle differences (Tsai & Machado, 2002; Waterhouse, 2005). Strategic evaluation begins with how words are defined and used (Ruhe & Zumbo, 2009). Not differentiating concepts reflects limited understanding of basic solutions and best practices—and a need to build evaluation capacity (Preskill & Boyle, 2008).

Navigational Map

It is important to be aware of influencers that shape evaluation. In education settings these include unique contexts (e.g., e-learning, distance education), modes of inquiry, conceptualization, and program components or objects to be evaluated. Evaluation purpose and questions are equally important (Patton, 2012). Influencers occur at the same time and unknowingly shape the direction of evaluation. The Navigational Map helps visualize intended purposes and questions addressed by an inquiry (Fig. 1).

The Navigational Map is not static—rather, it is dynamic. It is read vertically, starting with double arrows that point to "policy development/program implementation." The horizontal single-dotted arrow corresponds to bracketed terms "research/evaluation" that represent major paradigms of inquiry, along with four corresponding quadrants: (1) research, (2) evaluation research, (3) assessment, and (4) program evaluation. Each quadrant shapes the research-evaluation terrain in specific and purposeful ways. The quadrants may enlarge or contract, as arrows shift (side to side and/or up-down) depending upon purposes or types of questions asked. Terms listed on the map are described in subsections that follow.

Policy Development and Program Implementation

Viewing the map top-down are policy development and program implementation, which fuel expectations for evaluation and transparency. Policies create programs that generate unique implementations at the local level. Simultaneously, innovations

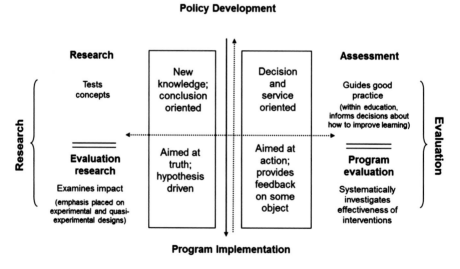

Fig. 1 Navigational map

and grassroots effort inform the need for program improvement or new policies, which foster additional programs. The up-and-down manner by which policies inform programs, and vice versa, is clearly evident in federal agencies within the United States government—and philanthropic sector. Administrators of public or privately funded programs and projects have to be responsive to funders, as they are guided by criteria and standards—or legislation. Similarly, programs within education settings must be responsive and justify their funding. Organizations learn about what is or is not working by way of evaluation, which informs decision-making and contributes to the knowledge base. The interplay of policy development and program evaluation represents this invisible reality (Fig. 1).

Research and Evaluation

These bracketed terms emphasize two major modes of inquiry that share common tools. Evaluation has many definitions, while research is understood to be empirical and aimed at truth. It tests hypotheses and informs science (Kuhn, 1970; Light, Singer, & Willett, 1990; Mertens, 2005). Succinctly stated, research knowledge affects what evaluation can contribute, whereas evaluation generates improvements, judgments, and actionable learning about programs. Michael Patton also points out that research generates knowledge about how the world works and why it works as it does. He differentiates research from evaluation as it pertains to purpose, question origin, persons judging quality and improvement, and ultimate test of value as depicted in Table 1 (Patton, 2014).

Research and Evaluation Research Quadrants

At the left of the map are research and evaluation research. Viewed separately, research is thought of as the scientific method and *not* evaluation. Although research and evaluation serve different purposes, they are *not* mutually exclusive. Inquiries

Table 1 Research vs. evaluation

Research	Evaluation
Purpose is testing theory and producing generalizable findings	Purpose is to determine the effectiveness of a specific program or model
Questions originate with scholars and a discipline	Questions originate with key stakeholders and primary intended users of evaluation findings
Quality and importance judged by peer review in a discipline	Quality and importance judged by those who will use the findings to take action and make decisions
Ultimate test of value is contribution to knowledge	Ultimate test of value is usefulness to improve effectiveness

Patton, Michael Quinn (2014). Evaluation flash cards: Embedding evaluative thinking in organizational culture. St. Paul, MN: Otto Bremer Foundation, ottobremer.org. http://www.ottobremer.org/sites/default/files/fact- sheets/OBF_flashcards_201402.pdf for education interventions can overlap and warrant evaluation research that involves more rigorous methods. In truth, it is not always possible to apply experimental designs in education settings. Evaluation research is "a systematic process for: (a) assessing strengths and weaknesses of programs, policies, organizations, technologies, persons, needs, or activities; (b) identifying ways to improve them; and (c) determining whether desired outcomes are achieved. It can be descriptive, formative, process, impact, summative or outcomes oriented—and, differs from program evaluation in that it is more likely to be investigator initiated, theory based, and focused on evaluation as the object of study" (Bickman, 2005, p. 141).

Assessment and Program Evaluation Quadrants

At the right of the map are assessment and program evaluation. These terms are used interchangeably. What is consistent about the word assessment is its formative purpose to determine whether intended learning outcomes are met (Palomba & Banta, 1999; Walvoord, 2010). While program evaluation may or may *not* be about learning outcomes (Smith, 2010). Rather, it could be to examine program effectiveness (Forsyth, Jolliffe, & Stevens, 1999). Assessment data collected to determine shifts in student learning can be part of a program evaluation depending on the purpose or questions asked (Comeaux, 2005; Suskie, 2004). Simply stated, assessment and program evaluation have different purposes and end goals. Consequently, you may wonder about the term program—especially at a course level of analysis. Program is a loosely used term defined in many ways for different purposes. For example, a program may be implemented at national and state levels, at various institutions, or could be multiple academic courses bundled together that lead to a degree, or a singular online course, project, event, etc. In fact, the term program can mean intervention or treatment. For the purposes of this chapter, we will think of a program or subprogram as listed in the Joint Committee on Standards for Educational Evaluation definition (Yarbrough et al., 2011).

What You Can Do

Although e-learning leaders want to know that education programs make a difference, they must resist temptation to cobble together evaluations without a plan. Meaningful evaluation meets primary users' information needs and requires critical thinking about design. Front-end evaluation planning helps with: (1) program design, (2) decision-making, (3) assessment, (4) evaluation and research, (5) monitoring and measurement, (6) grant-writing, (7) institutional review board (IRB) human subjects research applications, (8) conferences, (9) presentations, (10) publications, and (11) efficient use of time and resources. Evaluation is used to build transparency, make purpose and questions explicit, as well as to demonstrate that it was the program making a difference (Cousins & Bourgeois, 2014).

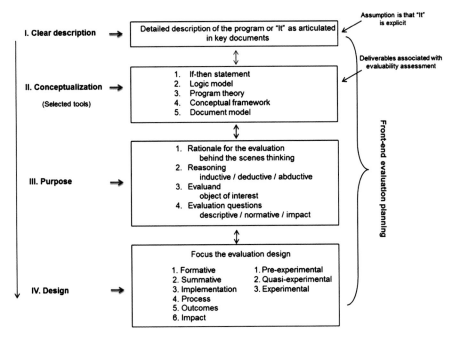

Fig. 2 Front-end evaluation planning framework

Front-End Evaluation Planning Framework

There are multiple ways to design an evaluation. The Front-end Evaluation Planning Framework is a guide that displays four phases of iterative processes (Fig. 2). Selected tools associated with an exploratory evaluation approach known as evaluability assessment (EA) are introduced. An aerial view of front-end planning averts the rush to measurement or "Garbage-in Garbage-out" (GIGO) phenomenon caused by hastily designed evaluations.

Phase I: Clear Descriptions and Context

e-Learning and distance education interventions should be clearly described before taking on evaluation (Yarbrough et al., 2011). Often it is assumed that they are; however, that is not always the case. Clear descriptions provide understanding for why an intervention or "IT" should achieve desired impacts—and make explicit the components, resources, activities, and people involved (Patton, 2008). "IT," according to Michael Patton, is what people ask about when they ask "Does "IT" work?" (Patton, 2008). Clear descriptions are the foundation for identifying evaluation questions—and capture an intervention's context, which is intertwined with evaluation theory and practice (Christie, 2003). Suffice it to say, context shapes how evaluation is approached, the types of questions asked, design and methods chosen, and how findings are reported (Rog, 2012; Yarbrough et al., 2011). e-Learning leaders implicitly know this to be true, because of the contextual differences between online and traditional face-to-face instruction. Context is unique to departments and programs within a department—as well as to courses, technologies, and students (Fig. 3). These varying levels of context are important to consider, as goals, objectives, and measures do not translate from one to another (McDavid, Huse, & Hawthorne, 2013). Aligning evidence to varying levels of impact is addressed in Phase II.

Phase II: Conceptualization

Conceptualization generates powerful tools that describe the main things to evaluate (Jaccard & Jacoby, 2010; Trochim & Linton, 1986). Complete understanding helps focus what is feasible within a given timeframe or budget (Bamberger, Rugh & Mabry, 2012). Conceptualization is best done graphically rather than in text (Miles & Huberman, 1994). Unfortunately, Phase II is often overlooked. The following subsections describe practical tools that generate deliverables associated with evaluability assessment.

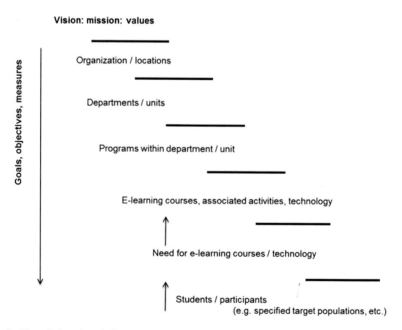

Fig. 3 Phase I clear description: context at varying levels

Phase II: Conceptualization—If-Then Statement

Basic if-then statements make interventions explicit and inform other models that capture changes expected to occur (Fig. 4). It is an easy way to identify program components, objectives, outcomes, and what to measure (Fig. 5). **If** something is done **then** something should change. Detailed if-then statements are logic models. For example, **If** program resources are available, **then** activities can be undertaken. **If** these program activities occur, **then** outcomes will be produced. **If** these activities and outcomes occur, **then** progress is made toward *xyz* goals, etc.

Phase II: Conceptualization—Logic Model

Logic models are linear and used to make assumptions explicit at varying levels of analysis, including policy. Anyone knowledgeable of the intervention can create one. Used for formative or summative evaluations (Knowlton & Phillips, 2013),

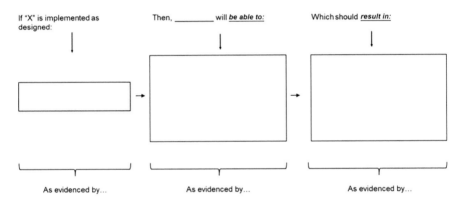

Fig. 4 Phase II conceptualization: "If-then" statement template

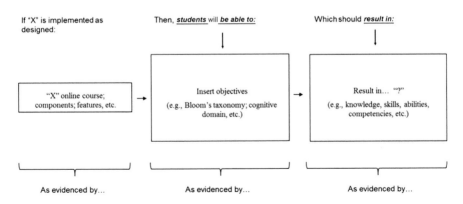

Fig. 5 Phase II conceptualization: "If-then" statement example

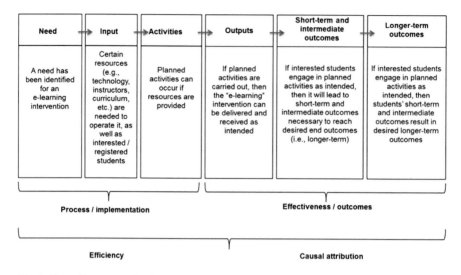

Fig. 6 Phase II conceptualization: logic model example

they help think through design, processes, implementation, effectiveness, outcomes, efficiency, and impacts.

As shown in Fig. 6, logic models describe events that: (a) connect need with results (b) identify evaluation questions, and (c) use different formats that depict major components: inputs, activities, outputs, and outcomes (Chen, 2005; Rogers, 2005; Funnell & Rogers, 2011; Shakman & Rodriguez, 2015; W. K. Kellogg Foundation, 2004a, 2004b). Data collected align to a logic model's chain of events and help answer questions such as these:

- To what extent were resources sufficient to implement the program effectively?
- Were activities conducted as intended?
- Did the program achieve its short-, intermediate-, and longer-term outcomes?

Administrators need to be aware that funders increasingly want logic models to be included in grant proposal submissions (Table 2).

Phase II: Conceptualization—Program Theory

The popularity of logic models overshadows program theory. Like logic models, program theory is used to guide evaluation (Bickman, 1987; Chen, 2005; Funnell & Rogers, 2011). What differentiates program theory from logic models is the program's design and implementation. Program theory is based on assumptions about what is needed to address a condition and why actions taken would remedy the situation (Chen, 2005; Wholey, 1987). Although program theory is similar in concept to

Table 2 Phase II: conceptualization—logic model; a tool for planning and matching data

Logic model	Program chain of events	Matching levels of evidence
Long-term	7. End results	7. Impact measures
Intermediate/long-term	6. Practice and behavior change	6. Measures of adoption of new practice and behavior overtime
Intermediate	5. Knowledge, attitude, and skill changes	5. Measures of students' changes in knowledge, attitudes, and skills
Short/intermediate	4. Reactions	4. What students have to say about the e-learning course/program or related components; satisfaction, etc.
Monitoring {	3. Participation	3. Characteristics of students, numbers, nature of involvement, background
	2. Activities	2. Implementation data on what the e-learning course/program actually does
	1. Inputs	1. Resources; number of students/ participants involved; times attended, etc.

Adapted from Rockwell, K., & Bennett, C. (2004). Taxonomy outcomes of programs: A hierarchy for targeting outcomes and evaluating their achievement. University of Nebraska-Lincoln Digital Commons @ University of Nebraska-Lincoln

logic models, it explains in detail (based on research evidence) connections that occur to bring about the desired outcomes. Program theory lays out evidence to show why you believe one thing leads to the next—and this approach is well suited for SoTL research.

Phase II: Conceptualization—Conceptual Framework

Conceptual frameworks guide research and evaluation (Chen, 2005; Dottin, 2001; Smyth, 2004). They perform a function that linear logic models cannot. According to Miles and Huberman, conceptual frameworks can be rudimentary or elaborate, theory-driven or commonsensical, descriptive or causal—and represent the current version of territory to be investigated (Miles & Huberman, 1994). The conceptual framework below helps with decision-making (Fig. 7). It displays overlapping considerations (e.g., criteria, standards, and quality principles), context, levels of analysis, and practices that shape e-learning contexts to capture recognizable assumptions and values not easily measured (Ruhe & Zumbo, 2009; Shelton, 2011, Waterhouse, 2005). Unique e-learning or distance education environments include: technology, curriculum and instructional delivery, organizational and policy domains.

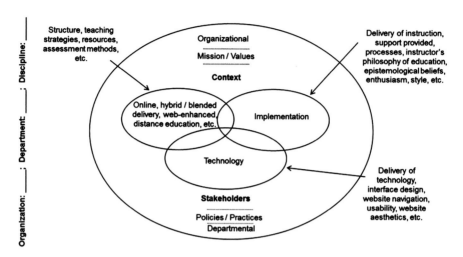

Fig. 7 Conceptual framework example

Phase II: Conceptualization—Document Model

One or more documents (e.g., grant proposals, web pages, syllabi) can be analyzed to create a graphic model that captures design, structure, logic, and expectations. Document models mirror the content of documents in an unbiased way; identify goals and objectives; expose problematic areas; identify faulty assumptions; and determine areas that need refinement (Rutman, 1980). Depending on the study, finalized evaluable models are created for evaluation purposes such as the example displayed in Fig. 8. Although information was redacted, the document model captures the essence of a course syllabus' design. The first draft showed gaps in learning objectives, and assumptions that needed clarification. Instructors thought their syllabus clearly described the course, but it did not. Rather, it presented challenges for assessment and program evaluation. Comparatively speaking, document models are used like logic models to clarify design, identify evaluation purpose, or match data measurement to a programmatic chain of events (Table 2). A second model was subsequently developed and design changes were made resulting in an evaluable model before taking on a comprehensive evaluation.

Phase II: Conceptualization—Evaluability Assessment

The tools described in Phase II generate deliverables associated with evaluability assessment (EA), which should be leveraged to determine whether "IT" is ready for evaluation. EA helps stakeholders agree on goals, intended uses of information, and

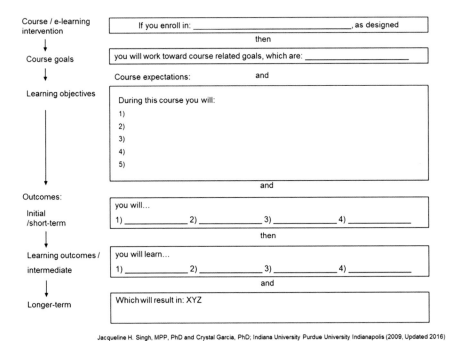

Course / e-learning
intervention
↓
Course goals
↓

Learning objectives

Outcomes:
Initial
/short-term
↓
Learning outcomes /
intermediate
↓
Longer-term

If you enroll in: _____, as designed
then
you will work toward course related goals, which are: _____
Course expectations: and
During this course you will:
1)
2)
3)
4)
5)
and
you will...
1) _____ 2) _____ 3) _____ 4) _____
then
you will learn...
1) _____ 2) _____ 3) _____ 4) _____
and
Which will result in: XYZ

Jacqueline H. Singh, MPP, PhD and Crystal Garcia, PhD; Indiana University Purdue University Indianapolis (2009, Updated 2016)

Fig. 8 Phase II conceptualization: document model

criteria (Smith, 1989; Davies, 2012; Wholey, 2015). It is well known among evaluation professionals—and internationally where there is widespread agreement on what evaluability means. The Organisation for Economic Co-operation and Development-Development Assistance Committee (OECD-DAC) definition is often cited:

> *The extent to which an activity or project can be evaluated in a reliable and credible fashion* (OECD-DAC, 2010, p. 21).

However, EA is lesser known to those outside the profession (Hatry, 2013). Within higher education contexts, EA presents opportunities to build evaluation capacity—and revisit interventions' design at the front-end before spending time on evaluation. Individuals often discover there is more design work to do (Trevisian & Walser, 2015). Familiarity with EA will cause e-learning leaders to question the value of traditional end-of-course student feedback surveys used by higher education—often for dual purposes (i.e., formative purposes *and* summative decision-making). Administrators must balance costs associated with evaluation and seriously weigh what it means to *not* use conceptualization tools. Not using EA can result in evaluations that produce little useful information (Hatry, 2013).

Phase III: Purpose

The purpose for engaging in evaluation can be difficult to articulate. So, what is an administrator to do? Several things can be considered. First, determine the extent that an evaluation's purpose is explicitly and genuinely addressed. Second, help stakeholders understand why evaluation is needed. Third, when value-added is questionable, the best action may be to *not* evaluate—or, use an alternate approach. Fourth, if evaluation is undertaken, ask why anyone should care? Why is it worth doing? What issues will it address? What best practices or decisions will an evaluation influence? Lastly, administrators *and* key stakeholders need to agree on the stated purpose for evaluation—preferably in writing, and address any conflicts that exist. Evaluation of e-learning interventions should make explicit who will learn about what—and by what means. For what purpose will information be used? Is it for formative purposes to improve a course or assess learning outcomes? To determine what works? To inform decisions regarding return on investments? These are important questions to consider, as purpose informs questions asked. Conversely, questions asked reveal intended purposes. In turn, questions *and* purpose inform evaluation design. One way to collaborate with key e-learning stakeholders is to start a conversation with the template below to create an agreed-upon evaluation purpose statement (Figs. 9 and 10).

Phase III: Purpose—Rationale, Reasoning, Evaluand

Stakeholders' rationale for engaging in evaluation should not be overlooked. It helps raise individuals' awareness of their collective reasoning and modes of inquiry used to evaluate an e-learning intervention (Rog, 1995; Ruhe & Zumbo, 2009;

The purpose of this evaluation is _____;

so, we can learn about _____,

which will enable us to make informed decisions about _____.

Fig. 9 Phase III purpose: evaluation purpose statement template

The purpose of this evaluation is: to collect relevant data that capture a hierarchy of outcomes;

so, we can learn about: program participant outcomes,

which will enable us to make informed decisions about: student engagement, retention, and returns on investment.

Fig. 10 Phase III purpose: evaluation purpose statement example

Shelton, 2011; Shank & Sitze, 2004). Recall the "IT" is the object of interest (e.g., e-learning program or course, technology, usability, teaching strategy, quality) captured in conceptualizations to help agree upon the evaluation's purpose.

Phase III: Purpose—Stakeholders' Questions

Evaluation questions address what primary information users want to understand. Generally speaking, there are three types of evaluation questions (described in the next section). Strategic questions accord transparency and confidence in evaluation. But, how does one engage key stakeholders to articulate strategic evaluation questions? And, do it well? Answers to these questions are important—and unfortunately beyond the scope of this chapter. Resources listed at the end offer practical guidance for developing evaluation questions.

Phase III: Purpose—Questions Inform Evaluation Approaches and Design

e-Learning leaders make better decisions when evaluation questions are clear and strategic. Questions fall on a continuum that range from need to return on investment (Fig. 11), which necessitates different evaluation and data collection approaches (Altschuld & Kumar, 2010; Phillips & Phillips, 2007; Tobin, Mandernach, & Tayor, 2015; Watkins, West Meiers, & Visser, 2012).

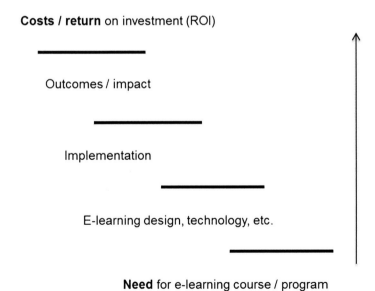

Fig. 11 Phase III purpose: varying levels of evaluation questions

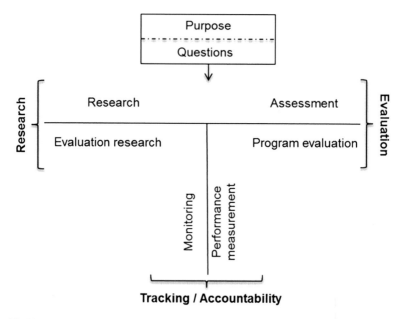

Fig. 12 Phase III: purpose—intersecting modes of evaluative inquiry

At the same time, other modes of evaluative inquiry intersect with evaluation as well as research (Fig. 12). It is important to be aware of the approaches other partnering organizations use and funders increasingly require. For example, monitoring and performance measurement are used to track indicators of progress or process and compare performance toward pre-existing goals or standards. Together, they provide data that guide strategic planning, design, and implementation of interventions, as well as resource allocation.

Although monitoring and performance measurement are complementary to program evaluation (Hunter & Nielsen, 2013; McDavid et al., 2013), e-learning leaders should not conflate terms—they are not the same (Patton, 2008). The major difference is program evaluation is episodic, while monitoring and performance measurement involves ongoing measurement as shown in Table 3 (GAO, 2011). Attribution of change due to the intervention is generally assumed (GAO, 2012; McDavid et al., 2013; Patton, 2008). Individuals assigned responsibility for managing interventions usually help develop performance measures and systematically track and report performance as part of program accountability. Program evaluation occurs less often. It is issue specific and the intended purpose is made explicit. Attribution of observed outcomes is often a question about efficiencies or impact (GAO, 2012; McDavid et al., 2013).

Because modes of inquiry often intersect, e-learning leaders should be aware of how questions are asked. According to the Government Accountability Office (GAO, 1991), evaluation questions are divided into three types: (1) descriptive,

Table 3 Program evaluation vs. performance measurement

Program evaluation	Performance measurement
Systematic study using research methods to collect and analyze data to assess how well a program is working and why	Systematic ongoing monitoring and reporting of program accomplishments, particularly progress toward preestablished goals
Answer specific questions about program performance & may focus on assessing program operations or results	
Can assess an entire program or focus on an initiative within a program	Typically conducted by program or agency (organization) management
Some attempt to isolate causal impacts of programs from other influences on outcomes, whereas performance measurement typically does not	And, may address the type or level of program activities conducted (process), the direct products and services delivered by a program (outputs) or the results of those products and services (outcomes)
Have been used to supplement reporting by measuring results that are too difficult or expensive to assess annually or by exploring why performance goals were not met	

GAO: Designing Evaluations: 2012 Revision (GAO-12-208G); http://www.gao.gov/assets/590/588146

(2) normative, and (3) impact (cause-and-effect). Descriptive questions provide information about conditions, context, or activities, number of people, etc. Normative questions are similar, but focus on what *should* be rather than what is. They evaluate against a criterion. Impact questions address cause-and-effect to reveal whether observed conditions or events are attributed to the intervention. The point of departure when planning evaluation is the question (GAO, 1991). For example, questions below necessitate different designs:

1. Is it *descriptive?* In what way(s) was the online course implemented? How was technology used?
2. Is it *normative?* Is this a quality online course? Which begs follow-on questions: By what criteria? Using what standards?
3. Is it *causal?* In what ways did "IT" have an impact on student learning? How can we know with certainty? How does "IT" impact the larger campus for its investment(s)?

The choice of design is linked with the level of certainty needed and constraints such as time and resources. There is no perfect design. But, most stakeholders ask a common question, "Is *it* working?" Not everyone defines what's working in the same way. e-Learning leaders want to know about outcomes related to student learning, such as engagement with technology. It's important to know that evaluation of online teaching and learning presents a different set of challenges (Tobin et al., 2015). Results from e-learning courses should not be compared to results from traditional courses—until thorough validation of data collection instruments. But, if individuals want to know how an e-learning course is implemented or why it leads to particular outcomes, then a descriptive study is most suitable. When questions are normative or directed toward aspects of quality, then use criteria, such as Quality *Matters Rubric Standards* or *Sloan-C Quality Framework and the Five Pillars*. Whether comprehensive evaluation for e-learning courses, or rigorous evaluation research, data collected should answer "As evidenced by what?" (see Fig. 4).

Phase IV: Design

At the heart of evaluation planning is design. Always begin with a clear description, conceptualizations, and questions that translate into an appropriate design. Evaluation is not an add-on activity—it is a way of thinking and doing (Patton, 2014; Preskill & Boyle, 2008). Examples of evaluation plans (adaptable to e-learning and distance education) are available at the Online Evaluation Resource Library (http://oerl.sri.com/home.html) to help visualize what this looks like. It is also important to consider program stages of maturation that range from needs assessment to dissemination (Altschuld & Kumar, 2010; GAO, 2012; U.S. Department of Education, 2008; Watkins et al., 2012). Some programs never mature (Patton, 2011) or reach dissemination (Trochim et al., 2012). Each stage necessitates a certain type of evaluation. Generally speaking, there are three major types of evaluation: developmental, formative, and summative (Fig. 13).

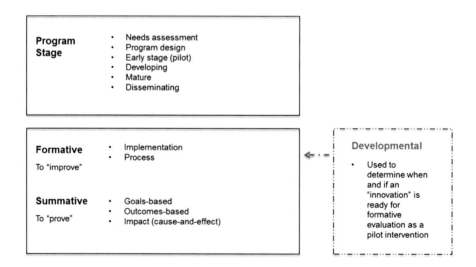

Fig. 13 Phase IV: program stage and common evaluation approaches

Table 4 Mapping program stage to evaluation type, approach, and questions asked

Program stage	Evaluation type	Plausible evaluation approaches	Examples of questions asked
Needs assessment	Developmental	Needs assessment; developmental evaluation	What is the problem or nature of the need? What are the needs of targeted students for the e-learning intervention? What or is anything being developed? What resources are available to address "it"?
Program design	Developmental; formative	Design assessment; evaluability assessment	What's being developed? Is there a well-formulated design? Is "it" or can its logic be made explicit? What aspects of the e-learning intervention need to be modified to achieve the intended outcomes? Is the e-learning intervention sufficiently designed and ready for implementation?
Early stage; pilot; or, new intervention within an existing program	Developmental; formative	Implementation or process evaluation; evaluability assessment	Is the e-learning intervention reaching targeted recipients? Is the e-learning intervention producing intended short-term outcomes? What progress has been made with new technologies or innovations? What gaps are there in the e-learning intervention's design that needs to be tweaked?
Developing	Developmental; formative	Implementation or process evaluation; evaluability assessment	What steps or progress has been in implementing the "it"? Is "it" being delivered as intended? To what extent has 'it' been implemented? Is "it" well managed? Are participants' satisfied with "it"? Is the e-learning intervention sufficiently designed and ready for an outcomes or impact evaluation?
Mature, stable, disseminating	Summative	Outcomes, goals, impact/cause and effects; impact/return on investment; program fidelity assessment; evaluability assessment	Are the desired outcomes achieved? Were desired goals reached? Did the intervention produce unintended outcomes? Why is the intervention not obtaining desired outcomes? Did the intervention "cause" the desired impact? What are the returns on investment for the "it"? Is the e-learning intervention ready for an outcomes or impact evaluation?

Adapted from Bernholz, E., et al. (2006, July). *Evaluation dialogue between OMB staff and federal evaluators: Digging a bit deeper into evaluation science.* Washington, DC. http://www.fedeval.net/docs/omb2006briefing.pdf

The program's stage of maturation should match the type of evaluation undertaken and align with a plausible evaluation approach as well as questions asked (Table 4). Additional resources are listed in the information section.

Conclusion

This chapter points out how to approach evaluative inquiries at the front-end. Two aerial view illustrations are introduced for quick reference: the Navigational Map (Fig. 1) that differentiates program evaluation from other complementary modes of inquiry and a Front-end Evaluation Planning Framework (Fig. 2), which helps navigate iterative evaluation processes and identifies selected deliverables associated with EA (Wholey, Hatry, & Newcomer, 2004). Strategic evaluation is possible when context is considered, purpose and questions are explicit—and front-end evaluation planning is not hurried or skipped.

For More Information

Websites

1. American Evaluation Association: http://www.eval.org/
2. Better Evaluation: http://betterevaluation.org
3. Online Evaluation Resource Library: http://oerl.sri.com/home.html
4. University of Wisconsin—Extension Program Development and Evaluation: http://www.uwex.edu/ces/pdande/

Resources, Evaluation Standards, and Quality Criteria

1. Preskill, H., & Jones, N. (2009). *A practical guide for engaging stakeholders in developing evaluation questions.* Retrieved from http://www.fsg.org/tools-and-resources/practical-guide-engaging-stakeholders-developing-evaluation-questions-0
2. Beginner guides to program evaluation: http://gsociology.icaap.org/methods/BasicguidesHandouts.html
3. Cornell University Cooperative Extension. (2012). *The guide to the systems evaluation protocol.* Retrieved from https://core.human.cornell.edu/documents/SEPGuide2_small.pdf
4. *Learning Consortium [OLC]; Quality framework.* Retrieved from http://online-learningconsortium.org/about/quality-framework-five-pillars/

5. Janet C. Moore. *The sloan consortium quality framework and the five pillars.* Retrieved from http://www.nova.edu/%7Esimsmich/best_practices/Sloan-C%20 Quality%20Framework%20and%20the%20Five%20Pillars.pdf
6. California State University, Chico. *Rubric for exemplary online instruction.* Retrieved from http://www.csuchico.edu/eoi/
7. *Rubric for online instruction.* Retrieved from http://www.csuchico.edu/eoi/the_ rubric.shtml

References

Altschuld, J. W., & Kumar, D. D. (2010). *Needs assessment: An overview.* Thousand Oaks: Sage Publications, Inc..

Bamberger, M., Rugh, J., & Mabry, L. (2012). *Real world evaluation: Working under budget, time, data, and political constraints* (2nd ed.). Thousand Oaks: Sage Publications, Inc.

Bernholz, E., Ginsburg A, Habibion M, Heffelfinger J., Introcasco, D., Oros, C., Scheers, N.J., Shipman, S., Stinson, L., Valdez B et al. (2006). *Evaluation dialogue between OMB staff and federal evaluators: Digging a bit deeper into evaluation science.* Washington, DC. Retrieved from http://www.fedeval.net/docs/omb2006briefing.pdf

Bickman, L. (1987). Using program theory in evaluation. *New directions for program evaluation,* No. 33. San Francisco: Jossey-Bass.

Bickman, L. (2005). Evaluation research. In L. Bickman (Ed.), *Encyclopedia of evaluation* (p. 141). Thousand Oaks: Sage Publications, Inc..

Cousins, J. B., & Bourgeois, I. (Eds.). (2014). *Framing the capacity to do and use evaluation. New directions for evaluation. Organizational capacity to do and use evaluation, No. 141.* San Francisco: Jossey-Bass.

Chen, H. T. (2005). *Practical program evaluation: Assessing and improving planning, implementation, and effectiveness.* Thousand Oaks: Sage Publications, Inc..

Christie, C. A. (2003). Understanding evaluation theory and its role in guiding practice: Formal, folk, and otherwise. *New Directions for Evaluation, 97,* 91–93.

Comeaux, P. (Ed.). (2005). *Assessing online learning.* San Francisco: Jossey-Bass.

Davies, R. (2012, November). *A bibliography on evaluability assessment.* Retrieved from http://mande.co.uk/2012/lists/evaluability-assessments-bibliography/a-bibliography-on-evaluability-assessment/

Dottin, E. S. (2001). *The development of a conceptual framework: The stimulation for coherence and continuous improvement in teacher education.* Lanham: University Press of America, Inc..

Forsyth, I., Jolliffe, A., & Stevens, D. (1999). *Evaluating a course.* Sterling: Stylus.

Funnell, S. C., & Rogers, P. J. (2011). *Purposeful program theory: Effective use of theories of change and logic models.* San Francisco, CA: Jossey-Bass.

Government Accountability Office (1991). *Designing evaluations: PEMD-10.1.4.* Published: May 1, 1991. Publicly Released: May 1, 1991 (Superseded by GAO-12-208G). Retrieved from http://www.gao.gov/products/PEMD-10.1.4

Government Accountability Office [GAO]. (2011). *Performance measurement and evaluation: Definitions and relationships GAO-11-646SP.* Retrieved from https://www.ise.gov/gao-11-646sp-performance-measurement-and-evaluation-definitions-and-relationships

Government Accountability Office [GAO] (2012). *Designing evaluations: 2012 revision GAO-12-208G.* Published: January 31, 2012. Publicly Released: February 1, 2012. Retrieved from http://www.gao.gov/products/GAO-12-208G

Hatry, H. (2013). Sorting the relationships among performance measurement, program evaluation, and performance management. In *Performance management and evaluation: New direction for evaluation* (pp. 9–32). San Francisco: Jossey-Bass.

Hunter, D. E. K., & Nielsen, S. B. (2013). Performance management and evaluation: Exploring complementarities. In S. B. Nielsen & D. E. K. Hunter (Eds.), *Performance management and evaluation. New directions for evaluation, 137*, 7–17.

Jaccard, J., & Jacoby, J. (2010). *Theory construction and model-building: A practical guide for social scientists*. New York: The Guilford Press.

Kellogg Foundation. (2004a). *Evaluation handbook*. Retrieved from http://www.wkkf.org/resource-directory/resource/2010/w-k-kellogg-foundation-evaluation-handbook

Kellogg Foundation. (2004b). *Logic model development guide*. Retrieved from http://www.wkkf.org/resource-directory/resource/2006/02/wk-kellogg-foundation-logic-model-development-guide

Knowlton, L. W., & Phillips, C. C. (2013). *The logic model guidebook: Better strategies for great results*. Thousand Oaks: Sage Publications, Inc..

Kuhn, T. (1970). *The structure of scientific revolutions* (2nd ed., enlarged ed.). Chicago: The University of Chicago Press.

Light, R. J., Singer, J. D., & Willett, J. B. (1990). *By design*. Cambridge: Harvard University Press.

Mathison, S. (Ed.). (2005). *Encyclopedia of evaluation*. Thousand Oaks, CA: Sage Publications, Inc..

McDavid, J. C., Huse, I., & Hawthorn, R. L. (2013). *Program evaluation and performance measurement: An introduction to practice* (2nd ed.). Los Angeles: Sage Publications, Inc.

Mertens, D. M. (2005). *Research and evaluation in education and psychology*. Thousand Oaks: Sage Publications, Inc..

Miles, M., & Huberman, M. B. (1994). *Qualitative data analysis: An expanded sourcebook* (2nd ed.). Thousand Oaks, CA: Sage Publications, Inc..

Organisation for Economic Co-operation and Development [OECD]. (2010). *Glossary of key terms in evaluation and results based management*. Retrieved from http://www.oecd.org/development/peer-reviews/2754804.pdf

Palomba, C. A., & Banta, T. W. (1999). *Assessment essentials: Planning, implementing, and improving assessment in higher education*. San Francisco: Jossey Bass.

Patton, M. Q. (2008). *Utilization focused evaluation* (4th ed.). Thousand Oaks, CA: Sage Publications, Inc..

Patton, M. Q. (2011). *Developmental evaluation: Applying complexity concepts to enhance innovation and use*. New York: Guilford Press.

Patton, M. Q. (2012). *Essentials of utilization-focused evaluation*. Los Angeles, CA: Sage Publications, Inc.

Patton, M. Q. (2014). *Evaluation flash cards: embedding evaluative thinking in organizational culture*. St. Paul, MN: Otto Bremer Foundation. Retrieved from http://www.ottobremer.org/sites/default/files/fact- sheets/OBF_flashcards_201402.pdf.

Phillips, P. P., & Phillips, J. J. (2007). *The value of learning*. San Francisco: Pfeiffer.

Preskill, H., & Boyle, S. (2008). A multidisciplinary model of evaluation capacity building. *American Journal of Evaluation, 29*, 443–459.

Rockwell, K., & Bennett, C. (2004). *Taxonomy outcomes of programs: A hierarchy for targeting outcomes and evaluating their achievement, University of Nebraska-Lincoln Digital Commons@*. Lincoln, NE: University of Nebraska-Lincoln.

Rog, D. J. (1995). Reasoning in evaluation: Challenges for the practitioner. *New Directions for Evaluation, 68*, 93–100.

Rog, D. J. (2012). When background becomes foreground: Toward context-sensitive evaluation practice. In D. J. Rog, J. L. Fitzpatrick, & R. F. Conner (Eds.), *Context: A framework for its influence on evaluation practice. New directions for evaluation* (vol. 135, pp. 25–40). San Francisco, Jossey Bass.

Rogers, P. (2005). Logic model. In S. Mathison (Ed.), *Encyclopedia of evaluation* (pp. 232–235). Thousand Oaks, CA: Sage Publications.

Ruhe, V., & Zumbo, B. D. (2009). *Evaluation in distance education and e-learning: The unfolding model*. New York: The Guilford Press.

Rutman, L. (1980). *Planning useful evaluations*. Beverly Hills: Sage Publications, Inc..

Scriven, M. (1991). *Evaluation thesaurus* (4th ed.). Newbury Park: Sage Publications, Inc..

Shank, P., & Sitze, A. (2004). *Making sense of online leaning*. San Francisco: Pfeiffer.

Shakman, K., & Rodriguez, S. M. (2015). *Logic models for program design, implementation, and evaluation: Workshop toolkit (REL 2015-057)*. Washington, DC: U.S. Department of Education, Institute of Education Sciences, National Center for Education Evaluation and Regional Assistance, Regional Educational Laboratory Northeast & Isands. Retrieved from http://ies.ed.gov/ncee/edlabs.

Shelton, K. (2011). A review of paradigms for evaluating the quality of online education programs. *Online Journal of Distance Learning Administration, 4*(1). University of West Georgia, Distance Education Center. Retrieved from http://www.westga.edu/~distance/ojdla/spring141/shelton141.html

Singh, J. H. (2011). *Navigational map*. Retrieved from http://comm.eval.org/communities/community-home/librarydocuments/viewdocument?DocumentKey=77a55f44-d544-4c68-862e-431a6cdee993&CommunityKey=00000000-0000-0000-0000-000000000000&tab=librarydocuments

Singh, J. H. (2016). *Front-end evaluation planning framework*. Retrieved from http://comm.eval.org/communities/community-home/librarydocuments/viewdocument?DocumentKey=c0bacdc8-ba66-49eb-a406-26919078da0e&CommunityKey=00000000-0000-0000-0000-000000000000&tab=librarydocuments

Smith, M. F. (1989). *Evaluability assessment: A practical approach*. Boston: Kluwer Academic Publishers.

Smith, N. L. (2010). Characterizing the evaluand in evaluation theory. *American Journal of Evaluation, 31*, 383–389.

Smyth, R. (2004). Exploring the usefulness of a conceptual framework as a research tool: A researcher's reflections. *Issues in Educational Research, 14*, 167–180.

Suskie, L. (2004). *Assessing student learning: A common sense guide*. San Francisco: Jossey-Bass Inc., Publishers.

Tobin, T., Mandernach, J., & Tayor, A. (2015). *Evaluating online teaching: Implementing practices*. San Francisco: Jossey-Bass.

Trevisian, M. S., & Walser, T. M. (2015). *Evaluability assessment: Improving evaluation quality and use*. Los Angeles: Sage Publications, Inc..

Trochim, W., Urban, J. B., Hargraves, M., Hebbard, C., Buckley, J., Archibald, T., ... Burgermaster, M. (2012). *The guide to the systems protocol*. Ithaca, NY: Cornell Digital Print Services.

Trochim, W. M., & Linton, R. (1986). Conceptualization for planning and evaluation. *Evaluation and Program Planning, 9*(4), 289–308.

Tsai, S., & Machado, P. (2002). E-learning basics: Essay: E-learning, online learning, web-based learning, or distance learning: Unveiling the ambiguity in current terminology. *eLearn, 2002*(7). doi:10.1145/566778.568597. Retrieved from http://elearnmag.acm.org/index.cfm

U.S. Department of Education (2008). *Evaluating online learning: Challenges and strategies for success*. Retrieved from http://www2.ed.gov/admins/lead/academic/evalonline/index.html

Walvoord, B. E. (2010). *Assessment clear and simple: A practical guide for institutions, departments, and general education* (2nd ed.). San Francisco: Jossey-Bass.

Waterhouse, S. (2005). *The power of eLearning: The essential guide for teaching in the digital age*. Boston: Pearson.

Watkins, R., West Meiers, M., & Visser, Y. L. (2012). *A guide to assessing needs: Essential tools for collecting information, making decisions, and achieving development results*. Washington, DC: The World Bank. doi:10.1596/978-0-8213-8868-6. Retrieved from https://openknowledge.worldbank.org/handle/10986/2231.

Wholey, J. S. (1987). Evaluability assessment: Developing program theory. In L. Bickman (Ed.), *Using program theory in evaluation. New directions for program evaluation* (Vol. 33, pp. 77–92). New York, NY: Wiley.

Wholey, J. S. (2015). Exploratory evaluation. In K. E. Newcomer, H. P. Hatry, & J. S. Wholey (Eds.), *Handbook of practical program evaluation* (4th ed.pp. 88–107). San Francisco: Jossey-Bass.

Wholey, J. S., Hatry, H. P., & Newcomer, K. E. (2004). *Handbook of practical program evaluation* (2nd ed.). San Francisco: Jossey-Bass.

Yarbrough, D. B., Shulha, L. M., Hopson, R. K., & Caruthers, F. A. (2011). *Joint Committee on Standards for Educational Evaluation [JCSEE]; The program evaluation standards: A guide for evaluators and evaluation users*. Thousand Oaks: Sage.

Scaling Online Learning: Critical Decisions for eLearning Leaders

Marie A. Cini and Matthew Prineas

Abstract Unlike most industries, higher education has largely failed to take advantage of economies of scale or the efficiencies gained through growth based on intentional methods to keep costs low and quality high. In the U.S., higher education has, from its inception, adopted a decentralized and fragmented system of thousands of institutions. While in some ways a strength, this disparate approach to higher education also militates against large-scale adoption of best practices and standardized approaches.

Yet the pressures to scale are increasing. Higher education is now grappling with the question of efficiency in light of reduced resources, and many institutions are focusing on scaling smartly so they can grow and yet remain cost effective. Some see scale as inevitable as the pressures on higher education increase. As resources have become more constrained, pressures on university leaders to leverage the benefits of scale will only grow.

This chapter is intended for the online learning leader who seeks to grow enrollments smartly, using a systematic process that will keep costs low and quality high, while providing greater access to those who seek a college education.

Keywords Business model • Change management • Cost disease • Economies of scale • Efficiency • Faculty development • Iron triangle • Learning design • MOOC • Online education

M.A. Cini (✉)
University of Maryland University College, Upper Marlboro, MD, USA
e-mail: marie.cini@umuc.edu

M. Prineas
Athabasca University, Athabasca, Canada
e-mail: mprineas@athabascau.ca

© Association for Educational Communications and Technology 2018
A.A. Piña et al. (eds.), *Leading and Managing e-Learning*, Educational Communications and Technology: Issues and Innovations,
https://doi.org/10.1007/978-3-319-61780-0_21

Decision-Making Guidance

This chapter will help you make decisions about:

- Building an institutional infrastructure that supports scale
- How to establish a common learning model
- Where to place course and learning design resources
- How to approach faculty training and development
- The model of student support
- The significance of Massive Open Online Courses (MOOCs)
- Managing the change process
- Organizations related to online education you may want to join

What You Need to Know

If you are reading this chapter, you likely are the leader of an online learning unit. Whether you are a vice provost for online learning, the dean of extension, or the director of online programs within a school or department, you will be facing some fundamental questions regarding how to build and lead a unit that achieves learning goals for students, grows enrollments and revenues, and yet follows a business model that does not create extraordinary costs. We wrote this chapter with you in mind as you negotiate these sometimes conflicting goals.

You are leading online education in your university during a time of intense financial pressure in higher education. With the exception of a few universities with large endowments, many universities today have an unsustainable business model (Denneen & Dretler, 2012). One solution is to grow enrollments in order to remain viable in today's crowded and competitive higher education landscape. You may even have been charged with growing enrollments through online education as part of your university's strategic plan.

Traditionally, universities have found it difficult to grow efficiently due to an entrenched assumption about the role of human capital. Baumol (2013) has described this as the "cost disease." In fields that are labor intensive (e.g., the arts) and cannot easily replace human labor with technology, costs will inevitably rise as the cost of labor increases over time. For a long time education was assumed to be in this category. Human beings did the teaching and could not be replaced by machines or other types of capital investment. Therefore, for more students to be educated in a quality manner, the cost of education would inevitably need to rise given the high cost of faculty talent.

This "iron triangle" of cost, quality, and access (Immerwhar, Johnson & Gasbarra, 2008) has generally constrained universities from being able to provide greater access with high quality at a reasonable cost. The iron triangle asserts that gains in any two of the triangle's vertices cannot come without a loss (e.g., higher costs, lower quality, or less access) in the third. The experience of the traditional model of education would seem to bear this rule out, and as long as the iron triangle has remained in force, the ability to serve greater numbers of students—in other words, to scale—has been limited. Online education promises a pathway out of the iron triangle, but only when it is based on a sound approach. Online education itself will not break the triangle; program development and delivery have to be carefully designed with low cost, high quality, and broader accessibility, all working together.

What Do We Mean by "Scale"?

Our intention in this chapter is walk you through the components you need to create an online model that works well for your university and your students. The underlying model should be based on the concept of "economies of scale" or "scale" for short. By economies of scale, we mean cost advantages gained through an organization's increased size based on an underlying model in which additional costs are intentionally kept lower than the additional enrollments served. Applied to academic programs, "scaling" means that you create a process by which, as you enroll more students, the additional costs to serve those students are kept low through a series of decisions to gain efficiencies where possible.

Some would argue that the goals of increasing enrollment and maintaining quality cannot coexist, but we know they can through our own experiences, and we have found ways to keep that relationship strong. Our goal is to help you make decisions that can actually help you increase learning quality and contain costs, even while growing your online programs.

We understand that in traditional academe the idea of "scale" is rarely discussed. If it is discussed there is often a negative reaction to the use of such "business" terms applied to higher education. Higher education has historically viewed itself as existing in a rarified atmosphere, not to be tainted by the base drive for money. Yet, we now face a time when the business model of higher education is increasingly viewed as broken; colleges and universities close or merge with others on a regular basis (Brown, 2014). In light of this fact, we need a new way of thinking about the business model of higher education, and applying economies of scale to current challenges in higher education provides a critically needed approach.

Are You Ready to Scale Your Online Programs?

For online leaders, it may seem strange to ask this question. Online education has been closely associated with outreach and access, allowing students who might otherwise not be able to attend location-based education to pursue a degree. In this way of thinking, the more students who access online higher education, the better in terms of serving new student segments, be they rural residents, those in the military, international students, adults with competing responsibilities, or even the disabled. At the same time, with the rising cost of physical facilities, many universities view online education as a way to grow enrollment and revenues.

If your university is seeking to grow online enrollments for these reasons, you will have to face the question of your institutional readiness to scale. Is your institution ready to explore more centralized and standardized ways to develop programs and courses? Do you have the resources to train and develop instructors for the online sections? Can you support students in technologically mediated ways at times that are outside of the traditional face-to-face advising hours? For those who can answer "yes" to these questions, you are ready to scale your operations. But for the larger numbers for whom the answer to these questions is "no"—this chapter is written with you in mind. And we will guide you through the steps, decisions, and resources to help you do so successfully.

The Right Approach to Scaling Online Learning

The growth of online education has benefitted from greater public acceptance and so the force of increased student demand requires a more scaled approach as well. Add to this an environment in which information is no longer a scarce resource—digital higher education content is now ubiquitous and inexpensive, allowing for new approaches to scale never before possible—and you have conditions that are ripe for smart growth through the right decisions about how to scale your programs.

In such an environment, it is tempting to see online education by itself as offering the promise of scale without a commensurate increase in costs. Unfortunately, this view underestimates the institutional infrastructure—and, in many cases, major changes—required to offer high quality online education at scale. Simply encouraging individual faculty members to place content online will not result in an effective and efficient learning experience for online students. The fact is that online education by itself cannot overcome the built-in inefficiency of the traditional academic model. Grafting new delivery platforms onto traditional approaches does not enable institutions to benefit from economies of scale. In the context of the traditional model, online education may in fact exacerbate inherent inefficiencies and actually yield lower educational outcomes, higher costs, and lower student satisfaction unless new approaches to course design, faculty development, and program delivery models are instituted.

Applying economies of scale that truly create lower costs, increased access, and high quality academic programs means that universities must first develop processes and systems that allow for rapid, additional growth at marginal cost, while maintaining or even increasing quality standards. Applied to online learning, among other things, this means that as new sections of a given course are added, growth of enrollment revenues will increase more quickly than any costs associated with adding additional sections.

For example, if adding an additional course section of 25 students increases revenue by x amount, the costs of adding that new section need to be well below x. The total cost of that hypothetical new section should include *all* costs, not limited to direct instructional costs, but also including indirect costs of student support, marketing, technology, and so on. The lower the total cost of adding that additional section, the greater the revenue that each additional section produces. But if the total cost to add an additional section is *more* than this hypothetical x, then the institution is in the unenviable position of potentially growing itself out of existence.

Most universities are simply not structured to sustain growth smartly. The ways in which universities have traditionally developed and delivered the curriculum virtually guarantee that costs will grow, quickly outstripping gains in revenue. For example, universities find it easy to add programs but very difficult to end them, no matter how low the enrollments, thus driving costs up (Saffron, 2014). And the plethora of course choices is not only inefficient, but also potentially harmful for student retention (Mathews, 2015). Yet, programs and courses proliferate, often presumed to be the province of faculty decision-making.

Many in higher education would reject as anathema even the notion of having or needing to have a "business model" or a plan for greater efficiency. But the need for a business model is ubiquitous across organizations of all kinds—even Mother Teresa had a business model (Hampson, 2012). It simply means that higher education institutions and their constituent departments need to articulate the underlying economic logic of how they plan to sustain themselves and meet the needs of the people they serve.

The largely unconscious "business model" of higher education is deeply rooted in the historical governance models of universities, in which faculty "own" content, learning design, and teaching approach. Faculty members choose the content they wish to cover in a course, determine how to design the course, and choose how to teach the course. These decisions are usually made by individual faculty members even when teaching different sections of the very same course.

With this fragmented approach to the curriculum and pedagogy, the iron triangle remains in force: growth in online education may lead to low quality or at best great variability and inconsistency in the student experience. While higher education faculty are expert in their discipline, very few have expertise in learning science, learning design, or teaching effectiveness. This is not to blame the faculty. Graduate school training rarely covers such subjects, and when it does so, tends to cover them only perfunctorily.

As they come under increasing pressure from a skeptical public and politicians to demonstrate learning outcomes and the value of a degree, higher education institutions are realizing the need to provide expertise and support in these critical areas of instruction and learning design. This recognition is reflected in the rise of Centers of Excellence in Teaching and Learning and the greater use of instructional designers in course development across the higher education landscape. These support units focus on the use of best practices and research-based approaches to achieving high quality learning outcomes.

Building an Institutional Infrastructure to Support Scale

A Common Learning Model

"Teaching philosophy" is traditionally treated as a matter of individual faculty expression, unique to each instructor. The very word "philosophy" connotes an art more than a science. Efforts to dictate how faculty should be teaching may be met with firm objections, if not outright hostility.

Yet, learning science has come a long way; we now know a great deal about how humans learn (Ambrose, Bridges, DiPietro, Lovett, & Norman, 2010), but most university faculty are not aware of this work. Chemists teach chemistry. Psychologists teach psychology. But they teach by modeling what they experienced throughout their education. Thus, for most faculty, teaching remains largely a self-taught art, based on individual experience, anecdote, and lore—and uninformed by the growing body of learning science now available.

The real question faculty should be asking is not "how should I teach mathematics?" but instead "how do I create a learning environment so that students are able to learn math most effectively?" Online education provides a unique opportunity to address this critical change. Most faculty new to online appreciate some orientation to teaching in this model, and this is a good opportunity to work *with* faculty to develop some common principles of an online "learning model" that fits your institution. Resources to support effective online teaching are readily available (e.g., Paloff & Pratt, 2013; Stavredes & Herder, 2014) and by working with a core group of online faculty, faculty development experts, and instructional designers, a model can be created.

At UMUC, our focus on adult students is moving us to explore a more experientially based pedagogy as a learning model. In our research, we discovered that Ryerson University in Canada has built a shared campus-wide learning model built on the concepts of experiential education (http://www.ryerson.ca/experiential/ELModelandVideo.html). Universities should start with their student base when designing a common learning model; others may adopt a more constructivist approach, a problem-based learning approach, or some combination of several models.

Exploring and adopting a common learning model across a university is a wonderful way to support a rich culture of faculty engagement in improved learning outcomes, and to create a far richer learning environment for students. It also nicely supports economies of scale in online learning. If faculty develop common standards, common designs, and common teaching approaches across courses and programs, they will be more likely to commit to and practice these best practices and standards. This is particularly important in the online environment where traditional modes of teaching cannot simply be applied without rethinking the educational space.

A university-wide core learning model shifts the emphasis from the solo work of individual faculty members as the source of curricular content to the pooled efforts of a team of professionals (including faculty subject-matter experts) who design optimum learning experiences. The late Nobel Laureate, Herbert Simon, predicted this occurrence years ago when he stated, "Improvement in post-secondary education will require converting teaching from a solo sport to a community based research activity" (Thille, 2012). Rather than viewing this shift as an encroachment on academic freedom, faculty should embrace this as their role and their purview—to design, along with experts in learning science and instructional design, the optimum pedagogy for their institution. Deep cultural change is not easy, and it may well take the move to a new online delivery model to help faculty understand the power and necessity of a common learning model.

Instructional Design

In most institutions, faculty who teach in the face-to-face classroom determine the "design" of a course and select the course materials. When this model is transferred to online education—allowing each section of a course to have varying learning outcomes, textbooks and materials, and a unique faculty-specific approach to teaching—total costs will increase rather than decrease for the institution. Learning outcomes will also vary widely across sections of a course. Therefore, it is important to create and follow a centralized model that can accommodate faculty variability without creating a unique course design for every faculty member.

For example, the personnel costs of having a textbook services team order six different textbooks for different sections of the same course, based on individual faculty preference, are much higher than the personnel costs of a common textbook chosen by the faculty as a team. Similarly, the cost of having sufficient instructional designers and technologists to provide customized support for each individual faculty member is simply prohibitive. A common design can increase quality while lowering costs.

Traditional models in which each faculty member's course is the "unit of production," guarantee that any growth in online education will increase, not decrease, costs, and at a rate far more costly than face-to-face instruction. If five faculty members each teach a slightly different face-to-face version of the same course, there will be fewer negative impacts on operational costs (negative impacts on student learning are another matter). Online, when course sections differ in learning outcomes, learning resources, and policies, the staff members who support and maintain these courses bear the extra work of uploading differing versions of a syllabus, ordering different textbooks for the same course, and responding to student questions about a variety of policies and practices. Although invisible to faculty members, this work comes at a real cost to the university.

To be fair, faculty take seriously their role as instructors in the discipline they love. But their lack of expertise in instructional design can be problematic in the online environment. Providing them with centralized course development resources is a cost-efficient way to maintain and even increase quality. Without prescribing the content, instructional designers can collaborate with departments to facilitate faculty teams who design the framework of a course. Then each faculty member who teaches a section adopts a certain number of agreed upon aspects such as learning objectives, textbooks, major assessments, or some other combination. Each faculty member can then add additional materials, learning activities, and assessments that fit her unique style. This hybrid model of a standard framework combined with individualized sections allows for quality, flexibility, and contained costs. It is the model we use at our university.

As we noted in the section on a common learning model, the faculty team approach to creating excellent courses and working together to improve learning outcomes over time yields a more engaging role for faculty. In our experience some of the most interesting breakthroughs in course designs came about when a faculty team worked together to design a new program or course. The solitary role of the faculty scholar is transitioning to a more engaged scholar who is also a cocreator of excellent learning designs.

Faculty Development

If you plan to grow your online programs, you will soon find that individual orientations for faculty will become time consuming and cost prohibitive. This one-to-one model was the only way to train faculty at the inception of online learning; indeed, there were no commonly agreed upon principles of effective online teaching in the early to mid-1990s when online education emerged.

This situation has greatly improved. In addition to university faculty development departments that have created online training experiences for faculty members, a number of associations and organizations have created training opportunities as well. The best of these create online classes for the faculty member to learn about online pedagogy while they experience model behaviors and learning activity designs within the course. At our university we have been developing faculty new to our online model in this way for 15 years (http://www.umuc.edu/facultydevelopment/).

Training, like education, is not a one-time event. Faculty who are trained to teach online will need continuing mentoring, feedback, and just-in-time assistance to help them grow as online instructors. A good faculty development program offers training as an ongoing process, using the optimum methods at the right times. For example, as an instructor teaches for the first time, a seasoned online instructor can be assigned to assist him to be successful throughout the semester. Scaling this approach is simple enough: a seasoned online instructor can be paid or given release time to mentor several faculty members new to online teaching. The more structured the role of the mentor, the easier it is to scale. At UMUC, faculty mentors work collaboratively with faculty new to UMUC online programs and help them achieve greater expertise in facilitating online learning. At the end of the course, both the mentor and mentee submit summary reports to the program chair to ensure that the mentoring relationship has achieved its goals.

Beyond the initial online course, online faculty, just like faculty in a face-to-face classroom, need feedback so that they can improve their teaching. Depending on your institution's model, there should be an agreed upon approach to faculty evaluation for online courses as there is in face-to-face courses. These can be peer evaluations, self-evaluations, program chair evaluations, or a combination of all three. Student evaluations of the course also provide important information about faculty behaviors in the online classroom.

Of particular importance is the "presence" of online faculty (Shea, Li, & Pickett, 2006). It is the norm for faculty in the face-to-face environment to show up regularly and hold class. If they fail to show up to class repeatedly, students will report this and an intervention will occur by an academic administrator. By contrast, in the online environment, where norms of presence and interaction are not as strongly held, faculty can be repeatedly missing for long periods before students report this fact to an administrator and an intervention occurs. Students are slower to sound the alarm in online classes due to a lack of understanding of the role of faculty, the inability to easily share concerns with other students in private ways, and the fear of being penalized by the instructor when she finally does return to the class. Thus, emphasizing the presence of faculty members in online courses and the types of instructor-led activities that lead to greater learning outcomes are important aspects of faculty expectations.

Student Support at Scale

Students in online programs have a plethora of needs outside the classroom. They need to apply, be admitted, enroll in courses, access financial aid, pay their tuition bill, learn how to use the online learning management system, and many other activities that are part of the university experience. With a small online enrollment, regular student service offices may be able to handle questions and transactions as part of the normal workload. But what happens when the number of online students begins to grow beyond what the current staff can handle? And what happens when online students expect an Amazon-like administrative experience with 24/7 access to answers and transactions?

As you scale online programs, you will reach a point that requires you to create a dedicated online student services unit. These "advisors" must be available for extended hours outside the normal workday (online students often do their work in the evenings) and students from international time zones may require a 24/7 staffing model with three shifts of advisors.

Because much of the information students require will be outside of traditional academic advising, these online student services personnel must be ready to serve students on a variety of topics via telephone, email, chat, or text. Essentially they must be a one-stop shop for students who wish to make one phone call to enroll for a course, pay their bill, apply for financial aid, and ask about an upcoming course deadline. Online students cannot be passed from one office to the next when the next office may be closed. It is also important to note that online students are often learning from a distance, and so they cannot be expected to navigate the myriad offices and functions that constitute a university. We must make the university transparent and simple to interact with.

To MOOC or Not to MOOC?

No discussion of scale in online education would be complete without a discussion of Massive Open Online Courses (MOOCs). Since 2012 we have seen the growth of Coursera, edX, and Udacity, all originally intended to offer large-enrollment online courses for free. MOOCs were open to literally any person from anywhere in the world who wanted to sign up. Elite institutions were the first to offer MOOCs, as a way to showcase their faculty and expertise. MOOCs are generally noncredit offerings, although the model is changing quickly and some credit-bearing MOOC options are now available.

As MOOC providers came to realize what "small, private, online course" or SPOC providers have known for 20 years, retention rates in online courses are not high unless there is a reason to complete, and then only when a student feels engaged with the instructor, peers, and content. So what began as an optimistic belief that MOOCs might just change the world and provide a world class education to the masses has transformed itself into more focused purposes: training and development and branding and marketing around the globe.

But don't count MOOCs out just yet. Platforms that offer MOOCs will become more flexible and fit the needs of not just massive courses, but also of smaller cohorts (SPOCs) within a MOOC; with these and other advances, we may see the resurgence of massive courses taught as hundreds or thousands of smaller sections for credit. Data collected about hundreds of thousands of students' behaviors will lead to rapid advances in predictive models that can help educators personalize learning pathways for individual students.

MOOCs represent an intriguing and still-evolving alternative to the current and "traditional" model of online education, which generally involves small class sizes (e.g., 16–35) in a Learning Management System classroom with a faculty member facilitating asynchronous discussions and grading student work. This model follows the "ideal" of the college classroom, but does not break out of the traditional boundaries of higher education. However, with the advent of MOOCs, learning science, and data analytics, scale may take on another form: we may be able to educate larger groups of students more effectively than is currently the case within a series of small online classrooms.

The wise online leader will keep an eye on MOOCs. They may not be commonly offered at your institution yet, but we suspect that they will become more common over time as the best MOOCs both in design and content are offered as hundreds of smaller sections, all facilitated by faculty or teaching assistants or mentors. The ability to scale using this model is something we believe will happen within the next few years.

A Primer on Change Management

Like all work being done at the frontier, applying economies of scale in a traditional university setting has both its rewards and its challenges. At this time in our history, when higher education is facing increasing pressures to contain the cost of education, an approach to growth that utilizes economies of scale will be welcome by most administrators. At the same time, creating a model for online programs that will scale in ways that keep quality high and costs low will create some challenges to the current culture of higher education. These challenges are not insurmountable. The wise online education leader will use the skills of change management and collaborative leadership to establish a model that can be good for all concerned.

Given that the topic of this chapter is about scaling online education and not a chapter on change management, we offer some resources here to help you create a strategic approach to change in your organization as it relates to online education. A thoughtful review of these works will provide ideas for a framework that you can apply in the work you are undertaking.

What You Can Do

Get Involved in the Field

Several organizations that focus on online education have sprung up over the past 20 years. The administrator new to his or her position should become connected with one or more of the following organizations:

National University Technology Network (NUTN)
http://nutn.org/
The Online Learning Consortium (OLC), formerly known as Sloan-C
http://onlinelearningconsortium.org/
Quality Matters
https://www.qualitymatters.org/
University Professional and Continuing Education Association (UPCEA)
http://www.upcea.edu/
United States Distance Learning Association (USDLA)
https://www.usdla.org/
WICHE Cooperative for Educational Technology (WCET)
http://wcet.wiche.edu/

An online administrator would do well to visit the website of each of these organizations to learn more about what each offers, attend a regional or national conference to assess their usefulness, and sign up for a few webinars to ascertain if they convey helpful information. One of the most important aspects of these organizations is the network of individuals who are usually very willing to share their expertise with a newcomer. Seek out opportunities to connect with those who have built a successful online unit to learn how they approached scaling their programs through these organizations.

Understand the Common Resistances to Change

We strongly believe that the changes to an institution that online learning will bring about follow some common patterns. The astute online leader will immerse himself in the literature on organizational change. In the end, moving to online models in our institutions elicits the same fears, concerns, and foot-dragging that any major change brings. These attitudes and behaviors are common and understandable; humans like their comfort zone and when asked to move outside it, they naturally balk. It's easy to blame those we are trying to change; but just remember than in many others situations you may be the recalcitrant one. Use your own sense of what behaviors and fears change elicits in you to understand and empathize with those new to online learning. If you understand what they are feeling and experiencing, and respond to it in your communications and actions, you will be more successful in engendering the change you hope to make.

Take a High Quality MOOC

You read that right. Sign up for a complete high quality MOOC. Be sure it focuses on content that you enjoy and want to learn more about. Find MOOCs that are well designed and produced. You will learn about and experience what a good online learning experience could be with another method of scaling.

It is somewhat difficult to locate well-designed MOOCs because there is no third party validator of MOOC quality—yet. A personal favorite of one of the authors is Introduction to Italian Opera from Dartmouth University offered through EdX. Videos are brief and engaging. The design of content and learning activities are well done. Learning activities and assessments are intriguing. See https://www.edx.org/course/introduction-italian-opera-dartmouthx-dart-mus-01x to investigate the course materials.

Another popular MOOC is entitled "Learning How to Learn" offered by faculty from the UC San Diego through Coursera. You can sign up for this course at https://www.coursera.org/learn/learning-how-to-learn#syllabus

Or find one of your own choosing from the links below:
https://www.coursera.org/
https://www.edx.org/
https://www.udacity.com/

Remember, we are not suggesting MOOCs as an example of how to scale online learning, but rather as one form of online learning that, as they emerge and transform, may hold promise as a centralized method to support scaled learning. But just as there are poor quality face-to-face courses, there are poor quality online courses and poor quality MOOCs. Be sure you pick one that follows good learning design.

Form an Internal Advisory Group to Help You Scale

You can't develop and build a scalable online unit alone. It is critical to collaborate with and draw on the wise counsel of influential individuals and opinion leaders. Each campus has a different set of these important peers. Ask everyone you know on campus who will be important to your unit's success. Over time you will hear a core set of names and positions that may include some or all of the following:

Faculty leaders
Deans
IT or academic technology leaders
The registrar
Center for teaching excellence leader
Instructional designers
Admissions and enrollment leaders
Advising lead
Financial aid
Student success support
Marketing and communications

Each of these functions may not directly and consistently need to be part of the decision-making and work of your unit, but keeping them apprised will make ongoing work relationships smoother. Consider creating an internal advisory board of the most important units and individuals to gain important insights and guidance, and to update on a regular basis.

Drawing from the list of individuals whose support you want and need from around the university form an internal advisory group. Meet with them four to six times a year to listen to their input and suggestions, to hear their concerns, and to brief them on your successes, challenges, and future plans. Talk to them about the need to scale your operations, and seek their support. The registrar, IT and admissions and enrollment services functions will especially understand your work and may be able to share valuable insights drawn from attempts to scale their own operations.

Conclusion

This chapter has been written with you, as an online leader, in mind. We presented a definition of scale, walked you through an assessment of your university's readiness to scale online learning, discussed the approach we use at our university, and described the institutional infrastructure necessary to support online learning at scale. We also discussed MOOCs as a future model of scaling in online learning—just not in the way they were offered at their beginning in 2012.

As academic administrators who lead online learning at scale, we believe strongly that with advances in learning science and educational technology, scale need not degrade quality. In fact, for the first time perhaps in our history, higher education can scale learning (online) while maintaining or even increasing learning quality. Unlike a face-to-face institution that equates scale to large lecture classrooms, online educators can create models that provide greater access and higher quality, while keeping costs low.

Admittedly, scaling online education at your institution is likely to be expensive, even if you make decisions to help keep costs low. You will need to work closely with your finance office to develop investment requests that show the ROI you will be providing the university. Some universities choose not to build online programs in-house; they seek out a commercial entity who will assist them to move online for a share of revenues. You will need to determine the best model for your university and, again, work closely with your finance office to determine the most affordable path forward.

The field of online education is advancing quickly. We would also encourage you to stay abreast of the advances in technology, learning science, and learning innovation that will soon create a breakthrough in personalized learning at scale. In the near future, online education will provide the underpinning for an advanced learning experience that allows each student to learn along a unique pathway, and this will occur for millions of students simultaneously. The faculty role will be that of a learning architect, creating the optimum combination of technology and human touch. And it will be scalable. You will want to be part of that exciting future.

For Further Information

Astin, A., & Astin, H.S. (2000). *Leadership reconsidered: Engaging higher education in social change.* W.W. Kellogg Foundation. Retrieved from http://eric.ed.gov/?id=ED444437

Fullan, M., & Scott, G. (2009). *Turnaround leadership for higher education.* San Francisco: Jossey-Bass.

Kotter, J. (2007). Leading change: Why transformation efforts fail. *Harvard Business Review*. Retrieved from https://hbr.org/2007/01/leading-change-why-transformation-efforts-fail

Lunenberg, F. (2010). Approaches to managing organizational change. *International Journal of Scholarly Academic Intellectual Diversity, 12*(1), 1–10. Retrieved from http://www.nationalforum.com/Electronic%20Journal%20Volumes/Lunenburg,%20Fred%20C%20Approaches%20to%20Managing%20Organizational%20Change%20IJSAID%20v12%20n1%202010.pdf

Acknowledgments The authors gratefully acknowledge M.J. Bishop, Ph.D., whose critical review of this chapter added immeasurably to its logic. The authors also thank Michelle Bennett for her patience and skill in formatting the chapter.

References

Ambrose, S. A., Bridges, M. W., DiPietro, M., Lovett, M. C., & Norman, M. K. (2010). *How learning works: Seven research-based principles for smart teaching.* San Francisco, CA: John Wiley & Sons.

Baumol, W. J. (2013). *The cost disease: Why computers get cheaper and health care doesn't.* New Haven: Yale University Press.

Brown, R. (2014, November). *College history garden.* Blog. Retrieved from http://collegehistorygarden.blogspot.com/2014/11/index-of-colleges-and-universities-that.html

Denneen, J., & Dretler, T. (2012, July). *The financially sustainable university.* The Bain Brief. Bain & Company. Retrieved from http://www.bain.com/publications/articles/financially-sustainable-university.aspx

Hampson, K. *Not quite right: Higher ed's business model & instructional technology.* Higher Education Management. Retrieved from https://higheredmanagement.net/2012/07/22/4338/

Immerwahr, J., Johnson, J., & Gasbarra, P. (2008, October). *The iron triangle: College presidents talk about costs, access, and quality.* The National Center for Public Policy and Higher Education & Public Agenda. Retrieved from http://www.highereducation.org/reports/iron_triangle/index.shtml

Mathews, J. (2015, October). Offering too many course choices can hurt community colleges and their students. *Washington Post.* Retrieved from https://www.washingtonpost.com/news/grade-point/wp/2015/10/01/offering-too-many-choices-can-hurt-community-colleges-and-their-students/

Paloff, R. M., & Pratt, K. (2013). *Lessons from the virtual classroom: The realities of online teaching.* San Francisco, CA: Jossey-Bass.

Saffron, J. (2014, September). *What's to be done about 'low-productivity' degree programs?* The John William Pope Center for Higher Education Policy. Retrieved from http://www.popecenter.org/commentaries/article.html?id=3073

Shea, P., Li, C. S., & Pickett, A. (2006). A study of teaching presence and student sense of learning community in fully online and web-enhanced college courses. *The Internet and Higher Education, 9*(3), 175–190.

Stavredes, T., & Herder, T. (2014). *A guide to online course design: Strategies for student success.* San Francisco, CA: Jossey-Bass.

Thille, C. (2012). *The Herb Simon connection.* Open learning initiative. Carnegie Mellon University. Retrieved from http://oli.cmu.edu/the-herb-simon-connection

Marketing Online Degrees to Adult Learners: Staff, Resources, and Key Strategies

Jessica DuPont, Stephanie Harff, Sanghoon Park, and Kathryn E. Linder

Abstract Marketing your e-learning program is a key component of its success. Although integrated marketing at most higher education institutions has become a strategic function, with staffing and resources generally housed in a centralized university marketing office, e-learning units may have different needs. In this chapter the authors discuss what you need to know and do to build a successful marketing team, how to collaborate with a centralized marketing unit, and how best to develop and assess successful marketing strategies. Practical strategies and examples are also offered for current marketing trends, defining your audience, and assessing the success of your marketing implementation. Lastly, the authors provide some concrete suggestions for creating marketing success with your e-learning unit.

Keywords Marketing • Staffing • Marketing plans • Assessment • Marketing trends

Decision-Making Guidance

This chapter will help you make decisions about:

- Defining marketing and its value in your e-learning unit
- Employing current trends with marketing online degree programs that integrate with more traditional marketing methods
- Key roles and resources critical to building a successful marketing team
- Defining your audience and using their communication preferences throughout the inquiry-to-enrollment funnel
- Tools and tactics commonly used in marketing planning and implementation
- Evaluating the success of marketing efforts

J. DuPont • K.E. Linder (✉)
Oregon State University, 4722 The Valley Library, Corvallis, OR 97331, USA
e-mail: jessica.dupont@oregonstate.edu; kathryn.linder@oregonstate.edu

S. Harff • S. Park
University of South Florida, 11739 Carrollwood Cove Drive, Tampa, FL 33624, USA
e-mail: sharff@usf.edu; park2@usf.edu

© Association for Educational Communications and Technology 2018
A.A. Piña et al. (eds.), *Leading and Managing e-Learning*, Educational Communications and Technology: Issues and Innovations,
https://doi.org/10.1007/978-3-319-61780-0_22

What You Need to Know

Marketing your e-learning programs will be a key component of their success. Although integrated marketing at most higher education institutions has become a strategic function, with staffing and resources generally housed in a centralized university marketing office, e-learning units may have different needs. Centralized marketing offices may be more used to working with on-campus students rather than with e-learners. It may become necessary to build a separate marketing team for your e-learning organization.

In this chapter we discuss what you need to know and do to build a successful marketing team, how to collaborate with a centralized marketing unit, and how best to develop and assess successful marketing strategies. We also offer practical strategies and examples of current marketing trends, defining your audience, and assessing the success of your marketing implementation. These topics are explored with the assumption that the reader is unfamiliar with strategic marketing planning and implementation in higher education. As you read through this chapter, keep in mind that marketing decisions and priorities for your e-learning unit will be dependent on your institution type, size, and mission.

Defining Marketing and Its Value in Your e-Learning Unit

Whether you are a brand new e-learning program, a veteran provider of distance education or somewhere in the middle, marketing plays a strategic role in your overall operations. As the online education marketplace has become increasingly mature and competitive, it is even more critical today to step back and understand how marketing adds value to your unit.

Most universities house a centralized marketing and communications unit that defines the brand of the institution. This is also where visual and brand identity guidelines are developed to ensure consistency and strength in marketing and communications. These include outlining specific fonts, a color palette, university logos, print and web templates, and core messages. This centralized unit works closely with others on campus, including college and unit marketing directors, and staff in admissions, alumni and other outreach departments. Often, these centralized units are set up like ad agencies in the private sector, providing creative and consulting services at a fee and in a queue format. They employ their own staff, including marketing managers and assistants, designers, writers, videographers, web developers, and often a media buyer.

Centralized marketing is a vital link for you, no matter how you structure marketing in your unit. Newer and smaller units will also appreciate that centralized marketing provides many templates for publications and digital assets, like photography and web templates. However, since centralized marketing tends to focus on campus initiatives and the traditional 18–24-year-old on-campus learner, hiring your own marketing staff will help to ensure that your e-learning needs will be met. In continuing and online education units nationwide, it is a recognized trend to have an in-house marketing team. At a minimum, you will want to consider hiring a marketing director or manager.

Within higher education, those with a limited understanding of marketing will often confuse its scope with advertising and sales or, worse yet, making something "look pretty." In a nutshell, the marketing function is a bridge connecting consumer needs with the programs and services you offer. Without this bridge, you have limited access to connect right-fit learners with the programs you develop and deliver.

Any definition of marketing for e-learning should start with market research. Market research will help you understand the needs of your consumers, or prospective students. Faculty might tell you they are sure there is a huge demand for an online degree in religious studies, rangeland resources, or Romanian. Without first conducting market research, though, you risk making costly mistakes and offering programs with low to no enrollment.

After market research, the functions of marketing planning and implementation begin. A marketing plan should always follow your strategic plan and business goals— whether it is for a specific degree program, an internal marketing plan to raise your visibility on campus, or a broad marketing plan for all of your offerings. Without clear organizational goals, marketing will lack direction and impact. In order to recruit students into your programs, building your brand awareness in the marketplace is another key function of marketing. Do consumers know that your institution offers online programs? How do they rank your programs compared to competitors? More often than not, they will affiliate your school's brand with your brick-and-mortar institution, which has been around for decades—maybe even centuries. There are a variety of integrated ways to build your brand, but usually purchased media gets the most attention. The marketing cycle should always include an evaluation of your efforts to know what has worked (and not worked), and the return on investment (ROI).

Additionally, inquiry or enrollment management is directly impacted by the marketing function, and should be woven into your marketing planning instead of being treated like an afterthought. Who will handle inquiries from prospective students when they do find you and want more information? How you manage prospective student leads is very much linked to your overall marketing efforts. In the end, marketing is like a well-constructed, energy-efficient home that takes into account all of the functions mentioned in this section. On the outside, it should not only look appealing and inviting, but its layout should also be built in a logical and integrated way, with each room designed to meet the specific needs of the homeowner.

Current Trends in Marketing

In the past, marketers used mass media such as outdoor billboards, newspaper ads, radio spots, TV commercials, and other traditional platforms to "spread the word" about products and services. The goal was to reach as many potential customers as possible, regardless of whether or not those customers were "in the market" for a particular offering. This approach was challenging because it often required a large budget, and success was difficult to track, as there was no way to ensure that the right prospects were seeing ads.

Over the past 15 years, however, technology has changed the landscape of marketing dramatically. It is now possible to target specific populations and to gather real-time, actionable data that allows marketers to make important decisions about how to allocate funds and which tactics are working most effectively. Digital marketing, or "the practice of promoting products and services using digital distribution channels to reach consumers in a timely, relevant, personal and cost-effective manner" (Reitzin, 2007), has become a central component of the e-learning marketing toolkit. There are many different tactics and tools that make up the digital marketing landscape. In this section, we explore some of the most popular.

Search Engine Marketing (SEM)

The purpose of search engine marketing is to promote online content through paid digital advertising. Marketers purchase ads designed to reach specific populations on popular digital platforms such as Google, Bing, Yahoo, Facebook, Twitter, and LinkedIn. The ad's reach is very targeted to a particular audience—i.e., women between the ages of 30 and 45 years old who are interested in pursuing an online MBA—and the content of the ad is tailored accordingly. When individuals who are in the market for a specific product or service search for information, the goal is to have your ad display at the top of the search engine results page (SERP) so that prospective customers find you. When prospects click on your ad, they are able to learn more about your offer and, hopefully, they will find your content to be helpful and compelling enough that they are willing to request more information from you.

Search Engine Optimization (SEO)

SEO "is an internet marketing technique that tailors a website—through the inclusion of keywords and indexing terms and the manipulation of HTML or other coding—to position it to receive a high, organic (unpaid) ranking within search engines such as Google or Bing" (Dewey, 2015). As with SEM, SEO is designed to ensure that your information displays at the top of a search engine results page (SERP). The primary difference between SEO and SEM is that with SEM you are paying for placement.

Content Marketing

Part of a successful SEO strategy is to develop useful content for prospective customers that goes beyond a sales pitch. Customers are more likely to find and consume your content if it helps them solve their problems. For example, if an individual is considering going back to school to earn a master's degree, they probably have a lot of questions about cost, the time commitment involved, how to select the program that is right for them, and more. Providing handy reference guides, resource manuals, checklists, and other helpful tools makes it easier for people to make tough choices, and aids them in taking action. When marketers develop these helpful resources and make them available on digital platforms such as social media sites, blogs, websites, and landing pages, customers feel like you have their best interests at heart and are trying to help them, which builds good will.

Social Media Marketing

Social media allows people to build social communities and actively participate in creating, publishing, and sharing content and ideas. Individuals can ask others for recommendations, share information about their experiences, and rate products and services. With this profound change in the role of customers, marketing strategies need to involve listening, engaging, understanding, and responding directly through conversation that not only satisfies customers but also encourages them to share their experiences with others (Evans & McKee, 2010).

There are also tools that make it easier for marketers to produce and publish digital content and to interact with customers including content management systems, marketing automation tools, and customer relationship management systems.

Content Management System

A content management system (CMS) is a tool that empowers marketers without advanced technical skills to build and manage a website. Web content stored in a CMS can be easily updated and maintained.

Marketing Automation Tool

A marketing automation tool allows marketers to build critical digital assets. Marketers use these tools to build landing pages with lead generation forms, empowering you to build a database of individuals who are interested in your programs. Prospective customers who request more information receive confirmation pages and emails that allow them to take advantage of a promised offer (i.e., "Download our free brochure to learn more about X program"), and are entered into a series of lead nurturing emails with each email focusing on a different program selling point.

All of these resources can be created in the marketing automation tool, and many also serve as a blogging platform, a social media management tool and more.

Customer Relationship Management Tool

Once you generate leads, it is important to track your interactions. A customer relationship management tool (CRM) serves as a system of record for all your customer interactions. In higher education, recruiters use a CRM to keep track of prospective students. They log interactions by email, phone, etc., and track the prospective student's status in the enrollment pipeline. It is critical to integrate your marketing automation tool and your CRM, so that data is consistent between the two systems.

Building a Successful Marketing Team: Key Roles and Resources

If no one is currently dedicated to overseeing the marketing function in your unit, your first hire should be a *marketing director* or *marketing manager*—someone who will not only be a strategic thinker and part of your leadership team, but also capable of managing hands-on tactics, resources, and staff. Modern marketers working in higher education consider themselves successful if they are able to meet enrollment targets while keeping their cost per acquisition low. They do this by building campaigns that focus on generating leads.

In order to generate leads, marketers must be familiar with the latest marketing tactics and technology, including marketing automation tools like HubSpot and customer relationship management tools like Salesforce. In order to implement these tools, and use them to their fullest, a specific set of skills is required. Whether you choose to build an internal team, outsource, or do a combination of both, the following functions will be critical to your success.

First you will need a *back-end developer* to build and manage your technology infrastructure. This person can help you select, implement, configure, test, launch, and manage the right technology tools. This person can also help integrate your selected tools so that your new technology can "talk to" your university's current enterprise tools. For example, if you implement a marketing automation tool, you will want it to share data with your university's customer relationship management (CRM) tool so that you can track leads through their entire lifecycle, from prospect, to applied, to admitted, to enrolled, and beyond.

Once your technology is in place, you will need a *front-end developer* to create marketing templates and to build digital assets. In smaller units, this person may also do back-end development, and is often called a *web developer* or *web designer.* This person can build templates for landing pages, inquiry forms, confirmation pages, confirmation emails, lead nurturing emails, and more. This person can also build the workflow behind your assets—in other words, they can program your marketing automation tool to send lead nurturing emails to your leads at various intervals or based on actions your lead completes. This technology becomes the home for compelling content designed to appeal to your target audience. Content includes written text, graphic elements, and sourced imagery.

Ideally, you would have a graphic designer and a writer on staff. Your *graphic designer* should have experience designing for both digital and traditional platforms and would be responsible for developing an appropriate look and feel for the academic program that is designed to resonate with your program's target audience. They would source imagery and design graphic elements and would collaborate with the front-end developer to build templates in your marketing automation tool.

Similarly, your *writer* should understand how to develop content for a variety of digital and traditional platforms including landing pages, ad copy, news releases, and email communication follow-up with inquiries. This person should be an expert in platform specifications and best practices and would be able to craft content designed to intrigue and influence your program's intended audience. Although a dedicated *videographer* is likely a luxury on most teams, producing high-quality video is an essential component to storytelling and content exchange in this digital age.

Of course, in order for your graphic designer and your writer to be successful, they need to know what they are selling. This is where revisiting the market research you originally conducted prior to developing a new program comes into play. Your *market researcher* or *market analyst* should document programmatic details and then perform a competitive analysis designed to see how the proposed academic program measures up against the competition. Analysis may include curriculum comparisons, cost comparisons, job market growth expectations, and more.

So now you have everyone you need to build a suite of assets in your marketing automation tool. But how do you drive prospects to your landing page? Because SEO and SEM work together, it is helpful to have someone responsible for managing your search engine optimization. On larger teams, this may be a dedicated *organic performance manager* (also known as a SEO strategy manager) to develop an organic strategy designed to promote your academic programs through owned and earned media. On smaller teams, it is often the web developer who assumes this duty. This person would be responsible for managing your websites, social media sites, blogs, and other owned platforms, as well as pushing out content to various earned platforms, such as news outlets, third-party websites, and others.

To boost you SEO efforts, this is where a *media buyer* comes in. Your media buyer is the person who creates your overall media strategy, which will include search engine marketing (SEM), and who will be responsible for purchasing paid advertising that drives customers to your landing page, allowing you to generate leads for your academic programs. Modern media buyers have expertise in purchasing advertising on digital platforms, including search engines (Google, Bing, Yahoo, etc.); social media platforms (Facebook, Twitter, LinkedIn, etc.); third-party websites that are designed to attract the prospects you are trying to reach; and other digital platforms, such as Pandora radio, etc. Media buyers may also recommend other mass-media tactics to raise your brand awareness, e.g., outdoor, radio, and airport.

To ensure that all of these professionals are working cohesively, it is helpful to have a *production manager* who manages your production schedule and assigns tasks to all team members. This person is responsible for keeping everyone on task, and ensuring that campaigns are produced as efficiently as possible. In larger units, the production manager may also be called a *marketing manager* or *assistant director of marketing*. In smaller units, this responsibility may be assumed by the director, or a marketing assistant—either way, this position should be someone with strong project management skills.

Once your campaigns are produced, and you are successfully generating leads, it is critical that you have a professional sales person—a *recruiter*—to manage the leads. This person, also commonly called an *enrollment counselor* or *admissions advisor*, proactively communicates with the leads you have generated through the marketing effort, answering questions and helping prospective students determine whether or not the prospective student and the academic program are a good fit. Without professional recruiters converting leads to enrolled students your marketing efforts will ultimately fail.

Additionally, it is critical to have a *marketing data analyst* who is charged with aggregating, analyzing, and reporting data, with an end goal of empowering your team to optimize your campaigns for performance, and reporting out to academic program owners and senior executives. An *analyst* working for the entire e-learning unit may assume this function, especially on smaller teams.

Keep in mind that depending on size of operation and scope of work, you may need more than one person in some of these roles; or for smaller units, multiple functions are often assumed by one person.

Defining Your Audience

Strategic and successful marketing hinges on clearly knowing your audience. Who are you trying to reach? Which of your programs will meet their specific needs? What are their preferred communication preferences so you can engage with them effectively? Additionally, for e-learning units, understanding the post-traditional *adult learner* is critical. It is no surprise that adult learners comprise a key segment in the online education market. When juggling career, family, and other personal commitments, online and blended learning meets their needs.

Understanding why adult learners go back to school is an essential part of your marketing strategy. Why are they specifically motivated to continue their education? In surveying your students, you will likely find that these results do not vary significantly from national data representing a broad range of institutions offering e-learning programs. Many prospective students cite career advancement as a primary motivation for continuing their education. Changing careers may also be a motivator. Demographics of your prospective students can vary from national data.

Fig. 1 The enrollment funnel

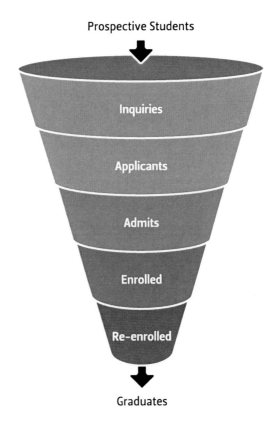

Consider surveying them to further segment your target audience and create content that resonates closely with their motivation.

Additionally, how you engage and communicate with your target audience will vary depending on where they are within the enrollment funnel. The enrollment funnel (see Fig. 1) is a common term in higher education marketing and recruitment that delineates the specific stages in which your target audience moves through the pipeline, from inquiry to the point of admissions and enrolled student status.

Top-of-the-funnel marketing tactics center on building awareness for your brand and positioning your strengths amidst the competition. Seasoned e-marketers can affirm that students will not come to you unless they first know you are there. In a nutshell, you need to be in their consideration set when they are at that discovery point of realizing they need to go back to school.

In our experience, at the pre-inquiry and inquiry stages, the number one preferred adult learner communication preference is an online search engine. Students are shopping online, comparing school websites to explore what's out there and to narrow down their choices. Ultimately, you want them to inquire with you if you have the program they want. This typically happens when they submit an inquiry form on your website capturing their contact information into your CRM. Contrary to popular belief, email and direct mail are not dead. On the flip side, we have found

Table 1 Sample CRM communication plan: undergraduate online degree-seeking inquiries

Day	Communication type	Content
0	Email	Thank you email with specific program info
0	Mailing	Welcome letter and program flier
1	Email	Tuition
2	Phone	Initial phone call[a]
2	Email	Admissions overview
3	Email	Online course demo
7	Email	Jobs and career counseling
10	Email	University prestige and accreditation

[a]To target audiences within inquiry pool, subsequent calls after this

that prospective students do not want to be contacted via text messages and social media. Phone calls lie somewhere in the middle.

As the funnel narrows, your marketing and communication efforts can and should become more personalized. Adult learners are generally shopping between a few schools. As savvy consumers, they will remember how you follow up with them and provide timely resources compared with other institutions they are shopping. In other words, your service matters greatly. This includes returning calls and emails promptly; checking in after time has passed to see what else you can do to help; inviting them to information sessions or webinars; and making sure that institutional roadblocks along the way do not prevent them from ultimately enrolling. In short, marketing's work does not end at the point when a lead or inquiry is generated. Table 1 shows a sample communication plan that continues to reach out to prospective students after their initial inquiry. Until inquiries move to admit, they will continue to receive regular campaign-style communications (e.g., invites to webinars, e-newsletters, postcard apply-now reminders).

Evaluating the Success of Marketing Efforts

As noted earlier, data is a critical component of the modern marketing effort. Marketers continuously collect, aggregate, analyze, and report on key data points, and then use that data to optimize marketing campaign efforts.

Your marketing team, and specifically your marketing data analyst if you have one, should be focused on measuring the effectiveness of every campaign tactic. They should continuously monitor real-time data, with a focus on identifying data trends that allow them to make critical recommendations on how to improve the performance of the campaign. There is an infinite amount of data that you can collect using modern tools and tactics, but the most critical ones to track during a student recruitment campaign include:

- *Landing page views*: The number of prospective students who visit your landing page, and the source of each visitor. The source of the visitor is critical as you need to know which tactics are working and eliminate those that are not producing the desired results.

- *Leads generated*: The number of leads, or inquiries, generated by your landing page and the source of each lead. Again, knowing which paid ads, blog posts, social media posts, etc. are effectively generating leads is critical.
- *Applicants*: The number of prospective students who submit a completed application to the program and the source of the applicant.
- *Admits*: The number of prospective students who are admitted to the program and the source of the admit.
- *Enrolled*: The number of admits who ultimately select your institution, pay any advanced deposit fees, and go on to enroll in their first class.

By tracking these and other data points, and carefully examining your results on a daily basis, you can begin to see which keywords, digital ads, social media posts, blog posts, landing pages, and lead nurturing emails generated the best results, and you can eliminate those tactics that do not work. This is critical, as you cannot afford to waste your team's time or marketing dollars on tactics that don't work.

Ideally, you will not only use this data for campaign optimization, you will also use it to develop weekly or biweekly campaign health reports that you can share with the colleges whose programs you are serving. Additionally, by the end of the campaign, you should be able to provide a detailed campaign recap that provides information about campaign performance and shows a complete sales funnel.

Your sales funnel should include the total dollars invested at the top, and should then highlight the number of landing page views, leads generated, applications and admits for the program, with a conversion rate between each funnel stage. At the bottom of your funnel, you should include the cost per acquisition, or CPA, which demonstrates how much it cost to recruit each student.

What You Can Do

Based on the information we have provided above, here are some concrete ways that you can set yourself up for marketing success with your e-learning unit:

Invite marketing to the table. Whatever internal leadership team you create, your marketing director should be part of this team and included in your strategic decision-making. Marketing works best when brought in early and not after a decision has been made. Your marketing director can help you strategize current and future direction of your e-learning unit.

Don't forget market research. One of the most important components of marketing, market research, is overseen by your marketing unit and will help you develop programs that will meet consumer *needs* versus faculty preferences. Research data you should seek includes consumer demand studies, industry trends, and competitive analyses. Partnering with an external market research firm focused on higher education is something you should strongly consider. Eduventures based in Boston and the Education Advisory Board (EAB) in Washington, DC, are two examples of firms focused on online higher education.

Get to know your centralized marketing unit. Whether you set up your own marketing team, or become a client of centralized marketing, it is important to connect with the centralized marketing office. In doing so, you will understand the current brand of the institution, the services and resources they provide, and also keep them in the loop regarding your initiatives and priorities so that they can help reinforce what it is you do.

Avoid reinventing the wheel, or going rogue. Tap into existing templates generally provided by your centralized marketing office (e.g., web banners, fliers) instead of creating your own, especially if you are short staffed in design resources. Get to know the brand of your institution and be a model brand ambassador. This means following brand identity guidelines and presenting a consistent image of your institution.

Document your business requirements. Specifically, what are you trying to do? If your goal is to increase enrollment in a particular program, you likely want to start by generating program leads, in which case, you will want to implement a marketing automation tool that allows you to build landing pages with lead generation forms and lead nurturing campaigns designed to help prospective students make choices.

Work with campus IT to document technical requirements. This is the only way to ensure that the technology you choose will be supported by IT, that the data you store in the system will be secure, and that your tools can "talk to" the other systems on your campus.

Get training when needed. Don't be afraid to ask for help or training for you and your team so that you can successfully implement and use the systems you choose.

Assess your own skill set. Be brutally honest here. What are your skills? Are you an excellent writer? Do you have a solid graphic design background? Have you spent years developing websites, or building social media communities? If so, you will most likely need to keep doing those things yourself, and invest in hiring someone whose skill set complements your own. For example, if you've never purchased advertising, you will probably want to hire a skilled media buyer, and if you've never written a word of advertising copy, you should consider hiring a content developer.

Consider your resources. Can you hire right now? Great! But what if you can't bring on another team member at this time? This is where freelancers come in. Think about what you need—a content developer, a graphic designer, a media buyer—and look for a qualified professional who can help you for an hourly rate.

Don't implement every tactic at once. You cannot simultaneously implement every tactic discussed in this chapter. Pick the ones that are likely to deliver the biggest impact the most quickly, and start there. You can always add other tactics later when you have more resources available to hire a bigger team. If you are a team of one, and you can only implement one strategy right now, start by making sure your websites are user friendly and feature accurate, up-to-date content about the program you are trying to promote. Then focus on building landing pages that allow you to generate leads for that program. Post links to those landing pages on university-owned digital media that targets the audience you are trying to reach, such as websites, social media sites, and student portals. Then follow up with those leads! Put them in a pipeline to receive your lead nurturing emails and follow up with them by phone.

Survey your prospective students and/or current students to better understand their motivations for continuing their education. Does this mirror national data for how the adult learner market is segmented? Know which of your programs appeal to career switchers, advancers, stop-outs, and/or lifelong learners.

Create content on your website and in your communications that addresses how your program will help to meet your inquiring students' needs. If they are career switchers, information and resources surrounding industry trends will be helpful. If they are stop-outs looking to start up again, be sure to include self-serve tools to give them an idea of what will transfer in prior to admissions.

Track conversion ratios for points along the enrollment funnel, e.g., the number of inquires who go on to apply, or admit-to-enroll ratio. This is one way of measuring your marketing impact along the way, and you certainly don't want to see these numbers go down over time.

*Mystery shop your own institution...*and some of your competitors. If you don't have time to do this, ask your marketing director or staff to routinely do this. What do you like or dislike about how competitors followed up? Track your impressions and share with your staff.

Support your marketing director and his/her staff in seeking professional development to stay on top of ever-changing marketing tools and tactics. The marketing landscape today has changed dramatically compared to 10 years ago. See "For more information" for examples.

Invest heavily in your website and the people who program and maintain it so that organic search engine optimization (SEO) tactics work well. Hire talented web programmers and writers who can make this happen. Searching online for your program is the number one way prospective adult learners find out about you. Let their first impression be a good one.

Be present on your university's homepage. Work hard to get a direct and visible link to your online programs. Your number one online referral source outside of SEO/SEM will stem from your institution's homepage.

Consider running a stop-out campaign targeting students who once attended your institution on-campus, but didn't complete their degree. If your online program is just starting or quickly adding new majors they likely don't know this is an option.

Develop a formula that demonstrates ROI for your marketing efforts. For example, if you know that you recruited 40 students for Program X, with a CPA of $500 per student, and that each student takes 6 credit hours per semester on average, at a tuition rate of Y, then you can calculate how much revenue the university is expected to receive in tuition dollars from this new cohort of students. This allows you to demonstrate an estimated ROI for your efforts.

Conclusion

Throughout this chapter, we have provided information to demonstrate how marketing is a key component of the success of an e-learning unit. Because e-learning units may have different needs than traditional on-campus courses, programs, and degrees it is important for e-learning leaders to be aware of how to build a successful marketing plan and a team that can implement the strategies of that plan. After reading this chapter we hope that you have a better sense of what you need to know and do to develop successful marketing strategies, learn about current marketing trends, and evaluate the success of your marketing implementation. Below, we offer some additional resources that may also be helpful to you as you begin your marketing planning.

For More Information

The University Professional and Continuing Education Association (UPCEA) has a specific member network devoted to Marketing, Enrollment and Student Services (MESS). Each year, UPCEA hosts an annual Marketing and Enrollment Management seminar for professionals in the field. There are also many opportunities for your marketing staff to get involved and network with their counterparts at other institutions. Lastly, through their research arm, UPCEA provides benchmarking data and marketing survey. Support your marketing team to get involved with UPCEA/MESS volunteer opportunities.

The American Marketing Association (AMA) is another professional organization for marketers in all professions. The AMA offers a variety of opportunities for professional development in both online and site-based formats.

Current research, studies, and publications from market research vendors focused on higher education and online learning can also be helpful to those just starting out in e-learning administration as well as those who are more seasoned in the field. Eduventures based in Boston and the Education Advisory Board (EAB) in DC are two potential sources for these resources.

References

Dewey, J. P. (2015, January). *Search engine optimization.* Salem Press Encyclopedia. Pasadena, California.

Evans, D., & McKee, J. (2010). *Social media marketing: The next generation of business engagement.* Indianapolis, IN: Wiley.

Reitzin, J. (2007). *What is digital marketing?* Retrieved from http://mobilestorm.com/mobile-marketing/what-is-digital-marketing/

Student Support and Retention Services: A Primer for Next Generation e-Learning Leaders

Alfonso Bradoch, Kyle Whitehouse, and Kathryn E. Linder

Abstract e-Learner support and retention can often be an afterthought when designing e-learning experiences. In this chapter, the authors discuss the main differences between e-learners and traditional on-campus students and share methods for thinking intentionally about the support services for e-learners. The authors outline the accreditation and policy guidelines that shape learner success initiatives at institutions of higher education and offer a comprehensive overview of the kinds of services and systems recommended by accrediting bodies as well as the student support components that are typically offered in e-learning units. Because an important component of providing student success services is networking and collaborating with academic departments and other institutional partners, the authors describe some of the more typical partnerships between e-learning units and various campus stakeholders in the provision of student success services and programs. The chapter concludes with a brief discussion of the growing trends of predictive modeling and real-time data analytics and concrete strategies that e-learning leaders can use in the development of strong student success models.

Keywords Online education • Student success • Adult learner • e-Learner • Program design • Accreditation • Regulations • Analytics

Decision-Making Guidance

This chapter will help you make decisions about:

- The kinds of e-learner support and retention services that you will want to implement

A. Bradoch • K. Whitehouse • K.E. Linder (✉)
Oregon State University, 4722 The Valley Library, Corvallis, OR 97331, USA
e-mail: alfonso.bradoch@oregonstate.edu; kyle.whitehouse@oregonstate.edu;
kathryn.linder@oregonstate.edu

© Association for Educational Communications and Technology 2018
A.A. Piña et al. (eds.), *Leading and Managing e-Learning*, Educational
Communications and Technology: Issues and Innovations,
https://doi.org/10.1007/978-3-319-61780-0_23

- How to collaborate with institutional partners to achieve your vision of e-learner success

What You Need to Know

e-Learner support and retention can often be an afterthought when designing e-learning experiences. Institutions may not consider the different needs of an e-learner versus a traditional on-campus student. Adapting current models, services, and systems already being used on a traditional campus is a significant component of building a successful e-learning program. A complicating factor is that e-learners are often blended with on-campus students who may be participating in online courses and programs, which can make providing support services more challenging.

This chapter will start with a discussion of the main differences between e-learners and traditional on-campus students. Given these differences, thinking intentionally about the support services for e-learners, and the logistical differences of providing those services to a population of students learning across time zones, is a foundational component to e-learner success. This chapter offers a comprehensive overview of the kinds of services and systems recommended by accrediting bodies, as well as the student support components that are typically offered in e-learning units.

An important component of providing student success services is networking and collaborating with academic departments and other institutional partners. In this chapter we offer examples of the key partnerships that can help create networked student services across an institution.

We conclude the chapter with a brief discussion of the growing trends of predictive modeling and real-time data analytics.

Who Are Your Online Learners?

Although students taking classes online and on campus share many common traits and life experiences, there are a few characteristics that uniquely shape the readiness of online learners for academic success. While there are many other characteristics that are worth considering, especially those that may distinguish your programs and audiences from other institutions, these foundational components will help shape the decisions you need to make about your own e-learning program design.

Adult Learners

The online student population often includes adults who have intentionally decided to pursue their education online. Online formats are an appealing option because adult learners tend to be place-bound by professional or family commitments.

Social and cognitive differences in self-efficacy, self-regulation, and motivation develop with maturity and can positively impact learning experiences, whether online or in person. This list of factors should be considered central to the adult learner's experience.

- *High motivation.* Adult learners have made the decision to return to school with much thought and often with the input of other people and situations that may be affected by their choice. Seeking education while working or raising a family is most often voluntary, so developing skills, increasing knowledge, and achieving goals is largely a personal choice driven by internal motivators.
- *Previous experience.* The history adult students bring to online learning is most certainly a mix of challenges and successes they have faced in other settings. These experiences have resulted in a set of personal skills, knowledge, and values. While some learners feel very comfortable translating these strengths into new academic territory, other adult learners need support recognizing the transferability of their experiences.
- *Previous credit.* Adult learners may have quite a history of previous education attempts, associate degrees in progress or earned, or may be actively taking classes at another institution that they will use to apply to your academic programs. Changing institutions comes with a considerable cost to the learner in time, commitment, and money. It is probable that the decision to return to school at your institution hinges on the ease of transferring previous credit, the requirements for being accepted into and completing a program, and the cost (time, money, energy) of doing so.
- *Time away from school.* Online learners have very often been away from the education system for some time, whether because of military, job, or family responsibilities. They may return to school feeling uncertain or lacking confidence about whether they are fully prepared. Think about all of the acronyms and myriad campus roles and resources at your institution. Systems and procedures may present like a foreign culture that will need to be figured out at the same time students are trying to master course requirements, deadlines, and faculty expectations.

Distance Learners

Surveys of online learners consistently reveal that students want to feel connected to their institutions and develop a sense of belonging to their program, despite the physical distance that may separate them from campus.

"Connection," though, often means something different than synchronous activities or campus events that draw e-learners together. Connection can be as simple as having a clearly designated, primary contact who is easily available to the student for answers to questions and assistance working through university processes. Ideally, however, the connection online students seek is a bit deeper and is created via multiple avenues and layers of support easily accessible when the student is looking for connection. One component of this is ensuring similar access to the services that on-campus students are using. Common barriers to access include technology (hardware and software), time zone differences between student and office hours, universal design issues that hinder disability access or user experience, student-fee funded services that historically serve on-campus students only, and other factors.

Busy Learners

While pursuing education may be a top priority for the e-learner, most often adding the role of student is a second or third or fourth "job" for otherwise busy people. e-Learners are juggling responsibilities to family, friends, workplace, and community. Time for learning can get crunched between other commitments and, because of the distance format, the time students have set aside for study can easily get pushed aside.

Online programs are attractive for their flexibility and selected precisely because of other life demands. Under stress, some busy learners default to practical and results-oriented habits and miss out on deeper learning or optional opportunities to engage meaningfully. They may whittle their involvement to meet minimal requirements at times or become frustrated as they fall further and further behind. The irony is that busy students are less likely to reach out for help when they are most likely to need it.

On the other hand, feeling the pressure of competing responsibilities can have the opposite effect altogether. Successful e-learners figure out—either on their own or with support—how to prioritize, intentionally schedule and protect their time allotted for academics, say "no" gracefully, and be proactive in communicating with their instructors and advisors. Helping online learners *learn how to learn online* helps students succeed.

An additional aspect of the busy learner is career ambition. Many online learners are pursuing schooling to advance, change, or achieve a career goal. When designing an online learning program, providing career development support and meaningful professional opportunities are important components to consider.

Support Resources for Online Learners

The types of services and the means for delivering them to students in your online courses and programs will partly depend upon your intended audience:

- "Traditional" distance students with the intent of expanding the institution's geographical reach and enrollments
- Campus-based student in need of more flexibly scheduled course offerings
- New audiences, such as life-long learners, professionals, and individuals abroad

Most institutions prefer a uniform pathway for admission and registration into online programs and courses, but these traditional pathways are often not designed to handle multiple modalities for program delivery. Admission applications, whether paper or electronic, must be adapted to allow for students to indicate their distance status and their preference for an online version of available majors. Registration systems may also need to be adapted to differentiate between on-site and online offerings.

To be successful, online learners require access to the variety of support services similar to those available to the campus-based student, such as academic advising, success counseling, and tutoring. Given the potential mix of traditional and nontraditional students in online programs, the challenge for the institution is to determine effective delivery methods, synchronous and asynchronous, that will accommodate students located across multiple time zones.

Course Materials

Unlike campus-based students who can go your institution's bookstore for textbooks and course materials on the first day of classes, online distance students must plan ahead and order their course materials in advance to ensure they have them for the first day of classes. This means that online instructors must be sure to have their orders for course materials posted well in advance of the start of the term so that distance students are not at a disadvantage.

Academic Advising

Online degree-seeking students can be at a disadvantage for advising, given that they may not be sufficiently close to campus to attend an in-office advising meeting. Advisors of online students, well meaning as they are, will often prioritize those advisees who are physically present over those at a distance. Due to differences in time zones and the student's availability due to work and other life commitments, it can take a greater amount of time to achieve an equivalent level of advising for the online student as it would for the campus-based student.

Academic Counseling, Tutoring, and Remediation

As with campus-based populations, online students will often need support in nonacademic areas to help ensure their success. Most campuses have academic success centers, remedial courses in mathematics and writing, and centers for specialized tutoring. Equivalent services are often difficult for campuses to provide to the online student, given staffing and the established office hours for those services.

Test Proctoring

In response to Federal guidelines for student authentication related to Title IV eligibility, online programs should consider test proctoring as a means to ensure the academic integrity of the course and to address the U.S. Department of Education's regulatory imperative for fraud prevention. In implementing test-proctoring programs for online courses, institutions will need to form guidelines for acceptable proctors, appropriate testing environment, and protocols. If your institution chooses to create its own testing center, you will need to consider staffing to administer the proctoring programs and supervise test proctors as well as test monitoring technologies. There are also third party providers of online test proctoring, using a variety of technologies to verify student identity, record the proctoring session, and report irregularities. These can be a good alternative for institutions with limited resources and students in need of greater flexibility for scheduling their proctoring sessions.

Regulatory and Accreditation Factors for e-Learning Programs

Much of the work we do in support of e-learners is mandated or regulated through a variety of legislative, regulatory, or accrediting bodies, some governmental, some professional. The services that are provided to e-learners, and institutional policies related to online learning, are often a response to the mix of laws, rules, and regulations surrounding the provision of online learning. As you consider the development of your e-learning initiatives, here are some of the key regulatory and accreditation drivers with which you should become familiar.

Federal Environment

The Higher Education Act of 1965 (HEA), and reauthorized in 2008 as the Higher Education Opportunity Act of 2008 (HEOA), articulate regulations and law surrounding the administration of federally supported educational programming. Originally slated for reauthorization in 2015, that effort is currently ongoing in the halls of Congress.

States Authorization

In 2010, the U.S. Department of Education (USDOE) set forth additional regulations as part of the "Program Integrity" rule making related to the Higher Education Act of 1965, which affects institutions offering online and distance education. For online programs the regulation meant that the offering institution was required to seek authorization from each state in which it proposed to offer online learning. This presented a huge task in that there is no centralized aggregation of information to aid institutions in determining the regulator bodies in a given state and what the laws and regulations are in those states.

Although the portions of the regulations related to states authorization were ultimately vacated pursuant to court challenges in 2011 and 2012, the requirement to obtain authorization in each operational state was reemphasized by the USDOE in a "Dear Colleague" letter in January 2013. Through a collaborative effort championed by higher education professional organizations and regulators in the states, a solution to mitigate the multi-state regulatory miasma was achieved through the formation of SARA, or the States Authorization Reciprocity Agreement (http://ncsara.org/) as an alternative to seeking authorization in individual states.

Credit Hour Definition

The USDOE provides a definition of credit hour and the assignment thereof in 34 CRF § 600.2 and 600.24. Under these regulations, it is important to note that distance education, correspondence courses, and direct assessment programs are treated as distinct delivery formats, each having separate regulatory definitions and requirements. Noncompliance impacts institutional and program eligibility for Title IV financial aid. It is also important to note that regional accreditors have a part in determining compliance with this and related regulations.

"Where to Complain" Rule

Under the USDOE Program Integrity rules, each state must have a formal process available for students with complaints against an educational institution. In addition, the USDOE regulation states that institutions must provide its students or prospective students with contact information for filing complaints with its accreditor and with its State approval or licensing entity and any other relevant State official or agency that would appropriately handle a student's complaint.

Accessibility

Accessibility regulations are enforced for online learning programs, just as they are for face-to-face education. The Americans with Disabilities Act of 1990, as amended, and section 508 of the Rehabilitation Act of 1973, amended in 1998, articulate institutional obligations in terms of accommodations for persons with disabilities.

Student Authentication

Through HEOA in 2008, the Department of Education issued a regulation to accreditation agencies that institutions must verify student identities through particular methods outlined by HEOA. In addition to this accreditor-enforced regulation, institutions must also demonstrate that the authentication process protects student privacy. If there are financial charges associated with the authentication process, disclosures must be made to students at enrollment. Note that the intent of this regulation, from the standpoint of the USDOE, is to support fraud prevention. The regulation is not motivated by a desire to enhance academic integrity, a theme that resonates more naturally with institutional priorities.

States Environment

Institutions, public and private, operate within the regulatory environment defined by the state in which it operates. Although the USDOE reminds institutions of their obligation to meet any and all laws and regulations governing distance and online education, the challenge for institutions is that states vary greatly in terms of their laws, regulations, and process through which authorization may be achieved. The underlying motivation for these regulations and authorization processes is fundamentally to ensure consumer protection.

For those seeking individual states' authorization, a useful but incomplete summary of the relevant states' authorizing agencies and regulations has been posted by the State Higher Education Executive Officers Association (http://www.sheeo.org/). A second pathway described earlier is through the States Authorization Reciprocity Agreement (SARA), a national consortium of regional education compacts where membership satisfies regulatory authorization in all participating states.

Accreditation

Regional accrediting agencies must observe federal regulatory requirements when assessing institutional compliance in order to achieve and maintain accreditation, and for the institution's eligibility for Title IV financial aid awarding. Each accreditor must comply with USDOE laws and regulations, but may also include additional guidelines such as those outlined by the Council of Regional Accrediting Commissions. Note that participation in SARA requires that the participating institutions have regional accreditation. Depending on the nature of the institution, accrediting bodies and their accreditation requirements for online education will vary and must be addressed in concert with other states and federal requirements.

Current Best Practices and Future Directions for Responding to e-Learner Needs

Online education is evolving as rapidly as are the technologies that support it. Here are the most recent developments that are most pertinent to student support services:

Analytics

Many institutions are now creating, "cleaning" and curating learning management system, student, and institutional data to allow for robust analyses of the factors that impact student performance, and to provide actionable insights to support informed decision-making.

Predictive Modeling

Using statistical techniques and supported by new technologies for data capture and analysis, predictive analysis takes into account prior student performance in the aggregate to predict future performance on the individual level. This approach can help identify potential areas of weak performance, and the creation and delivery of interventions. Systems can be created in-house or are available by a host of leading private providers.

Machine Learning

A recent advent in artificial intelligence systems is the ability to use machine learning techniques that are able to analyze very large data sets and develop predictive models independently based on that data analysis. Machine learning systems can adapt predictive models on a continuous basis, adjusting as new data are acquired for individual student performance. Essentially, the system teaches itself and self-adjusts over time so that a rich portrait of student performance and intervention impacts is generated.

The use of these methods will make it possible to provide a technology-enabled, personalized learning experience wherein each student receives the support they need, when they need it, from the service or person best suited to respond to that need. This unified, holistic strategy is exemplified through initiatives such as EDUCAUSE's iPASS and Next Generation Digital Learning Environment (NGDLE) efforts, which attempt to create a network of approaches that utilize technology to enhance student success. These initiatives are built on the assumption that the use of technology will allow us to increasingly acquire a deeper understanding of our students, their challenges, and their needs in order to respond in personalized ways that can enhance student success.

Real-time support strategies are enhanced by real-time information that tells us something about how students are doing, both informed by trends and based on current performance data. These systems are not limited to e-learning programs but are influencing teaching and learning across the globe. Some institutions are actively engaging in data-driven decision-making, and others are just becoming aware of the possibilities. Using predictive modeling along with real-time data analytics will help you develop processes to inform, monitor, and assess your student support initiatives. And, clearly, developing predictive and data-intensive student support systems necessitates both specific staffing choices and institutional investment. The most effective e-learning programs employ an ecosystem approach that takes into consideration technological solutions and human support services that work together to respond to individual student needs.

The future of these efforts includes a number of major advances in data-informed decision-making including privacy/data sharing governance, dashboard visualization, and communication system development that allow full-cycle, data-informed learning to take place. Questions informing best practices include: who owns the data? What is ethical use of big and real-time data? And how can data be used to positively impact learning? Systems and strategies that inform and empower the student with real-time feedback regarding performance and standards for success are the new developments in e-learning. Initial work in this area suggests a powerful evolution in learning and support systems that will allow the student to adjust as needed, seek additional support, and understand how his or her own engagement with course content, peers, instructors, and other support professionals is impacting learning. Simultaneously, institutions will be able to proactively understand individual student's needs and engage the student with appropriate and personalized interventions.

What You Can Do

Providing a rich, engaging, and responsive learning experience is an aspirational goal for all education modalities. The challenge is how we can achieve this in light of institutional preparedness and competition for resources. A starting point for developing and enhancing your online program is to review current best practices for the effective delivery of student support services. Here are a few key resources:

- American Council on Education (http://www.acenet.edu)
- Education Advisory Board (http://eab.com)
- EDUCAUSE (http://www.educause.edu/)
- University Professional and Continuing Education Association (http://www.upcea.edu/)

- WICHE Cooperative for Educational Technologies (http://wcet.wiche.edu/)
- University Innovation Alliance (http://www.theuia.org/)
- NextGenerationLearning.org

Creating a Plan for Student Success

Once you have reviewed these resources, we recommend the following steps:

Define Student Success for Your e-Learning Unit

This definition will help you to develop priorities for your student success programs.

Map Existing Services

Once your definition of success has been established, a needs assessment and a gap analysis are important next steps. A full range of services required to support and retain students already exists at your institution and, as you design new e-learning programs, consider who your partners are in extending those resources to e-learners. Some services may need to be replicated with technological solutions; others may need to be created from scratch to meet the unique needs of e-learners as addressed above. Your institution will need to assess the degree to which your campus is prepared to offer existing support services to distance students, with expanded or altered hours of service for students in other time zones. If that is not feasible, you may consider contracting with third party providers for forms of nonacademic support.

Identify Your Partners and Allies

Central to your intentional design process will be many conversations with your institutional partners to identify the success resources that are already effective and highly valued by your institutional culture, and where the gaps might develop when extending educational programs to the distance learner (see Table 1 for potential stakeholder groups to consider).

We recommend developing a matrix for evaluating current and proposed student support and retention programs to help guide this process.

Table 1 Potential institutional partners for e-learning student success

Partner	Student success initiatives
Academic success or tutoring center	Align with campus-based resources and initiatives to ensure that the unique needs of online learners are understood and incorporated in decision-making
Career services	Design solutions for the distance online student to actively participate in career-related events, such as virtual career fairs
Registrar's office	Develop flexible course scheduling options and fully online registration processes
Financial aid	Create supplemental aid for the nontraditional distant online learners
Wellness center	Provide alternative means to provide health services and psychological counseling for students at a distance
Veteran's support services	Develop centralized resources to ensure veterans and active military who are studying at a distance have the support they need throughout the student life cycle
Institutional research/ information technology	Partner closely to collect, share, and analyze data and to develop systems for improving teaching and learning, understanding who your students are, informing retention efforts, and aligning information governance policies
Institutional leadership	Consider reporting models, the role e-learning will play, the vision leadership has, and how distance education will impact strategic planning at your institution for student support
Professional associations	Identify historically relevant and leading organizations to guide best practices and future visioning for effective e-learning programs

Watch for Trends

There are institutional trends to become aware of and to monitor for patterns demonstrated by e-learners: major migration (timing and frequency of major changes), D/F/W (drop, fail, withdrawal) rates in key courses, murky middle GPAs, and credit attempt versus completion ratios, among other patterns. Given the unique characteristics and needs of e-learners, you will want to watch for emerging patterns that tell the story of success and retention at your institution. Proactive outreach to e-learners when they begin to demonstrate indicators of concern as well as encouraging the effective behaviors of students progressing in a positive direction is essential to your e-learners' success.

Additional strategies can serve as a guide to conversations with various campus stakeholders when designing student success initiatives:

Value Background

Allow the online learner to draw upon their experiences, both past and present. In some e-learning programs, previous experience may be evaluated to meet academic requirements, which is a formalized process for valuing skills and knowledge.

Engagement is Key

Welcoming a distance learner as one of your own is an important move institutions can make to help e-learners identify as part of the community. There is a natural desire to belong, and this is also true for e-learners. Help create an affinity by building upon natural connections to your institution.

Language on your institution's website (not only the webpages you control, but institution-wide webpages), interactions with the admissions processes and representatives, academic on-boarding and registration for classes, ordering course materials, understanding degree requirements, and other systems that support the students' successful navigation must be clear and inclusive from a student's first glance and through to graduation.

Make Learning Meaningful

We know that e-learners begin their online education inspired, self-directed, and with a commitment to achievement. Making learning personally relevant or individually meaningful is a challenge, but by actively engaging the student, it is attainable. Giving each e-learner the tools for self-reflection, identifying short- and long-term action plans, measuring progress, and achieving individual goals directly engages the student, ties learning objectives to personally/professionally relevant goals, and taps into the motivators that led to the decision to learn online.

Plan for Part-Time

Student retention and success initiatives are getting a lot of attention in higher education, which is warranted. Unfortunately, the metrics for evaluating student progress as well as the programs that are designed to positively impact persistence may not fit the online learner. Students in online programs involved in other commitments like full- and part-time or seasonal employment, families, and care-giver support to aging parents or children with special needs very often take classes on a part-time basis. Examples of metrics that often miss the mark for part-time e-learners include:

- Time to graduation, which is often measured in 4-, 5-, and even 6-year comparisons rather than the longer timeline many online learners require
- Progress to degree calculations tracking credit hours and typical course loads that many e-learners do not maintain
- Rigid program requirements, whether mandated at the federal, state, or institution level, that may not be flexible enough to meet the online learner's needs and responsibilities to job and family

Provide Real-Time Supports

Helping students engage with content, with their instructors and academic supports, and with students so that they do not feel isolated but connected, may involve synchronous opportunities to connect.

Evaluate Your Efforts

Once student support services and retention efforts have been established, evaluating these efforts is imperative to measuring the effectiveness of e-learner support. Additionally, decisions regarding the creation of new services or interventions when e-learner or institutional needs change over time can be influenced by data collected regarding current efforts. Student support services should be systematic so that they can be informed by an assessment cycle, but they should also be responsive to the changing needs of e-learners.

Conclusion

In this chapter, we have provided information about what e-learning leaders need to know and do to create strong e-learner success initiatives and partnerships. Although e-learner support and retention can often be an afterthought when designing e-learning experiences, this chapter provides evidence for why e-learner success efforts should be a central component to the design of an e-learning unit. The differences between e-learners and traditional on-campus learners can have an incredible impact on the kinds of services provided to both populations. Given these differences, we have shared some of the ways that e-learning leaders can think intentionally about the support services for e-learners.

In this chapter, we have also offered a comprehensive overview of the policy and accreditation landscape for e-learner support services. This landscape is both complex and still developing as technologies change and develop over time. e-Learning leaders will be best served if they can remain aware of the policy developments related to e-learner success.

The success of e-learners is dependent on a network of stakeholders who work together across a campus to ensure that e-learner needs are met. This chapter has also offered suggestions of key partnerships that an e-learning unit will need to pursue to ensure the success of their students.

We concluded this chapter with a brief discussion of the growing trends of predictive modeling and real-time data analytics, areas that will deeply impact student success initiatives in the coming years. In the following section, we offer additional resources that e-learner leaders can review to stay up-to-date on these trends and other issues directly related to e-learner support services and programs.

For More Information

The following resources offer helpful information about the topics in this chapter.

Adult Learners

Hagelskamp, C., Schleifer, D., & DiStasi, C. (2013). *Is college worth it for me? How adults without degrees think about going (back) to school.* Public Agenda. Retrieved from http://kresge.org/sites/default/files/Is-College-Worth-It-For-Me-Public-Agenda-2013.pdf

Soares, L. (2013). *Post-traditional learners and the transformation of postsecondary education: A manifesto for college leaders.* American Council on Education. Retrieved from http://kresge.org/sites/default/files/Is-College-Worth-It-For-Me-Public-Agenda-2013.pdf

Support Resources for e-Learners

Benke, M., & Miller, G. (2013). Optimizing student success through student support services. In G. Miller et al. *Leading the e-learning transformation of higher education: Meeting the challenges of technology and distance education.* Sterling, VA: Stylus.

The National Association of Foreign Student Advisers (NAFSA; www.nafsa. org). International students can present a unique set of issues for e-learning units in terms of visa regulations and allowed participation in online curriculum. If your institution will allow international students to enroll into your online programs, you will want to learn more about regulations governing online attendance, which differ depending upon the type of visa the student holds.

Accreditation and Policy

Chaloux, B. (2013). Policy leadership in e-learning. In G. Miller et al. *Leading the e-learning transformation of higher education: Meeting the challenges of technology and distance education* (pp. 177–199). Sterling, VA: Stylus.

Council of Regional Accrediting Commissions. (2011). *Interregional guidelines for the evaluation of distance education.* Middle States commission on higher education. Retrieved from https://www.msche.org/publications/Guidelines-for-the-Evaluation-of-Distance-Education-Programs.pdf

USDOE-OIG. (2014). Title IV of the higher education act programs: Additional safeguards are needed to help mitigate the risks that are unique to the distance education environment. Retrieved from http://education.gov/about/offices/list/oig/rpauditfsa.html

Future Directions for Responding to e-Learner Needs

EDUCAUSE library of analytics resources: https://library.educause.edu/topics/information-systems-and-services/analytics

EDUCAUSE Next Generation Digital Learning Environment Initiative: https://library.educause.edu/resources/2014/9/next-generation-digital-learning-environment-initiative

EDUCAUSE iPASS resources: http://www.educause.edu/grants/ipass-grant-challenge/ipass-resources

EU General Data Protection Regulation (GDPR): http://www.algoodbody.com/EU_General_Data_Protection_Regulation

Journal of Learning Analytics: http://learning-analytics.info/

Leading the Implementation of a Successful Community College e-Learning Program

Amy Valente

Abstract This chapter provides the reader with an understanding of what it takes to successfully develop and implement an e-learning program for a community college campus. A case study of Cayuga Community College (Cayuga), a small community college in Central New York that is part of a larger state-wide system, State University of New York (SUNY) is analyzed. As a result of reading this chapter, the reader will:

- Gain an understanding of the challenges and opportunities to implement successful e-learning programs at community colleges.
- Explore the critical success factors, project management approach, and leadership skills that must be present in community college settings to enable successful e-learning program implementations.
- Review the implementation of a specific program—a fully online, credit-based event management certificate program at SUNY's Cayuga Community College, a small, rural college in central New York.
- Consider practical implications for leading the implementation of successful community college e-learning degree programs.

Keywords e-Learning program • Community college • Online learning • Distance education

Decision-Making Guidance

This chapter helps the reader make decisions about how to effectively plan, organize, lead, and implement e-learning programs in an existing community college setting. An institutional analysis of critical success factors will be reviewed to provide practical recommendations for the reader in the following areas:

A. Valente (✉)
Cayuga Community College, Auburn, NY, USA
e-mail: amy.valente@cayuga-cc.edu

© Association for Educational Communications and Technology 2018
A.A. Piña et al. (eds.), *Leading and Managing e-Learning*, Educational
Communications and Technology: Issues and Innovations,
https://doi.org/10.1007/978-3-319-61780-0_24

- Organizational culture.
- Transformational leadership.
- Strategic planning.
- Program development process.
- Project management process.
- Organizational structure and roles.
- Cross-departmental teamwork and communication.

What You Need to Know

The Situation, Challenges, and Opportunities

Community college e-learning degree programs comprise a substantial portion of all undergraduate e-learning degree programs (Johnson & Berge, 2012). Although overall student enrollment at community colleges has been trending downward in recent years, e-learning enrollments continue to grow more rapidly than at 4-year institutions (Lokken & Mullins, 2014). Often community colleges consider implementing new e-learning programs as a way to increase enrollment given a challenging local economy (Jaggars, 2013). e-Learning programs provide a unique opportunity for community colleges to attract students outside of their service area (Capra, 2014). This is particularly true in locations experiencing a declining population of high school graduates. In fact, for a substantial number of community colleges, continued growth in e-learning programs is of utmost importance to the institution's future sustainability (Jaggars, 2013). Many community college leaders consider new e-learning programs a significant opportunity to increase enrollment while improving program offerings.

Thus, it is imperative for community college leaders to recognize the challenges related to e-learning programs and consider how their institution can achieve successful implementations. Community colleges seldom have the organizational structure required to embark on new e-learning programs without rethinking the necessary roles and responsibilities. Further, community colleges may face resource constraints, given recent budget shortfalls due to declining enrollment. Thus, it is necessary for leaders to recognize limitations and determine how to address gaps. Who will champion the initiative through the necessary approval channels? Who is accountable for a successful e-learning program implementation? Who is responsible for marketing the program? How will the tasks and activities that must occur be managed? These questions and more must be considered up-front. Implementing a successful e-learning program requires new and varied roles within the college as well as cooperation across different functional areas (Barefield & Meyer, 2013).

Beyond the organization's structural challenges, the institution must also consider who they are serving—the online student. Students are attracted to e-learning programs at community colleges due to the open access admission policies and affordability. They are a diverse group, ranging from traditional students, adult learners, at-risk learners, multicultural learners, nonlocal students, and learners requiring accommodation. Several state-wide research studies have concluded that the retention rate for students in online programs is generally lower than in a traditional classroom-based program (Allen & Seaman, 2013). However, a recent national study found that community college students who took online courses "early in their college careers were more likely to attain a degree than students who had not done so" (Shea & Bidjerano, 2014, p. 110). To accommodate varied student needs and the risks involved in e-learning student retention, community colleges must envision how they plan to assist online students. What is the admissions process for the program? Who do students contact when they have questions about the program? What do students do if they have started the program and are struggling? Is online tutoring offered? How can learning activities be structured in such a way as to engage students in a learning community and leverage their diverse backgrounds? While diversity can pose a challenge, it can also be viewed as an advantage in that students have the opportunity to work with and learn from others who have different perspectives and backgrounds (Korobova & Starobin, 2015). To assist students in community college e-learning programs, faculty, staff, and administrators must think strategically to overcome the challenges inherent in supporting student success in the online environment.

Finally, community colleges must consider whether their e-learning program will be competitive in the marketplace and attract students. Community colleges are often part of a larger public college system. If the larger system has not centralized the development and implementation of their online programs, institutions may find themselves competing with other community colleges within their system for online programs. It is also important to evaluate the e-learning programs offered outside of the system in which the community college belongs. Thus, it becomes important to conduct market research on e-learning program offerings both within and outside of your college system when considering program viability.

What You Can Do

The critical success factors include a collection of best practices that enable a successful e-learning program implementation. When considering these factors, educational institutions can learn from business disciplines such as human resource management, project management, business analysis, and marketing.

Organizational Culture

The institution's culture must be flexible, open to change, and innovative to encourage new e-learning program development. Rogers (2003) discusses organizational characteristics that facilitate the initiation of innovative ideas: decentralized structure, less bureaucratic, and a high degree of interconnectedness. Often, an institution's culture is defined by its institutional leaders. A high degree of policies and procedures can hinder innovative ideas. While it may be advantageous to centralize approval of new program implementations, campus leaders can foster new e-learning program ideas from faculty using an approach that encourages collaboration and innovation. Faculty who are provided with professional development opportunities, incentives, stipends, release time, and recognition are often those who explore and ultimately lead the implementation of new e-learning programs (Baran & Correia, 2014; Moloney & Oakley, 2010; Owen & Demb, 2004). Embracing a culture of innovation can position the community college to value new ideas for e-learning programs.

Transformational Leadership

Transformational leaders are those who inspire and motivate others through their vision, integrity, and empowerment (Schemerhorn & Bachrach, 2016). Online education programs must be envisioned, implemented, and evaluated through strategic leadership. For many community colleges, e-learning programs are essential to the institution's ongoing growth and viability, yet, are often treated peripherally. To effectively manage successful e-learning programs, community colleges require transformational leaders who envision the strategic importance of e-learning and empower faculty and staff to realize this vision (Beaudoin, 2013). The presence of a project champion who will advocate for the new e-learning program is also vital to a successful implementation (Rogers, 2003). In smaller community colleges, the champion is often the faculty member who envisioned the new e-learning program.

Strategic Planning

Organizations typically develop strategic plans to prepare for the future and guide decision-making. Strategic planning involves the establishment of the mission or purpose of the organization and a vision for the future. The organization must then analyze where they are today and what it will take for them to realize their vision. A common approach for businesses to analyze themselves internally and externally is the SWOT analysis in which strengths (S), weaknesses (W), opportunities (O), and threats (T) are analyzed to consider the organization's current situation. The results of a SWOT analysis are used to develop goals that take advantage of opportunities that match the organization's strengths, while minimizing threats and overcoming weaknesses (Armstrong & Kotler, 2015). In situations with a high number of competitive e-learning programs, college leaders must consider how to differentiate their e-learning program from the programs that are offered by other colleges.

Community colleges embarking on e-learning programs should ensure that their strategic plan clearly identifies the goals for e-learning programs and articulates the strategy to achieve the goals.

Product Development Process

When businesses consider new products or services, it is common to follow a systematic product development process to improve the chances for success. These steps generally include:

1. Idea Generation—ideas are generated for new products from customers, sales, suppliers, engineering, research, and development.
2. Screening—product ideas that suit the firm's abilities and objectives are selected.
3. Concept Development and Testing—the firm obtains customer input on selected product ideas.
4. Marketing Strategy Development—target market(s), sales, profit, and marketing mix are determined.
5. Business and financial analysis—costs and benefits are compared.
6. Product development—a prototype is produced.
7. Test marketing—the product is tested in a realistic marketing setting.
8. Commercialization—full-scale production and introduction of the product to market (Armstrong & Kotler, 2015).

At every step throughout the product development process, the product should be analyzed by various external and internal stakeholders to ensure that it continues to meet the goals and objectives of the organization. Similarly, community colleges can follow a systematic process to develop and implement new e-learning programs to ensure that the programs meet the needs of the organization and the community.

Project Management Process

A project is defined as a "temporary endeavor undertaken to create a unique product, service or result" (*A Guide to the Project Management Body of Knowledge*, 2013). Project management is utilized in many organizations to ensure that initiatives are implemented in a quality manner, on time and within budget. Project management involves management of scope, time, cost, quality, human resources, communications, risks, and stakeholders related to the project (Project Management Institute, 2015). While e-learning initiatives and project management have largely remained disconnected, recent researchers have stressed the importance of integration. For example, Eby and Yuzer (2013) emphasize the importance of educational institutions using project management methodologies, tools, and techniques to oversee e-learning initiatives through the use of a framework called the Project

Management Based Design for Online Learning (PMDOL). Their work focuses on how to successfully meet online learning goals through planning and resource management using project management principles.

College leaders should consider the value of managing new e-learning initiatives as a "project" to implement the best possible online programs. Project management of an e-learning initiative involves managing the scope of the project, the budget, the timeline, risks, and resources. Software tools can be used to develop a project schedule to plan and manage tasks, resources, dependencies, and milestones. Risks can be managed through a thorough analysis of risks and the development of a risk mitigation plan.

Organizational Structure and Roles

Community colleges must consider the organizational roles and responsibilities necessary to successfully develop and implement e-learning programs. Ideally, organizational structures are selected to complement the primary goals of an organization. Businesses whose focus is developing new products or implementing new programs often choose a "projectized" organizational structure to effectively and efficiently organize resources to meet these goals (Tahri & Drissi-Kaitouni, 2013). Projectized organizations are characterized by full-time project managers who control project budgets, have full authority for the project and resources who are dedicated to complete activities on projects. In projectized organizations, the organizational structure seamlessly accommodates new project implementations.

Community colleges are rarely projectized and often organized functionally, by department and academic disciplines. e-Learning program implementations require specific roles that are likely not aligned to the institution's organizational structure. Thus, it becomes important for the institution to establish specific project roles such as a project sponsor, project manager, and to determine the process by which resources are assigned to the project. Depending on the community college size, one person may play multiple roles. Frequently, faculty members perform nontraditional roles when developing and implementing e-learning programs (Barefield & Meyer, 2013).

At a minimum, community colleges must have people in key roles when implementing new e-learning programs:

Project Sponsor

Initially, a new e-learning program may be championed by a faculty member. But ultimately, an administrator should "sponsor" and support the curriculum, obtaining necessary approval through university channels and the State Education Department.

Project Manager

It is critical that someone oversee the e-learning implementation throughout all phases of the project (program conception, design, development, implementation, and evaluation). In a small community college setting, faculty members may play the role of project manager.

Faculty

Community college faculty often serve as the project champion, leading the development of new program proposals, working closely with a project sponsor. Upon approval of a program proposal, faculty design and develop course syllabi and course content for the new program within the learning management system. Once new courses are developed, faculty members then work with administration to determine course schedules. And most importantly, faculty teach the new courses in the online system.

Online Instructional Designer

Online course design and development of course content in community colleges is regularly completed by faculty members. Assistance with online course design may be provided by an instructional designer, if available.

Learning Management System Expert

This person assists the faculty member in setting up the new e-learning courses within the e-learning management system.

Marketing Resources

The project manager must work with the college's marketing staff to market the online program to prospective students through various media (brochures, web site, direct marketing, advertising, etc.) to promote enrollment.

Student Support

Resources and staff must be provided for online students in areas of academic support, program advisement, library, educational counseling, bookstore, and help desk.

Admissions

Admission's staff must be trained on the new e-learning program so they can communicate effectively with prospective students.

Registrar

The Registrar's office must set up the new e-learning program within the student information system and set up the course schedules so that students may register for courses offered as part of the new e-learning program.

Cross-Departmental Teamwork and Communication

A key component of successful e-learning program implementations is teamwork and communication. The project manager is often considered the "hub" of the project team and is responsible for mitigating potential risks and ensuring that activities are on track. Regular project team meetings are essential to confirm that the project is meeting the objectives. Frequent communication of project accomplishments serves to motivate the team towards overall e-learning program implementation success.

Community college leaders must analyze their institution's unique situation and determine how to best prepare their institution for successful e-learning program implementations. It can be helpful for educational leaders to consider the success of other e-learning programs when evaluating their own situation. The next section of this chapter will inform the reader of the process of developing a new e-learning program at a community college, reflecting on what went well and lessons learned throughout the process of conception through implementation.

Cayuga Case Study

Cayuga Community College is one of 64 campuses within one of the largest statewide public educational institutions in the United States, SUNY. Cayuga is a small, rural campus in Central New York serving approximately 4600 students across two campuses, through high school and online programs. Cayuga's mission states that the college is "dedicated to providing students with diverse learning opportunities to discover their passions and advance their personal and professional growth" (Cayuga Community College's Catalog, 2015, p. 1). Cayuga is considered an early adopter of fully online programs within SUNY, offering programs since 1998, currently offering ten fully online programs and approximately 30% of all students enrolled in online courses (Cayuga Community College's Catalog, 2015).

OpenSUNY is SUNY's e-learning platform currently delivering nearly 400 online degrees and 12,000 course sections to over 200,000 students throughout its campuses (OpenSUNY, 2016). OpenSUNY is enabled through a centralized structure providing campus access to the Blackboard Learning Management System, a portal for students to find online programs offered by individual campuses, faculty training, and a help desk for faculty and students. While SUNY campuses benefit from the centralization of the services offered through OpenSUNY, each individual campus is responsible for the development and implementation of new programs within their campus, including e-learning programs. However, approval of new programs is a centralized decision made by SUNY and the State Education Department (as shown in Fig. 1):

The College fosters ongoing innovation through its Planning Council, a cross-functional team that oversees strategic direction, planning and ongoing communications with the college community (*Self-Study Report Cayuga Community College Submitted to: Middle States Commission on Higher Education*, 2016). Due to declining enrollment in campus-based courses, Cayuga's strategic plan identified online learning as an ongoing area of growth. Moreover, Cayuga's Program Development Committee regularly conducts research to determine gaps in program offerings.

In 2013, the Program Development Committee recognized the event management industry as an area of growth for Cayuga to consider. Concurrently, a faculty member expressed interest in developing online programs in the event management discipline to enhance the College's online program offerings. As a result, in 2013–2014, a new fully online credit-based event management proposal was developed and approved through SUNY and the State Education Department. In 2015 the new event management e-learning program enrolled its first students. As of this publication date, the program has experienced early success based on student enrollment and positive feedback from College administrators, faculty, the community, employers, and students. To fully appreciate how Cayuga achieved this initial success, the critical success factors of this specific e-learning implementation will now be examined.

Fig. 1 Cayuga's online education organization

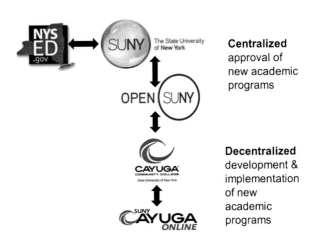

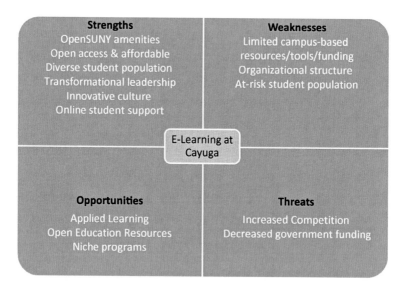

Fig. 2 Cayuga's SWOT analysis results

When an institution considers a new e-learning program, it is important to perform an analysis of the institution's current situation. While Cayuga did not conduct a formal SWOT analysis and document the results as precisely as shown below, an informal analysis revealed the information shown in Fig. 2.

Strengths

Cayuga has been offering e-learning programs for many years, and currently provides online student support services including online tutoring through NetTutor, and access to library databases online. Cayuga is affiliated with OpenSUNY, a significant asset that provides access to a robust e-learning management system, faculty training, and helpdesk for faculty and students. As a community college, Cayuga provides open access to a diverse student body in an affordable manner. Lastly, Cayuga is a small college with transformational leadership known for a culture of innovation and flexibility, responding nimbly to community opportunities that present themselves.

Weaknesses

While Cayuga is strong in many areas, it is a small rural community college, lacking an extensive campus-based e-learning organizational structure, resources, and tools. Often, faculty play the role of an instructional designer working with the Director of

Distance Learning. The organizational structure is primarily functional in nature and not prepared to handle projects as easily as in a projectized organization.

Further, as a community college, many of Cayuga's students are considered "at-risk," magnifying the issue of student success in e-learning programs. It becomes important to consider how to support online students in unique ways.

Opportunities

As Cayuga considers new e-learning programs, the College must determine how to make their programs unique to attract students and differentiate their programs from those offered by other institutions. One such opportunity is to explore ways to infuse applied learning into the e-learning curriculum. Recent studies in this area have shown that students are motivated and inspired when they have an opportunity to learn through an authentic real-world experience in their online programs (Mundkur & Ellickson, 2012).

Another opportunity involves the cost of the e-learning program for students. Although community college tuition is significantly lower than 4-year institutions, additional steps can be taken to make e-learning programs even more affordable. Textbook accessibility is a barrier for students as prices have risen by 80% in the last 10 years to an average of $1200/year per student (Quick Guide: College Costs, 2015). As textbook prices continue to rise, 65% of students choose not to purchase textbooks, recognizing that their own success could be negatively impacted by doing so (Bidwell, 2014). Open Education Resource (OER) use influences student success in terms of better grades, higher engagement, and retention (Whissemore, 2015). Since 2012, Cayuga has been instrumental in creating and using OERs for select courses. As new e-learning programs are developed, OERs should be used where possible.

Threats

While there are several opportunities for Cayuga to develop new e-learning programs, Cayuga may experience increased competition within and outside of SUNY. Differentiation of a new e-learning program is essential to gain enrollment. At the same time, funding from state and local government is decreased, creating a challenging situation given the pervasive resource constraints.

This informal SWOT analysis provides Cayuga with important internal and external factors to consider when planning, developing, and implementing new e-learning programs. Cayuga has clear strengths when coupled with opportunities to create appealing e-learning programs, but the institution must overcome its weaknesses and minimize the threats. The analysis prepared Cayuga as it embarked on the program development process.

One of the weaknesses identified from the SWOT analysis is that Cayuga primarily utilizes a functional organizational structure with departments focused on particular functions such as academic affairs, student affairs, and administration. When embarking on new e-learning program development, it was necessary to establish a cross-functional team to represent the various functional areas requiring representation. It was essential that the faculty member play additional roles, including the role of the project manager, project champion, and instructional designer (in conjunction with the Director of Distance Learning) to ensure that program implementation was successful. The Provost played the role of the project sponsor. Several marketing staff were on the team, including the Vice President of Student Affairs who had oversight of marketing and communications operations.

Fig. 3 e-Learning program implementation roles

Cayuga utilized a program development process similar to a product development process for the new event management certificate program. Figure 4 depicts a variation of the product development process (adapted from Armstrong & Kotler, 2015) specific to e-learning program development. The steps of the program development process are outlined below from the initial idea through implementation.

1. Program Idea Generation—Cayuga identified an idea for a new event management e-learning program through both internal and external research.
2. Idea Screening—The program was identified as feasible by the academic division and a good fit with the College's mission and vision for the future.
3. Program Concept Development and Testing—Cayuga obtained feedback from its Business Program Advisory Board and stakeholders to ensure the program concept met expectations.
4. Marketing Strategy Development—Cayuga considered its target market (what students would be best served by this program) and its promotional strategy (how to best reach the target market). The SWOT analysis provided valuable insights to consider.

Fig. 4 Cayuga's program development process

5. Program Proposal—Once Cayuga envisioned a solid program and target market, work on the program proposal was completed and approvals were obtained through SUNY and the New York State Department of Education.
6. Program Development—After the program was approved, faculty then developed new courses, determined course schedules, faculty teaching assignments, and worked with organizations on internship opportunities.
7. Program Implementation—New e-learning program implementations require many tasks and cross-departmental coordination. The project manager worked with admissions to ensure that the application was updated to incorporate the new program. The project manager collaborated with the Marketing area to ensure that the website was updated to incorporate program information, including course requirements and contact information for questions. Direct mail and social media promotions were implemented to communicate program benefits to potential students.
8. Program Evaluation—Obtain feedback from students, employers, faculty, and staff to continuously improve the program.

Throughout the program development process, project management was utilized (although not formally) to plan and manage tasks, resources, and timelines. A sample of a rudimentary timeline used to track assignment, due dates, and status of tasks for the implementation plan is shown in Table 1.

As a result of the planning efforts, Cayuga developed a robust e-learning program in event management that prepares students for careers in hotels, conference centers, corporations, non-profit organizations, wedding planning, or event planning organizations. Students learn the knowledge and skills to effectively plan and manage events in organizations or consider self-employment as an event planner. The program incorporates opportunities for students to share learning reflections through discussion boards while also gaining applied learning through projects. For example, students plan and manage real events such as weddings or community events using tools learned in class. Students also attend, experience, and critique actual conferences or conventions based on concepts learned in class. The program includes road trips to organizations that host events, both locally and recorded via video. An internship is a key component of the program providing students with the opportunity to gain professional experience while in the program. Open Education Resources, such as free textbooks, have been incorporated into many of the courses, reducing overall costs for students. Cayuga was able to develop and implement a unique program that attracted students.

As with any new initiative, lessons are learned to improve future e-learning program implementations. Recommendations include:

• Formalizing the program development and project management process for new e-learning programs to assist colleagues throughout the organization and gain efficiencies.
• Establishing a forecasted budget for marketing prior to program development to ensure that money is allocated to market the program. While Cayuga was still able to market the program, it was challenging since the budget was not allocated initially.

Table 1 Sample implementation plan

Task	Responsible	Date due	Status
Develop initial print marketing piece for orientation	Marketing	Xx/xx/xx	Done
Create degree sheet for the certificate program	Marketing	Xx/xx/xx	Done
Add degree sheet to website, update web pages	Web Master	Xx/xx/xx	Done
Add program to MyCayuga	Registrar	Xx/xx/xx	Done
Add program to application	Web Master	Xx/xx/xx	Done
Add a slide on homepage slide show	Web Master	Xx/xx/xx	Done
Create/implement Facebook marketing campaign	Web Master	Xx/xx/xx	Done
Add the program to OpenSUNY	Director of Distance Learning	Xx/xx/xx	Done
Press release announcing program	Marketing/Faculty	Xx/xx/xx	Done
Send out email promotion to current students, prospective students, our business advisory board, and local community contacts	Faculty	Xx/xx/xx	Done
Develop and schedule new courses	Faculty	Xx/xx/xx	Done
Work with organizations on internship opportunities, guest speakers, and road trips	Faculty	Xx/xx/xx	Done
Send out postcards to venues that hold events	Marketing	Xx/xx/xx	Done

- Considering student success advocates, also called concierges, to serve as a single point of contact dedicated to online students, reducing barriers to student success in e-learning programs. Concierges are used in many community colleges to proactively assist e-learning students, in particular returning adult students, in overcoming administrative and academic obstacles, thus improving retention and completion rates (Michelau & Lane, 2010).

Conclusion

For many community colleges, e-learning initiatives are paramount to their continued success, often to mitigate risks associated with continued declining enrollment in their local service area. Given this situation, it is important for community college leaders to understand the challenges and opportunities when developing and implementing e-learning programs at their institution.

Community college leaders who are considering new e-learning programs should evaluate their institution both internally and externally prior to undertaking such initiatives. This evaluation considers a variety of critical success factors that can influence the success of new program implementations including organizational culture, leadership, planning process, organizational structure, teamwork, and communications. As a result of this evaluation, community colleges can develop and implement new e-learning programs that capitalize on institutional strengths, take advantage of external opportunities while overcoming existing challenges, and minimizing threats.

For More Information

For additional information on this topic, please consider the following resources:

Jaggars, S. S. (2013). Online learning in community colleges. In M. G. Moore (Ed.), *Handbook of distance education* (3rd ed., pp. 594–608). New York, NY: Routledge.

Kearsley, G. (2013). Management of online programs. In M. Moore (Ed.), *Handbook of distance education* (3rd ed., pp. 425–436). New York, NY: Routledge.

Project Management Institute. (2015). Retrieved from http://www.pmi.org/About-Us/About-Us-What-is-Project-Management.aspx

References

Allen, I. E., & Seaman, J. (2013). *Changing course: Ten years of tracking online education in the United States*. Newburyport, MA: Sloan Consortium.

Armstrong, G., & Kotler, P. (2015). *Marketing: An introduction* (12th ed.). Upper Saddle River, NJ: Pearson Education.

Baran, E., & Correia, A.-P. (2014). A professional development framework for online teaching. *TechTrends: Linking Research & Practice to Improve Learning, 58*(5), 95–101. doi:10.1007/s11528-014-0791-0

Barefield, A. C., & Meyer, J. D. (2013). Leadership's role in support of online academic programs: Implementing an administrative support matrix. *Perspectives in Health Information Management, 10*(Winter), 1f. Retrieved from http://www.ncbi.nlm.nih.gov/pmc/articles/PMC3544146/.

Beaudoin, M. F. (2013). Institutional leadership. In M. G. Moore (Ed.), *Handbook of distance education* (3rd ed.pp. 467–480). New York, NY: Routledge.

Bidwell, A. (2014). *High textbook prices have college students struggling*. U.S. News & World Report. Retrieved from http://www.usnews.com/news/articles/2014/01/28/report-high-textbook-prices-have-college-students-struggling

Capra, T. (2014). Online education from the perspective of community college students within the Community of Inquiry paradigm. *Community College Journal of Research and Practice, 38*(2–3), 108–121. Retrieved from http://doi.org/10.1080/10668926.2014.851949.

Cayuga Community College. (2016). *Self-Study Report Cayuga Community College Submitted to: Middle States Commission on Higher Education*. Retrieved from https://www.cayuga-cc.edu/wp-content/uploads/2016/03/2016-Cayuga-Community-College-Self-Study.pdf

Cayuga Community College's Catalog. (2015). Retrieved from http://www.cayuga-cc.edu/pdf/brochures/ccc_catalog_2015-2016.pdf

Eby, G., & Yuzer, T. (2013). *Project management approaches for online learning design*. Hershey, PA: IGI Global. Retrieved from http://doi.org/10.4018/978-1-4666-2830-4.

Jaggars, S. S. (2013). Online learning in community colleges. In M. G. Moore (Ed.), *Handbook of distance education* (3rd ed.pp. 594–608). New York, NY: Routledge.

Johnson, S., & Berge, Z. (2012). Online education in the community college. *Community College Journal of Research & Practice, 36*(11), 897–902. doi:10.1080/10668920903323948

Korobova, N., & Starobin, S. S. (2015). A comparative study of student engagement, satisfaction, and academic success among international and American students. *Journal of International Students, 5*(1), 72. Retrieved from http://ufl.summon.serialssolutions.com/2.0.0/link/0/eLvH-CXMw3V05T8MwFLYoExJC3Dd6E0ubKokTlw4MFVAFmMDtXCWxIyFKIvWAv4_PHK0qdlbHcRx_zrvy_D2EsN91nRWZgIUnFPgp9zDhoZvyjIcJCZNexlws3DkZ4h1HvbchGT4GUZVlVLX9B-AH-hs3jN7UkkZTTWIpCQhNvosOCFeHG2wiZ5kyT5eqmqIpSNSMHaqO9m-.

Lokken, F., & Mullins, C. (2014). Trends in eLearning: Tracking the impact of eLearning at community colleges. In *ITC 2014 distance education survey results* (10th ed.). Instructional Technology Council. Retrieved from http://www.itcnetwork.org/component/content/article/1171-itc-2014-distance-education-survey-results.html

Michelau, D. K., & Lane, P. (2010). *Bringing adults back to college: Designing and implementing a statewide concierge model*. Boulder, CO: Western Interstate Commission for Higher Education.

Moloney, J. F., & Oakley, B. (2010). Scaling online education: Increasing access to higher education. *Journal of Asynchronous Learning Networks, 14*(1), 55–70.

Mundkur, A., & Ellickson, C. (2012). Bringing the real world in: Reflection on building a virtual learning environment. *Journal of Geography in Higher Education, 36*(3), 369–384. doi:10.1080/03098265.2012.692073

OpenSUNY. (2016). Retrieved from http://open.suny.edu/about

Owen, P. S., & Demb, A. (2004). Change dynamics and leadership in technology implementation. *Journal of Higher Education, 75*(6), 636–666.

Project Management Institute. (2013). *A guide to the project management body of knowledge* (5th ed.). Newtown Square, PA: Project Management Institute.

Project Management Institute. (2015). Retrieved from http://www.pmi.org/About-Us/About-Us-What-is-Project-Management.aspx

Quick Guide: College Costs. (2015). Retrieved from https://bigfuture.collegeboard.org/pay-for-college/college-costs/quick-guide-college-costs

Rogers, E. M. (2003). *Diffusion of innovations*. New York, NY: The Free Press.

Schemerhorn, J., & Bachrach, D. (2016). *Exploring management* (5th ed.). Hoboken, NJ: John Wiley & Sons, Inc..

Shea, P., & Bidjerano, T. (2014). Does online learning impede degree completion? A national study of community college students. *Computers & Education, 75*, 103–111. Retrieved from http://doi.org/10.1016/j.compedu.2014.02.009.

Tahri, H., & Drissi-Kaitouni, O. (2013). IT project management in non-projectized organization. *Procedia—Social and Behavioral Sciences, 75*, 318–327. Retrieved from http://doi.org/10.1016/j.sbspro.2013.04.036.

Whissemore, T. (2015). Community colleges take a lead on OER. *Community College Journal, 86*(1), 7–8. Retrieved from http://search.proquest.com/docview/1776144320?accountid=10920.

Leading e-Learning Schools from a Systemic Perspective: A Guide for K-12 Leaders

Victoria Raish, Stephenie Schroth, and Alison Carr-Chellman

Abstract This chapter is directed towards leaders of K-12 e-learning schools who do not have a background in online learning or instructional design. The systemic perspective taken in this chapter gives the e-learning leader a holistic understanding of the various people and parts that comprise e-learning K-12 schools. Introducing the variety of colloquial terms used in online schooling gives new leaders some standard language. Tackling issues of supporting students, giving clear expectations for parents, selecting curricula, ensuring equitable access to resources, and maintaining a sense of innovativeness balanced with transparency are discussed. Each of these issues has significant potential impact to the system and should not be selected in isolation from other decisions. Embracing a bottom-up change approach where power is reimagined among stakeholders should be adopted to gather buy-in from your school community. Following this, practical suggestions are given to react to these issues systemically by considering reactions to change and including stakeholders in important decisions. These suggestions should be taken with consideration of your local context and modified to fit your school population. Readings identified as critical for the implementation of these suggestions are identified and should be used in association with the action you implement.

Keywords K-12 • e-Learning • Systemic perspective • Student support • Parental expectations • Curricula • Innovation • Transparency • Accountability • Resources • Equivalent access

V. Raish (✉) • S. Schroth
Penn State University, 222 Outreach Building, University Park, PA 16802, USA
e-mail: vrc112@psu.edu; Victoria@PSU.edu; sss177@psu.edu

A. Carr-Chellman
University of Idaho, Moscow, ID, USA
e-mail: alicarrchellman@uidaho.edu

© Association for Educational Communications and Technology 2018
A.A. Piña et al. (eds.), *Leading and Managing e-Learning*, Educational
Communications and Technology: Issues and Innovations,
https://doi.org/10.1007/978-3-319-61780-0_25

Introduction

Online learning has a great deal of scholarship already existing, although primarily up until 2009 this scholarship has centered on higher education, with a modicum of corporate training applications. Very little research has been conducted on leading K-12 e-learning schools, which leaves those who wish to lead online environments, whether they are cyber charter schools or virtual academies, with very little to go on in terms of guidance (Kowche, 2009). This chapter will lay out specific guidance for decision-making, student success, parent communications, curriculum selection, resource access, and transparency. As leaders consider the issues associated with leading online spaces, it is important to balance the needs for effective learning outcomes and the public good (Conn, 2002). Leadership involves a good dose of values mixed in with good strategy and basic management skills. Those values need to be tightly focused on the public good applications of schooling whether this is within a cyber charter or virtual academy embedded within a traditional public school.

Decision-Making Guidance

As an e-learning leader, you are expected to make crucial decisions related to the e-learning program at your school. This chapter will help prepare you for your leadership position by focusing on decisions related to leading a K-12 e-learning program. Specifically, this chapter will help you to make decisions about:

- Supporting students who choose to learn in the online environment and prepare students to be successful in this environment.
- Setting clear expectations for the parent/guardian/learning coach at the various grade levels.
- Choosing curricula that support students in their learning through knowledge on how people learn from orientations to assessments.
- Providing equitable access to resources.
- Being innovative and responsive to issues of transparency.

The goal of this chapter is to equip leaders with a systemic perspective on e-learning leadership so that when they encounter policy decisions, they can approach them with this powerful perspective.

What You Need to Know

e-Learning, or online learning, is the newest model of distance education. Distance education efforts have been recorded since the twentieth century (Sumner, 2000). The basic premise of distance education is that the student, teacher, and the other students are geographically separated. Distance education was predominantly a one-way communication format that promoted passive learning and a lack of personalized feedback on learning—what we have colloquially thought of as correspondence courses or radio/television courses. The continued development of information and communication technologies (ICTs) has enabled a transition from one-way communication to interactive and responsive learning environments (Guri-rosenblit, 2005).

This development has allowed for the creation of active learning environments in which students, although geographically separated, can communicate with their peers and teachers through asynchronous or synchronous methods. Although the creation of an active learning environment is possible in an e-learning course, it is not a condition of using e-learning. Frequently, the design of the e-learning system prevents students from deeply learning about content through a variety of factors (Sawyer, 2006). Making decisions from a systemic perspective can help you plan for and possibly prevent some of the most common criticisms and stumbling blocks of K-12 e-learning programs (Moore & Kearsley, 2011). For the purpose of this chapter, it has been assumed that the most frequent systemic change e-learning leaders will embrace is school-wide systemic change and during this change "the purposes of schooling and the goals of education" are retooled (Squire & Reigeluth, 2000, p. 144).

A critical point that the e-learning leader needs to know when discussing e-learning with their peers and institutions is the differences in standard terms used in K-12 online learning. Online learning is a delivery mechanism for education. In this delivery, all of the coursework and instructional experience is delivered through an online format. Online learning is used interchangeably with e-learning or cyber learning (iNACOL, 2015). Hybrid learning environments have the same primary delivery mechanism for instruction as online schooling, but there is an opportunity for students to meet for face-to-face experiences as well. Blended learning environments are environments that were initially face-to-face and have since included an online component. This online component can range from having course resources in a learning management system (LMS) to completing some activities in a physical classroom and other activities in the virtual classroom. Some online programs use synchronous classes where the class uses video conferencing software to meet. Other programs use asynchronous classes where required classes are nonexistent. And yet still, some schools choose to use a blend of synchronous and asynchronous classes. In remaining consistent with the book and for the focus of this chapter, e-learning will refer to entirely online K-12 programs or schools.

There are subtypes of K-12 e-learning schools. Public cyber charter schools can accept students from any area of a state and do not charge tuition. The actual governance, charter, and accountability for cyber charter schools differ by state. Some of these schools are run by educational management organizations (EMOs) while local leaders run others. An example of an EMO is K-12, Inc. An e-learning leader in charge of one of these schools needs to become very familiar with their state's policy for cyber charter schools. There are also private cyber charter schools that charge tuition. An example of a private cyber charter school is the Stanford Online High School (https://ohs.stanford.edu/). As a response to public cyber charter schools, some districts have created their own e-learning schools/programs. These can be single-district or multi-district and are offered partially in response to the pressure these schools face in losing enrollment to cyber charter schools (Stone, 2008). Equipped with standard terminology, you are now ready to consider the issues surrounding decisions you will need to make as an e-learning leader.

Preparing Students to Be Successful Online Learners

There are two common misconceptions with online learning. The first is that online learning will be less rigorous than face-to-face learning, and therefore easier. It is imperative that you do not think of online teaching as the same as face-to-face teaching (Sieber, 2005). There is a perception among a minority of administration (23%) that online learning is inferior to face-to-face teaching (Allen & Seaman, 2013). This number has continued to trend downward when tracking online learning trends. There are several parts necessary to create a successful e-learning environment. A systemic perspective reminds leaders of this complexity. Without an understanding of this complexity, leaders may think that online learning is less rigorous than face-to-face learning (Moore & Kearsley, 2011). Students who do not understand the rigor and self-regulation required to be successful online will likely struggle and fail to adjust to the online learning environment (Cho & Shen, 2013). These students run the risk of being unprepared and having negative associations with their education. Parental/guardian supervision is essential in the K-12 online learning environment (Waters & Leong, 2014). Students in the younger grades, especially, require a whole family commitment to be successful online learners.

The second misconception is that students and teachers believe the notion "anywhere, anytime, anyplace" with online learning, which implies that schoolwork can be completed at any pace and in any setting (Dawley, 2007). Online K-12 schools increase the flexibility for students to complete their coursework. No longer is school tied to a physical classroom. Anywhere means that walls do not bind online learning. A student could complete their coursework at their house, in a cafe, on their mobile device, or on their desktop. Anytime means that, in an asynchronous environment, students can complete their schoolwork when it is convenient for them. In a synchronous environment this means that, besides class, schoolwork can be completed anytime. For students who are unable to attend a synchronous session, video conferencing software, such as Zoom © or AdobeConnect ©, allows sessions to be recorded and viewed later. Touting an e-learning K-12 school as being "anywhere, anytime, anyplace" without guided regulations or policies to help students be successful in this environment can be compared to expecting students to construct their own knowledge without guidance or scaffolding (Mayer, 2004). In the similar situation of an employee telecommuting, the company has typically had guidelines/policies to structure this type of work. For example, "the state of Oregon provides a very detailed, easy-to-follow workbook to help a company devise its own guidelines" (Kurland & Bailey, 1999, p. 60). These guidelines are for a company who is going to have telecommuting employees.

Expectations for the Parent/Guardian

As a person in a leadership role at the K-12 level, you may have considered how important the parent/guardian is to support students in their education. However, being a leader of a K-12 e-learning school brings an entirely new perspective when considering the role of the parent/guardian. Huerta, Gonzalez, and d'Entremont (2006) consider the policy changes needed to accommodate education in the e-learning environment. The role of the parent as teacher assistant is very integral to the e-learning environment. This is because the onus of direct supervision of students moves from the teacher to the parent/guardian. This move is a considerable systemic change in an educational organization. Ahn (2011) researched the role of the parent in three different e-learning schools and found that the teacher communicates with the whole family on a regular basis and relies on the parent for direct supervision of student work. However, Waters and Leong emphasize that the actual engagement by the parents remains amorphous. Raish (2016) found that while the teachers would love to have more parent involvement and supervision over student work at the middle school level, schools are hesitant to define the parent role because of possible home life instability. As a virtual academy or cyber charter leader, it is imperative that you are able to align the parent participation and communication to the needs of the school and learners, this is no easy task, but it is an essential one. In order for e-learning to work for most K-12 students, parents need to have heavy involvement as teachers, essentially. This is a dramatic departure from the e-learning environment in higher education or corporate training where adult learning theories are at play. As a leader, it is your responsibility to ensure that parent expectations are set, communication is clear, and regulations are followed.

Selecting Curricula

There is a range of options to choose from when deciding what the curricula for a school will be. Huerta et al. (2006) note that for teaching the primary sources for learning materials come from "software, third-party curriculum...and the library" (p. 112). Moore and Kearsley (2011) emphasize the most common system of design for the online environment is for the teachers to be facilitators of the curricula but not expected to design it. Raish (2016) found in a sample of five cyber charter schools in Pennsylvania that three schools did not follow this model and that the teachers were able to design their curricula. These schools used a range of curricula from third-party to teacher-designed to open, educational resources and a combination of the three.

The e-learning environment expands curricula in some ways and narrows options in others. In an e-learning school, it might not make sense to have the majority of the curricula be in the form of textbooks. Students have access to a wealth of interactive information at their fingertips and can also use e-books when a text is required. There are advantages and disadvantages of the various curricular options. Table 1 highlights the advantages and disadvantages.

Table 1 Curricular options for e-learning schools

Curricula options	Advantages	Disadvantages
Third-party curricula (typically provided by an Educational Management Organization (EMO))	• Uniform experience • Learning analytics likely provided • Less time-consuming • External technical support	• Cannot be personalized for students • Typically does not allow for modification • Cost prohibitive • Dependent on external provider for quality
Teacher-designed	• Responsive to student needs • Adaptable for students with individualized educational plans (IEPs) • Gives the teacher authority and ownership over the course • Allows the teacher to become intimately aware of the curriculum	• Time-consuming for the teacher to develop the curriculum • Dependent on teacher to have instructional design expertise • Not a consistent educational experience for students in the same school • Takes teacher attention away from helping students
Embedded in Learning Management System (LMS)	• Reduces the need for students to learn multiple websites/resources for their courses • Creates a consistent educational experience for the students • Ideal for courses from a third-party subscriber	• Limited by what is possible in the chosen LMS • Dependent on learning technology interoperability to get external software/plug-ins to work in the LMS • Can be used by the teacher but requires a certain level of technical expertise to effectively integrate a variety of sources into the LMS • Concerns about FERPA (Family Educational Rights and Privacy Act) requirements
Composite of resources	• Can select to use a variety of resources to make up the curricula • Allows students the opportunity to learn how to interact with different websites • Is less reliant on a consistent LMS experience • Teacher can select different resources or websites for students at different levels	• Concerns about FERPA requirements • Teacher needs to take time to investigate a variety of resources • Requires students to learn how to use a variety of different software to learn in their course • Can create a situation where students have to learn from multiple resources for every single course

(continued)

Table 1 (continued)

Curricula options	Advantages	Disadvantages
Licensed software	• Have a certain level of support from the company providing the software • Varying levels of services dependent on license • Can streamline and reduce the workload of teachers • Can be used in multiple courses for students	• A certain cost involved • If the school chooses not to renew the software then the teacher work using that software is lost • Need to be concerned with FERPA and if student data would be collected/stored
Open software	• Affordable • Can increase access to information for students • Teachers can choose to use different software that the school does not license	• Will frequently require teacher to manually enter class roster for every single class • Does not always track learning progress for the students • Will not have in-house or software technical support

These are a few of the most common decisions that you will need to make as the e-learning leader when it comes to selecting curricula for your school. This is not a decision to be taken lightly as the curricula chosen will speak highly of the mission and learning philosophy of your school. A combination of solutions can be chosen, or a singular provider can be selected to deliver the curricula. The most important aspect of choosing the curricula is to keep the system in mind and how these choices will interact with other parts of your school system. The other very important issue to be aware of is that for many online K-12 settings, the curricula is already determined, and will not be up to you. In too many cases, this has been a business decision, often following specific agreements that may not be best for learners, but rather are part of contractual agreements for using certain curricula. Too often, the curriculum is provided at prohibitive costs because this allows the nonprofit of K-12 online learning to function as a business model. This moves the financial focus away from the public good of public online schools and toward a more capitalist model of schooling in which for profit curriculum delivery is seen as a cash cow and a wise investment on Wall Street. As an e-learning leader it is incumbent upon you to see these particular injustices that can impact the educational experience of students and work to right the ship. This commitment to the public good needs to be communicated to everyone in your organization that your educational purpose is educating not profit extending to curriculum decisions.

Equitable Access to Resources

One of the most innovative aspects of an e-learning school at the K-12 level is that students are no longer geographically limited to the school they attend. A student from a northern rural school district could be enrolled in the same class as a student from a large urban area. However, it is this very innovation that can create new educational inequalities. If an e-learning school is not designed with equitable access to resources in mind, then decisions made could provide an inconsistent educational experience for students.

Equity, in an e-learning school, should provide equal access to resources and the ability of the school to meet the needs of students and provide all students with the same level of support (Mann & Barkauskas, 2014). Decisions made can affect the equity of the e-learning school. For example, a school could choose to have physical learning support centers, learning tutors, or specialized education centers. From a systemic perspective, it is important to remember that geographic boundaries do not limit school choice in an e-learning school (except district cyber schools). Therefore, when designing resources for students, they need to be designed with the lack of geographic boundaries in mind. Designing physical support centers that only a certain number of students have the ability to access can put other students at a disadvantage. In an e-learning school, the budget typically does not account for transportation, so even students who would live close enough to use a center might not be able to get there.

Another way that inequity is introduced into the e-learning environment is through the creation of specialized learning centers. For example, PA Cyber Charter School proposed building a STEM (Science, Technology, Engineering, and Mathematics) Center in the Pittsburgh area (PA Cyber Charter, 2012) to connect students with universities or industries involved in STEM and begin their hands-on STEM learning. If a center like this were established, it would put other PA cyber students who cannot travel to Pittsburgh on an uneven playing field for their learning opportunities. Ensuring an equivalent level of access is imperative for students in an e-learning environment (ACRL, 2008). Equal access in e-learning schools is typically thought of in relation to students in brick-and-mortar schools (Mann & Barkauskas, 2014) but also deserves consideration for students in the same school.

Being Innovative and Transparent

As the leader of a K-12 e-learning school, you have a tremendous opportunity to be innovative in the education for students. Access to technology, which can be a limiting factor in a brick-and-mortar school, is no longer a limit to students engaging with a variety of different learning experiences. Barbour and Reeves (2009) emphasize that the chance to be innovative is a common descriptor of K-12 online schools and Tucker (2007) in the report, *Laboratories of Reform: Virtual High Schools and Innovation in Public Education*, highlight that the innovation can go beyond curricula to how teachers are hired and how students communicate.

While being innovative is important, it is essential to ensure the quality of the school. Using an evaluative tool such as Quality Matters © can help your school to focus on learning outcomes and valid measures of assessment while still being innovative in how students are experiencing their education. Quality is a piece of being transparent. Depending on the type of K-12 e-learning school that you lead, you may have to deal with issues of funding and accountability. This aspect is likely not applicable to leaders of private K-12 schools and less applicable to those leading district e-learning K-12 initiatives as those schools likely have an existing structure in place for transparency. Controversies surrounding public cyber charter schools frequently highlight the finances of the schools (McCorry & Socolar, 2015). Part of the confusion comes with a lack of transparency when seeing how the money is spent (Carr-Chellman & Marsh, 2009; Raish & Carr-Chellman, 2015). Keeping a budget record and other means of staying transparent is essential as a leader in the K-12 e-learning educational movement.

What You Can Do

Successful leaders identify student outcomes, obtain appropriate curriculum to meet the needs of the students, possess vision, and recognize areas for improvement (Berge & Clark, 2005). A system is not inert. Similar to the manner in which forces are constantly interacting in a physics diagram, the system is never in a completely stable state. In the field of e-learning, there are continual changes that a leader must be able to respond to. Effective leaders will respond to these changes by taking into consideration the entire system. Responding to changes without considering the process, outcomes, and potential consequences is not a systemic perspective (Hutchins, 1996). A critical component of being an effective leader is to approach decisions from a bottom-up perspective valuing the input and expertise of the team and stakeholders. When making decisions on the factors identified in the previous section for issues in e-learning, it is essential to institute a culture where the opinions of various stakeholders are taken seriously and respected. As much as possible, a bottom-up, stakeholder-based approach to decision-making should be used to empower faculty, staff, students, parents, community members, and other stakeholders. Similar to the way an ecological system considers all of the different parts that will impact the ecosystem, in a human system you need to "involve multiple perspectives and a variety of stakeholders in the change process" (Squire & Reigeluth, 2000, p. 146).

Preparing Students to Be Successful Online Learners

There are many strategies to help students be successful online learners in e-learning K-12 schools. Understanding your student population, networking with peers who have strategies for success, and reading literature on how to support online students are all sound strategies for helping students and families from the time they enroll in your e-learning school until the time they leave the school. In addition, specialized plans should be made for students who have transferred in the middle of the school year, or whose academic record indicates a high rate of transfer. Teachers need to be committed to helping families transition into the online learning environment and providing as much support as the students need in learning how this school setting works (Raish, 2016). However, teachers need to be supported in this effort through a whole school system for preparing and supporting students to be successful. The following ideas are ways to address the issues raised in this chapter:

- Creating a successful online learning environment requires a level of commitment towards building a community. The community can foster a sense of belonging to their school (McInnerney & Roberts, 2004). First-time online students can be resistant to full participation in the community (Conrad, 2002). From a community of practice perspective, do not require students to jump into the middle of the community, legitimate peripheral participation is a valid form of involvement (Lave & Wenger, 1991).

- Have students take a self-readiness assessment so they can evaluate how prepared they are to learn online. These self-readiness tests are freely available online. For example, Penn State Online offers readiness assessment and provides prompt feedback for students on their strengths and weaknesses for online learning (https://pennstate.qualtrics.com/jfe/form/SV_7QCNUPsyH9f012B). A copy of this survey is included in Appendix section "Penn State Qualtrics Survey Online Readiness."

- Create orientations for students and families. In the K-12 e-learning school, it is essential to consider the whole family as part of the learning unit. Therefore, the orientation should go over the expectations for both students and their learning coaches. These orientations should stress important parts of being successful in your school ranging from technical requirements, to the delivery of classes, to the time expected for learning online. These orientations could be text-based, have multimedia components, be synchronous, or asynchronous. The most important part is to consider your population and make an orientation that is relevant for them.

- Personally connect students to their teachers. As a leader of a K-12 e-learning school, it is essential that the importance of the teacher is never neglected. An effective and caring teacher is the most important factor in a student's educational experience. The teacher is critical in the online learning environment (Maor, 2003). However, the types of spontaneous interactions and relationship building that can occur in physical buildings are qualitatively different online. There needs to be intentional design to foster meaningful interactions between students and their teacher. Having the teacher introduce themselves with a personal video and allowing them to personalize their course as much as possible can make the students feel a bit more connected to their teacher. But two things are important, *ongoing* teacher engagement with learners and making sure that the teachers who are engaged with learners have proper pedagogical preparation. Too often there is an overreliance on tutors or paraprofessionals in the online space. As a leader, it is your role to ensure that the teachers are well prepared not just to teach, but to teach in an online space.

- There is a fine line in online education between standardization and personalization of the learning experience. One of the perceived benefits of K-12 online learning is the ability to personalize the learning environment (Barbour & Reeves, 2009). The flexibility of "anytime" learning speaks to students working through lessons at their pace. To help students succeed, the learning environment should be personalized for students, adjust to any educational plans for particular students, and provide guidelines for the student on how flexible the school is with their assignments and progress. These decisions need to be made with the teachers as they know best how their workflow can be balanced to deliver a degree of personalization for the students while maintaining the quality of the course.

These are some concrete ways to support students so they succeed in the e-learning environment. Undoubtedly, there are more ways to support students. For more information, consider resource four, *Supporting Students in Open and Distance Learning,* in the further resources section Supporting Students in Open and Distance Learning.

Parent/Guardian Role

There are two common assumptions of K-12 e-learning schools. The first assumption is that online learning requires students to be able to self-regulate and be independent learners. The second is that the parent is expected to play a role in monitoring their child's learning. The parent's role is not consistent across K-12 e-learning schools, and it is important to make their role very explicit. From a systemic perspective, you should consider gathering input from all of the parents/guardians and forming a parent stakeholder group to include their perspective from the very beginning of establishing expectations. For example, you may find that a large portion of the parents of children in your e-learning K-12 school work and are only available to help their student at night or that they have never been comfortable using the computer. The design of the school experience then could have parents able to review student work but not complete it with them or include tutorials/lessons for parents, so they become comfortable using the technology that their child is using for school. The following list are suggestions for making parents/guardians explicitly aware of their role in their child's online education.

- Form a parent stakeholder group and take seriously their perspective on how they can help their child be successful in school.
- Have very clear expectations before students even enroll in your e-learning school. Information on parent/guardian expectations should be included in information given to prospective student families. It needs to be stressed that in this learning environment parental guidance/teaching is expected and crucial for the success of students. Does this involve checking work, communicating with the teacher, or helping complete assignments? These are all decisions that need to be made for your particular school audience.

- Be realistic in the types of families who may not be the best fit for the demands of your e-learning school. Davis (2011) remarks that having parental support is vital to the success of the student in the online learning environment. If the parent is not available, are there extra supports available for the student like a grandparent? Or does the school need to provide transportation to and assistance from learning support coaches who help students complete their work? The best interest for a particular student should always take precedence over the bottom line of recruitment and enrollment numbers.
- Keep support available for parents/guardians as student's progress through their education. While families may need a more heavy-handed approach to support in the first few months of school, their needs will differ over time. Work closely with the stakeholder group to identify changing needs and serve families at their point of need.
- Make sure that any employees of your school who speak with parents have a list of FAQs and expectations for parental involvement.
- Send out communication/feedback/surveys to parents/guardians as a whole to assess how this group feels about the education of their child at your school.

Selecting Curricula

There are unlimited combinations that could be made to deliver an effective educational experience for students. It is essential to keep a systemic perspective when making decisions on which products and curricula to use. For example, will you support the professional development of your teachers to be effective designers of course content? Do you expect teachers to be able to learn this information on their own? Will you have the budget to subscribe to closed-access sources? Are the sources you choose Learning Tools Interoperability (LTI)? LTI means that the tools can "talk" to each other and work within the learning management system. Making these decisions will force you to rely on a team. To increase ownership of that team, give them authority over suggesting decisions for the curriculum. To balance competing interests, make sure to have regular meetings with the group as a whole so that one group understands the perspective of another group. For example, a teacher may see the pedagogical use of a particular tool, but it might not be sufficient for use with your FERPA requirements or budget. Ideally, a design conversation framework will be used from a systemic perspective for selecting/changing the curricula. A design conversation framework "is a group endeavor in which a group searches for common meaning and designs a new entity" (Stokes & Carr-Chellman, 2007, p. 91). This framework can help to create a unified vision for the goal of using a specific curriculum.

- Embrace the expertise of your faculty and staff to make curricular decisions. Hold regular design conversations when the time is ripe to create or implement a new curriculum. Follow the design framework to ensure real input from stakeholders and not shallow opinions/perspectives.

- Use the information provided in Table 1 to guide your focus for selecting the ideal team for the design conversations. Choose a team that has expertise in instructional design, enrollment plans for the school, security and student privacy interests, budgetary knowledge, and any other areas you identify as having a role to play in the curriculum design for your school.
- Communicate clearly to all stakeholders what the curriculum will be. This can include a sample lesson or week to students who are looking to enroll in your school, parent features in the curriculum, support when using different parts of the curriculum, and updates to licensing. This communication can come in the form of a newsletter, email, blog site, or updates on the school website.
- Weigh the pros and cons of different curricula combinations. For example, should teachers be able to choose their preferred software or have to use purchased curricula from the school? How many different software are students expected to master to use different resources? Should everything be embedded into the LMS? These are all critical decisions to be made when deciding on the educational sequence for students.

Equitable Access to Resources

It can be very tempting to create physical centers for students to go to, to host field trips, to promote social gatherings, and to geo-target a certain population of students. However, if these decisions are made without a systemic perspective of your whole student population, you run the risk of isolating and disadvantaging the very student body you are trying to serve. This could create a very real problem. While issues of equity certainly exist across school districts, issues of inequity within the same school are much more problematic. This leads to an uneven distribution of tuition money where some students benefit from a program or building and others do not have access to this program or building.

- If you have a physical support center for some students, a virtual support center needs to be built for students who cannot go to the physical support center, and it needs to be staffed by the same level of employee so that students receive an equal level of support.
- Consider rotating through regional field trips so that all students enrolled in the school have an opportunity to go on that field trip. For students who cannot go on field trips, consider using a virtual alternative that includes a virtual field trip or a community-building experience for a cohort of students.
- Do not build specialized STEM or Arts centers if all students do not get to use them. This is not fair to students who cannot use them just because they live in a different part of the state.
- Make a commitment to deliver a minimum level of technology for the students. This may mean that students who live in remote areas may need additional technology support to reach the same level of connection as a student who lives in an area with better internet.

Being Innovative and Transparent

Being innovative should be a primary goal of a K-12 e-learning school. However, this goal should not be in conflict with being transparent about issues or accountability, student enrollment, budget, and student success. When taking over an existing or leading the creation of a new K-12 e-learning school, create a strategy for being transparent about accountability, student enrollment and marketing, budget, and student success.

A key strategy for being innovative while being transparent is to assess the success or failure of the innovations and communicate what happened with a particular innovation. Considering the assessment when planning and implementing an innovation will also lead to a systemic perspective on the innovation in which it is considered within a system, rather than for the sake of implementing an innovation. Heidegger (2010) stresses that technology should not be used for the sake of using technology. Being clear and accountable about innovations can help to give a purpose to why they are being used.

- Use an outcomes-based model of objectives for the implementation of innovations. This should help to focus on how these innovations will be assessed and ensure they are being used for a specific purpose.
- Ensure that your school is reporting accurate measures of accountability as defined by the state's department of education. Generally, e-learning schools do not have as many measures of accountability as a traditional brick-and-mortar public school. However, this does not mean that the measures of accountability that are required should not be reported. This should be made clear somewhere on the website or through communication to all relevant stakeholders.
- A criticism of some cyber charter schools is that they have questionable recruiting tactics that are more concerned with enrollment and money than about the best-fit for a particular student. Always care more about the best-fit for the student than about total enrollment for the school.
- Be very clear about the budget and what money is going where. Carr-Chellman and Marsh (2009) address this as a concern of cyber charter schools. If a school was completely transparent about what money was going where and why, then they would have a strong case for the money needed and why, and there would be less mysticism about what they are doing with the money. This might not apply if you are leading a K-12 e-learning school sponsored by the brick-and-mortar district. However, good recordkeeping of expenditures and costs is still helpful for these schools, so they have evidence on which to base their monetary requests to the district.
- The final area in which to be transparent is with student outcomes, scores on standardized tests, and possible portfolio samples of student work. The more tangible products upon which student success can be based, the less important one of those outcomes becomes. For example, if students can demonstrate what they learned through applying technological innovations such as a blog post or Web 2.0 presentation, this can be used in consideration with their standardized test score to help document their progress for the year.

Conclusion

The decisions described in this chapter represent only a segment of the decisions that you will need to make as a K-12 e-learning leader. It was the goal of this chapter to introduce considerations that need to be taken from a systemic perspective and at the level of someone without the background in online learning. e-Learning is synonymous with online learning. However, within the field of e-learning, there are many different models for K-12 schools to consider. A school could be private or public, associated with a district or independent, singular, or part of a chain of schools. The system in which your school exists will have an impact on the decisions made. However, keeping a systemic perspective in which stakeholders are involved on a level playing field is essential for creating a school where the stakeholders feel valued and empowered to better the school.

When students are first exploring enrollment options, the goal(s) of the e-learning school need to be publicly stated. The experiences of the student within that school should then be consistent with that goal. By considering issues of preparing students to be successful online learners, providing clear expectations for the parent/guardian, engaging in a design conversation for the curricula decisions, ensuring that students are given equivalent access to resources, and maintaining an acceptable level of transparency you will be prepared to lead a K-12 e-learning school in the twenty-first century.

For More Information

The following resources were selected as ones that can provide you with additional information to help with the decisions described in this chapter.

1. Moore, M., & Kearsley, G. (2011). *Distance education: A systems view of online learning.* Belmont, CA: Wadsworth Cengage Learning.
2. Molnar, A., Huerta, L., Barbour, M. K., Miron, G., Shafer, S. R., & Gulosino, C. (2015). *Virtual schools in the U.S.: Politics, performance, policy, and research evidence.* Retrieved from http://nepc.colorado.edu/publication/virtual-schools-annual-2015
3. Quality Matters K-12 Program. Retrieved from https://www.qualitymatters.org/grades-6-12
4. Simpson, O. (2002). *Supporting students in open and distance learning.* New York: Routledge Falmer
5. Stokes, H., & Carr-Chellman, A. (2007). Seeds of engagement: Design conversation for educational change. *Systems Research and Behavioral Science 24*(1), 91–101. doi: 10.1002/sres.812

Appendix: Penn State Qualtrics Survey Online Readiness

Welcome to the world of online learning. Before you enroll in an online course, take some time to think about yourself as a learner and see whether your characteristics would help you be a successful online learner. Your answers to these questions can help you decide whether or not to take an online course. You can also talk to your adviser before you decide.

Please indicate whether you agree or disagree with the following statements.

	Agree	Somewhat Agree	Disagree
I am good at setting goals and deadlines for myself.	○	○	○
I have a really good reason for taking an online course	○	○	○
I finish the projects I start.	○	○	○
I do not quit just because things get difficult.	○	○	○
I can keep myself on track and on time.	○	○	○

Please indicate whether you agree or disagree with the following statements.

	Agree	Somewhat Agree	Disagree
I learn pretty easily.	○	○	○
I can learn from things I hear, like lectures, audio recordings or podcasts.	○	○	○
I have to read something to learn it best.	○	○	○
I have developed a good way to solve problems I run into.	○	○	○
I learn best by figuring things out for myself.	○	○	○
I like to learn in a group, but I can learn on my own, too.	○	○	○
I am willing to e-mail or have discussions with people I might never see.	○	○	○

Please indicate whether you agree or disagree with the following statements.

	Agree	Somewhat Agree	Disagree
I usually work in a place where I can read and work on assignments without distractions.	○	○	○
I can ignore distractions around me when I study.	○	○	○
I am willing to spend 10-20 hours each week on this online course.	○	○	○
I keep a record of what my assignments are and when they are due.	○	○	○
I plan my work in advance so that I can turn in my assignments on time.	○	○	○
People around me will help me study and not try to distract me.	○	○	○
I am willing to use e-mail and other online tools to ask my classmates and instructors questions	○	○	○

Please indicate whether you agree or disagree with the following statements.

	Agree	Somewhat Agree	Disagree
I am pretty good at using the computer.	○	○	○
I am comfortable surfing the Internet.	○	○	○
I am comfortable with things like doing searches, setting bookmarks, and downloading files.	○	○	○
I am comfortable with things like installing software and changing configuration settings on my computer.	○	○	○
I know someone who can help me if I have computer problems.	◉	○	○

Please indicate whether you agree or disagree with the following statements.

	Agree	Somewhat Agree	Disagree
My computer runs reliably on Windows or on Mac OS X.	○	○	○
I have access to a printer.	○	○	○
I am connected to the Internet with a fairly fast, reliable connection such as DSL or cable modem.	○	○	○
I have access to a computer with virus protection software on it.	○	○	○
I have headphones or speakers and a microphone to use if a class has a videoconference.	○	○	○
My browser will play several common multimedia (video and audio) formats.	○	○	○

Where are you located?

References

ACRL. (2008, July 1 *Standards for distance learning library services*. Retrieved from http://www.ala.org/acrl/standards/guidelinesdistancelearning.

Ahn, J. (2011). Policy, technology and practice in cyber charter schools: Framing the issues. *Teachers College Record, 113*(1), 1–26.

Allen, I. E., & Seaman, J. (2013). *Changing course: Ten years of tracking online education in the United States*. Babson Park, MA: Babson Survey Research Group.

Barbour, M. K., & Reeves, T. C. (2009). The reality of virtual schools: A review of the literature. *Computers & Education, 52*(2), 402–416. doi:10.1016/j.compedu.2008.09.009.

Berge, Z., & Clark, T. (Eds.). (2005). *Virtual schools: Planning for success.*New York, NY: Teachers College Press.

Carr-Chellman, A. A., & Marsh, R. (2009). Pennsylvania cyber school funding: Follow the money. *TechTrends*, *53*(4), 49–55. doi:10.1007/s11528-009-0306-6.

Cho, M.-H., & Shen, D. (2013). Self-regulation in online learning. *Distance Education*, *34*(3), 290–301. doi:10.1080/01587919.2013.835770.

Conn, K. (2002). For-profit school management corporations: Serving the wrong master. *Journal of Law & Education*, *31*(2), 129–148.

Conrad, D. (2002). Deep in the hearts of learners: Insights into the nature of online community. *International Journal of E-Learning & Distance Education*, *17*(1), 1–19.

Davis, M. R., (2011, February 4). Full-time e-learning not seen as viable option for many. *Education Week: Digital Directions*. Retrieved from http://www.edweek.org/dd/articles/2011/02/09/02elearning. h04.html.

Dawley, L. (2007). *The tools for successful online teaching*. Hershey, PA: Information Science Publishing.

Guri-rosenblit, S. (2005). 'Distance education' and 'e-learning': Not the same thing. *Higher Education*, *49*(4), 467–493. doi:10.1007/s10734-004-0040-0.

Heidegger, M. (2010). The question concerning technology. In C. Hanks (Ed.). Technology and values: Essential readings (99–113) Chichester: Wiley-Blackwell.

Huerta, L. A., Gonzalez, M. F., & d'Entremont, C. (2006). Cyber and home school charter schools: Adopting policy to new forms of public schooling. *Peabody Journal of Education*, *81*(1), 103–139. doi: 10.1207/S15327930pje8101_6.

Hutchins, C. L. (1996). *Systemic thinking: Solving complex problems*. Aurora, CO: Professional Development Systems.

iNACOL. (2015). *Keeping pace with K-12 digital learning: An annual review of policy and practice* (12th ed.). Durango, CO: Evergreen Education Group.

Kowche, E. (2009). New capabilities for cyber charter school leadership: An emerging imperative for integrating educational technology and educational leadership knowledge. *TechTrends*, *53*(4), 41–48. doi:10.1007/s11528-009-0305-7.

Kurland, N. B., & Bailey, D. E. (1999). Telework: The advantages and challenges of working here, there, anywhere, and anytime. *Organizational Dynamics*, *28*(2), 53–68. doi:10.1016/S0090-2616(00)80016-9.

Lave, J., & Wenger, E. (1991). *Situated learning: Legitimate peripheral participation*. Cambridge: Cambridge University Press.

Mann, B., & Barkauskas, N. (2014). Connecting learning or isolating individuals? The social justice frames in cyber charter schools in Pennsylvania. *International Journal of Cyber Ethics in Education*, *3*(2), 39–50. doi:10.4018/ijcee.2014040104.

Maor, D. (2003). The teacher's role in developing interaction and reflection in an online learning community. *Educational Media International*, *40*(1–2), 127–137. doi:10.1080/0952398032000092170.

Mayer, R. (2004). Should there be a three-strikes rule against pure discovery-based learning? *American Psychologist, 59*(1), 14–19. https://doi.org/10.1037/0003-066X.59.1.14.

McCorry, K., & Socolar, P. (2015, May 29). Pa. cyber charters not happy with Gov. Wolf's proposed steep cuts [Multiple Choices, Part 11]. *Keystone Crossroads*. Retrieved from http://crossroads.newsworks.org/index.php/local/keystone-crossroads/81326-pa-cyber-charters-not-happy-with-gov-wolfs-proposed-steep-cuts.

McInnerney, J. M., & Roberts, T. S. (2004). Online learning: Social interaction and the creation of a sense of community. *Educational Technology & Society*, *7*(3), 73–81. doi:10.1207/S15327930pje8101_6.

Moore, M. G., & Kearsley, G. (2011). *Distance education: A systems view of online learning* (3rd ed.). Belmont, CA: Wadsworth Cengage Learning.

PA Cyber Charter (2012, April 2. Congressman Altmire: PA cyber STEM epicenter to train youth for tech jobs of the future. Retrieved from http://www.prnewswire.com/news-releases/congressman-altmire-pa-cyber-stem-epicenter-to-train-youth-for-tech-jobs-of-the-future-145824565.html.

Raish, V., & Carr-Chellman, A. A. (2015). Cyber charter schools: An alternative to traditional brick-and-mortar schooling? In T. Clark & M. Barbour (Eds.), *Online, blended, and distance education in schools: Building successful programs* (pp. 59–70). Sterling, VA: Stylus Publishing.

Raish, V. (2016). *A content analysis of virtual science labs in cyber charter school* (Unpublished doctoral dissertation). Pennsylvania State University, University Park, PA.

Sawyer, R. K. (2006). Introduction. In R. K. Sawyer (Ed.), *The Cambridge handbook of the learning sciences* (pp. 1–15). Cambridge: Cambridge University Press.

Sieber, J. E. (2005). Misconceptions and realities about teaching online. *Science & Engineering Ethics, 11*(3), 329–340.

Squire, K. D., & Reigeluth, C. M. (2000). The many faces of systemic change. *Phi Delta Kappa International, 78*(3), 143–152.

Stokes, H., & Carr-Chellman, A. (2007). Seeds of engagement: Design conversation for educational change. *Systems Research and Behavioral Science, 24*(1), 91–101. doi:10.1002/sres.812.

Stone, A. (2008). The holistic model for blended learning: A new model for L-12 district-level cyber schools. *International Journal of Information and Communication Technology Education, 4*(1), 56–71. doi:10.4018/jicte.2008010106.

Sumner, J. (2000). Serving the system: A critical history of distance education. *Open Learning, 15*(3), 267–285. doi:10.1080/02680510075003688l.

Tucker, B. (2007). Laboratories of reform: Virtual high schools and innovation in public education. *Education sector report.* Retrieved from http://www.k12hsn.org/files/research/Online_Learning/Virtual_Schools.pdf.

Waters, L. H., & Leong, P. (2014). Who is teaching? New roles for teachers and parents in cyber charter schools. *Journal of Technology and Teacher Education, 22*(1), 33–56. Chesapeake, VA: Society for Information Technology & Teacher Education.

Index

© Association for Educational Communications and Technology 2018
A.A. Piña et al. (eds.), *Leading and Managing e-Learning*, Educational Communications and Technology: Issues and Innovations, https://doi.org/10.1007/978-3-319-61780-0